A Concise Dictionary of Theology

by
Gerald O'Collins, S.J.
and
Edward G. Farrugia, S.J.

PAULIST PRESS
New York/Mahwah, N.J.

De licentia superiorum ordinis

Library of Congress Cataloging-in-Publication Data

O'Collins, Gerald.
    A concise dictionary of theology/by Gerald O'Collins and Edward G. Farrugia.
        p. cm.
    ISBN 0-8091-3235-4 (pbk.)
        1. Theology—Dictionaries. 2. Catholic Church—Doctrines—Dictionaries. I. Title.
    BR95.025 1991
    230'.03—dc20   91-7187
                                                     CIP

Published by Paulist Press
997 Macarthur Boulevard
Mahwah, New Jersey 07430

Printed and bound in the
United States of America

PREFACE

Over the past three decades programs of Christian theological study have, by and large, been considerably improved. Historical and biblical sources are generally used more scientifically and fairly. Narrow debates have given way to dialogue and a readiness to learn from the best available authorities. Professors and students of the Latin west have discovered more and more the rich treasures of eastern Christianity. A rigid reliance on just one philosophical tradition has been superseded by a healthier philosophical pluralism. In most quarters theologians have appreciated and faced two great challenges: What is involved when we interpret our basic texts? What method(s) should we employ in developing our theological systems? Dialogue with Judaism, Islam and other religions has flourished in a new and surprising way. In various parts of the world local and regional expositions of Christian faith have emerged.

Despite some loss, there have been very many gains in Christian theology. At the same time, change, growth and the new diversity have created a language problem—especially for those beginning the study of theology. Students can be confused about the meaning of important and even basic theological terms.

To help relieve this situation we offer this concise dictionary. Our aim is not to smuggle in some system but simply to clarify key words and phrases which are used in contemporary theology, sometimes in a variety of ways. We have included some biblical, catechetical, ethical, historical, liturgical and philosophical terms that theological students will come across sooner or later. Although this dictionary is primarily designed for westerners (particularly Roman Catholics), increased contacts with eastern Christians have encouraged us to add some terms from the east.

In brief, the aim of this work is to clarify theological terminology and to promote accuracy in its usage. We shall be thoroughly satisfied if we make some contribution toward achieving these goals. In its entirety this dictionary has been authored by both of us, and we assume equal responsibility for its whole content.

It did not seem appropriate to burden a concise theological dictio-

1

nary with bibliographies. But we wanted to indicate some major sources: The Bible, whose two main parts, the Old and the New Testaments, are abbreviated as OT and NT, respectively; the documents of the Second Vatican Council (1962–65); the 1983 Code of Canon Law (abbreviated as CIC); and the latest edition of H. Denzinger and A. Schönmetzer's *Enchiridion Symbolorum, Definitionum et Declarationum de Rebus Fidei et Morum* (Freiburg i.Br., 1976; abbreviated as DS). Those who have difficulty with Latin are referred to the translations of the DS documents provided by J. Neuner and J. Dupuis, *The Christian Faith* (Westminster Md., 1975; rev. ed. London, 1983).

The expertise of various friends and colleagues has helped us clarify many terms more successfully: Giorgio Barone-Adesi, Jean Beyer, Charles Conroy, Mariasusai Dhavamony, Clarence Gallagher, Edouard Hambye, Eduard Huber, John Long, Antonio Orbe, Ronald Roberson, Tomas Spidlik, Frank Sullivan, Javier Urrutia, Jos Vercruysse, Jared Wicks and Boutros Yousif. In a special way we wish to thank most sincerely John Michael McDermott and Robert Taft, who provided us with numerous corrections and challenges.

With gratitude and affection we dedicate this dictionary to those great supporters of theology and theologians, Eugene and Maureen McCarthy.

Gerald O'Collins, S.J. and
Edward G. Farrugia, S.J.
Rome, June 16, 1990

After we delivered our manuscript to the publishers, the *Codex Canonum Ecclesiarum Orientalium* ("Code of Canons of the Oriental Churches") was promulgated by Pope John Paul II on October 18, 1990. Many of its 1546 canons are relevant to this dictionary: for example, the entries on *Patriarch* (canons 55–150; in particular, 78, 110), *Eparchy* (117–310), *Religious Life* (410–572) and all the entries on the sacraments (667–895). In the eastern churches, for instance, the blessing of a priest (rather than a deacon) is essential for the ordinary celebration of marriage (canon 828). The new code is an indispensable reference work on eastern Christianity.

G. O'C and E.G.F.
February 11, 1991

2

ABBREVIATIONS
FOR DOCUMENTS
OF VATICAN II

AA **Apostolicam Actuositatem** (Decree on the Apostolate of Lay People)

AG **Ad Gentes Divinitus** (Decree on the Church's Missionary Activity)

CD **Christus Dominus** (Decree on the Pastoral Office of Bishops in the Church)

DH **Dignitatis Humanae** (Declaration on Religious Liberty)

DV **Dei Verbum** (Dogmatic Constitution on Divine Revelation)

GE **Gravissimum Educationis** (Declaration on Christian Education)

GS **Gaudium et Spes** (Pastoral Constitution on the Church in the Modern World)

IM **Inter Mirifica** (Decree on the Means of Social Communication)

LG **Lumen Gentium** (Dogmatic Constitution on the Church)

NA **Nostra Aetate** (Declaration on the Relation of the Church to Non-Christian Religions)

OE **Orientalium Ecclesiarum** (Decree on the Catholic Eastern Churches)

OT **Optatam Totius** (Decree on the Training of Priests)

PC   **Perfectae Caritatis** (Decree on the Up-to-Date Renewal of Religious Life)

PO   **Presbyterorum Ordinis** (Decree on the Ministry and Life of Priests)

SC   **Sacrosanctum Concilium** (The Constitution of the Sacred Liturgy)

UN   **Unitatis Redintegratio** (Decree of Ecumenism)

Other Abbreviations

Arab.   Arabic

Gr.   Greek

Heb.   Hebrew

Lat.   Latin

NT   New Testament

OT   Old Testament

A

ABBA. The familiar word in Aramaic for father. Where it occurs in the NT (Mk 14:36; Rom 8:15; Gal 4:6), the Greek equivalent is always given. See *Adoption as God's Children.*

ABSOLUTION. Pronouncing over repentant sinners the forgiveness of personal sins through Christ (see DS 1673). The absolution may be in the indicative form (e.g., "I absolve you") or the precatory form (e.g., "May almighty God have mercy on us and forgive us our sins"). Eastern formulas of absolution are generally precatory (e.g., "May God forgive you"). Absolution forms an essential part of the sacrament of penance, and recalls Christ's ministry of forgiveness (Matt 18:21–35; Mk 2:1–12, 15–17; Lk 5:17–26; 7:36–50; 15:1–32; 19:1–10; Jn 8:3–11) and the powers he left to the church to "bind" and to "loose" (Matt 16:19; 18:18; Jn 20:22–23). In the Latin rite, the prayer of absolution runs as follows: "God, the Father of mercies, through the death and resurrection of his Son has reconciled the world to himself and sent the Holy Spirit among us for the forgiveness of sins; through the ministry of the Church may God give you pardon and peace, and I absolve you from your sins in the name of the Father, and of the Son, and of the Holy Spirit." The Council of Trent (1545–63) defined absolution to be not only a statement, but also a juridical act (DS 1684, 1709). Absolution is given by the bishop who heads the diocese and by the priests to whom he gives jurisdiction to hear confessions (see DS 1323). According to the 1983 Code of Canon Law, they then have jurisdiction everywhere in the world, unless the bishop of another diocese expressly forbids them from hearing confessions in his diocese (see CIC 959–60, 966). Where there is imminent danger of death or large numbers who want to receive the sacrament of penance but cannot confess individually, general absolution may be given (CIC 961). But those who receive the sacrament should be told to confess individually at their earliest convenience. The absolution at the beginning of mass or during the liturgy of the hours is a sacramental, not a sacrament. See *Confession; Diocese; Epiclesis; Forgiveness of Sins; Jurisdiction; Ordinary; Penance, Sacrament of; Sacraments; Sacramentals.*

ABSTINENCE. Refraining from otherwise legitimate activities like eating meat. In the west, the Catholic Church enjoins abstinence from meat on Ash Wednesday and every Friday, especially Fridays in Lent. Episcopal conferences, however, may adapt the practice to local needs (see CIC 1249–53). In the east, abstinence days are much more frequent and, as a rule, identified with fasting. See *Episcopal Conference; Fasting; Lent.*

ACCIDENT. A characteristic that inheres in a substance and cannot exist independently of it, but which as such is not essential to that substance. Aristotelian philosophy recognizes nine classes of accidents, which include quality, quantity, space and time. See *Substance and Accidents; Transubstantiation.*

ACOEMETAE (Gr. "non-sleepers"). Monks who took seriously the injunction of St. Paul to "pray without ceasing" (1 Thess 5:17), lived in absolute poverty and devoted themselves to prayer, group by group, for twenty-four hours a day. Their founder was Abbot St. Alexander (ca. 356–ca. 430). They upheld the Council of Chalcedon (451), but were later unjustly accused of being Nestorian. With their center in Constantinople, they survived till the thirteenth century, having mitigated their poverty and built up a famous library. The Pauline ideal has also inspired western contemplatives, in particular institutes of perpetual adoration. Both east and west have widely accepted the proposal of Origen (ca. 185–ca. 254) to unite prayer with necessary work, so that the whole of life becomes "prayer without ceasing." See *Hesychasm; Liturgy of the Hours; Monasticism; Prayer.*

ACOLYTE (Gr. "follower"). See *Lector; Tonsure.*

ADAM (Heb. "man"). The biblical designation for the first man, created with Eve in the image of God (Gen 1:26–27) and the original ancestor of Jesus (Lk 3:38). As Second or Last Adam (Rom 5:14; 1 Cor 15:45) Christ restored to the human race the righteousness and life lost by the first Adam (see DS 901). See *Eve; Life; New Eve; Original Sin; Polygenism; Righteousness.*

AD LIMINA VISIT (Lat. "at the threshold"). The visit which bishops pay to the pope in order to give an account of the state of their dioceses (see CIC 395). See *Bishop; Collegiality; Diocese; Pope.*

ADOPTION *as God's Children.* A Pauline way of expressing the new relationship to God of those redeemed through Christ. No longer slaves to sin but adopted children who cry "Abba, Father" (Rom 8:15; Gal 4:5–7), believers have become heirs with Christ, the Son of God by natural right

(Rom 8:17; Gal 4:7). Their adoption will be completed by the bodily resurrection (Rom 8:21–25). See *Deification; Grace, Sanctifying; Redemption; Regeneration; Resurrection.*

ADOPTIONISM. An eighth-century Spanish heresy which held that, as God, Christ was by nature truly Son of God but, as man, only God's adopted son (see DS 595, 610–15). Its chief proponents were Elipandus (ca. 718–802), archbishop of Toledo, and Felix (d. 818), bishop of Urgel. The Muslim domination of Toledo, at the time the capital of Spain, and Islamic theology, one of whose main tenets is that God cannot have a son, provide the background. This heresy had precedents in Ebionitism and dynamic Monarchianism, which became associated with Adoptionism through Adolf von Harnack's (1851–1930) study. See *Ebionitism; Islam; Monarchianism; Nestorianism.*

ADORATION. The highest reverence to be offered only to God (Exod 20:1–4; Jn 4:23), our creator, redeemer and sanctifier who alone should be "worshipped and glorified" (Nicene Creed). Believers adore God through various images (e.g., the cross); they also adore Christ present in the eucharist (see DS 600–01). See *Cross; Icons; Latreia; Veneration of Saints; Worship.*

ADVENT. In western Christianity the four weeks which prepare for Christmas and form the beginning of the liturgical year. They are characterized by the curtailing of festivities: no Gloria is said (except on the Feast of the Immaculate Conception) and the liturgical color is penitential violet (except for the third Sunday of Advent, when rose may be used). "Advent" also refers to Christ's "second coming" at the end of history. See *Christmas Preparation; Gloria; Immaculate Conception; Calendar, Liturgical; Parousia.*

AESTHETICS. The principles for judging beautiful objects. Theology needs aesthetic criteria drawn from artistic, cultural and contemplative experience, so as to appreciate the material images that manifest and communicate the spiritual and divine realities (see IM 6; GS 57). See *Beauty, Theology of.*

AGAPE (Gr. "love"). The characteristic term used in the NT, especially in John's gospel, the letters of John and Paul, to designate the love of God (or Christ) for us and, derivatively, our love for God and one another (e.g., Jn 15:12–17; 1 Jn 4:16; 1 Cor 13). The word also applies to the common meal early Christians held in connection with the eucharist. See *Eucharist; Love; Philanthropy.*

AGNOSTICISM (Gr. "not knowing"). The view that we cannot know anything with certainty about God, the "other" world and the afterlife (see DS 3475–77; 3494–95; GS 57). In popular usage the term covers various forms of religious skepticism. See *Atheism*.

AKATHISTOS (Gr. "not sitting"). One of the oldest and most beautiful songs of praise to the Mother of God in the Byzantine east. It is usually sung standing (hence its name) during the Saturday vigil service of the fifth week in the Greek Lent. The first part of the text is based on the infancy narrative of St. Luke, interspersed with some apocryphal elements and the repetitive "Hail, Mary," whereas the second part contemplates Jesus' birth in its salvific impact on the whole cosmos. See *Theotokos*.

ALBIGENSIANISM. A medieval heresy named after its center, Albi, in southern France. It understood redemption as the soul's liberation from the flesh, dismissed matter as evil, and hence rejected Christ's incarnation, the sacraments and the resurrection of the body. Its adherents were divided into the perfect, who did not marry and lived an extremely austere existence, and ordinary believers, who led normal lives until they came to be in danger of death. In 1215 the heresy was condemned at the Fourth Lateran Council (see DS 800–02). See *Bogomils; Cathars; Dualism; Manichaeism*.

ALEXANDRIAN THEOLOGY. A theology that began in Alexandria as a catechetical school toward the end of the second century A.D. It interpreted the scriptures with an allegorical bias and, as the classic christology from above, focused on the Word becoming flesh and the divine nature of the incarnate Christ. The many famous exponents of Alexandrian theology include St. Pantaenus (d. ca. 190), St. Clement of Alexandria (ca. 150–ca. 215), Origen (ca. 185–ca. 254), St. Athanasius of Alexandria (d. 373), Didymus the Blind (ca. 313–398) and St. Cyril of Alexandria (d. 444). See *Antiochene Theology; Christology From Above; Christology From Below; Logos-Sarx Christology; Monophysitism; Origenism; Senses of Scripture*.

ALLEGORY (Gr. "speaking under the guise of something else"). A point-by-point interpretation that goes beyond what a narrative says on the surface to find deeper and further links with reality (e.g., the allegory of the vine in Isa 5:1–7; Ps 80:9–17). In places St. Paul follows Jewish exegesis of his time by interpreting the OT allegorically (e.g., Gal 4:21–31). Unlike the Antiochene writers, Origen (ca. 185–ca. 254) and the school of Alexandria sometimes favored an allegorical over a literal meaning of the OT narratives. Like other Latin fathers St. Augustine

(354–430) recognized both the literal and the allegorical meaning of the scripture. See *Alexandrian Theology; Antiochene Theology; Exegesis; Haggadah; Hermeneutics; Origenism; Parable; Senses of Scripture.*

AMERICANISM. A late nineteenth-century movement among Catholics in the U.S.A. who were open to the best ideals of American Puritanism, the Enlightenment, incipient ecumenism and contemporary culture and who were influenced by Fr. Theodore Isaac Hecker (1819–88), the founder of the Paulist Fathers. In 1899, Rome censured Americanism (DS 3340–46). Some themes of Americanism, such as religious liberty, were later vindicated in Vatican II (see DH 2–8). See *Ecumenism; Enlightenment; Liberty, Religious; Puritanism; Vatican Council, Second.*

ANABAPTISTS (Gr. "rebaptizers"). A sixteenth-century movement (found mainly in Germany, Holland and Switzerland) which considered infant baptism invalid and so promoted the "rebaptism" of adults. There were several groups, the most famous of which was that headed by Thomas Münzer (ca. 1490–1525), who led the Peasants' Revolt (1522–25). Another group of Anabaptists tried to set up a theocratic type of government in Münster (1533–35) under Jan Mattys and John of Leyden. The heirs of the Anabaptists are the Mennonites, the followers of Menno Simons (1496–1561), who are mainly found in North America. See *Infant Baptism; Theocracy.*

ANACHORETISM (Gr. "withdrawing onself"). Term applied to eastern monks who live in solitude as hermits do in the west. Like western hermits, anchorites may be attached to a monastery. See *Athos, Mount; Cenobite; Monasticism.*

ANAKEPHALAIOSIS (Gr. "recapitulation" or "summing up"). A term which in its verbal form refers to Christ bringing into unity everything in the universe (Eph 1:10). Along these lines, such church fathers as St. Irenaeus (ca. 130–ca. 200) presented Christ as the head of the Church who fulfills God's design in creation and redemptive history.

ANALOGY (Gr. "proportion"). The use of a common term to designate realities which are both similar and dissimilar with regard to the same point (e.g., "love" as predicated of God and human beings). Analogy is to be distinguished from (a) the case of equivocal terms, i.e. terms which are the same but designate totally dissimilar realities (e.g., "pen" as an enclosure for cows and as a writing instrument), and (b) the case of univocal or perfectly synonymous terms, i.e. different terms which refer to an identical reality (e.g., "king" and "sovereign" for the male hereditary ruler of an independent state). See *Equivocity; Univocity.*

9

ANALOGY OF BEING. In theology, analogy regulates talk about God in human words and indicates that all information communicated in this way does not violate the absolute mystery of God. As the Fourth Lateran Council points out, any similarity between the creator and creatures is characterized by an even greater dissimilarity (see DS 806). There exists an infinite difference between saying "God is" and "creatures are." See *God; Mystery; Theologia Crucis; Thomism.*

ANALOGY OF FAITH. An expression drawn from Romans 12:6 and used in Catholic theology to recall that a passage of scripture or an aspect of faith should be interpreted in the context of the one, whole and indivisible faith of the church (DS 3016, 3283). Karl Barth (1886–1968) used the expression to designate the similarity and dissimilarity that simultaneously exist between the human decision to believe and God's decision to bestow grace. See *Faith; Grace; Mystery; Theologia Crucis.*

ANALYSIS OF FAITH. A study of the motives which lead to faith in God as freely revealed in Jesus Christ. The analysis of these motives shows that the *auctoritas Dei revelantis* (Lat. "the authority of God who reveals") is the decisive factor in believing. See *Experience, Religious; Faith; Mystery; Preambles of Faith.*

ANAMNESIS (Gr. "remembrance"). The bringing to mind of God's saving interventions in history, especially in Christ's passion, death, resurrection and glorification. In the eucharist the Lord's command "do this in memory of me" (1 Cor 11:24,25; Lk 22:19) invites the assembly to appropriate the salvation he has effected once and for all. See *Epiclesis; Paschal Mystery.*

ANAPHORA (Gr. "offering"). The eucharistic prayer or canon of the mass. Normally it includes an introductory dialogue, thanksgiving, the words of institution from the last supper, the *anamnesis,* the *epiclesis* and the doxology. East Syrians call the anaphora *"quddasha"* (Syriac "hallowing"). In the east it bears the name of an apostle or some other saint. See *Doxology; Epiclesis; Eucharistic Prayer.*

ANATHEMA (Gr. "curse" or "object which is accursed"). A solemn form of excommunication or exclusion from the community. St. Paul uses the term against anyone who preaches a false gospel (Gal 1:9) or refuses the love of Christ (1 Cor 16:22).

ANAWIM (Heb. "the afflicted"). Poor people unsupported by wealth and social position. Although poverty was sometimes considered the result of idleness (Prov 10:4) and the sign of God's displeasure, the prophets demanded justice for the oppressed (Isa 10:2). The term came to designate those who place their trust in God (Zeph 2:3). The messianic king will ride on a donkey like a poor man (Zach 9:9; Matt 21:5). According to the Magnificat, God endorses the cause of the poor (Lk 1:46–55), who come first in Jesus' beatitudes (Matt 5:3; Lk 6:20). See *Beatitudes; Poverty.*

ANGELOLOGY. That treatise in systematic theology which studies the function, nature and hierarchies of angels, as well as their cult and iconography.

ANGELS (Gr. "messengers"). God's spiritual envoys, recognized, albeit differently by the Jewish, Christian and Islamic faiths. In earlier OT traditions angels are hardly distinguishable from God (Gen 16:7–13), their purpose being to mediate between God and human beings and protect God's transcendence. Teaching about angels greatly developed in late Judaism, where the names "Michael," "Gabriel" and "Raphael" appear. In the NT angels play a prominent role (e.g., Matt 1:20,24; Lk 2:9–15; Jn 20:12–13). They serve humanity's salvation (Heb 1:14). Church teaching distinguishes between the spiritual reality of angels and that of material beings and affirms their personal existence (see DS 3891). While angels are more agents of revelation than its object, both scripture and church teaching take their existence for granted (see DS 3320). See *Choirs of Angels; Guardian Angels.*

ANGLICAN COMMUNION. The communion of churches which arose from the reform of the English Church in the sixteenth century and which recognized the leadership of the Archbishop of Canterbury. It understood itself as the church of the fathers, and aimed at a middle road between papal authority and Lutheran reform (see DS 2885–88; 3315–19). See *Episcopalians; Fathers of the Church; Lambeth Conferences; Lutheranism; Reformation, The; Thirty-Nine Articles.*

ANGLO-CATHOLICISM. A term first employed in the mid-nineteenth century to designate High Church Anglicans who shared Catholic doctrines, traditions and sacramental practice. See *Ecumenism; Oxford Movement.*

ANHYPOSTASIA (Gr. "without a hypostasis"). A term used of Christ's human nature which, while complete, does not subsist on its own as a human person or *hypostasis,* but rather in the divine Logos. See *Enhypostasia; Hypostasis; Logos; Neo-Chalcedonianism; Person.*

ANIMISM (Lat. "soul," "spirit"). A term once widely applied to the belief of less developed peoples that certain plants and material objects have a spirit or soul of their own.

ANNULMENT. An official declaration by a church court that a sacrament, especially a marriage or ordination, all appearances to the contrary notwithstanding, never existed because of some impediment, a lack of consent or some failure to observe the proper form or procedure in being married or ordained. If the nullity of marriage is established, both parties are free to remarry, but only after an appeals court has confirmed the verdict (see CIC 1671–85; 1708–12). See *Canon Law; Holy Orders; Marriage; Validity.*

ANNUNCIATION. The feast celebrating the message of Christ's conception brought to Mary by the angel Gabriel (Lk 1:26–38). Of Byzantine origin, the feast seems to have been observed in Rome from the seventh century. The date of March 25 comes nine months before Christmas, the traditional but not historically reliable date for the birth of Jesus. See *Advent; Christmas; Virginal Conception.*

ANOINTING. Smearing or pouring oil on persons (or sometimes on things) to change them and their relationship to God and the community. The OT speaks of kings, priests and prophets being anointed and so endowed with God's Spirit (see Exod 29:22–30; 30:25; 1 Sam 10:1; Ps 2:2; 20:7; Isa 45:1). Christians anoint with oil the sick and those being baptized, confirmed, ordained to ministry (in the west) or installed as kings. See *Chrism; Confirmation; Messiah.*

ANOINTING OF THE SICK. The new name for "extreme unction" after the reforms of the Second Vatican Council. As a sacrament it recalls the NT ministry to the sick (see Mk 6:13; Jas 5:14–15) and expresses the whole church's solidarity with the sick, the old and the dying by enabling them to draw spiritual and physical healing from Christ's victory over sickness and death (DS 1694–1700). In the west the sacrament is administered by one priest, in the east by several. See *Sacrament.*

ANOMOEANS (Gr. "dissimilar"). The extreme Arians of the second generation, led by Aetius (d. ca. 370) and Eunomius (d. 394) who held that the Son is only the first creature and unlike the Father in essence. Moreover, Eunomius taught that the Spirit was simply the highest creature produced by the Son. Hence his disciples baptized only "in the name of the Lord." See *Arianism; Cappadocians; Eunomianism; Filioque.*

ANONYMOUS CHRISTIANS. Karl Rahner's (1904–84) term for those who are saved by Christ's grace, even if (through no fault of their own) they remain unbaptized and outside the Christian community (see LG 16 and GS 16). Rahner developed this term and thesis in the light of God's will to save all people (1 Tim 2:4). See *Church; Salvation.*

ANTHROPOCENTRICISM. An approach to theological questions which takes human experience as its point of departure and subsequent guide. When this approach degenerates into making human beings the center and sole measure of all things, anthropocentricism makes genuine theology impossible. See *Mystery; Theocentricism; Theology.*

ANTHROPOLOGY. The interpretation of human existence (in its origin, nature and destiny) in the light of Christian faith. See *Creation; Deification; Eschatology; Grace; Image of God; Original Sin; Protology.*

ANTHROPOMORPHISM. The attribution to God of human characteristics, both physical (e.g., face, mouth and hands) and emotional (e.g., sorrow, joy and anger). See *Apophatic Theology; Negative Theology.*

ANTICHRIST. Christ's supreme opponent, connected with the end of the world (1 Jn 2:18, 22; 4:3) and personified by those who deny the incarnation (2 Jn 7). He has also been identified with "the man of sin" (2 Thess 2:3–10) and "the beast" (Rev 11:7; see DS 916; 1180). See *Messiah.*

ANTICLERICALISM. An attitude which denies the right and duty of church leaders to speak out on political issues of public morality and have any real role in a country's political and sociocultural life. See *Church; Clergy; Clericalism; Political Theology.*

ANTIDORON (Gr. "in place of the gift"). See *Eulogy.*

ANTIMENSION (Gr. "instead of the table"). See *Veneration of Saints.*

ANTINOMIANISM (Gr. "against the law"). A disregard of or even contempt for law. In general this rejection may be supported by philosophical or theological reasons, spring from a psychological rejection of authority, or simply be dictated by economic greed. Since NT times various sects have claimed that Christians are no longer bound by law. They have justified this attitude by misrepresenting Paul's teaching (see Rom 3:8, 21) or claiming a special guidance of the Holy Spirit that delivers them from ordinary moral obligations. See *Anabaptists; Gnosticism; Law; Sects.*

ANTIOCHENE THEOLOGY. An orientation in theology, connected with the Christian community of Antioch, where it emerged with a very distinct exegetical profile in the fourth century. It stressed the literal and historical interpretation of the Bible, but also looked for a *theoria* (Gr. "insight") that went beyond the mere letter of the text. While open to the danger of inadequate *dyophysism* (Gr. "two-natures") by not properly relating the divine and human natures in the one person of Jesus Christ, its emphasis on his full humanity partly anticipated modern christology from below. Antiochene theology is generally thought to have been shaped by the martyr St. Lucian of Antioch (d. 312), who had studied at Edessa; it was developed in particular by Diodore of Tarsus (d. ca. 390) and reached its high point with St. John Chrysostom (ca. 347–407), Theodore of Mopsuestia (ca. 350–428) and Theodoret of Cyrrhus (ca. 393–ca. 466). See *Alexandrian Christology; Christology From Above; Christology From Below; Edessa; Nestorianism; Senses of Scripture; Three Chapters.*

ANTISEMITISM. Hostility toward Jews on racial, religious and political grounds. The Second Vatican Council rejected the charge against the Jews of collective guilt in the death of Jesus, and deplored "the hatred, persecutions and displays of antisemitism directed against the Jews at any time and from any source" (NA 4). See *Holocaust; Jews.*

APATHEIA (Gr. "lack of passion or suffering"). A Stoic term sometimes used by the church fathers to indicate the serenity that comes through growing freedom from one's evil passions and deepening union with God. See *Asceticism; Deification; Hesychasm; Impassibility; Mortification; Stoicism.*

APHTHARTODOCETISM (Gr. "incorruptibility" and "appearance"). A sixth-century monophysite heresy, founded by Julian of Halicarnassus (d. after 518). It claimed that from the first moment of the incarnation Christ's body was incorruptible and immortal, but he freely accepted suffering for our sake. See *Chalcedon, Council of; Docetism; Monophysitism.*

APOCALYPTIC LITERATURE (Gr. "uncovering," "revealing"). A style of writing that ran from 200 B.C. to A.D. 100 and claimed to reveal divine mysteries, above all the signs which will precede the (already determined) end of all history, the resurrection of the dead and the general judgment which will lead to the final transformation of the world. Apocalyptic writings include both noncanonical works (e.g., Enoch) and canonical works (e.g., Daniel, Revelation and Mark 13). See *Eschatology; Parousia; Resurrection of the Dead; Revelation.*

APOCATASTASIS (Gr. "universal restoration"). A theory, developed by

Origen (ca. 185–ca. 254), and later condemned as heretical, that all angels and human beings, even the demons and the damned, will ultimately be saved (see DS 409, 411). See *Hell.*

APOCRYPHA (Gr. "hidden" or "not genuine"). OT books written in Greek (mostly between 200 B.C. and A.D. 70), printed in Catholic Bibles but often omitted in Protestant Bibles. They include such works as Tobit, Judith, Sirach, Wisdom, and I and II Maccabees (see DS 213, 354). See *Bible; Canon of Scripture; Deuterocanonical Books; Old Testament; Vulgate.*

APOCRYPHAL GOSPELS. Christian writings from the second to the fourth centuries which aim to supplement and revise what the canonical gospels tell us of Jesus' birth, life, teaching, death and resurrection. They include "The Gospel of James," "The Gospel of Peter," "The Gospel of Thomas" and "The Gospel of Truth." See *Gospels.*

APOLLINARIANISM. A christological heresy coming from a bishop of Laodicea, Apollinarius (ca. 310–ca. 390). Intent on defending Christ's full divinity against the Arians, he undercut his full humanity by holding that Christ had no spirit or rational soul, this being replaced by the divine Logos (see DS 146, 149, 151). His overriding concern was thus to establish a strict unity in Christ, as is shown in his formula, "the one incarnate nature of the Logos." See *Arianism; Christology; Monophysitism.*

APOLOGETICS. The intellectual defense of Christian beliefs about God, Christ, the church and our common human destiny. The arguments may be addressed to adherents of other religions, members of separated Christian communities, wavering members of one's own church or simply to believers who want to see how responsible their faith is (see 1 Pet 3:15). See *Dialogue; Fundamental Theology.*

APOLOGISTS. The name given to St. Justin Martyr (ca. 100–ca. 165), St. Theophilus of Antioch (late second century), Athenagoras (who ca. 177 addressed his *Apology* to Emperor Marcus Aurelius), Tatian (d. ca. 160) and other Christian writers, who defended their faith against Jewish and pagan objections. Whereas some, like Justin, became the first Christian authors to make serious use of philosophy others, like Tatian, were hostile to Greek philosophy. The apologists offered educated outsiders a case for the Christian religion. Latin apologetics came of age somewhat later with Tertullian (ca. 160–ca. 220). See *Apostolic Fathers; Fathers of the Church; Philosophy; Platonism; Stoicism.*

APOPHATIC THEOLOGY (Gr. "prohibiting," "negative"). Central concept in eastern theology, often translated as negative theology. It points out the inadequacy of all attempts to describe the absolute mystery of God. Any affirmation about God has to be qualified by a corresponding negation and the recognition that God surpasses in an infinite way our categories. Knowledge of God is never purely intellectual, but calls for an ascent to God through moral and religious purification, classically described in *The Life of Moses* by St. Gregory of Nyssa (ca. 330–ca. 395). See *Cataphatic Theology; Dark Night; Essence and Energies; Negative Theology.*

APOPHTHEGMATA PATRUM (Gr./Lat. "sayings of the Fathers"). A collection in Greek of anecdotes and sayings from the desert fathers of Egypt and elsewhere, who include St. Anthony the Abbot (ca. 251–356), St. Syncletica (fourth century) and Poemen (fifth century). Some extravagances apart, the work is characterized by wisdom and discretion. It offers an invaluable source for the origins of monasticism and Christian spiritual life. See *Anachoretism; Cenobites; Monasticism.*

APOSTASY (Gr. "standing apart"). A word occurring in the Greek OT (Jer 2:19) and Acts 21:21 to describe falling-off from the faith and defection from the believing community. In its current usage it means the deliberate and complete abandonment of the faith by a baptized Christian and is thus to be distinguished from mere heresy and schism. See *Faith; Heresy; Schism.*

APOSTLE (Gr. "somebody sent," "ambassador"). In a narrower sense the twelve disciples chosen by Christ (Matt 10:2; Lk 6:13–16) who were to witness to his ministry, death and resurrection through the power of the Holy Spirit (Acts 1:5,8). In a broader sense the apostles include Paul (1 Cor 9:1; Gal 1:1,17), Barnabas (Acts 14:4,14), James (1 Cor 15:7) and others (Rom 16:7) who served as leaders in the original Christian mission and were invested with Christ's authority in founding the church (Eph 2:20). See *Apostolic Succession; Petrine Ministry.*

APOSTOLIC FATHERS. The name for the oldest, nonbiblical and orthodox Christian writings, commonly adopted after Jean Baptiste Cotelier published in 1672 the so-called Epistle of Barnabas (first century), St. Clement of Rome (d. ca. 96), St. Ignatius of Antioch (ca. 35–ca. 107), the *Shepherd of Hermas* (second century) and St. Polycarp of Smyrna (ca. 69–ca. 155), as well as the account of the latter's *Martyrdom*, the oldest of this literary genre. In 1765 Andrea Gallandi added the *Epistle to Diognetus*, a defense of Christianity, and Papias of Hierapolis (ca. 60–130). Philotheos Bryennios published in 1883 what may be the oldest work in this whole group, the anonymous *Didache* (Gr. "teaching"). These writ-

16

ings shed invaluable light on the passage from the NT church to post-apostolic Christianity. Some modern scholars wish to exclude those authors who probably were not directly connected with the apostles, or whose mentality is not so close to the NT. This suggests listing as apostolic fathers only St. Clement, St. Ignatius of Antioch, St. Polycarp and Papias, as well as St. Quadratus (second century), who around 124 addressed to Emperor Hadrian the oldest apology for Christian faith. See *Apologists; Didache; Fathers of the Church.*

APOSTOLIC SUCCESSION. The unbroken continuity in essential belief and practice between the church today and the church founded by Christ through the apostles. This continuity is expressed by calling the bishops the successors of the apostles. As a visible sign of this succession and of an individual bishop's union with his fellow-bishops, the consecrating bishops lay hands on the bishop-elect. See *Apostle; Bishop; Petrine Ministry.*

APOSTOLICITY. The identity in Christian faith and practice of the present church with the church of the apostles. Along with unity, holiness and catholicity, the Nicene Creed names apostolicity as one of the four marks of the church. See *Catholicity; Creed, Nicene; Holiness; Marks (Notes) of the Church; Unity.*

APPEARANCES OF THE RISEN LORD. A special series of encounters with the risen Jesus which were the primary ways the first Christians knew that he had risen from the dead. He appeared to such individuals as Mary Magdalene (Matt 28:9–10; Jn 20:11–18), Peter (1 Cor 15:5; Lk 24:34) and Paul (1 Cor 9:1; Gal 1:12,16; Acts 9:1–19) and to groups, above all "the eleven" (e.g., Mk 16:7; Matt 28:16–20; 1 Cor 15:5). As first Corinthians 15:8, John 20:29 and other NT texts (e.g., 1 Pet 1:8) indicate, the appearances of the risen Christ were experiences reserved to the original witnesses, whose preaching and ministry inaugurated the Christian mission and church. See *Apostle; Ascension; Resurrection.*

APPROPRIATION (Lat. "to make one's own"). Assigning a divine action or attribute, which is actually common to all three persons of the Trinity, to only one of them. Thus creation is appropriated to the Father, redemption to the Son and sanctification to the Holy Spirit. In fact, all *opera ad extra* (Lat. "outward actions") are common to the three persons (see DS 545–46; 1330). See *Attributes, Divine; Immanent Trinity.*

ARCHBISHOP. Title used from the fourth or fifth century for bishops of particularly prominent sees, and later applied in the west to metropolitans or heads of an ecclesiastical region. In the Latin church, "archbishop" can also be used as a purely honorific title. In the east, patriarchs were called archbishops, a title later extended to metropolitans. See *Bishop; Metropolitan: Patriarch.*

ARCHDEACON. Originally, the head of the college of deacons, who helped the bishop with the administration and discipline of his diocese. The term came to designate a priest in charge of important functions in the diocese. See *Deacon; Diocese.*

ARCHIMANDRITE (Gr. "ruler of a fold"). A title in the Byzantine east applied to the superior of a large monastery or group of monasteries, or used to honor certain celibate priests.

ARGUMENTS FOR THE EXISTENCE OF GOD. Philosophical ways of showing the ultimate reasonableness of belief in God by moving, for example, from design in the world to a divine Designer (see DS 3004, 3026). So far from replacing belief, these arguments come from a prior faith in and experience of God. See *Experience, Religious; Five Ways, The; God; Mystery; Natural Theology; Teleological Argument.*

ARIANISM. A heresy condemned at Nicaea I (325) and derived from an Alexandrian priest Arius (ca. 250–ca. 336), who asserted that God's Son did not always exist and consequently was not divine by nature but only the first among creatures (see DS 125–26, 130). After seriously disturbing church peace down to 381, Arianism survived in a mitigated form for several centuries among the Germanic tribes. See *Anomoeans; Filioque; Homoeans; Homoousios; Nicaea, First Council of; Semi-Arianism; Subordinationism.*

ARISTOTELIANISM. A philosophical orientation, originating with Aristotle (384–22 B.C.) and characterized by a greater realism than the earlier and often rival school of Platonism. After being neglected or opposed by some fathers of the church, Aristotelian ethics, logic, theory of causality (with efficient, final, formal and material causes) and view of the human soul as the form of the body (not its prisoner as in Platonism) came into their own in the middle ages through the support of Arab philosophers, Moses Maimonides (1135–1204) and St. Thomas Aquinas (ca. 1225–74). Aquinas elaborated his proofs for the existence of God on an Aristotelian basis, but championed the natural immortality of the soul, apparently denied in Aristotelianism. See *Causality; Five Ways, The; Neoplatonism; Platonism; Soul; Thomism.*

ARMENIAN CHRISTIANITY. A nation now partitioned between Turkey, the Soviet Union and Iran, Armenia claims to have been evangelized by

18

the apostles Thaddaeus, Bartholomew, Simon and Jude. Although Christianity had arrived by the end of the first century, the real credit for establishing Christianity belongs to St. Gregory the Illuminator (ca. 260–ca. 328). He converted the king, who made Christianity the state religion in 301—the first time this had happened in any country. Prevented by war from sending delegates to the Council of Chalcedon (451), Armenia remained united with Constantinople till 518, when the latter definitely accepted Chalcedon, after which Armenia stayed non-Chalcedonian. During the crusades (1198) and at the Council of Florence (1439) a temporary union was reached with Rome (see DS 1006–20; 1310–28; 1344–45). In 1743 a section of the Armenian Church recognized the pope (see DS 2534); its primate or *catholicos* resides in Lebanon. See *Chalcedon, Council of; Eastern Churches; Florence, Council of; Monophysitism.*

ARS MORIENDI (Lat. "art of dying"). Late medieval teaching on the way Christians ought to face death. Books on this topic, e.g., the work of Jean Gerson (1363–1429), enjoyed great popularity and influenced the portrayal of death in art. See *Death.*

ASCENSION. The risen Christ's "going up" into heaven to enter into full and final glory at "the right hand of the Father," where he intercedes for us and exercises his power over the whole universe (see DS 10–30; 189). Marking the close of the post-resurrection appearances (except for the unique case of Paul), the ascension inaugurates Christ's new presence through the Holy Spirit, which is the church with her worldwide mission. Hence, the two mysteries were initially celebrated together at Pentecost, but around 370 the feast of the Ascension was fixed at forty days after Easter (Acts 1:3). See *Pentecost; Resurrection.*

ASCETICISM (Gr. "exercise"). Ways and means adopted by Christians under the action of the Spirit to purify themselves from sin and remove obstacles in the way of freely following Christ. Genuine asceticism brings a growth in contemplation and the love of God that is not detrimental to personal maturity and social responsibility. See *Contemplation; Imitation of Christ; Mortification; Penance.*

ASSENT, NOTIONAL. A merely abstract assent to some truth without fully grasping or being grasped by the reality of that truth. See *Theology.*

ASSENT OF FAITH. The confession of God's saving self-revelation in the crucified and risen Jesus (e.g., Rom 10:9) that involves a personal commitment to Christ as Lord (e.g., Rom 1:5; 1 Cor 12:3) and a hopeful confidence in the resurrection to come (Rom 6:8). This free and reasonable act, made possible through the power of the Holy Spirit, enables one to be baptized and enter the church. See *Baptism; Faith.*

ASSENT, REAL. A full assent to truth, especially concrete rather than abstract truths. Observing how many people accept only notionally the realities mediated by the concrete truths and language of Christian revelation, John Henry Newman (1801–90) popularized the distinction between real and merely notional assent. See *Faith.*

ASSUMPTION OF THE BLESSED VIRGIN. The dogma defined in 1950 by Pope Pius XII that at the end of her earthly life Mary was taken up body and soul into eternal glory (see DS 3900–04). Where Christ "ascended" of his own power, Mary was "assumed" by divine power. From the fifth century eastern Christians celebrated the *koimesis* ("falling asleep") of our Lady. "Assumption" replaced *dormition* ("falling asleep") when Rome adopted the feast in the seventh century. See *Dogma.*

ATHEISM (Gr. "godlessness"). The denial of God's existence, in theory or in practice. The many forms of atheism range from tolerant indifference to a militant rejection, which varies according to the particular concept of God being rejected and the socio-ecclesiastical setting for the conflict. For a time it is possible to be an atheist in good faith, but to bracket off consistently the question of God's existence is irresponsible and blameworthy. See *Agnosticism; God; Mystery; Negative Theology.*

ATHOS, MOUNT. The famous holy mountain at the end of the most eastern promontory of the three-pronged Chalcidice peninsula in northern Greece. On this promontory there are twenty principal monasteries, the first one being founded by St. Athanasius the Athonite in 962. All types of Orthodox monks are to be found on Mount Athos: (a) the anchorite or hermit, (b) the semi-hermit or anchorite living in a colony of hermits under the spiritual guidance of an experienced monk, (c) the cenobite or monk living in community. Cenobitism came to predominate throughout the east, especially after St. Basil the Great (ca. 330–79) wrote his two rules. The rule St. Athansius the Athonite adopted for Mount Athos followed closely those of St. Basil and St. Theodore the Studite (759–826), the great eastern reformer of monasticism. (d) A fourth type, the *idiorrhythmic* (Gr. "own style") monk, who enjoys some measure of financial independence, was introduced on Mount Athos in the fourteenth century. In general, monks of the Holy Mountain enjoy a considerable degree of administrative autonomy; ecclesiastically, they are under the Patriarch of Constantinople. No women may set foot on the peninsula. See *Anachoretism; Cenobites; Hermit; Hesychasm; Monasticism; Palamism; Philocalia; Theocracy.*

ATONEMENT. Often used as a synonym for redemption, "at-one-ment" refers to the end-effect of the process of redemption: being at one with God (from whom we were previously alienated) and so sharing in the divine life. The language of atonement also points to the means for removing guilt and reconciling sinners with God: in particular, various ceremonies in the OT (e.g., those prescribed for *Yom Kippur* or the annual Day of Atonement) and the death and resurrection of Christ in the NT. See *Deification; Justification; Redemption; Salvation; Yom Kippur.*

ATTRIBUTES, DIVINE. Properties predicated of God on the basis of philosophical thought (e.g., immutability) and/or biblical revelation (e.g., faithfulness), and expressing, within the limits of analogy, the ineffable essence of God, from which in the final analysis they are not really distinct. See *Analogy; Palamism.*

ATTRITION (Lat. "remorse"). A term coined in the twelfth century to designate that sorrow for sins, (a) produced by shame or fear of punishment rather than by love of God, and (b) sometimes called "imperfect contrition." The Council of Trent (1545–63) taught that attrition suffices for the fruitful reception of the sacrament of penance when it is animated by the hope of being forgiven and the resolution not to sin again (see DS 1678). See *Contrition; Penance, Sacrament of.*

AUGSBURG CONFESSION. The first confessional statement of the Lutheran Church. Composed mainly by Philipp Melanchthon and presented to Charles V at the Diet of Augsburg in 1530, it consists of 21 articles summarizing essential Lutheran doctrines and seven articles directed against abuses in the Roman Church. In the 450th anniversary year (1980) Pope John Paul II joined the German bishops in recognizing that the Augsburg Confession expresses fundamental truths of our common Christian faith. See *Dialogue; Lutheranism.*

AUGUSTINIANISM. The philosophical and theological system of St. Augustine of Hippo (354–430), a synthesis emphasizing (a) God's sovereign freedom in granting grace and (b) the primacy of God's illumination in human knowledge. Augustine's own views are sometimes called *Augustinism*, to distinguish them from the Augustinianism which was developed by Thomas Aquinas' pupil Aegidius Romanus of the Colonna family (= Giles of Rome, ca. 1243–1306) and became dominant among the Hermits of St. Augustine. See *Grace; Semi-Pelagianism.*

AUTHORITY. The justified expectation that a command will be obeyed or that a statement will be accepted as true. In the church all authority comes from Christ and is to be exercised under the guidance of the Holy

Spirit as a service, not as an assertion of power (see Lk 22:24–27; LG 24). See *Analysis of Faith; Antinomianism; Autonomy; Charism; Heteronomy; Jurisdiction; Magisterium; Obedience; Theonomy.*

AUTOCEPHALOUS (Gr. "having its own head"). A term mainly used of churches governed by their own synods and belonging to the communion of eastern and oriental orthodox churches. All patriarchates are autocephalous, but not all autocephalous churches are patriarchates. For the eastern Orthodox, the Patriarch of Constantinople enjoys a primacy of honor, and a general council could legislate for all autocephalous churches. See *Eastern Churches.*

AUTONOMY (Gr. "self-government"). A term often used since Immanuel Kant (1724–1804) of the right to be self-determining in the spheres of moral freedom and religious thought. As this independence is exercised in a universe created and conserved in being by God, our autonomy can only be relative. See *Enlightenment; Heteronomy; Theonomy.*

AZYMES (Gr. "without yeast"). Thin bread baked without yeast (see Gen 19:3), eaten during a week-long, OT feast commemorating the exodus from Egypt (Exod 23:15; 34:18). On account of its fermentation, leavened bread came to signify corruption (Matt 16:6; 1 Cor 5:7). Since the synoptic gospels report the last supper to have taken place on the first day of the Feast of Azymes (Matt 26:17; Mk 14:12; Lk 22:7), unleavened bread is used in the Latin mass. Most eastern churches, however, follow St. John, who dates the last supper and crucifixion to just before the Feast of Azymes began (Jn 13:1; 18:28; 19:14). This difference provided one of the immediate pretexts for the schism of 1054 between east and west. Archbishop Leo of Ohrid accused the Latins of being "azymites" or "infermentari," while the easterners were nicknamed "prozymites" or "frumentari." The Council of Florence (1439) taught that both unleavened and leavened bread may be used for the eucharist (see DS 1303). All easterners, except the Armenians and the Maronites, use leavened bread. See *Florence (Basle, Ferrara), Council of; Passover.*

B

BAPTISM (Gr. "washing" or "dipping"). The basic sacrament of "rebirth" that makes one a member of the church and thus capable of receiving the other sacraments. Washed with water and consecrated by the Holy Spirit (Jn 3:5; Matt 28:19), with faith and repentance the baptized are cleansed from sin, share in the dying and rising of Christ and begin a new life in him (Rom 6:3–11). In the first centuries baptism was normally followed at once by confirmation and communion, a practice still maintained by the Orthodox. Baptism is necessary for salvation, but can be replaced by baptism of blood (martyrdom) or baptism of desire (the implicit or explicit wish to be baptized; DS 1524). See *Catechumen; Character; Initiation; Sacraments.*

BAPTISM BY AFFUSION (or Infusion). A way of baptizing by pouring water three times on the head of the candidates. First introduced for the sick who could not be immersed or submerged, in the thirteenth century it became the standard western way of baptizing.

BAPTISM BY ASPERSION. A way of baptizing under emergency circumstances by sprinkling (instead of pouring) water three times on the candidates.

BAPTISM BY IMMERSION. A way of baptizing, once popular but now found only among east and west Syrians, which consists in pouring water three times on candidates when they are already in the water or are going down into it. See *Syrian Orthodox.*

BAPTISM BY SUBMERSION. The normal way of baptizing among eastern Orthodox and among many Baptists in the west. The candidates' whole body, or at least their head, is completely submerged three times in the water. See *Eastern Churches.*

BAPTISTS. Members of a very large evangelical church that trace their immediate origins to the early seventeenth century, when they broke with the Anglican Church. John Smyth (ca. 1554–1612), called the "Se-Baptist" because he baptized himself, founded the first Baptist Church in Amsterdam in 1609. Baptists reserve baptism for those who consciously profess repentance for their sins and faith in Christ, and maintain the relative autonomy of the local congregations. See *Anabaptists; Evangelicals; Infant Baptism.*

BASIC (BASE) COMMUNITIES. A term coming from Latin America to describe those many local groups of Christians who strive to revitalize their church life by worshiping and studying the scriptures together, by using their personal gifts in the service of others and by becoming involved in common social action. This movement has been encouraged by the general conferences of the Latin American bishops held at Medellin, Colombia (1968) and Puebla, Mexico (1979). The texts of Puebla speak of "Basic Ecclesial Communities," to distinguish them from other groups which may have weaker links with church authority. See *Church; Liberation Theology; Option for the Poor.*

BASLE, COUNCIL OF (1431–49). Convoked by Pope Martin V (1417–31) and then by Pope Eugenius IV (1431–47), this council was still tainted by the conciliarism of the previous Council of Constance (1414–18). Partly for this reason and partly because the Greek Church agreed to attend a general council in Ferrara, Pope Eugenius ordered the council transferred there in 1437. A minority at Basle obeyed, but the majority stayed to elect an anti-Pope, Felix V. This tried the patience of western Christian nations, who gave their allegiance to Pope Eugenius when Basle became schismatic. Felix V abdicated in 1449. In spite of some unacceptable conciliarist teaching, Basle decreed a series of reforms for the church (see DS 1445). See *Conciliarism; Florence (Basle-Ferrara-Florence), Council of.*

BEATIFIC VISION. That immediate and fulfilling vision of God in heaven which will constitute the core of eternal happiness for the redeemed (see DS 1000–02; 1304–06). See *Heaven; Light of Glory; Palamism.*

BEATIFICATION. The solemn approval for the public veneration after death of a Christian of heroic virtue. In 1747 Benedict XIV reserved to the Pope the right to beatify. See *Canonization.*

BEATITUDES. The eight (or nine) blessings in Christ's "Sermon on the Mount" (Matt 5:3–11), which have analogies in the OT (e.g., Ps 1:1; Isa 32:20) and sum up perfection for all Christians. In the parallel "Sermon on the Plain" (Lk 6:20–26), the four blessings, coupled with the four woes, are more specific in their demands. The beatitudes, which present the kingdom of God in its central requirements and promises, have proved inspiring to many non-Christians. See *Imitation of Christ; Kingdom of God.*

BEAUTY, THEOLOGY OF. In aesthetics, beauty is that quality or combination of qualities which gives pleasure. The harmony of God's own perfections and the interplay of forces in the drama of salvation produce delight through their beauty. We can contemplate this beauty in the glory or splendor that Christ revealed as the only-begotten Son of the Father (Jn 1:14). In recent times, Hans Urs von Balthasar (1905–1988) in the west and Pavel Florenskij (1882–ca. 1943) and Paul Evdokimov (1900–70) in the east did much to develop the theology of beauty. See *Aesthetics; Glory; Transcendentals.*

BEING. Anything that is or exists. As applicable to everything, "being" as

24

such has a minimal conceptual content. Exod 3:14 ("I am who am"), interpreted in the light of Greek philosophy, led Christians to speak of God as the Supreme Being or Being itself.

BENEDICTION. A eucharistic devotion which became common in the west from the sixth century. A consecrated host is placed in a monstrance on the altar and exposed for veneration. After hymns, prayers and the use of incense the celebrant blesses the congregation by making a sign of the cross with the monstrance. See *Blessing.*

BERAKAH (Heb. "blessing"). Jewish prayer of thanksgiving to God (e.g., Gen 24:27; Ps 28:6). The Christian term "eucharist" is a translation of *berakah.*

BERITH (Heb. "obligation" or "covenant"). Central Jewish concept which might have originally indicated simply an obligation imposed by God or (occasionally) a promise made by God. Later it denoted the reciprocal, covenantal relationship between God and the chosen people. See *Covenant.*

BIBLE. The sacred writings inspired by God and expressing the Jewish and Christian faith in a way that is normative for all time. See *Apocrypha; Canon of Scripture; Deuterocanonical Books; Hermeneutics; Inspiration; Marcionism; New Testament; Old Testament.*

BIBLICAL CRITICISM. That modern search for a richer understanding of the Bible which follows various scholarly approaches. Textual criticism seeks to establish as closely as possible the original wording of the scriptures. Historical criticism tries to clarify the date, first context and intention of each biblical book, using evidence from the other scriptures and from such external sources as archeological remains and nonbiblical literature. Form criticism analyzes and classifies the styles of biblical speech and writing (e.g., parables and miracle stories). Tradition criticism investigates the handing down of the oral and written units that entered the books of the Bible as we now have them. Redaction criticism studies (a) the motivation and mindset of the biblical authors in editing their inherited traditions, and (b) the meaning and message they wished to convey to their particular audience. Literary criticism deals with the value and impact of the biblical texts as pieces of literature (see DS 3829–31). See *Hermeneutics; Parable; Quelle; Redaktionsgeschichte; Senses of Scripture; Synoptic Gospels.*

BIBLICAL THEOLOGY. Any theology which bases itself primarily on the scriptures. Particular biblical theologies develop such OT and NT themes as covenant, justification, promise, prophecy or salvation history to draw from the scriptures a unified message for today. See *Hermeneutics; Theology.*

BINITARIANISM. A modern term for some brief NT confessions (e.g., 1 Tim 2:5–6; Rom 4:24; 2 Cor 4:14) that name only the Father and the Son and are found alongside trinitarian formulae (e.g., Matt 28:19; 2 Cor 13:13). Binitarianism may also denote the heretical denial of the Holy Spirit's divinity and belief that there are only two persons in God. See *Constantinople, First Council of; Creed; Trinity.*

BISHOP (Anglo-Saxon corruption of Gr. *"episcopos," "overseer"*). One who has been ordained to the fullness of the priesthood and is entitled to lead a particular church or diocese by his teaching, pastoral care and liturgical ministry. As successor of the apostles he shares with the whole body or college of bishops a responsibility for the entire church (see LG 22–23). He confers holy orders and, in the west, is the ordinary minister of confirmation; the blessing of the sacred oils is also reserved to him (see CIC 375–430). See *Apostolic Succession; Cathedra; Collegiality; Diocese; Enthronement; Episcopal Conference; Jurisdiction; Ordinary; Sacraments.*

BLACK THEOLOGY. North-American theological school developed by Black Christians in the aftermath of Martin Luther King's (1929–68) civil rights movement. It has opposed racist and exclusively white interpretations of the Christian faith, supported further struggles for social rights and joined forces with such similar movements as feminist theology and Latin American liberation theology. See *Feminist Theology; Liberation Theology; Political Theology.*

BLASPHEMY (Gr. *"damage to reputation"*). Showing contempt for God and religious matters through one's words, thoughts and actions (see Exod 22:27; Lev 24:10–23).

BLESSED. In a narrower sense all those who have been officially beatified; in a broader sense all human beings in heaven. See *Beatification.*

BLESSED SACRAMENT. A term employed for the bread and wine after their consecration in the eucharist. See *Consecration; Eucharist; Transubstantiation.*

BLESSING. In Christian usage, an authoritative declaration, invocation or

26

bestowal of divine approval and grace, usually accompanied by a sign of the cross. See *Berakah; Consecration; Sacramentals.*

BLOOD OF CHRIST. Understood against its OT background, the blood of Jesus expresses and effects deliverance from death to life (Exod 12:7, 13, 22–23; 1 Pet 1:18–19), cleansing from sin (Lev 16; Rom 3:25; Heb 9:12, 14; 1 Jn 1:7; Rev 7:14) and a new loving relationship with God (Exod 24:3–8; Mk 14:24). See *Covenant; Expiation.*

BODY OF CHRIST. A term designating (a) the human body of Jesus, (b) the risen Christ present in the eucharist, (c) the church (or the mystical body of Christ) made up of those incorporated into him through baptism and the Holy Spirit, and (d) the feast celebrated in the Latin rite after Trinity Sunday to honor the blessed sacrament. See *Blessed Sacrament; Church.*

BOGOMILS (Slavic "pleasing to God"). A dualistic, docetic medieval sect which for a time enjoyed some support in Byzantium. Its founders were reputed to be a priest Jeremias (mid tenth-century Bulgaria), and a certain Theophilus, who was active between 927 and 950. (Bogomil is the Slavic translation of Theophilus). Their abhorrence for matter led the Bogomils to reject (a) the OT (except for prophetic passages which point to Christ and the psalms) and (b) various "material" practices such as veneration of images (including the crucifix), baptism by water, any kind of infant baptism, and marriage. The only prayer allowed was the Lord's Prayer. The sect spread rapidly through the Balkans, especially in Bulgaria but, with the coming of the Turks, many of its adherents became Muslims. Bogomils had an influence on the rise of Albigensianism. See *Albigensianism; Cathars; Docetism; Dualism; Gnosticism; Manichaeism; Marcionism; Priscillianism.*

BREVIARY. In the west, the book or books used for daily prayer by priests and others and containing all the psalms, a variety of hymns, readings from scripture, prayers, and lessons from the fathers and other spiritual writers (see SC 83–101; PO 5, 13). See *Liturgy of the Hours.*

BUDDHISM (Sanskrit "enlightened one"). A world religion, founded in India by Siddharta Gautama Buddha (ca. 563–ca. 483 B.C.). It exists in two forms: *Hinayana* (Sanskrit "little vehicle") or *Theravada* (Pali "old doctrine") Buddhism (found in Burma, Sri Lanka, Thailand and elsewhere), and *Mahayana* (Sanskrit "great vehicle") Buddhism (found in China, Japan, Korea, Mongolia, Tibet and elsewhere). Under the Bodhi tree (tree of enlightenment) the prince Gautama became enlightened about the four basic truths: (a) human existence is pain; (b) the cause of pain is desire; (c) pain ceases with the emancipation from every form of desire; (d) the cessation of pain may be attained through the eightfold way of deliverance. This way involves right knowledge of these four truths, right intention, right speech, right action, right occupation, right effort, right control of sensations and ideas, and right concentration. This way promises to end suffering (which feeds on desire) and lead to *nirvana* (Sanskrit "being extinguished") or a complete state of peace (see NA 2). The Buddhist scriptures exist in Pali (Sri Lanka) and Sanskrit (India). Two basic doctrines of Buddhism are: (a) that of *karma* (Sanskrit "action, faith"), the belief that old deeds are rewarded or punished in this life or subsequent lives, and (b) that of rebirth or the transmigration of souls. *Mahayana* Buddhism, which arose around the time of Christ, teaches individuals not only to attain *nirvana* but also to become Buddhas themselves and so save others. This form of Buddhism includes the worship of gods and various syncretistic features. See *Reincarnation; Salvation; Syncretism; World Religions; Zen.*

BYZANTINE CHRISTIANITY. A common name for Christians who belong to the Byzantine liturgical, canonical, spiritual and theological tradition, deriving from the fact that in 330 Constantine the Great moved his capital from Rome to Byzantium on the Bosphorus and renamed the city Constantinople. (a) *Greek Byzantines.* Claiming from 381, and especially from 451, a position second only to Rome, Constantinople became the undisputed center for the majority of Christians in the east. In 1054 its patriarch and the pope's legates mutually excommunicated each other. After the Turks captured the city in 1453, the patriarchs have continued to enjoy a primacy of honor over all eastern Orthodox. In 1965 Pope Paul VI and Patriarch Athenagoras of Constantinople mutually lifted the excommunication, which in any case had often been ignored. (b) *Byzantine-Slavonic Christians.* Those Christians of the Byzantine tradition who use Old Church Slavonic instead of Greek for their liturgy. There are churches in communion with Constantinople (e.g., Russians, Ukrainians, Serbians, Bulgarians, Ruthenians, etc.) and their counterparts who are in communion with Rome. The mission of Saints Cyril and Methodius in 863 began the conversion of the Slavic nations to Christianity. Cyril devised for Old Church Slavonic an alphabet, Glagolitic, later superseded by the "Cyrillic" alphabet, not created by the saint but named after him, and still in use today. With the baptism of Prince Vladimir of Kiev in 988 Christianity became the official religion of the Kievan Rus'. (c) *Other Byzantine Christians.* Besides Greek and Slavic-speaking Byzantines there are several other ethnic groups, including the Georgians, some Arabs and, most importantly, the Romanians, who have the second-largest Orthodox Church today. See *Chalcedon, Council of; Constantinople, First Council of; Eastern Churches; Ruthenians.*

C

CAESAROPAPISM. State's practice of constantly interfering in church matters, under the pretext of protecting the faithful's interests. The Roman emperors had been supreme pontiffs in the pagan state religion; after conversion to Christianity they often failed to respect the independence of church order. When the empire survived primarily in the east, the Byzantine rulers dominated the patriarchs, especially in the period before the 1054 crisis between east and west. See *Church and State; Symphony.*

CALENDAR, GREGORIAN. The reform of the calendar which Pope Gregory XIII introduced by dropping the days from 5 to 14 October 1582. The earlier Julian calendar, created by Julius Caesar in 46 B.C., had not taken into account that, in addition to 365 days, the earth takes about six hours more to go round the sun. By the time of the Gregorian reform the calendar was running ten days late. To avoid future errors, a leap year of 366 days was inserted every four years and century years were to count as a leap year if divisible by 400. While the Gregorian reform had immediate effect in Catholic countries of western Europe, England and the American colonies accepted it only in 1752. Orthodox Christians began to accept it only in 1924, but continue to follow the Julian calendar for Easter and the feasts which depend on it. Those who, like the monks on Mount Athos, still accept only the Julian calendar, are now thirteen days behind. See *Athos, Mount; Calendar, Liturgical.*

CALENDAR, LITURGICAL. The calendar used in the various Christian churches to regulate the weekly celebrations (above all, Sunday), movable feasts (especially Easter and Pentecost, whose dates vary) and immovable feasts like Christmas, which always fall on the same date. See *Christmas; Easter Triduum; Liturgy; Liturgy of the Hours; Old Believers; Pentecost; Sunday.*

CALVINISM. That branch of Protestantism which traces its origin to the Swiss reformer John Calvin (1509–64). Within these churches his theology (characterized by the unity of the OT and NT, an emphasis on God's sovereignty, the predestination of the elect to heaven and the reprobate to hell, and the church as a well-ordered community living in solidarity) exercises a decisive influence, even if his theory of double predestination has been modified. See *Congregational Theology; Predestination; Presbyterianism; Protestant; Puritans; Reformation, The; Theocracy; Zwinglianism.*

CANON. (a) A title often given to priests who help staff a cathedral or a collegiate church (see CIC 564–72). Under the direct jurisdiction of the local ordinary, they are obliged to celebrate together certain liturgical ceremonies and sometimes fulfil other duties such as taking part in selecting a new bishop when the see is vacant. (b) "Canon" is also a traditional western term for the eucharistic prayer or anaphora of the mass. See *Anaphora; Bishop; Cathedral; Eucharistic Prayer; Jurisdiction; Ordinary.*

CANONIZATION. Church's solemn and final declaration that one of its dead and previously beatified members belongs among the saints in heaven and as such is to be publicly invoked and venerated (see CIC 1186–90). This proclamation is reserved to the Holy See. See *Beatification; Communion of Saints; Holiness; Saint.*

CANON LAW. That body of codified law to be observed by Catholics, either individually or through various groups which they form within the church. In particular, it refers to the code which was promulgated by John Paul II in 1983, superseding that of 1917, and the Code of Canon Law for the eastern churches, not yet promulgated. See *Code of Canon Law; Code of Canon Law for Eastern Churches; Corpus Juris Canonici; Nomocanon.*

CANON LAW, SOURCES OF ORIENTAL. Prescriptions about the conduct of church members and ministers, usually coming from ecumenical councils and synods. Once the church was officially recognized by the state, church precepts automatically became law of the empire, and entered the *Theodosian Code* and, even more, the *Justinian Code.* Under Emperor Theodosius II (401–50) all the general laws enacted since Constantine the Great (d. 337) were codified in one collection, officially in force from 439. In 529 Emperor Justinian I (483–565) published a new code, revised in 534. The Justinian Code aimed at procuring a *symphony* (Gr. "harmony") and *synalleleia* (Gr. "autonomous cooperation") between the imperial court and church leaders by making the emperor the executor of canonical legislation.

The Justinian Code helped canon law to emerge in the west during the later middle ages. But a codification of eastern canon law was long in coming. St. Nicodemus of Mount Athos (1749–1809) attempted such a compilation and added a commentary, called *Pedalion* (Gr. "rudder"), which was quickly recognized in the praxis of the patriarch of Constantinople. This rudder was meant to guide the ship of the universal church, with dogmas and traditions for its beams and planks, Jesus for its navigator and the apostles and the clergy for the officers and crew. This image recalls the name for the chief code of Russian canon law, *Kormcaja Kniga* (Russ. "navigator's chart"), a collection of canons first printed in 1653. The work of St. Nicodemus reflects the close ties between law and spirituality and the interpenetration of law and dogma. Two terms summarize the spirit of eastern canon law: *akribeia* (Gr. "rigor") and *oikonomia* (Gr. "house management"). See *Church and State; Corpus Juris Canonici; Economy; Nomocanon; Philocalia; Trullan Synod; Symphony.*

CANON OF SCRIPTURE (Gr. "rule, measuring rod"). List of biblical books authoritatively recognized by the church as inspired and normative for her teaching and practice. Among various Christian denominations, the lists differ considerably. See *Apocrypha; Bible; New Testament; Old Testament.*

CAPPADOCIAN FATHERS. Title used chiefly for three Cappadocian saints: Basil the Great (ca. 330–79), bishop of Caesarea in Cappadocia and organizer of monastic life in the east; his brother Gregory, (ca. 335–ca. 395), bishop of Nyssa and a theologian of great mystical depth; and Gregory of Nazianzus (329–89), first bishop of Sasima and then for a while bishop of Constantinople during the First Council of Constantinople. A cousin of Gregory of Nazianzus is sometimes listed among the Cappadocians: St. Amphilochius (ca. 340–ca. 394), bishop of Iconium. See *Constantinople, First Council of; Essence and Energies; Eunomianism; Fathers of the Church; Three Theologians, The.*

CASUISTRY. The application of general moral principles in judging particular cases in their specific circumstances as one searches for God's will. See *Moral Theology; Probabilism.*

CATAPHATIC THEOLOGY (Gr. "affirmative"). Complementary concept to "apophatic theology" and sometimes called "positive theology." Despite the radical inadequacy of our categories, we may nonetheless assert much that is true of God as revealed unsurpassably in Jesus Christ and known to us now through the Holy Spirit. However, apophatic theology insists that even after the divine self-revelation and self-gift in grace, God remains the primordial mystery. See *Apophatic Theology; Positive Theology.*

CATECHESIS (Gr. "teaching"). In the early church, either the instruction given to those preparing for baptism or the books used for that purpose. Nowadays, the word is applied to any instruction meant to deepen Christian faith, even if it is given to those already baptized (CIC 773–80). The ultimate responsibility for catechesis lies with the whole community. See *Catechumens; RCIA.*

CATECHISM. The instruction given to candidates for baptism as well as any book used for such purposes. Often the term refers to popular manuals explaining basic beliefs, moral teachings and prayers.

CATECHUMENATE. In the early church, the period of preparation for baptism, culminating in the scrutinies or prayers of healing on the third, fourth and fifth Sundays of Lent and the actual reception of baptism during the Easter Vigil. To a large extent this practice has been restored for adults (see SC 64–66). See *Eastern Triduum; Neo-Catechumenate; RCIA.*

CATECHUMENS. In the early church, those preparing to receive the sacraments of initiation. They occupied a special place during the liturgy of the word. Then the deacon solemnly dismissed them before the prayers of the faithful. See *Initiation; Liturgy of the Word.*

CATECHUMENS, MASS OF THE. A common, now outdated and misleading term for the liturgy of the word. All those present, and not just catechumens, have the serious duty of listening to God's word. See *Liturgy of the Eucharist; Liturgy of the Word; Faithful, Mass of.*

CATEGORICAL IMPERATIVE. According to Immanuel Kant (1724–1804) an unconditional moral principle that binds in an absolute way—unlike a *hypothetical imperative*, which has binding force only in view of a chosen goal. See *Ethics.*

CATHARS (Gr. "pure"). Name for several sects (mainly medieval sects in France, Germany and Italy) which admitted to membership only the morally and doctrinally pure (see DS 127; 800–02). See *Albigensians; Bogomils.*

CATHEDRA (Gr. "seat"). The bishop's throne in his cathedral and which is the oldest sign of his office, predating later (western) episcopal emblems like the mitre and the ring. Flanked by lower chairs for concelebrating priests, the bishop's throne was placed behind the altar. From there he preached and presided over the eucharist. The expression "ex cathedra" applies to solemn pronouncements made by the pope in virtue of his highest authority. The word "see" for a diocese indicates that it possesses its own episcopal "cathedra." See *Bishop; Diocese; Enthronement; Infallibility; Office; Ordinary.*

CATHEDRAL. The chief church of a diocese where the bishop has his throne. See *Bishop; Diocese; Enthronement.*

CATHOLICITY (Gr. "universality"). The all-embracing character of the true and undivided church that gathers into the one People of God those

32

of different races, languages and cultures (see LG 13). See *Inculturation; Marks (Notes) of the Church.*

CATHOLICISM. That worldwide unity in belief and conduct, frequently identified with the Roman Catholic Church and also claimed by Anglicans and Orthodox. See *Churches; Ecumenism.*

CAUSALITY. The influence exercised by one being or partial being on another. An efficient cause produces effects in an already existing being or brings another being into existence. A material cause is the "stuff" out of which a being is made. A formal cause shapes and organizes something, making it to be what it is. A final cause is the purpose for which something is made. An exemplary cause serves as the model or pattern in the production of a being. To show that human and divine activity are on different levels, God is called *causa prima* (Lat. "first cause") inasmuch as all other things depend on God for their coming into being, continuing existence, and activity. Creatures are termed *causae secundae* (Lat. "secondary causes") insofar as it is only in radical dependence on God that they influence each other. See *Analogy; Arguments for the Existence of God; Aristotelianism; Creation; Hylomorphism; Matter and Form; Ontologism.*

CELIBACY. The renunciation of marriage for religious reasons. Nuns, monks and other men and women in religious life express this commitment as a vow. In the Latin tradition celibacy is required of candidates for the priesthood; permanent deacons are not permitted to marry after ordination (CIC 247, 1037). There is also a married clergy among eastern Catholics. Orthodox priests and deacons are generally married, but they may not marry or remarry after ordination. In the east bishops must be celibate. See *Deacon; Priests; Vow.*

CENOBITES (Gr. "living in community"). In the east, vowed religious, who live in community and observe the same spiritual rule. See *Athos, Mount; Monasticism; Religious Life.*

CHALCEDON, COUNCIL OF. Fourth ecumenical council, held in 451 at a city now called Kadi-Köy (Turkey) on the other side of the Bosphorus from Constantinople. The council was convoked to deal with the monophysite heresy of Eutyches (ca. 378–454), whose strong opposition to those who divided Christ into two sons seems to have led him into the opposite error, which was to reduce Christ to one of his two natures, the divine, or to a third nature which originated from both and was the only one to remain after the incarnation. Condemned in 448 at a home synod held in Constantinople, Eutyches was rehabilitated the following year at

33

a synod in Ephesus summoned by Emperor Theodosius II (401–50). Leo I (Pope, 440–61) branded the synod of Ephesus (449) as a *"latrocinium"* (Lat. "brigandage") because its violence and uncanonical procedure robbed him of his right to judge, expressed in the famous *Tome to Flavian*, the Patriarch of Constantinople (d. 449). When Theodosius II fell from his horse and died, Emperor Marcian, in agreement with the pope, convoked a new council at Chalcedon. This brought together between 500 and 600 bishops, all of them easterners, except for three papal legates and two bishops from Africa. The council fathers condemned Eutyches, as also did Dioscorus, Patriarch of Alexandria, his former patron. Dioscorus (d. 454), however, was himself deposed for having dared to excommunicate Pope Leo. The council affirmed the one person of Christ in his two natures, divine and human. It specified that "the one and the same Christ, Son, Lord and Only begotten" was made known in these two natures which, without detriment to their full qualities, continue to exist "without confusion or change, and without division or separation," while belonging to only one person and not two (DS 300–02). Moreover, the council enacted 27 canons concerning disciplinary matters. Jerusalem became a patriarchate, the fifth, but Pope Leo refused to recognize the twenty-eighth canon, which assigned Constantinople, "the new Rome," wide jurisdictional powers, second only to old Rome itself. See *Constantinople, First Council of; Constantinople, Second Council of; Ephesus, Council of; Eutychianism; Jerusalem; Monophysitism.*

CHALCEDONIAN CHURCHES. Originally, those churches which accepted the Council of Chalcedon. The term is still used for Orthodox churches in the east which did not separate from Constantinople over this council. See *Eastern Churches; Oriental Orthodox.*

CHALICE (Lat. "cup"). A goblet used to hold the wine to be consecrated at the eucharist. In the west, chalices became smaller when the congregation no longer received communion under both kinds—a state of affairs ratified at the Council of Constance in 1415 (see DS 1198–1200). In the east, where the faithful have always received under both kinds, chalices have remained bigger. See *Ciborium.*

CHANT (Lat. "song"). The singing or recitative proclamation of poetical or prose passages (often taken from the Bible) during liturgical ceremonies—a practice coming from our Jewish heritage. The NT quotes Christian hymns (e.g., Lk 1:46–55; Phil 2:6–11; 1 Tim 3:16) which antedated the writing of the scripture. St. Ephraem the Syrian's (ca. 306–73) hymns on church feasts and other liturgical occasions earned him the reputation of being "the harp of the Spirit." Through St. Hilary of Poitiers (ca. 310–67) chant seems to have spread from the east to the west. In the eastern rites, the liturgy is always sung and in most traditions only percussion instruments are allowed, if at all. See *Gregorian Chant; Liturgy*.

CHAPLAIN. A priest who is normally not in charge of a parish, but provides church services for the armed forces or in such institutions as schools, hospitals and prisons (see CIC 564–72). See *Parish*.

CHARACTER (Gr. "seal"). An indelible and unrepeatable spiritual sign (DS 1303; 1609) marking those who become Christ's members (through baptism and confirmation) or his ministers (through ordination). See *Priest; Res et Sacramentum; Sacraments; Sphragis*.

CHARISMATIC. In a general sense, every Christian who is called and graced by God. More specifically, the term refers to those who receive special gifts of the Holy Spirit, such as celibacy (1 Cor 7:7), miraculous powers, discernment and the gift of tongues (1 Cor 12:10). See *Grace; Pentecostalism*.

CHARISMATIC RENEWAL. See *Pentecostalism*.

CHARISMS (Gr. "gifts"). Special gifts of the Holy Spirit, over and above those strictly necessary for salvation. For the benefit of the church and the world, they are given to individuals or groups (see 1 Cor 12; LG 10–12) and are always to be animated by charity (1 Cor 13:1). See *Glossolalia*.

CHARITY. Third theological virtue, which presupposes the other two (faith and hope) and gives life to all the virtues. Its primary object is God; secondarily it is directed towards ourselves and other human beings (Deut 6:5; Jn 13:34; 1 Jn 4:7–5:4; 1 Cor 13:1). See *Agape; Love; Virtues, Theological*.

CHASTITY. That virtue which enables human beings to integrate sexuality within their whole personality according to their vocation in life: for the celibate, through complete abstention, for the married, through fidelity and for single persons, through self-control. See *Marriage; Religious Life*.

CHILIASM (Gr. "thousand"). A movement in early and later Christianity which interprets Revelation 20:1–5 as promising that before the end of the world, Christ will establish a kingdom of a thousand years with the saints who have already risen from the dead (see DS 3839). See *Millenarianism*.

35

CHOIRS OF ANGELS. A way of classifying angels in nine choirs, which goes beyond the limited data of the Bible and was popularized by Pseudo-Dionysius, an anonymous Christian writer of the fifth or sixth century. His nine choirs were arranged in groups of three: Seraphim, Cherubim and Thrones; Dominations, Virtues and Powers; Principalities, Archangels and Angels. See *Angels; Guardian Angels.*

CHRISM (Gr. "oil for anointing"). In the western church, the oil that the bishop consecrates (along with other oils) on Maundy or Holy Thursday during the Chrism mass held in the morning. Normally a mixture of olive oil and balsam, it is used during baptism and confirmation, and to consecrate priests, bishops, churches and altars. In the eastern church, this oil is called *myron* (Gr. "oil for anointing"); "chrismation" refers to what the Latin church calls the sacrament of confirmation. See *Anointing.*

CHRIST. See *Messiah.*

CHRISTENDOM. A collective name for Christians, Christian countries and Christianity's cultural and religious influence.

CHRISTENING. Being named with a Christian name and received into the church. In the west this is done by baptism; in the east confirmation and communion are also administered. See *Baptism; Initiation.*

CHRIST EVENT. Term used to designate Christ's coming as the decisive fact of salvation history. See *Salvation History.*

CHRIST OF FAITH. An expression to indicate the gap between the results coming from a merely historical study of Jesus and the stance of faith, which accepts Jesus as Son of God and savior of the world. See *Historical Jesus.*

CHRISTIANITY. The religion of those who belong to Christian churches and communities.

CHRISTIANS. Followers of Christ, a term used first in Syrian Antioch (Acts 11:26).

CHRISTMAS. The celebration of the birth of Jesus Christ on December 25, a feast of western origin, which replaced the pagan feast of the Unconquered Sun and which eventually became common to all Christian churches except the Armenian. The Roman liturgy allows for mass to be said during the night (normally at midnight), at dawn and during the day: to celebrate the threefold birth of the Son—in the bosom of the Father, from the womb of Mary and in the heart of the believer. See *Armenian Christianity; Epiphany.*

CHRISTMAS PREPARATION. Called Advent in the west. The east Syrians call their preparation, which covers four Sundays before Christmas *subára* (Syriac "annunciation"), as do the west Syrians their six Sundays prior to Christmas. Both celebrate in this season the annunciation to Mary and the birth of St. John the Baptist. In the Byzantine tradition this pre-Christmas season starts on November 15 and involves a forty-day fast, sometimes called "Philip's fast," because it begins a day after the Feast of St. Philip the Apostle. See *Advent; Annunciation; Calendar, Liturgical; Fasting; Liturgy.*

CHRISTOCENTRICISM. A systematic focusing of all theology and devotional life on the person and work of Jesus Christ.

CHRISTOLOGICAL TITLES. Such NT designations for Jesus as Christ, Son of God and Son of man. They entail various approaches to understanding who Jesus was/is and what he did/does. See *Kyrios; Messiah.*

CHRISTOLOGY. The theological interpretation of Jesus Christ, clarifying systematically who and what he is in himself for those who believe in him. In a less systematic way the NT contains various christological approaches to Jesus. See *Functional Christology; Hypostatic Union; Soteriology.*

CHRISTOLOGY FROM ABOVE. The kind of christology developed from the theme of the preexistent Logos or Son of God who descended into our world (Jn 1:14). See *Alexandrian Theology; Logos-Sarx Christology.*

CHRISTOLOGY FROM BELOW. The kind of christology developed from an examination of Christ's human history, especially as it is presented by the synoptic gospels. See *Antiochene Theology; Logos-Anthropos Christology.*

CHRISTOPHANY (Gr. "manifestation of the Anointed One"). The revelation of Jesus as God's Anointed One or messiah. This happened not only at Jesus' baptism in the Jordan (Matt 4:16–17; Mk 1:9–11; Lk 3:21–22) and his transfiguration on Mount Tabor, but above all in the Easter appearances. See *Anointing; Appearances of the Risen Lord; Messiah; Transfiguration.*

CHURCH (Gr. "thing, building belonging to the Lord"). The community founded by Jesus Christ and anointed by the Holy Spirit as the final sign of God's will to save the whole human family. God's abiding presence among human beings is expressed in the preaching, sacramental life, pastoral ministry and organization of this community that consists in a communion of local churches presided over by the church of Rome. See *Body of Christ; Marks (Notes) of the Church; People of God.*

CHURCH AND STATE. The relationship between these two bodies that are independently competent in their own spheres but should work together harmoniously to advance the comprehensive welfare of human society and maintain a proper civil and religious freedom. While church members as such have no right to dictate in political matters, the state and its leaders should not pretend to be independent of the moral law which the church upholds (see DH *passim*). See *Canon Law, Sources of Oriental Church; Liberty, Religious; Symphony.*

CHURCH, DEDICATION OF. The solemn rite, reserved to the bishop or his delegate, whereby a building is set apart for Christian worship and thus indicates a special presence of God and the church in the world. In the west the rite generally consists of the eucharist and a ceremony during which the building is blessed and relics of saints fixed in the altar. In the east, before the first liturgy is celebrated, the altar is sprinkled with holy water and anointed as in the rites of initiation. See *Blessing; Consecration; Initiation; Sacramentals.*

CHURCHES. Various Christian communities that may differ, to an extent, in beliefs, liturgy and discipline, but have some measure of union with one another by holding to "one Lord, one faith, one baptism" (Eph 4:5; see AG 19–22; LG 26; CIC 368–572; and OE and UR *passim*). See *Church; Ecumenism; Local Church.*

CHURCH MILITANT. The visible, pilgrim church here on earth, to be distinguished from the Church Expectant (or Suffering) or the souls in purgatory and the Church Triumphant or the saints already in heaven. See *Heaven; Purgatory.*

CHURCH OF THE EAST (ASSYRIAN). A Middle-Eastern church, the oldest, still surviving church to have separated from the Great Church, present in both east and west. This form of Christianity developed under less Greek influence, since it had been founded in very early Christian times apparently from Palestine and Edessa. It became independent at the time of the Council of Ephesus (431), which it rejected, after having already proclaimed itself independent of the patriarchate of Antioch in 424 and established its center in Seleucia-Ctesiphon in Persia, outside of the Byzantine Empire. The Church of the East regarded Theodore of Mopsuestia (ca. 350–428) as its chief theologian. His orientation in christology was sharpened by like-minded theologians, who were expelled from Edessa in 489 by Emperor Zeno and fled to Persia. This church goes by the name of "Church of the East," because it lay east of the Roman Empire. Later on, because of its rejection of Ephesus (431), it was widely known in the west as the "Nestorian Church." Today, the Catholic heirs of this church are called Chaldeans, while those not in union with Rome are called "Assyrians." See *Antiochene Theology; Eastern Churches; Edessa; Ephesus, Council of; Nestorianism; Malabar Christians; Three Chapters, The.*

CIBORIUM (Gr. "seed-like cup obtained from water-lily"). A cup bigger than a chalice that holds the wafer-hosts to be consecrated for communion or for reservation in the tabernacle. The baldacchino or canopy over the altar in some old churches like St. Clement's in Rome is also called a ciborium. See *Chalice.*

CIRCUMCISION. Cutting off the foreskin of male infants to symbolize their admission to the religious community. The Jews made this rite the hallmark of their alliance with God (Gen 17:10–14; Exod 12:48; Lev 12:3). The early church refused to impose on male converts circumcision, as baptism replaced it (Acts 15:5, 28–29; Gal 5:2–6; 6:15; Col 2:11–15). The feast of the Circumcision of Our Lord is celebrated on 1 January. See *Baptism; Judaism.*

CIRCUMINSESSIO (Lat. "sitting around"). See *Perichoresis.*

CIVIL RELIGION. The use of religious traditions to support public activities in a country where there is no established religion. In the U.S.A. a civil religion derived from a Jewish-Christian heritage expresses itself in various ways: when, for example, political leaders appeal to the nation's "manifest destiny," use the Bible on taking their oath of office and echo the basic belief "in God we trust." See *Church and State; Religion.*

CLASSICAL CONSCIOUSNESS. Expression used by Bernard Lonergan (1904–84) to describe how culture conditions awareness in its progress from naive to philosophical knowledge. Classical consciousness is a developed form of awareness that believes one culture to be the normative and superior criterion by which to judge other cultural experiences and expressions. After centuries of domination in the west, classical consciousness has given way to a *pluralistic consciousness*, which is more descriptive than normative. In theology this means that many classical answers, though not necessarily invalidated, can no longer be maintained as the exclusive interpretations of Christian faith. See *Pluralism; Theology, Methods in.*

CLERGY (Gr. "lot, fate, portion"). Collective term for ordained deacons, priests and bishops (see CIC 232, 266). See *Bishop; Deacon; Priest.*

CLERIC (Gr. "one chosen by lot," "an inheritor"). Somebody who has received an ecclesial ministry entailing precise obligations and rights over and above those of lay persons, but different from those of religious (see CIC 232). One becomes a cleric by receiving the diaconate. See *Laity; Religious; Tonsure.*

CLERICALISM. An effort by clergy to enhance their influence in nonecclesial affairs; an approach to pastoral and theological problems that seeks to concentrate everything in the hands of the clergy. See *Anticlericalism.*

CODE OF CANON LAW (CIC). The highest code of law for the Latin church. A revision was first announced by Pope John XXIII in 1959, in view of the forthcoming Ecumenical Council, Vatican II (1962–65). The code was drawn up after extensive collegial consultation with bishops and episcopal conferences (see LG 9, 48). The CIC promulgated by John Paul II in 1983 contains 1,752 canons arranged in seven books (as compared with the first CIC promulgated by Benedict XV in 1917, which contained 2,414 canons in five books). The 1983 code aimed to express in juridical terms the teaching of Vatican II and its subsequent implementation. See *Canon Law; Corpus Juris Canonici; Episcopal Conferences.*

CODE OF CANON LAW FOR THE ORIENTAL CHURCHES. Projected scheme of canon law for the Oriental churches already presented to Pope John Paul II (b. 1920) but not yet promulgated. As early as 1927— ten years after the promulgation of the *Codex Juris Canonici* (= CIC) by Pope Benedict XV—the Congregation for the Oriental Church [now: Churches] proposed that these churches should have their own code of canon law, a suggestion accepted in 1929 by Pope Pius XI (1857–1939). The first drafts included too much Roman centralism and Latin patterns of church life. After Vatican II, which clearly acknowledged the special traditions, rights, privileges and sacramental discipline of the eastern churches (OE 5–23), Paul VI (1897–1978) set up the New Commission for the Code of Canon Law for the Eastern Churches. Despite inspiration from Oriental sources and consultation with the Catholic Eastern Patriarchs, the main source for the projected Oriental code has remained the Latin code promulgated in 1983. Drafts published so far have caused discussion about the role of the patriarchs and the local church. If properly balanced, the Oriental code could open the way for mergers with non-Catholic eastern churches. See *Eastern Churches; Local Church; Patriarch.*

COLLECT. First variable prayer in the mass of the Latin rite after the Kyrie or, on Sundays and feast-days, after the Gloria. It expresses what the congregation may have been silently praying, thus "collecting" their prayers and setting the tone for the particular feast or mystery being celebrated. See *Gloria; Kyrie.*

COLLEGIALITY. The responsibility for the whole church shared by the bishops in communion among themselves and with the head of the college of bishops, the pope (LG 22–23; CIC 336–41). The primary place for the exercise of this collegiality is an ecumenical council, but collegiality is also expressed, to a lesser degree, through episcopal conferences and synods. See *Council, Ecumenical; Episcopal Conferences; Sobornost; Synod.*

COMMUNICATIO IDIOMATUM (Lat./Gr. "interchange of properties"). Exchange of attributes because of the union of divinity and humanity in the one person of the incarnate Son of God. This means that attributes of one of his natures may be predicated of him even when he is named with reference to the other nature: e.g., "the Son of God died on the cross," and "the Son of Mary created the world" (see DS 251). This method of attribution calls for certain distinctions, so as not to confuse the two natures. The Son of God precisely as divine did not die on the cross, nor did the Son of Mary precisely as human create the universe. See *Chalcedon, Council of; Constantinople, Second Council of; Ephesus, Council of; Hypostatic Union; Monophysitism; Trisagion.*

COMMUNICATIO IN SACRIS. Participating in the liturgy of a church other than one's own. Ecumenism encourages sharing the word of God, but sacraments normally express (and further) a union already present (see UR 8). In case of necessity and in the absence of Catholic clergy, Catholics may confess, communicate and receive the anointing of the sick from Orthodox priests (see OE 26–27). Orthodox churches, in most cases, are reluctant to administer sacraments to the non-Orthodox. See *Eastern Churches; Orthodoxy.*

COMMUNION. Sharing in the body of Christ by receiving the consecrated host during mass and after due preparation (e.g., by confessing grave sins). When communion is received on other occasions (e.g., at home by the sick), the link with the mass should not be ignored. Church law prescribes that communion should be received at least once a year, but

41

not necessarily under both species (see DS 1198–1200; CIC 912–23). See *Eucharist; Koinonia; Mass.*

COMMUNION, SPIRITUAL. Receiving communion in desire when actual communion is not possible. Those who wish to partake spiritually in the body of Christ ought to prepare themselves as if they were attending mass (e.g., by asking pardon for their sins, reading the scriptures and expressing perfect love for God).

COMMUNION OF SAINTS. The spiritual union between Christ and all Christians, whether already in heaven (or purgatory) or still living on earth (LG 49–50). See *Church Militant; Heaven; Koinonia; Purgatory.*

COMMUNITY. Christians united for prayer, ministry and life in common. See *Basic Communities; Church; Parish; Religious Life.*

COMPARATIVE RELIGION. That science which developed in the late nineteenth century and which studies the parallels and differences between the beliefs and practices of various religions. Comparative religion as such does not pronounce on the relative merits and ultimate truth of religions. See *Religion; World Religions.*

COMPUNCTION. The "pricking of conscience" occasioned by an awareness of one's sins. It should lead to a healthy sorrow and divine pardon rather than to a morbid scrupulosity over one's faults. See *Attrition; Contrition; Penance, Virtue of.*

CONCELEBRATION. The joint celebration of the same sacramental act by several ministers led by a main celebrant. This practice, found in the early church, continued in the east, whereas in the Latin rite it was limited to a few occasions like ordination to the priesthood. By once more encouraging concelebration of the eucharist in the west, the Second Vatican Council did not abolish "private" masses or masses celebrated without a congregation (but preferably with an altar server). Rather, the council acknowledged the social character of the eucharist and the unity of ministerial priesthood, in particular, that of the bishop with the priests of his diocese (SC 57–58). In the eastern churches, "private" masses are unknown, and concelebration once a day at the same altar the norm. See *Anointing of the Sick; Communicatio In Sacris.*

CONCILIARISM. A theory which flourished at the time of the Great Schism (1378–1417), when the west was divided in allegiance between two or even three popes. It held that supreme authority is vested in an ecumenical council independently of the pope, unlike the teaching of

Vatican II which situates the college of bishops with and under the pope. See *Basle, Council of; Collegiality; Constance, Council of; Council, Ecumenical; Pentarchy; Pope; Vatican Council, Second.*

CONCILIARITY. See *Sobornost.*

CONCUPISCENCE. In general, desire or covetousness. More specifically, it refers to the disordered desire that comes from original sin and remains after baptism (see DS 1515). See *Original Sin; Trent, Council of.*

CONCURSUS DIVINUS (Lat. "divine concurrence"). God's constantly needed cooperation that enables creatures to initiate, continue and complete their actions. Since rational creatures sometimes sin, we face the problem of accounting for God's collaboration in actions that deliberately run counter to the divine will. See *Freedom; Grace; Molinism; Omnipotence; Pelagianism; Synergism.*

CONFESSION. The whole sacrament of penance or that part of it when penitents acknowledge their sins to the priest (CIC 959–991; see 915–16). Confession usually takes place individually, but general absolution (or absolution of a group without previous confession), may be given under certain circumstances (see CIC 961). Confession once a year is obligatory on all Catholics who have reached the age of reason (CIC 989). Confession of venial sins is recommended, whereas all mortal sins must be confessed. See *Absolution; Attrition; Contrition; Lateran Council, Fourth; Penance, Sacrament of; Satisfaction; Sin.*

CONFESSION OF DOSITHEUS. A profession of faith approved by the 1672 Synod of Jerusalem and recognized as authoritative in the eastern Orthodox Church. It was mainly composed by Dositheus (1641–1707; Orthodox Patriarch of Jerusalem from 1669) who opposed Protestant influence in the Byzantine Church and, in particular, the ideas of Cyril Lukaris. See *Eastern Churches; Orthodoxy.*

CONFESSION OF LUKARIS. A profession of faith showing Calvinist tendencies and written by the Patriarch of Constantinople Cyril Lukaris (1572–1638), the most important theologian of eastern Orthodoxy since the fall of Constantinople (1453). Although repeatedly condemned in the eastern church, the confession exercised an influence on subsequent Orthodox theology. See *Calvinism; Eastern Churches; Eastern Theology.*

CONFESSION OF PETER MOGHILA. A profession of faith composed by the Orthodox Metropolitan of Kiev, Peter Moghila (1597–1646), in reaction to Cyril Lukaris' Calvinist trends. Approved in a modified form by the

Synod of Jassy, in modern Romania (1642) and the foremost Orthodox patriarchs in 1643, it remains the most pro-Latin document accepted by the Orthodox.

CONFIRMATION. The western name for one of the seven sacraments, the second of the sacraments of initiation. The minister imposes hands on the candidates and anoints their foreheads with chrism while saying: "Be sealed with the gifts of the Holy Spirit." In the east confirmation, called chrismation, is administered by the priest immediately after the baptism of an infant. In the west confirmation has been administered by the bishop and for pastoral reasons comes later (e.g., at the age of reason or even during adolescence). Adult converts, however, are confirmed immediately after baptism and before receiving their first communion. The east recognizes the presence of the bishop by the fact that the chrism has been blessed by him. In the west a simple priest may be the extraordinary minister of confirmation (see CIC 882; 879–896). See *Baptism; Character; Charisms; Chrism; Holy Spirit; Initiation; RCIA; Sacraments.*

CONFUCIANISM. The beliefs and practices drawn from the ancient Chinese classics and transmitted in a special way by Confucius or K'ung Fu-tzu (ca. 550–478 B.C.). He may have authored the last of the five classical or "canonical" books: the Shu King (historical documents), Shih King (poems), Li Ki (ceremonies and institutions), Yi King or book of change, and the Annals of Lu. Confucius approved the traditional religion of his time, emphasizing religious rituals and firmly believing in T'ien, a supreme cosmic power which assigns to human beings and all things their destinies. On that basis Confucius developed his ethical teaching. He insisted on sincerity, loyalty to principles, and the cultivation of kindness (*jên*) and good character. He taught that inward goodness is fully expressed in all human relationships through decorum, propriety, and the observance of rites (*li*). The marks of true nobility are kindness, filial piety, loyalty, reciprocity, propriety and a harmonious balance between extremes. From about 200 B.C. to A.D. 1912 Confucianism was the official state doctrine in China. See *Buddhism; Taoism; Zen.*

CONGREGATIONAL THEOLOGY. A form of Protestant Christianity which developed out of the reformation and which maintains the right of local churches to regulate their own affairs in complete independence, a principle seen to be anchored in the Bible. See *Church; Protestantism; Reformation.*

CONSCIENCE. The capacity to evaluate and choose a course of action according to the law God has written in our hearts (Rom 2:12–16). Conscience cannot simply be identified with God's law, because it may fail through scrupulosity and laxity or insensitivity to the guidance of the Holy Spirit. See *Heart; Moral Theology.*

CONSECRATION. The solemn act whereby someone or something is set apart for God. Persons are consecrated for sacred office, buildings dedicated for worship, and bread and wine consecrated at the climax of the eucharist.

CONSENSUS FIDELIUM. See *Sensus Fidelium.*

CONSTANCE, COUNCIL OF (1414–18). Generally considered the sixteenth general council by Roman Catholics and convened to resolve the Great Schism (1378–1417), in the last phase of which three popes claimed the allegiance of Christians: John XXIII, who convoked the council at the instigation of the German Emperor Sigismund and was deposed by the council; Gregory XII, who resigned; and Benedict XIII, who was deposed. In their place Martin V was elected. The council condemned John Wycliffe (ca. 1329–84) and John Huss (ca. 1369–1415) (DS 1151–1195; 1201–79) and also defined that in the eucharist Christ is wholly present under the appearance of either bread or wine (DS 1198–1200). *Conciliarism; Hussites.*

CONSTANTINOPLE, FIRST COUNCIL OF (381). Convoked by Emperor Theodosius I to consolidate the unity of faith after the long Arian controversy, it was attended by 186 bishops, all from the east. Neither Pope Damasus I nor the west were represented. When the first president of the council, Melitius of Antioch, died, St. Gregory of Nazianzus presided for some time before resigning; the council then chose Nectarius as its president and Bishop of Constantinople. The council proclaimed the divinity of the Holy Spirit against the Pneumatomachians, and the full humanity of Christ against the Apollinarians. It gave the see of Constantinople the place of honor in Christendom after Rome. It was recognized later as the second ecumenical council—partly through Chalcedon, which promulgated its creed (see DS 150, 300). See *Apollinarianism; Chalcedon, Council of; Creed, Nicene; Holy Spirit; Macedonianism; Pentarchy; Pneumatomachians.*

CONSTANTINOPLE, SECOND COUNCIL OF (553). The fifth general council, convened by Emperor Justinian (527–65) to bring peace to the church in the east. In order to win over the Monophysites, Justinian encouraged the 165 bishops present (practically all easterners) to condemn Theodore of Mopsuestia (ca. 350–428), Theodoret of Cyrrhus (ca. 393–ca. 458) and Ibas of Edessa (435–457) for Nestorianism. After considerable harassment, Pope Vigilius (d. 555) dropped his opposition to the proceedings and accepted the council (see DS 421–38). See *Monophysitism; Neo-Chalcedonianism; Nestorianism; Quinisext; Three Chapters.*

CONSTANTINOPLE, THIRD COUNCIL OF (680/681). The sixth general council, convoked by Emperor Constantine IV to resolve the issue of Monotheletism. Pope Agatho was represented through three delegates who, however, did not preside; the Emperor did. The council reaffirmed the Chalcedonian profession of faith and taught, as a necessary corollary, that Christ has two distinct wills (divine and human) which nonetheless operate together in perfect moral harmony (see DS 550–59). See *Chalcedon, Council of; Lateran Councils; Monotheletism; Quinisext.*

CONSTANTINOPLE, FOURTH COUNCIL OF (869/870). Considered by Roman Catholics the eighth general council, it asserted Rome's jurisdictional primacy, condemned iconoclasm and tried to win over the supporters of Photius (ca. 810–ca. 895), the deposed Patriarch of Constantinople, who was later reinstated and deposed again, but is acknowledged as a saint by the Orthodox. In the twenty-first canon issued by the council, Pope Hadrian II acknowledged for the first time Constantinople's precedence over Alexandria (see DS 650–64). See *Iconoclasm.*

CONSUBSTANTIAL. See *Homoousios.*

CONSUBSTANTIATION (Lat. "along with the substance"). The view, condemned at Trent (1545–63), that after the words of eucharistic consecration the substances of bread and wine continue to exist alongside the body and blood of the Lord (DS 1652). See *Transubstantiation.*

CONTEMPLATION. That form of silent prayer in which the mind and imagination are less active, and the believer looks with love at God and the divine mysteries. When contemplation comes through diligent exercise, it is called "acquired." When it is simply granted as a special gift of God, it is called "infused." See *Meditation; Prayer.*

CONTINGENCY. The characteristic of beings and events that do not exist or occur by necessity, but only in dependence—ultimately on God, the only Being that necessarily exists.

CONTRITION. A heartfelt sorrow for past sin accompanied by the intention not to sin again (see Ps 51; Lk 15:11–32; 18:9–14; DS 1676–78). Contrition is necessary for the sacrament of penance to be valid (see DS 1451–65; 1704). See *Attrition; Penance, Sacrament of.*

CONVERSION. A turning from sinful priorities to God, in a way that enhances both personal integrity and the good of the Christian community. Conversion is required by the coming of God's kingdom (Mk 1:15; Matt 4:17). See *Metanoia*.

COPTIC CHRISTIANITY (Arabic "qubti," from the Gr. for "Egyptian"). That church which claims to have originated with the evangelist Mark, supposedly martyred in Alexandria in A.D. 68. By the late second century it had its own self-identity, and after the Council of Chalcedon (451) went its own way by maintaining a verbal form of Monophysitism. Coptic, a late form of the old Egyptian language, is now used only in the liturgy, since Arabic has become the language of the country. Through efforts at a wider communion, a Coptic church recognizing Rome emerged in the late eighteenth century (see DS 1330–53). The challenge facing all Copts is to show how their form of Christianity, rich in monasticism and literature, can contribute to a predominantly Islamic Egypt. See *Eastern Churches; Jacobites; Melkites; Monophysitism; Oriental Orthodox*.

CO-REDEMPTRIX. A title applied to Our Lady to express her cooperation in the work of salvation. While remaining strictly subordinate to Christ, the sole source of grace, she collaborates in the incarnation (Lk 1:26–38) and the redemptive death of her son (Jn 19:25–27) (see DS 3370). See *Atonement; Eve; Incarnation; New Eve; Redemption*.

CORPUS CHRISTI (Lat. "Body of Christ"). A feast in the western church celebrated after Trinity Sunday and commemorating Christ's gift of the eucharist. Its institution was largely due to Blessed Juliana of Liège (d. 1258). See *Blessed Sacrament; Eucharist*.

CORPUS JURIS CANONICI (Lat. "Body of Canon Law"). The main collection of laws of the Catholic Church until Pope Benedict XV promulgated the *Codex Juris Canonici* in 1917. The *Corpus Juris Canonici* was composed in six stages. (a) Gratian, a twelfth-century monk from Bologna, created the discipline of canon law by putting together in an organized way legal rulings from councils, popes and church fathers in his *Concordia Discordantium Canonum* (Lat. "Concordance of Discordant Canons"), usually called *Decretum Gratiani* (Lat. "Decree of Gratian") (1141). (b) Pope Gregory IX (ca. 1148–1241) ordered the renowned canonist St. Raymond of Peñafort (1185–1275) to complete Gratian's *Decretum*. The result was the *Liber Decretalium Extravagantium* (Lat. "Book of Decretals not [yet] Included") divided into five books and promulgated by the pope's authority. (c) Boniface VIII (ca. 1234–1303) added a sixth book in 1298, *Liber Sextus Decretalium*. (d) In connection with the Council of Vienne (1311–12), Clement V (1264–1314) added further legislation. These decretals were promulgated in 1317 and are known as the *Clementinae*. (5) The decrees of Pope John XXII (1249–1334) were collected and published as the *Extravagantes Joannis XXII*. (6) Finally, the *Extravagantes comunes*, or papal decrees enacted between 1261 and 1471, entered the *Corpus Juris Canonici*, which was revised and promulgated in 1582 by Pope Gregory XIII (1502–85). See *Codex Juris Canonici*.

COSMOLOGICAL ARGUMENT. See *Arguments for the Existence of God; Five Ways, The.*

COSMOLOGY. A coherent interpretation of the universe in its ultimate origin, nature, order and destiny. See *Creation; Eschatology; Protology.*

COSMOS (Gr. "world," "adornment"). The universe as an orderly whole. In the NT "cosmos" can denote simply our wider environment (Gal 4:3) or else the world as hostile to Christ (Jn 1:10). In eastern theology cosmos refers to the beauty of creation as opposed to the disgust caused by chaos (see Gen 1:1–2:4). See *Beauty, Theology of; Doxa; World.*

COUNCIL, ECUMENICAL (GENERAL). An occasional assembly of the bishops of the whole church who, with and under the pope, teach and legislate as one college and may even pronounce infallibly on matters of revealed faith and morals. On the basis of a list first drawn up by St. Robert Bellarmine (1542–1621), Roman Catholics usually accept twenty-one ecumenical councils, from Nicaea I (325) to Vatican II (1962–65). Under current legislation, it belongs to the pope to call a council, preside over it personally or through his legates, determine its program, extend an invitation to those who are not strictly entitled to attend, and confirm the council's decrees. A council has to be reconvoked if the pope dies while it is still in session (CIC 337–41). See *Conciliarism; Episcopal Conferences; Reception; Seven Councils, The; Synod of Bishops.*

COUNTER-REFORMATION. The revival and reaction of the Catholic Church (from ca. 1520 to the end of the Thirty Years War in 1648) to the forces of the reformation. The term itself is problematic, because earnest efforts to reform the church had been undertaken long before Martin Luther's initial protest in 1517. Spain remained practically untouched by Protestantism partly through the reforms already introduced by Cardinal Francisco Ximénez de Cisneros (1436–1517) and supported by the Spanish crown. In Italy Girolamo Savonarola (1452–98) died in the cause of ecclesiastical reform. Lateran V (1511–17) decided to correct abuses. After the initial shock at what Luther's protest triggered off, reforming forces within the Catholic Church gained momentum. Such new religious orders came into being as the Theatines (founded by St. Cajetan [1480–1547] and Giovanni Pietro Caraffa, later Pope Paul IV [1476–1559]) and the Capuchins (founded by Matteo di Bassi [d. 1552]). Although every schoolbook says that St. Ignatius of Loyola (1491–1556) founded the Jesuit Order to combat Protestantism, this was still not a major objective when he received papal approbation (1540). He aimed rather at the reform of Catholic life within Europe and mission work abroad. Later, especially through St. Peter Canisius (1521–97) Jesuits became deeply involved in the struggle to save Germany, Austria, Poland, England and other countries for the one Catholic Church. Further leading figures in the counter-reformation include St. Philip Neri (1515–95), St. Charles Borromeo (1538–84), St. Francis de Sales (1567–1622) and Mary Ward (1585–1645). The Council of Trent (1545–63) was of immense importance through its careful restatement and/or reformation of a whole range of church beliefs and practices. Any full account of the counter-reformation will also deal with the influence of Jesuit colleges, baroque culture, missions in the Americas, Asia and Africa, and the reigns of Charles V (1500–58) and Philip II (1527–98) of Spain. See *Calvinism; Inquisition; Lateran, Fifth Council of; Presbyterianism; Lutheranism; Protestant; Puritans; Reformation, The; Trent, Council of; Tübingen and Its Schools.*

COVENANT. God's alliance of friendship with all humanity represented by Noah (Gen 9:8–17) and with Abraham and his descendants (Gen 15:18; 17:1–22). At Sinai God made a covenant through Moses (Exod 19:5–6; 24:7–8), and the ten commandments summarized Israel's corresponding duties (Exod 20:1–17; Deut 5:1–21; Jer 11:1–8). The major prophets announced the interior holiness to be offered and effected by God (e.g., Jer 31:31–34). The new and eternal covenant was sealed by the blood of Christ (Lk 22:20; 1 Cor 11:25; Heb 7:22; 8:8–13). See *Berith; Decalogue.*

CREATION. The act whereby in sovereign freedom and out of nothing God has brought about and constantly maintains in existence all that exists (DS 800; 3002). The Bible is less interested in the starting-point than in the end-product of creation, the world created for God's glory (e.g., Isa 43:7; Psalm 8; see DS 3025). See *Causality; Contingency; Deism; Evolution; Pantheism.*

CREATIONISM. (a) The doctrine that each human soul is created directly by God (see DS 3896) and not generated by the parents, as traducianism claims. (b) Creationism also refers to the anti-evolutionary view of those who interpret the Genesis accounts of creation in a fundamentalist way and argue that our universe came into being through a series of separate divine interventions "from the outside." See *Evolution; Fundamentalism; Soul.*

CREATURE. Whatever is not God and depends for existence on God. While all creatures share in the divine goodness (Gen 1:31), men and women have been created in the image and likeness of God (Gen 1:26–27) and fulfill their destiny by truly loving God and their fellow human beings. See *Image of God.*

CREED. A concise version of the chief points of Christian faith. As answers to questions about the Father, Son and Holy Spirit, creeds developed in connection with baptism. Debates and heresies forced the church to clarify further the doctrines expressed in creedal form.

CREED, APOSTLES'. The creed promoted by the Emperor Charlemagne (ca. 742–814) and used at baptism in the western church. It has a simple tripartite scheme, constructed around the Father, the Son and the Holy Spirit (see DS 16). Rufinus (ca. 345–410) reports the legend that the twelve apostles composed it, each one being responsible for a phrase.

CREED, ATHANASIAN. Profession of faith, also called *Quicumque vult* (Lat. "Whoever wants") after its opening words, falsely attributed to St. Athanasius of Alexandria (ca. 296–373) and probably originating in southern France in the fifth century. It has much to say about the Trinity, the incarnation and redemption (see DS 75–76).

CREED, NICENE. The creed ratified at Nicaea I (325). Against the Arians, it proclaimed the eternal divinity of the Son, who is "of the same substance" (*homoousios*) with the Father (DS 125–26). Often, the "Nicene Creed" refers to what is more precisely called the Nicene-Constantinopolitan Creed, associated with Constantinople I (381). This creed presupposes that of Nicaea, but is more specific about the divinity of the Holy Spirit, who is to be "worshiped and glorified" with the Father and the Son (DS 150). Widely used during the eucharist and at baptism, this is the most commonly accepted creed among Christians. See *Constantinople, First Council of; Filioque; Homoousios; Nicaea, First Council of.*

CROSS. The characteristic Christian sign, expressing Christ's death for our salvation and used by Paul to sum up his message (1 Cor 1:17–18). A feast on September 14, the sign of the cross, the veneration of the cross on Good Friday and, in the Latin tradition, the stations of the cross are some of the many ways for recalling Christ's death. In any case it is always being remembered and re-presented through the church's sacraments. See *Icon; Theologia Crucis.*

CRUSADES (Lat. "cross"). Military expeditions undertaken by western Christians to liberate from Islamic domination the land where Jesus lived and died. Between 1096, when Peter the Hermit preached the first crusade, till 1270, when what is usually considered the last crusade ended with the death of St. Louis IX, there were five major crusades. Christian expeditions against the Turks continued in later centuries. The crusades have fired the imagination of writers and painters, but their evil effects included a deepening of the break between eastern and western Christianity. In 1204, when the crusaders sacked Constantinople and set up the Latin empire and patriarchate, they practically sealed the schism between Rome and Constantinople. At the same time, however, the crusades increased cultural contacts. See *Aristotelianism; Byzantine Christianity; Schism.*

CULT. The religious homage due to God as creator, redeemer and sanctifier. Christian cult stresses praise and thanksgiving more than petition. See *Adoration; Worship.*

CULTIC MEAL. The meal through which in the highest way worshipers acknowledge and identify themselves with their deity. In Christianity the supreme act of worship is the eucharist, the sacrificial and spiritual meal given to us by Jesus Christ in his death and resurrection, so that in anticipation of his final coming we may thank and unite ourselves with God. See *Eucharist; Mass; Sacrifice of the Mass.*

D

DAMNATION (Lat. "condemnation"). The fate of those who die in unrepented mortal sin. Having radically rejected God and their fellow human beings (Matt 25:31–46), they will suffer forever in hell. See *Hell; Judgment; Reprobation.*

DARK NIGHT. At night the visible world disappears, making way for the invisible world. For mystics "night" becomes the privileged place to encounter God. "Dark" indicates that this privileged experience comes through trials that purify the soul from earthly attachments. With St. John of the Cross (1542–91) one may distinguish between the dark night of the senses, which weakens the grasp of sensual attractions, and that of the spirit, which detaches the soul from spiritual consolation. See *Mysticism; Spirituality.*

DEACON (Gr. "server"). Inspired in part by the seven men chosen to care for the material needs of the Jerusalem community (Acts 6:1–6), deacons flourished in the early centuries of the church. Later their importance declined in the west, and the diaconate became simply a temporary stage before priesthood. The Second Vatican Council endorsed the restoration of the permanent diaconate for older, married men (LG 29), a decision implemented in 1967. Besides being entrusted with administrative and pastoral duties, deacons may, when authorized, baptize, solemnly preach, distribute the eucharist and officiate at marriages and funerals. See *Clergy; Cleric; Ministry; Ordination.*

DEACONESS. Woman in the early church holding an office similar to that of the deacon. Besides caring for the sick and the poor, deaconesses assisted the minister in baptizing women. The office of deaconess died out in the middle ages, but was revived in the nineteenth century by Anglicans and Protestants. See *Anglican Communion; Protestant.*

DEAD SEA SCROLLS. See *Qumran Scrolls.*

DEATH. The definitive end of our biological existence whereby the history of our life before God assumes its complete, irreversible shape. The Bible sees death both as natural (e.g., Ps 49:11–12; Isa 40:6–7) and as the consequence of sin (Gen 3:19; Rom 5:12). Death will be the last enemy to be overcome (1 Cor 15:26) through our sharing in Christ's resurrection. See *Immortality; Resurrection; Soul.*

DEATH OF GOD THEOLOGY. A theological movement of the 1960's, found chiefly in the USA, which at times merely entered into dialogue with contemporary atheism, but at other times represented the world as truly God-forsaken or even followed Friedrich Wilhelm Nietzsche (1844–1900) in proclaiming God's death at the hands of men.

DECALOGUE (Gr. "ten words"). The ten commandments, which sum up our religious and moral responsibilities. They are found in two versions: Exod 20:1–17 and Deut 5:6–21. Jesus did not abolish the ten commandments but, drawing on Deuteronomy 6:4–5 and Leviticus 19:18, summarized them in terms of love toward God, our neighbor and ourselves (Mk 12:29–31). He also indicated that observance of the decalogue may lead to perfect detachment and discipleship (Mk 10:17–21). See *Imitation of Christ; Love; Moral Theology; Perfection.*

DE FIDE (Lat. "pertaining to faith"). Theological statements possessing the highest degree of certitude coming from divine revelation and being proclaimed as such by the teaching authority of the church. See *Dogma; Magisterium; Qualification, Theological.*

DEIFICATION. The purpose of the incarnation, according to St. Irenaeus (ca. 130–ca. 200), St. Athanasius (ca. 296–373) and other Greek fathers. Already created in God's image and likeness (Gen 1:26), human beings are called by grace to share in the divine life (1 Pet 1:3–4). See *Grace; Incarnation.*

DEISM. An umbrella-term for the beliefs of many British, European and American writers of the seventeenth and eighteenth centuries, who in various ways stressed the role of reason in religion and rejected revelation, miracles and any providential involvement in nature and human history. See *Miracles; Providence.*

DEMIURGE (Gr. "artisan, craftsman"). A name used by Plato (427–347 B.C.) for the divine architect who fashioned the world according to the eternal ideas. Gnostics reduced the demiurge to an inferior deity, responsible for the creation of the material universe which they despised. See *Creation; Gnosticism.*

DEMONOLOGY. The study of demons, their nature as fallen angels and their role in tempting and harming human beings. See *Angelology; Angels; Exorcism.*

DEMONS. Spiritual beings which, in the Jewish-Christian tradition, correspond to devils, angels in revolt against God and bent on harming human beings. See *Devil.*

DEMYTHOLOGIZATION. The attempt by Rudolf Bultmann (1884–1976) to translate what he calls biblical mythology into contemporary language. Although the term suggests elimination, Bultmann's intention was positive: to interpret myths existentially. See *Existentialism; Hermeneutic; Myth.*

DENZINGER. A collection of excerpts from church documents, first published by Heinrich Joseph Denzinger in 1854. Its thirty-fifth edition, revised by Adolf Schönmetzer, appeared in 1973. Among his other works may be mentioned a still useful collection of eastern liturgical texts, *Ritus Orientalium, Coptorum, Syrorum et Armenorum* (Würzburg 1863–64).

DEPOSIT OF FAITH. All that God definitively revealed through Christ for our salvation, considered as a treasure entrusted to the church to be preserved, interpreted and proclaimed faithfully to all people till the end of time (1 Tim 6:20; 2 Tim 1:12, 14; see DV 10; GS 62). See *Magisterium; Revelation; Tradition.*

DEPRAVITY, TOTAL. A term used by Calvinists to express the view that human beings were radically corrupted by the fall into sin. See *Calvinism; Fall, The.*

DESCENT INTO HELL. A traditional term for Christ's (a) stay among the dead after his death on the cross and (b) his victory over death, often expressed in Byzantine iconography by his liberation of Adam and Eve. In fact, this latter scene is the characteristic icon for Easter and is also called the *anastasis* (Gr. "resurrection"). See *Easter Triduum; Icon.*

DETERMINISM. An interpretation of the universe according to which all states of affairs and events come about inevitably and without any exercise of freedom. Our experience of choosing between alternatives contradicts this view of reality as rigidly predetermined. See *Foreknowledge; Freedom; Predestination.*

DEUTEROCANONICAL BOOKS. A Catholic name for those books found in the Greek (Septuagint) version of the OT but not in the Hebrew version. See *Apocrypha; Septuagint.*

DEVELOPMENT OF DOCTRINE. Growth in church's teaching since the apostolic age. Authentic development requires identity-in-change between the new teaching and the original deposit of faith or revelation that reached its climax with Christ. The fathers compared doctrinal development to the identity-in-change between a child and the same person as an adult. In grappling with the issue much depends on one's theory of understanding and interpretation. See *Deposit of Faith; Doctrine; Tradition.*

DEVIL, THE (Gr. "accuser," "tempter"). Name used for Lucifer or Satan, chief of the fallen angels. Allusions to Satan and his followers are frequent in the Bible (e.g., Wis 2:24; Matt 25:41; Lk 10:18; Jude 6, 9; Rev 12:9–12; 16:14). See *Angels; Demons.*

DEVOTION. That prayerful and affective dedication that makes believers deeply responsive to God's will. See *Religion.*

DEVOTIONS. Such non-liturgical prayers and practices as the way of the cross and the rosary that develop one's spiritual life and deepen one's religious convictions. See *Liturgy; Prayer; Rosary; Sacramentals.*

DIACONIA (Gr. "service"). NT term indicating that ministry and mission in the church is for the service of the community (Acts 1:17, 25; 21:19; Rom 11:13; 1 Tim 1:12). The Second Vatican Council describes the office of bishops in this way (LG 24). See *Ministry.*

DIALECTICAL THEOLOGY. An important movement in Protestant theology during the 1920's that was led by Karl Barth (1886–1968) and radically dissented from the prevailing Liberal Protestantism. Emphasizing the infinite qualitative difference between God and human beings, dialectical theology revelled in paradoxes (e.g., eternity and time) that allowed for no intellectual synthesis. See *Liberal Protestantism.*

DIALOGUE (Gr. "conversation"). Courteous discussion between individuals who hold different beliefs with a view to reaching or at least drawing closer to a consensus. Vatican II (1962–65) encourages Catholics to dialogue with the world at large (GS 85), with members of non-Christian religions (AG 16), with other Christians, both those of the churches of the east (UR 14–18) and those of churches in the west which became separated from Rome during the reformation (UR 19–23). Dialogue with non-Christian religions is called "interreligious" or "interfaith," whereas dialogue between Rome and other Christian churches is called "ecumenical" or "interconfessional." From time to time, guidelines for dialogue have been issued by various Vatican offices. In the case of the eastern churches one distinguishes between (a) the "dialogue of charity," which consists in signs and gestures that express both the common faith already shared by all members of the dialogue and their desire to remove obstacles blocking full communion; and (b) official theological dialogue, sometimes called the "dialogue of truth," in which through discussion representatives of various churches seek to reach full communion in faith and sacramental life. See *Ecumenism; Faith and Order; Vatican Council, Second; World Religions.*

DIASPORA (Gr. "dispersion"). Initially applied to Jews deported under the Assyrian (722 B.C.) and Babylonian (597 B.C.) conquests, the term eventually designated all Jews living outside Palestine (Jn 7:35), of whom there may have been a million in Alexandria alone at the time of Jesus. To some Greek-speaking Jews of Alexandria the church owes the Septuagint translation of the OT. The Christian proclamation outside the Holy Land first took place in Jewish synagogues (Acts 9:19–20; 11:19; 13:5, 14–44; 17:12 etc.). With the destruction of the temple and the advance of Christianity the diaspora Jews became more isolated and their religion developed into the Talmudic Judaism of medieval and modern times. The NT in places uses "diaspora" of Christians spread around the world and living in strange and sometimes hostile environments (Jas 1:1; 1 Pet 1:1). Modern persecution and emigration have brought a large-scale diaspora of eastern Christians. In Germany, "diaspora" refers to confessional minorities, whether Catholic or Protestant. See *Church; Mission; Septuagint; Talmud*.

DIDACHE (Gr. "teaching"). A work from around the end of the first century, compiled from various sources by a Jewish-Christian author of western Syria or eastern Asia Minor. It presents the ways that lead to life or death, as well as material concerning baptism, fasting, prayer, prophets and the eucharist. After the NT writings, the *Didache* and 1 Clement are our oldest documents on church order. See *Apostolic Fathers*.

DIOCESE (Gr. "house management," "administration"). (a) An administrative division of the Roman Empire, resulting from the reorganization initiated by Emperor Diocletian (ca. 245–316; emperor 284–305). By the beginning of the fifth century there were fifteen such dioceses in the Roman Empire, by then divided into east and west. (b) When the term passed into the vocabulary of the church, its meaning varied greatly—from what we would nowadays call a parish right through to an exarchy or an ecclesiastical district including several provinces. (c) In current usage, "diocese" or "archdiocese" refers to a territory under the immediate jurisdiction of a bishop or an archbishop, who governs in his own name and not as someone else's vicar. Hence he is called a "diocesan bishop" or "ordinary." A diocese corresponds to an eparchy in the eastern churches. The CIC defines a diocese (or see) as that portion of the people of God which is guided by its bishop as a pastor who with his priests gathers his faithful, in the Spirit, to hear the word of God and celebrate the eucharist (CIC 369). See *Archbishop; Bishop; Eparchy; Exarch; Holy See; Metropolitan; Ordinary; Patriarch*.

DIPTYCHS (Gr. "twofold, double(d), a double writing tablet"). The names of people, living and dead, to be read during the eucharist, originally written on two wooden tablets, joined together by hinges, hence the name. Naming prominent persons meant communion with them, whereas striking their names off the list signified excommunication. The use of diptychs of the living continues on more solemn occasions in Byzantine pontifical liturgies. See *Eucharistic Prayers*.

DISCERNMENT OF SPIRITS. The special gift of being able to distinguish divine charisms from merely natural or evil influences (1 Cor 12:10). To decide whether a particular state of affairs comes from the Spirit of God or from the spirit of evil and error (1 Jn 4:1–6), many fathers of the church and later authors have devised rules, such as those elaborated by St. Ignatius of Loyola (1491–1556) for people doing his Spiritual Exercises. See *Charism; Experience, Religious; Prudence.*

DISCIPLINA ARCANI (Lat. "discipline of the secret"). The early church's practice involving reticence about her most sacred rites and teachings, to ensure that catechumens and pagans did not treat them with irreverence. See *Catechumenate.*

DIVINE OFFICE. See *Breviary; Liturgy of the Hours; Office.*

DIVINIZATION. See *Deification.*

DOCETISM (Gr. "appearance"). The early heresy which held that the Son of God merely seemed to be a human being. Christ's bodily reality was considered heavenly or else a body only in appearance, with someone else, such as Simon of Cyrene, suffering in his place. Against Docetic views, which were already rejected in the NT (1 Jn 4:1–3; 2 Jn 7), the church taught that Christ took from Mary a genuine body like ours and suffered in a really human way (DS 76, 292, 1338, 1340–41). See *Christology; Johannine Theology.*

DOCTOR OF THE CHURCH. A title given to certain saints for their outstanding, orthodox teaching. From the eighth century the west recognized four such doctors: Pope Gregory the Great (ca. 540–604), Ambrose of Milan (ca. 339–97), Augustine of Hippo (354–430) and Jerome (ca. 342–420). A century later in the east, Basil the Great (ca. 330–79), Gregory of Nazianzus (328–89) and John Chrysostom (ca. 347–407) came to be known as "the Three Hierarchs and Ecumenical Teachers." The west added Athanasius of Alexandria (ca. 296–373), so as to have four eastern doctors paralleling four western doctors. Pope Benedict XIV (1675–1758) elaborated the norms for qualifying as a doctor of the church. Pope Paul VI added two women saints to the list of doctors of the church: Catherine of Siena (ca. 1347–80) and Teresa of Avila (1515–82). See *Cappadocian Fathers; Three Theologians, The.*

DOCTRINE. Church teaching in all its many forms, which is intended not only to communicate orthodox beliefs but also to feed Christian life and worship. See *Magisterium; Orthodoxy.*

DOGMA (Gr. "opinion" or "decree"). A divinely revealed truth, proclaimed as such by the infallible teaching authority of the church, and hence binding now and forever on all the faithful (DS 3011, 3073–75;

LG 25). Despite their importance, dogmas are not ultimate norms. "The supreme rule of faith" is found rather in "the Scriptures, taken together with sacred Tradition" (DV 21), and celebrated in the church's worship. In the Orthodox church, dogma denotes conciliar teaching (especially that of the first seven ecumenical councils), accepted by all the particular churches in communion with each other and nourishing the faithful in liturgy and life. See *Council, Ecumenical; Deposit of Faith; Hierarchy of Truths; Magisterium; Revelation; Seven Ecumenical Councils, The.*

DOGMATIC THEOLOGY. The chief branch of theology, which, drawing on scripture and tradition for the data of revelation, examines and presents coherently all major Christian doctrines. Current attempts to renew this discipline reflect on the common faith in the light of the whole history of Christianity and the changing circumstances of our times (OT 16). See *Dogma; Systematic Theology; Theology.*

DONATISM. A schism that arose ca. 311 over the episcopal consecration of Caecilian of Carthage, by a bishop (Felix of Aptunga) who was accused of being a traitor during the persecution of the Emperor Diocletian. The dissenting bishops chose instead Majorinus, later succeeded by Donatus—hence the name of the schism. The Donatists seem to have denied the validity of sacraments administered by unworthy ministers, and to have required the rebaptism of Christians who lapsed back into sin (see DS 123, 705 and 913). St. Augustine of Hippo (354–430) strongly opposed the Donatists; a conference organized at Carthage in 411 weakened them, and they finally disappeared when the Saracens destroyed the church in North Africa. See *Novatianism; Schism; Validity.*

DOUBT. Uncertainty about or suspension of assent to particular Christian beliefs or even to the faith as a whole. Serious questions and the honest facing of difficulties do not amount to sinful doubt. See *Assent of Faith; Faith.*

DOXA (Gr. "glory"). The sublime majesty and radiant splendor of God revealed in Israel's history (especially in the Exodus [Exod 14:4, 17–18; 15:1–21]), through nature (Exod 24:15–17; Ps 104:31–32) and in the experience of the divine holiness (Isa 6:1–7). Luke associates God's glory with Jesus' birth (Lk 2:9), transfiguration (Lk 9:31–32), triumphal entry into Jerusalem (Lk 19:38), resurrection from the dead (Lk 24:26) and ascension (Acts 1:9, 11; 7:55). John's gospel begins with the contemplation of the divine glory (Jn 1:14) which is already revealed in Christ's life and especially through his miraculous signs (Jn 2:11). In Jesus Christ the glory of God has been disclosed (2 Cor 4:4–6) and will be fully manifest at the end (Tit 2:11–13). *Doxa* is one of the key theological ideas in eastern theology and is exercising increasing influence in the west. See *Beauty, Theology of; God; Revelation; Theology, Methods in; Theologia Gloriae; Transfiguration.*

DOXOLOGY. Giving glory to God. The psalms frequently glorify God (Psalms 8; 66; 150), and so does the NT (Rom 16:27; 1 Tim 6:16; 1 Pet 4:11; Rev 4:11; 5:12). (a) The early church developed what came to be known as the subordinate doxology: "Glory be to the Father through the Son in the Holy Spirit." When the Arians abused it to argue that the Son was inferior to the Father and the Spirit inferior to the Son, St. Basil the Great (ca. 330–79) helped to introduce a coordinate doxology: "Glory be to the Father and the Son and the Holy Spirit." This latter doxology became dominant and is known as the "short doxology," the "long doxology" being "Glory to God in the highest!" of the Latin mass (see Lk 2:14). (b) A doxological start of theology, shaped by worship and the rule of prayer, has been developed in the west by G. Wainwright (b. 1939) and others. See *Eastern Theology; Gloria.*

DUALISM. Any interpretation of reality which explains everything through two quite independent primordial principles. An example of dualism in philosophy is that of René Descartes (1596–1650), who interpreted the universe in terms of two irreducible principles, mind and matter, even if he held that God ultimately created both. Radical theological dualism normally proposes two antagonistic deities, a good and an evil one, as did the Manichaeans and some Gnostics in the early church and, in the middle ages, the Albigensians and the Cathars in the west, and the Bogomils in the east. Christianity acknowledges a qualified dualism (between soul and body and, above all, between God and the created universe, but proclaims that in Christ all things are reconciled to God (2 Cor 5:18–20). See *Albigensianism; Bogomils; Cathars; Gnosticism; Manichaeism.*

DYOTHELETISM (Gr. "two wills"). The doctrine of the church that in Christ there are two wills, which belong to his two natures. Although separate, his divine and human wills work together in a perfect moral unity (see DS 2531). See *Constantinople, Third Council of; Monophysitism; Monotheletism.*

E

EASTER. The earliest and most important feast of the Christian year, which recalls the rising from the dead of Jesus Christ. Initially it seems to have been celebrated every Sunday, while Jewish Christians still kept up the Jewish Passover. This was bound to create friction, since the Christian message proclaimed that Israel's deliverance from Egypt had been fulfilled and superseded by Christ's resurrection (1 Cor 5:7). The practice of setting aside one special day each year to celebrate the resurrection led to controversy between the Christians of Asia Minor, who kept the feast on whichever day the Jewish Passover (14 Nisan) fell, and other Christian communities, who celebrated on the following Sunday. Such controversies continue. The Orthodox, even when they have accepted the Gregorian reform of the Julian calendar, still follow the Julian calendar for the Easter feast. Recent ecumenical development, however, has brought an agreement between eastern Catholics and the Orthodox over the date of Easter every four years. In the Gregorian calendar the dates for Easter vary between March 21 and April 25. See *Exodus; Calendar, Gregorian; Passover; Resurrection*.

EASTERN CHURCHES. Those churches which gradually evolved into independent communities after the death of Theodosius I (395), when the Roman Empire was divided into east and west. There are four groups. (1) The (Assyrian) Church of the East recognizes the first two general councils, but not Ephesus (431), which condemned Nestorius. Hence its members used to be called Nestorians. (2) The Oriental Orthodox Churches recognize the first three general councils, but not Chalcedon (451) and their adherents used to be called "Monophysites." This group includes five independent churches: the Armenian, the Coptic, the Ethiopian and the Syrian Orthodox churches, as well as Oriental Orthodox in India, who are evenly divided between the autocephalous Malankar Orthodox Syrian church and an autonomous church under the supervision of the Syrian Orthodox Patriarch in Damascus. (3) The (Eastern) Orthodox churches, whose break with Rome is conventionally dated to 1054, are all in communion with each other and recognize the Patriarch of Constantinople as the first among equals. They include the old patriarchates of Constantinople, Alexandria, Antioch and Jerusalem; the new patriarchates of Russia, Serbia, Romania, Bulgaria and Georgia; the autocephalous churches of Cyprus, Greece, Poland, Albania and Czechoslovakia; and the Orthodox Church of America, whose autocephaly is recognized by Moscow, but not by Constantinople; the autonomous churches of St. Catherine's Monastery (Sinai); and the Orthodox churches of Finland, Japan and China. (Constantinople does not recognize the autocephalous status granted by Moscow to the Orthodox church in Czechoslovakia, but it does recognize this church as autonomous. There is a similar problem regarding the autonomous Orthodox churches of Japan and China. Since they were made autonomous by Moscow without Constantinople's consent, Constantinople does not recognize them as such.) (4) The eastern Catholic churches are in communion with Rome. Parallel to the Assyrian Church of the East there are the Chaldean and the Malabar Catholic churches. Parallel to the Oriental Orthodox churches there are the Armenian, the Coptic, the Ethiopian, the Syrian and the Malankara Catholic churches. Parallel to the Eastern Orthodox churches we have the Melkite, the Ukrainian, the Ruthenian, the Romanian, the Greek, the Bulgarian, the Slovak and the Hungarian Catholic churches; besides there are the Byzantine Catholics in Yugoslavia. The Maronite and the Italo-Albanian Catholic churches do not correspond to any other church. See *Armenian Christianity; Autocephalous; Church of the East (Assyrian); Coptic Christianity; Ethiopian Christianity; Jacobites; Malabar Christians; Maronites; Monophysitism; Nestorianism; Oriental Orthodox; Patriarch; Rite; West Syrian Church.*

EASTERN THEOLOGY. A theology developed by the Greek and Syrian fathers of the church. In general, eastern theology is committed to preserving the whole of tradition, as guided by the Holy Spirit, recorded by the Bible, taught especially by early general councils and celebrated in worship and icons. It is characterized by the primacy of the spiritual, spirituality being considered as lived dogma and dogma as that spirituality which has found official endorsement in its verbal expression. In uniting harmoniously church teaching, spirituality and discipline, this theology is maintained and shaped by liturgy and monasticism. See *Alexandrian Theology; Antiochene Theology; Apophatic Theology; Council, Ecumenical; Doxa; Doxology; Fathers of the Church; Fools for Christ's Sake; Holy Spirit; Icon; Johannine Theology; Liturgy; Monasticism; Origenism; Seven Councils, The; Symbol, Theology of; Theology, Methods in; Three Theologians; Tradition; Worship.*

EASTER TRIDUUM (Lat. "three days"). The liturgical celebrations starting with evening mass on Maundy Thursday and ending at Vespers on Easter Sunday. The Thursday mass recalls the last supper and Christ's institution of the eucharist. On Good Friday, after the reading of the passion according to St. John, special prayers for the whole world and the adoration of the cross, comes the "Mass of the Presanctified," in which there is no consecration, but hosts already consecrated are distributed. After sunset on Holy Saturday the Easter vigil celebrates Christ's resurrection and our dying and rising with him in baptism. A service of light and the blessing of the paschal candle introduce a series of scriptural readings that recapitulate the whole history of salvation from creation to the resurrection. Then catechumens are baptized and/or the whole community renews its baptismal promises before the eucharist is celebrated. See *Catechumens; Holy Week; Mass of the Presanctified; Paschal Mystery; Resurrection.*

EBIONITES (Heb. "poor men"). An ascetic group of Jewish Christians in the first and second centuries who considered Jesus to be the human son of Mary and Joseph, a mere man on whom the Spirit descended at baptism. They stressed adherence to the law of Moses, and for this reason they rejected St. Paul. See *Christology; Encratites.*

ECCLESIOLOGY (Gr. "study of the church"). That branch of theology which systematically reflects on the origin, nature, distinguishing characteristics and mission of the church. Although no articulated ecclesiology can be found in the Bible, the NT offers various images for the church: such as the spouse of Christ (Eph 5:25–32; Rev 21:2; 22:17), the body of Christ (Rom 12:4–5; 1 Cor 12:12–27; Eph 1:22–23; Col 1:18, 24), the People of God (1 Pet 2:10; Rom 9:25), the temple of the Holy Spirit (1 Cor 3:16; 6:19), the family and the household of God (Eph 2:19–22) (see LG 6-8). St. Irenaeus of Lyons (ca. 130–ca. 200), in his struggle with the Gnostics and their purported revelations accessible only to an elite, initiated an apologetic of criteria (or marks) for the church which could be recognized by everybody. St. Cyprian of Carthage (d. 258) wrote the first treatise on the unity of the church. Almost all breaches in the church's unity would be related, directly or indirectly, to different interpretations of her visibility. The *Summa de Ecclesia* by John of Torquemada (1388–1468), uncle of the Grand Inquisitor, signalled the development of ecclesiology as a distinct discipline, which then became more important through the reformation controversies. The break between east and west led the Orthodox to develop a more pneumatological ecclesiology to account for the union of local churches in the same faith. Notable influences in the growth of Catholic ecclesiology were St. Robert Bellarmine (1542–1621) and the teaching of Vatican I (1869–70). In this century the ecumenical movement, Vatican II and the work of such theologians as Yves Congar (b. 1904), Avery Dulles (b. 1918), Karl Rahner (1904–84) and Jean-Marie-Roger Tillard (b. 1927) have contributed to the growth of the discipline. Orthodox theologians like Nikolai Afanas'ev (1893–1966) and John Zizioulas (b. 1931) have developed an ecclesiology centered on the eucharist. Ecclesiology's major themes include: the origins of the church in the OT, the ministry of Jesus, his resurrection from the dead, and the outpouring of the Holy Spirit; the relationship between the church and the kingdom of God; the variety of models for the church; her mission in and for the world; her pneumatological, charismatic, institutional, hierarchical and eschatological nature. See *Augsburg Confession; Body of Christ; Charism; Church; Communion of Saints; Conciliarism; Eschatology; Extra Ecclesiam Nulla Salus; Febronianism; Gallicanism; Gnosticism; Hierarchy; Holy Spirit, The; Magisterium; Marks of the Church, The; Mission of the Church; Office; Primacy; People of God, The; Reformation, The; Sects; Sobornost; Synod; Ultramontanism; Vatican Council, First; Vatican Council, Second; World Council of Churches.*

ECOLOGY, HUMAN (Gr. "study of the house"). The study of human beings in their interaction with their environment. As God's representatives men and women were to be responsible stewards of creation (Gen 1:26–31; see Job 28:1–2, 9–11). The Messianic Age was to restore what nature lost through sin (Isa 11:6–8; see Ezek 47:1–12). The Christian hope is for the whole of creation to share in the risen glory (Rom 8:19–33) of "the new earth and the new heavens" (2 Pet 3:13–14). Such a hope encourages here and now a conscientious concern for and management of our environment—a theme developed in the teaching of John Paul II (b. 1920) and the theology of creation coming from Jürgen Moltmann (b. 1926) and others. See *Creation; Messiah; Nature.*

ECONOMY (Gr. "house management"). God's saving plan for the human race revealed through creation and, above all, through the redemption effected in Jesus Christ (Eph 1:10; 3:9). In eastern theology, economy also denotes concessions to human weaknesses made by the church, which in particular cases dispenses from its own canonical prescriptions. See *Canon Law, Sources of Oriental; Economic Trinity; Immanent Trinity; Salvation.*

ECUMENISM (Gr. "inhabited world"). A worldwide movement between Christians who accept Jesus as Lord and savior and, inspired by the Holy Spirit, seek through prayer, dialogue and other initiatives to eliminate barriers and move towards the unity Christ willed for his church (Jn 17:21; see Eph 4:4–5; UR 1–4). Christian communities separated over the Council of Ephesus (431), over the Council of Chalcedon (451), through the east-west schism conventionally dated 1054, at the reformation in the sixteenth century, and later. Vatican II taught that the true church "subsists in" but is not simply identified with the Catholic Church (LG 8). Belief in Christ and baptism establish a real, if imperfect, union among all Christians (LG 15). In particular, the Orthodox share with Catholics very many elements of faith and sacramental life, including the eucharist and apostolic succession (see OE 27–30). See *Apostolic Succession; Communicatio in Sacris; Dialogue; Faith and Order; Hierarchy of Truths; Oikumene; Schism; Vatican Council, Second; World Council of Churches.*

EDESSA (now Urfa in Turkey). The most important center of Syriac Christianity, which, in spite of the Muslim invasion in 639, was active until the twelfth century. According to legend, Jesus sent a letter and his portrait to the king of Edessa, Abgar V Ukkama (4 B.C.–A.D. 50). Christianity was certainly known there from the second century. Its most significant writer was St. Ephraem the Syrian (ca. 306–373) who started the "School of the Persians" in Edessa after his native Nisibis was abandoned by the Romans in 363. Emperor Zeno closed the school in 489 because of acute conflicts between Nestorians and Monophysites. Edessa served as headquarters of the Syrian Orthodox Church. See *Antiochene School; Church of the East (Assyrian); Eastern Churches; Nestorianism; Monophysitism; Syrian Orthodox Church.*

ELDERS. Men having responsibility in Jewish synagogues (Lk 7:3), the Jerusalem Sanhedrin (Mk 14:43, 53; 15:1) and in early Christian communities (Acts 11:30; 14:23; 15:22). At times in the NT elders or "presbyters" seem synonymous with overseers or "bishops" (Phil 1:1; Titus 1:5, 7). John Calvin (1509–64) distinguished between "teaching elders" (ordained pastors) and "ruling elders" (laymen), a division still found in Reformed and Presbyterian churches. See *Bishop; Laity; Presbyter.*

ELECTION. God's free choice of individuals and groups. In the OT Israel was conscious of being God's "chosen people" (Deut 4:32–40; Isa 41:8–16). A new community of believers gathers through Christ's choice (Jn 15:1–17). In spiritual theology, "election" refers to the choice of one's state in life or the improvement of one's life-style, especially according to rules found in the Exercises of St. Ignatius of Loyola (1491–1556). Canon law uses "election" of the choice made by the authorised voters for appointment to an office in the church: e.g., the election of the pope by cardinals in conclave (see CIC 349). See *Predestination.*

ELEVATION. The raising of the consecrated host and chalice at mass to invite adoration of Christ now eucharistically present and to express our offering to God. In the Ambrosian, Latin and Mozarabic rites the canon or eucharistic prayer ends with a second or minor elevation when the priest holds up both the host and the chalice. See *Adoration; Canon; Real Presence.*

EMANATION. A reality that issues from a source (God) as light comes from the sun. This language, which goes back to the Neoplatonism of Plotinus (205–70) and was used by St. Thomas Aquinas (ca. 1225–74), has been opposed by many Christians because it seemed to make the world necessary and even identical with God, instead of being freely created by God (see DS 3024). See *Gnosticism; Neoplatonism; Pantheism.*

EMBER DAYS. Four periods of fasting and abstinence that originally may have been linked with crop festivals and subsequently formed a preparation for ordination. The Ember Days are the Wednesday, Friday and Saturday after Ash Wednesday, Pentecost Sunday, the Triumph of the Cross (September 14) and the feast of St. Lucy (December 13). See *Abstinence; Fasting.*

EMMANUEL (Heb. "God is with us"). The symbolic name for a child announced by Isaiah to King Ahaz (Isa 7:14). Matthew interprets this sign as a prophecy of Jesus' birth (Matt 1:23), and concludes his gospel with the related promise "I am with you always" (Matt 28:20). See *Christology; Virginal Conception of Jesus.*

ENCRATITES (Gr. "abstainers"). A name used for various early Christian extremists who commonly abstained from meat, wine and even marriage. It was among such fringe groups that the Apocryphal gospels were written. See *Apocryphal Gospels; Asceticism; Docetism; Ebionites; Gnosticism.*

ENCYCLICAL (Gr. "circular letter"). A bishop's letter intended for wide circulation. From the eighteenth century western Catholics have applied the term to letters addressed by the pope to the whole church or a part of it. As such, papal encyclicals are not infallible pronouncements, but rather authoritative statements of the ordinary magisterium (see DS 3884–85). Eastern Christians still call authoritative letters from their patriarchs "encyclicals," a term also used by Anglicans since the first Lambeth Conference (1867) for the message issued at the end of those conferences. See *Magisterium; Lambeth Conferences.*

ENHYPOSTASIA (Gr. "in the person"). The doctrine of Christ's fully human nature, personalized through being assumed by the *hypostasis* or person of the Logos. To clarify the teaching of Chalcedon (451) on Christ's two natures in one person, Leontius of Byzantium (sixth century) developed this doctrine which was later supported by St. John of Damascus (ca. 650–ca. 750). See *Anhypostasia; Chalcedon, Council of; Hypostasis; Logos.*

ENLIGHTENMENT. A movement starting in seventeenth-century Europe (and spreading to North America) that resisted authority and tradition, defended freedom and human rights, encouraged empirical methods in scientific research, and aimed at deciding issues through the use of reason. In religious matters many representatives of the movement supported biblical criticism, rejected special divine revelation and miracles, and could be strongly opposed to mainline Christianity. The prominent figures of the Enlightenment include Denis Diderot (1713–84), Benjamin Franklin (1706–90), David Hume (1711–76), Immanuel Kant (1724–1804), Gotthold Ephraim Lessing (1729–81), John Locke (1632–1704), Moses Mendelssohn (1729–86), Jean-Jacques Rousseau (1712–78) and Francois-Marie Arouet (= Voltaire) (1694–1778). Although the Enlightenment fostered some false hopes for social progress and encouraged an anti-doctrinal rationalism, it did hand on a healthy respect for human reason and religious freedom. See *Authority; Autonomy; Deism; Liberty, Religious; Miracle; Rationalism; Revelation.*

ENTELECHY (Gr. "bearing its own perfection"). The realization of what is potential, the actualization of the goal for which something exists. See *Aristotelianism; Causality.*

ENTHRONEMENT. A bishop's being seated after consecration on the *cathedra* in his own cathedral, symbolizing the beginning of his teaching and pastoral government of his diocese. *Cathedra; Cathedral; Diocese.*

ENTHUSIASM (Gr. "possession by God"). Ecstatic or emotional behavior, attributed to the special influence of the Spirit of God. St. Paul warns against stifling the Spirit at work in prophecy and other unusual gifts (1 Thess 5:19–22), yet recognizes love as the highest gift (1 Cor 12:13–13:13). In the history of Christianity religious enthusiasm, when directed with discernment, has often produced lasting benefits. Misguided claims to the special influence of the Spirit can cause considerable harm (see DS 803–08). See *Charism; Discernment of Spirits; Experience, Religious; Prophecy.*

EPARCHY (Gr. "province"). A word which frequently occurs in the canons of general councils in the east and which designates an ecclesiastical province governed by a metropolitan. Today it means diocese. See *Diocese; Metropolitan.*

EPHESUS, COUNCIL OF. Third ecumenical council, and the first of which we possess the conciliar acts. It was convoked by the eastern Emperor Theodosius II (408–50) to settle the debate provoked by Nestorius (d. ca. 451), Patriarch of Constantinople, who had expressed reservations about the popular title for Mary, "Theotokos" (Gr. "Mother of God"). Without waiting for the papal legates or the Syrian bishops headed by John, the Patriarch of Antioch (d. 441), St. Cyril of Alexandria (d. 444) on June 22, 431 opened the council, which condemned Nestorius' teaching and excommunicated him. Ephesus coined no new dogmatic formula, but rather proclaimed St. Cyril's second letter to Nestorius to be consonant with the faith of Nicaea (325) (see DS 250–68). By declaring Mary to be Mother of God, the council acknowledged Jesus Christ to be "one and the same" divine person. This primarily christological teaching paved the way for the formula of Chalcedon (451). The "eighth" canon of Ephesus recognized the church of Cyprus to be autocephalous. See *Apollinarianism; Chalcedon, Council of; Church of the East; Constantinople, Second Council of; Nestorianism; Theotokos; Three Chapters, The.*

EPICLESIS (Gr. "invocation"). In general, any invocation of God to bless and sanctify material creation (see 1 Tim 4:1–5). In the anaphora or canon of the mass, the epiclesis is the prayer asking that the Spirit or the Logos descend upon the gifts to change them into the body and blood of Christ for the spiritual profit of those who receive them. In the middle ages there was a controversy as to whether the consecration was complete with the words of institution, as the Latins maintained, or only with the subsequent prayer of epiclesis, as in most Greek and Oriental anaphoras (see DS 1017, 2718 and 3556). The reform of the liturgy after the Second Vatican Council put into the new canons an epiclesis before the consecration (praying that the gifts be changed) and after the consecration (praying that the communicants be changed). It is still debated whether the prayer "quam oblationem" before the consecration, and the "supra quae" and "supplices te" after the consecration in the old Roman canon (= the first eucharistic prayer) are prayers of epiclesis. See *Anaphora; Canon; Consecration; Eucharistic Prayer; Holy Spirit.*

EPIPHANY (Gr. "manifestation"). In general, any appearance of the divine in space and time (Exod 3:12; 19:18; Acts 2:3–4). The Johannine literature sees the incarnation and the whole of Christ's life as an epiphany (Jn 1:14; 1 Jn 1:1–3). As a major feast, held on January 6 in the east from at least the fourth century, the Epiphany celebrated the entire cycle of Christ's appearance in his birth, adoration by the Magi, baptism and first miracle at Cana (Jn 2:1–12). Gradually Christmas came to be observed everywhere on December 25, although in the Armenian tradition Christ's birth is still commemorated on January 6. In the east, where baptism is also called *photismos* (Gr. "enlightenment"), the Epiphany is celebrated with lights, and the waters of rivers, etc. (representing the Jordan) are blessed by plunging a cross into them. In the west, the feast of the Epiphany celebrates the coming of the Magi, and the revelation of Christ to the Gentiles; the following Sunday is invariably dedicated to the baptism of the Lord, while, in cycle C, the next Sunday recalls the marriage at Cana. Even so, the Magnificat antiphon for the second vespers of the Epiphany retains the original, inclusive character of the feast: "Three wonders mark this day we celebrate: today the star led the Magi to the manger; today water was changed into wine at the marriage feast; today Christ desired to be baptized by John in the river Jordan to bring us salvation." See *Christmas; Doxa; Johannine Theology; Theophany.*

EPISCOPACY (from Gr. "bishop," "overseer"). Church government by bishops who together, as the successors to the collegiate system of apostles found in the NT, form the present college of bishops responsible for that government. See *Apostolic Succession; Bishop; Collegiality; Diocese; Ordinary.*

EPISCOPAL CONFERENCE. The assembly of Catholic bishops of a certain country or region, held at least every five years to plan collective pastoral initiatives for the good of the church in the whole territory. When decisions enjoy a two-thirds majority and are endorsed by the Holy See, they have the force of law for the area (see CD 38; CIC 447–459). See *Bishop; Collegiality; Motu Proprio.*

EPISCOPALIANS. Members of a church led by bishops and, in particular, those Christians in the United States who are in communion with the Archbishop of Canterbury. See *Anglican Communion.*

EPISTEMOLOGY (Gr. "theory of knowledge"). That branch of philosophy which investigates human knowledge, its nature, sources, criteria, possibilities and limits. See *Philosophy.*

EPISTLE (Gr. "letter"). Term traditionally used for the 21 letters of the NT and for the reading at the Sunday eucharist that precedes the gospel.

EQUIVOCITY (Lat. "using the same word"). The use of words with double meanings (e.g., "star," for a heavenly body and for an outstanding actor). This makes arguments fallacious because the point is valid only for one of the meanings. See *Analogy; Univocity.*

EROS (Gr. "love of desire"). Love that seeks self-fulfillment. It is distinguished both from *agape,* which is God's self-giving love in Christ that calls for a human response (1 Jn 4:7–12), and *philia* or the love between friends and relatives. See *Agape; Love.*

ERROR. False belief or incorrect conduct. People held to be in error should, however, be treated with courtesy and love, and their religious liberty should be respected (GS 28; DH 14). See *Heresy.*

ESCHATA (Gr. "the last things"). The current term for what used to be called *novissima* (Lat. "the latest things"): death, judgment (both the particular judgment of the individual and the universal judgment of all humanity), heaven and hell. These elements of our destiny, necessarily shrouded in mystery during this life, find their focus in Christ himself, who is the Alpha and the Omega, the beginning and the end (Apoc 22:13). Without taking an explicit position about modern debates over purification at the moment of death and the possibility of all humans being finally saved through God's infinite mercy, a 1979 letter of the Congregation for the Doctrine of the Faith drew attention to church teaching on resurrection for the whole person, purgatorial purification and our two final possibilities (heaven or hell). See *Apocatastasis; Beatific Vision; Death; Last Judgment; Heaven; Hell; Mystery; Purgatory.*

ESCHATOLOGY (Gr. "knowledge of the last things"). That branch of systematic theology which studies God's final kingdom as expressed by its OT preparation (e.g., the messianic hopes), the preaching of Jesus and the teaching of the NT church. According to Albert Schweitzer (1875–1965), Jesus mistakenly expected the imminent coming of the kingdom. According to the opposite thesis of realized eschatology, represented by Charles Harold Dodd (1884–1973), Jesus announced that with his ministry the essential elements of the kingdom had already come. Mediating positions argue for a kingdom already inaugurated with the ministry, death and resurrection of Jesus (see Lk 11:20; 1 Cor 10:11), but still to be consummated (see Mk 13; Lk 11:2; 1 Cor 15:20–28) when Christ comes in glory to judge the living and the dead (see Matt 25:31–46; Rev 22:12–13). See *Apocalyptic Literature; Hope; Johannine Theology; Kingdom of God; Messiah; Millenarianism; Parousia; Resurrection.*

ESCHATON. See *Parousia.*

ESSENCE AND ENERGIES. A key distinction in the theology of St. Gregory Palamas (ca. 1296–1359), according to which the divine essence remains unknowable, but not God's self-disclosing and life-giving "energies" or activities. This differentiation in God was meant to safeguard both our deification and the inaccessible otherness of God. See *Apophatic Theology; Deification; Eunomianism; Hesychasm; Palamism.*

ESSENCE AND EXISTENCE. In the philosophy of St. Thomas Aquinas (ca. 1225–74), the basic, real distinction between the two principles of being that account for the ultimate composition of whatever exists in the created world. The act of existence actualizes the potentiality of essence, and thus enjoys a primacy over essence. See *Being; Thomism.*

ESSENES. An ascetic and highly organized Jewish group mentioned by Philo (ca. 20 B.C.–ca. A.D. 50), the elder Pliny (ca. 23–79) and Flavius Josephus (ca. 37–ca. 100). They seemed to have originated in the second century B.C., and were probably identical with the Qumran community. See *Qumran Scrolls.*

ETERNITY (Lat. "endless duration"). Having neither beginning nor end, but being unchangeably full of life. Eternity is a divine attribute, but through grace God lets us share in "eternal life" (Jn 11:25–26). See *Attributes, Divine; Grace; Heaven; Hell; Resurrection.*

ETHICS (Gr. "custom, ethos"). That branch of philosophy which studies moral principles to clarify what is right and wrong or what human beings should freely do or refrain from doing. *Deontological ethics*, represented by Immanuel Kant (1724–1804), considers human conduct morally good when, guided by a sense of duty, it fulfills its obligations independently of their consequences. *Utilitarian ethics*, represented by Jeremy Bentham (1748–1832), takes consequences to be the ultimate norm of morality and tries to effect "the greatest happiness of the greatest number." See *Freedom; Moral Theology.*

ETHIOPIAN CHRISTIANITY. Founded by two Syrians, St. Frumentius and Edesius, the Ethiopian church came under the Patriarch of Alexandria when Frumentius was consecrated bishop (ca. 350) by St. Athanasius of Alexandria. Christianity soon became the state religion, with the religious capital at Axum and a metropolitan or "abuna" ("our father"). Through the Egyptian connection and the "Nine Saints," probably Syrian monks who had came to Ethiopia because they were opposed to the Council of Chalcedon (451), the Ethiopian church became non-Chalcedonian without a struggle. The union reached with Rome at the Council of Florence (1442) proved short-lived (see DS 1330–53). The emperor's conversion to Catholicism in 1621 ended with his abdication in 1632. In the twentieth century, Emperor Haile Selassie reformed the church and promoted the establishment of an independent Ethiopian Patriarchate in 1959. The Oriental Orthodox Patriarchate of Alexandria retains a primacy of honor over the Ethiopian church. Ethiopian Oriental Christianity is characterized by certain Jewish elements such as the practice of circumcision and the observance of the Sabbath. The language used for the liturgy is the classical Ge'ez. A small group of Ethiopian Christians in communion with Rome makes up the Ethiopian Catholic Church, uses the Ethiopian rite and, since 1961, has its metropolitan see in Addis Ababa. See *Autocephalous; Chalcedon, Council of; Coptic Christianity; Eastern Churches; Metropolitan; Monophysitism; Oriental Orthodox.*

ETIOLOGY (Gr. "account of causes"). A story "explaining" how something came into existence by recounting a particular event supposed to have originally caused it. Thus an act of Lot's wife accounts for a strange geological formation (Gen 19:26). Etiological explanations are offered for names of persons like Abraham (Gen 17:5) and Moses (Exod 2:10), "Israel," the new name given to Jacob (Gen 32:28), and such places as Beersheba (Gen 21:31). Hermann Gunkel (1862–1932) did important work in analyzing and classifying biblical etiologies. Following Karl Rahner (1904–84), some call Genesis 1–11 an "historical etiology." The OT writers experienced, on the one hand, the goodness of God as savior and creator and, on the other hand, the reality of sin and its consequences. They explained the tension between grace and sin in present reality by referring it to the origins of the human race. This is not to say that the opening chapters of the Bible offer us an historical report. But it is to say that real, primordial events account for the present human condition. See *Biblical Criticism; Creation; Original Sin; Protology*.

EUCHARIST (Gr. "thanksgiving"). Word used for the whole service of the mass and especially for the second part, which follows the celebration of the word of God, reaches its highpoint with the consecration of the bread and wine into the body and blood of Christ, and ends with communion. "Eucharist" refers besides to Christ's real presence under the appearances of bread and wine (DS 1640, 1651). The greatest of the sacraments and the center of Church life, the eucharist was instituted by Christ at the last supper (DS 1637, 1727). A sacrifice of praise and thanksgiving, in which Christ is present as priest and victim, the eucharist (a) re-presents the new covenant (1 Cor 11:25; Lk 22:20) effected through his death and resurrection that reconciled us with God (DS 1740, 1742), and (b) anticipates the consummation of the divine kingdom. As a meal, the eucharist (Acts 2:46; DS 847) makes us guests at God's own banquet and expresses our deepest unity in the church. As sacrifice and meal, the eucharist efficaciously symbolizes the self-sacrificing service of others to which Christians are called. See *Agape; Anaphora; Blessed Sacrament; Church; Communion; Covenant; Liturgy; Lord's Supper; Mass; Sacrament; Sacrifice; Transubstantiation*.

EUCHARISTIC PRAYER. The prayer at the heart of the eucharist, called "the canon" in the Roman liturgy. Some later forms seem to be variants of the first fully developed eucharistic prayer, found in the *Apostolic Tradition* (ca. 215), which is often attributed to St. Hippolytus of Rome. With some variations in order, a eucharistic prayer contains the following elements: an introductory dialogue between the priest and the congregation; a prayer of praise and thanksgiving; the narration of the institution of the eucharist; the *anamnesis* recalling God's salvific actions; the *epiclesis* inviting the descent of the Spirit; the commemorations or intercessions; and the final doxology. See *Anamnesis; Anaphora; Canon; Doxology; Epiclesis; Intercession*.

EULOGY (Gr. "blessing," "thing blessed"). In the latter sense the blessed but not consecrated bread distributed to the faithful at the end of the eucharist. As "pain bénit" or blessed bread, the practice has survived in some French-speaking areas. Its counterpart in eastern liturgies is "antidoron" (Gr. "instead of the gift"), distributed in practice to all present at the service. See *Blessing*.

71

EUNOMIANISM. Heresy propagated by a bishop of Cyzicus, Eunomius (d. 395), who belonged to the most radical wing of the Arians. He asserted that God is an ungenerated, utterly simple and absolutely knowable substance. The Son is the first being created by the Father, with the Holy Spirit then being created by the Son. Against such pronounced rationalism both in method and content, St. Basil the Great (ca. 330–79) and St. Gregory of Nyssa (ca. 335–ca. 395) reasserted the orthodox teaching of the church and proper sense of mystery which characterizes genuine theology. See *Anomoeans; Apophatic Theology; Cappadocian Fathers; Essence and Energies; Nicaea, First Council of; Pneumatomachians; Rationalism.*

EUTYCHIANISM. Heresy associated with Eutyches (ca. 378–454), head of a large monastery in Constantinople. He was accused of acknowledging only one (divine) nature or *physis* in Christ after the incarnation—a "mono-physite" view which denies that Christ also has a human nature like ours. Condemned in 448 at a home synod in Constantinople, through the influence of the emperor and the patriarch of Alexandria he was rehabilitated the following year at a synod held in Ephesus and dubbed by Pope St. Leo the Great the "Latrocinium" (Lat. "brigandage"). However, at the Council of Chalcedon (451) Eutyches was condemned and disowned by all parties (see DS 290–300). See *Chalcedon, Council of; Monophysitism.*

EVANGELICAL COUNSELS. Three radical ideals for Christian discipleship that involve freely embracing a life of poverty, celibacy and obedience for the sake of the coming kingdom of God (see DS 1087–94, 1810, 3911; CIC 573; LG 44). See *Celibacy; Kingdom of God; Obedience; Perfection; Poverty; Religious Life.*

EVANGELICALS (from Gr. "Gospel"). In general, Protestant Christians who stress justification through faith and the supreme authority of the Bible. "Evangelical" is also the name for the Protestant Church in Germany, and for Anglicans who (a) highlight personal conversion, the authority of the scriptures and atonement through Christ's death and (b) do not fully share High Church views about grace, the eucharist and other sacraments. See *Anglican Communion; Episcopalians; Justification.*

EVANGELIZATION. The proclamation to all peoples (Matt 28:19–20; Rom 10:12–18) and cultures of the good news about Jesus Christ (Mk 1:1). Through the power of the Holy Spirit (Acts 1:8) the gospel message goes out both to Christians alienated from the church (evangelism) and to non-Christians (missions). See *Gospel; Inculturation; Missions, Church.*

EVE (Heb. "living"). In the creation story, the first woman, the "mother of all the living" and wife of Adam (Gen 3:20; 4:1; Tob 8:6) who followed her into sin (Gen 3:1–7; 2 Cor 11:3; 1 Tim 2:13–14). See *Adam; New Eve.*

EVIL, MYSTERY OF. The mystery of a God who is infinitely good and powerful allowing so much sin, pain and other suffering in our world. Only partial solutions are available; they appeal to (a) the divine respect for our created freedom, (b) Christ's enduring the mystery of evil through his death on the cross, and (c) the glorious consummation of our world (Rom 8:18–23) when the forces of evil will be definitively overcome (1 Cor 15:24–28). See *Apophatic Theology; Mystery; Theodicy.*

EVOLUTION. A theory launched by Charles Darwin (1809–82) and claiming that, through natural selection, present living beings developed gradually from less complex forms. Some fundamentalists wrongly hold that the theory of biological evolution conflicts with the Genesis account of creation, instead of appreciating the admirable picture it offers of God working with wisdom and power "from the inside" to bring about higher forms of life and eventually the emergence of human beings. See *Creationism; Fundamentalism; Polygenism.*

EXARCH (Gr. "ruler"). Originally a civil title for the ruler of a province in the Byzantine Empire. See *Eastern Churches.*

EX CATHEDRA DEFINITION (Lat. "from the throne"). Solemn and binding definition made by the pope with his full apostolic authority as the pastor and teacher of all Christians (DS 3074–75) in revealed matters concerning faith and morals. See *Cathedra; Enthronement; Infallibility; Magisterium; Pope.*

EXCOMMUNICATION (Lat. "exclusion from communion"). Exclusion from the reception of the sacraments and the exercise of full rights in the church (CIC 1331). Excommunication either follows automatically from certain acts or is pronounced by a church tribunal or authority. See *Anathema; Ferendae Sententiae; Latae Sententiae.*

EXEGESIS (Gr. "bringing out the sense"). Interpreting the meaning of sacred texts, usually biblical texts (DV 12, 23; OT 16). As well as trying to establish what the authors of the Bible intended to say in their original contexts (= what the text meant), exegetes also interpret the message of the text for today (= what it means). See *Alexandrian Theology; Antiochene Theology; Biblical Criticism; Hermeneutics; Senses of Scripture.*

EXEMPLARISM. Any theory which highlights exemplary causality in explaining reality. Thus the value of Christ's saving action on our behalf has been understood to consist largely or even solely in the example he gave of self-sacrificing love—a theory which goes back to Peter Abelard (1079–1142; see DS 721–39). See *Atonement; Causality; Redemption.*

EXISTENTIAL, SUPERNATURAL. A term coined by Karl Rahner (1904–84) to indicate that even prior to their accepting or rejecting salvation, in the basic structure of their existence ("existential") all human beings are already affected by the freely offered ("supernatural") grace of God communicated through Christ. See *Anonymous Christians; Grace; Justification; Salvation; Supernatural.*

EXISTENTIALISM. A philosophical, religious and literary trend which is exemplified by such writers as Søren Kierkegaard (1813–55), Fyodor Dostoyevsky (1821–81) and Miguel de Unamuno (1864–1936), Karl Jaspers (1883–1969) and Martin Heidegger (1889–1976), and which has enjoyed considerable influence in Catholic and Protestant theology. In general existentialists highlight individual persons in their freedom and search for authentic existence. They vary from avowed atheists like Jean-Paul Sartre (1905–80) to Christian believers like Rudolf Bultmann (1884–1976) and Gabriel Marcel (1889–1973). See *Dialectical Theology.*

EX OPERE OPERANTIS (Lat. "on the basis of the one acting"). The subjective dispositions for receiving a sacrament, which function not as a cause but rather as the condition for the full effectiveness of God's grace (see DS 781, 1451, 1601–13). See *Sacraments.*

EX OPERE OPERATO (Lat. "on the basis of the act performed"). The objective efficacy and fruitfulness of sacraments, which do not primarily depend on the attitudes or merits of those receiving or administering the sacraments. See *Donatism.*

EXORCISM (Gr. "adjuring under oath"). Expelling evil spirits (or even the devil himself) from persons possessed by them or at least affected by their power. A form of exorcism is found in the prayers preceding baptism. In the case of a person possessed by the devil, an exorcist acting with the permission of the bishop performs a rite consisting of prayers, sprinkling with holy water and the laying on of hands. The practice of exorcism imitates what Christ and his disciples did in similar cases (Matt 10:1; Mk 1:21–28; Lk 4:31–37; 11:14–23; Acts 19:11–12). See *Demons; Devil; Possession, Diabolical; Sacramental.*

EXPERIENCE, RELIGIOUS. Immediate, personal contact with God and the things of God (Heb 6:4–6; DS 3033, 3484; DV 8, 14). In the second "annotation" of his Spiritual Exercises St. Ignatius of Loyola (ca. 1491–1556) followed a tradition which goes back to Origen (ca. 185–ca. 254) and ultimately to St. John (Jn 1:39; 13:23; 1 Jn 1:1–3; see Ps 34:9) in expecting that prayer will bring us to "feel and taste interiorly" the things of God. Whether intense or ordinary, religious experiences need to be tested and interpreted in the church and under the guidance of the Holy Spirit (1 Thess 5:21)—especially dramatic, mystical experiences. See *Contemplation; Discernment of Spirits; Holy Spirit; Modernism; Mysticism; Prayer.*

EXPIATION (Lat. "atone," "purify"). Making amends for sin and repairing the damage caused in the moral order and one's relationship to God. The need for their sins to be expiated was institutionalized by the Jews in the day of atonement, *Yom Kippur.* The NT, in a particular way the letter to the Hebrews, understands Christ to be the priest and victim who has representatively expiated our sins and cleansed a contaminated world (Heb 2:17–18; 9:6–10:18; see Rom 3:24–25; Tit 2:13–14). See *Atonement; Penance, Sacrament of; Redemption; Heart, Sacred; Priests; Sacrifice; Salvation; Satisfaction; Sin; Yom Kippur.*

EXTERNAL FORUM. See *Forum Internum.*

EXTRA ECCLESIAM NULLA SALUS (Lat. "no salvation outside the Church"). An adage which goes back to St. Cyprian of Carthage (d. 258) and highlights the necessity of belonging to Christ's church in order to be saved (Mk 16:16; LG 14). This is not, however, to deny salvation to those who in good faith do not belong to the church and follow their consciences in living by truths they know (LG 16). See *Anonymous Christians; Church; Salvation; Supernatural.*

EXTREME UNCTION. See *Anointing of the Sick.*

F

FAITH (Lat. "belief"). The objective, revealed truth believed in (*fides quae*) or the subjective, personal commitment to God (*fides qua*). Made possible through the help of the Holy Spirit (Acts 16:14; 2 Cor 3:16–18), faith is a free, reasonable and total response (DV 4) through which we confess the truth about the divine self-disclosure definitively made in Christ (Jn 20:31; Rom 10:9), obediently commit ourselves (Rom 1:5; 16:26) and entrust our future to God (Rom 6:8; Heb 11:1). See *Analysis of*

Faith; Analogy of Faith; Deposit of Faith; Fideism; Justification; Rationalism; Revelation; Semi-Pelagianism; Sola Fides; Truth.

FAITH AND ORDER. An ecumenical body which was founded to study theological problems underlying the divisions of Christians and which organized world conferences at Lausanne (1927), Edinburgh (1937), Lund (1952) and Montreal (1963). It is now a sub-unit within the World Council of Churches. See *Ecumenism; World Council of Churches.*

FAITH AND WORKS. A question already raised in the NT (e.g., Jas 2:14–26) that was vigorously debated at the time of the reformation. St. Paul insists that justification comes by grace through faith, and not by the works of the law (Rom 3:20–26; Gal 2:16; 3:2, 5, 10). Nevertheless, God works in believers (Phil 2:12–13) to produce the fruits (Gal 5:22–23) of a faith that issues in love (Gal 5:6). See *Decalogue; Faith; Grace; Imputation; Justification; Law; Lutheranism; Merit; Reformation; Righteousness; Sola Fides; Torah.*

FAITH DEVELOPMENT. A growth in living and understanding Christian faith that follows the stages of human maturation. St. Paul notes how he has outgrown the ways of a child (1 Cor 13:11), and interprets the life of faith as our being steadily "changed" into Christ's "likeness from one degree of glory to another" (2 Cor 3:18). Trials test and perfect faith (Jas 1:2–12), and "discipline" brings growth in holiness (Heb 12:5–13). Maturing in faith requires not only a full sacramental life, constancy in prayer and practical love toward the neighbor in need, but also a regular study of Christian revelation that keeps pace with one's intellectual growth. See *Catechesis; Moral Development; Mystagogy; Neo-Catechumenate; Perfection; Sanctification.*

FAITHFUL, MASS OF. Old-fashioned term for the second part of the mass, which follows the Liturgy of the Word. The term belonged to a situation when many catechumens (adults preparing for baptism) were instructed to leave before the second part of the mass began. The correct expression used nowadays for the second part of the mass is Liturgy of the Eucharist. See *Catechumens, Mass of; Liturgy of the Eucharist; Liturgy of the Word.*

FALL, THE. The vivid story of how Adam and Eve freely disobeyed God and so lost their innocent, ideal existence (Gen 3:1–24; see Wis 2:23–24; Rom 5:12–18). The doctrine of the fall teaches that it was the earliest human beings (not God) who brought moral evil into our world—a sinful condition which affected all subsequent generations and from which Christ has redeemed us. See *Adam; Eve; Redemption; Original Sin.*

FASTING. Abstention from food motivated by religious reasons such as repentance (Joel 1:14; Jonah 3:7) or the preparation for a special mission (Matt 4:12; Acts 13:2–3), and normally accompanied by prayer (Acts 14:23). Fasting may be quantitative (when the amount of food to be consumed is limited) or qualitative (when certain kinds of food like meat are not taken [= abstinence]). After fasting in the desert (Lk 4:2), during his ministry Christ was criticized for not fasting like the Pharisees (Matt 11:18–19), and he in turn criticized those who made a self-righteous practice out of fasting (Matt 6:16–18; Lk 18:12). In the Latin tradition Catholics observe Ash Wednesday and Good Friday as obligatory fast-days, whereas the eastern Christians prepare for Easter especially, but also for Christmas, by a forty-day fast. Besides they fast, e.g., from the Sunday after Pentecost to the vigil of Sts. Peter and Paul as well as during the fortnight before August 15, the *koimesis* of Our Lady. See *Abstinence; Christmas Preparation; Ember Days; Holy Week; Lent.*

FATHERS OF THE CHURCH. A popular title for certain early Christians who wrote in Greek, Latin, Syriac and Armenian and whose doctrine and personal holiness won general approval in the church. "Each in a different way and to a different degree," they remain "classics of Christian culture" (1989 *Instruction on the Fathers* by the Congregation for Catholic Education). In theological controversy, it became customary to appeal to the eastern and western fathers, their unanimous consent being considered a decisive argument (see DS 271, 510–520, 2856, 3541). In the west the church fathers are understood to have ended with St. Isidore of Seville (ca. 560–636), in the east with St. John of Damascus (ca. 675–ca. 749). See *Cappadocian Fathers; Patristics; Patrology.*

FEAR OF GOD. In the OT that deep sense of religion and filial piety which summarizes our proper attitude toward God (Job 28:28; Prov 1:7; 9:10; Sir 1:11–20), which is not to be taken as slavish terror. See *Hesed; Holy; Love; Religion.*

FEAST. A day of special celebration in the church's liturgical calendar. Sunday commemorates Christ's resurrection from the dead, and in the east is often called the "eighth day" or the first day of the new creation brought about by Christ. Movable feasts are those like Easter and Pentecost, the dates of which vary from year to year. Immovable feasts (e.g., Christmas and feasts of saints) are always celebrated on the same day. See *Calendar, Liturgical; Resurrection; Sabbath; Sunday.*

FEBRONIANISM. A German theory of church-state relations which rejected certain papal powers as medieval accretions. The movement was named after Johann Nikolaus von Hontheim (1701–90), coadjutor bishop of Trier, who in 1763 under the pseudonym "Justinus Febronius" published *On the State of the Church and the Legitimate Authority of the Roman Pontiff*. The book recognized the pope as head of the church but denied his jurisdiction on most issues beyond the diocese of Rome (see DS 2592–97). See *Church and State; Gallicanism; Pope.*

FEMINIST THEOLOGY. An approach to theology (developed largely in the U.S.A. since 1968) that protests against the long-standing, masculine bias in Christian theology, exegesis and church life. Its demands include the ordination of woman and the use of an inclusive language that does not reflect and support a male power structure. See *Black Theology; Liberation Theology; Political Theology.*

FERENDAE SENTENTIAE (Lat. "by imposed sentence"). An ecclesiastical penalty which is binding only if formally imposed by a church judge (see CIC 1314, 1318). Because of the complexity of individual cases and the subtlety of the law, most penalties in the Church are of this nature. See *Latae Sententiae.*

FIDEISM. The tendency (a) to undervalue the role of reason in examining religious claims and (b) to overemphasize the free decision of faith. At best fideism rightly challenges attempts to demonstrate scientifically the truth of Christianity. At worst it represents faith as a blind leap in the dark. See *Analysis of Faith; Modernism; Natural Theology; Rationalism; Preambles of Faith; Traditionalism.*

FIDES FIDUCIALIS (Lat. "faith as trust"). The major element of faith according to Martin Luther (1483–1546). While maintaining the priority of this confident trust (*fiducia*) in the salvation effected by Christ, later Lutheran theologians included the role of knowledge and assent in their account of faith. See *Faith; Lutheranism.*

FIDES QUAERENS INTELLECTUM (Lat. "faith seeking understanding"). The title which St. Anselm of Canterbury (ca. 1033–1109) originally gave to one of his works (later renamed *Proslogion*). The title, a variant on the Augustinian *credo ut intelligam* (Lat. "I believe in order to understand"), indicates that in theology, faith inspires and guides intellectual understanding rather than the reverse. See *Augustinianism; Ontological Argument.*

FILIOQUE (Lat. "and [from] the Son"). A phrase added to the Nicene-Constantinopolitan Creed at the Fourth Synod of Braga, Spain (675)— its addition at the Third Synod of Toledo (589) seems to be an interpolation (see DS 470)—indicating (a) that the Holy Spirit proceeds from the

Father and the Son and (b) that the three persons of the Trinity are perfectly equal. The Greek Orthodox Church objected strongly to this insertion in the Creed. Since Patriarch Photius of Constantinople (ca. 810–95), the "Filioque" has often been considered the greatest point of difference separating east and west. The Council of Florence (1439) did not insist that the Greeks accept the "Filioque" addition, provided they acknowledge the truth behind it (DS 1301–03), as they did. See *Arianism; Creed, Nicene; Florence, Council of; Holy Spirit; Lyons, Second Council of; Processions; Trinity.*

FINALITY. A principle in scholastic philosophy according to which beings act always for a purpose or end, even if this principle applies in a different way to intelligent and nonintelligent agents. See *Scholasticism.*

FIVE WAYS, THE. Five arguments for the existence of God found in the *Summa Theologiae* of St. Thomas Aquinas (ca. 1225–74). From the fact of change (motion) in the world the First Way infers the existence of a first Unmoved Mover. The Second Way argues from our experience of causes producing effects to an ultimate Uncaused Cause. The Third Way moves from the observed contingency of our world to a first Necessary Cause. The Fourth Way begins with the limited grades of perfection found in the universe to arrive at a first Unlimited Cause. The Fifth Way observes the world's orderly design, which can only be explained through the purposeful activity of a divine Designer. The Five Ways have been radically challenged by the work of David Hume (1711–76), Immanuel Kant (1724–1804) and other philosophers, but still offer valuable perspectives on our (limited) knowledge of God. See *Arguments for the Existence of God; Causality; Finality; Teleological Argument.*

FLORENCE, COUNCIL OF (1438–45). Reckoned the seventeenth ecumenical council of the Roman Catholic Church, and sometimes dated from 1431 because the first part of the Council of Basle was a preparation for Florence. Principally convened to achieve reunion with the Greek church, it met at Ferrara (1438–39) when the Greek prelates arrived, and was transferred first to Florence in 1439 and then to Rome in 1443. On July 6, 1439 the bull of union was signed with the Greeks; on November 22, 1439 followed the union with the Armenians. The council achieved reunion with the Copts and Ethiopians (February 4, 1442) and some other eastern Christians. Florence insisted on the doctrine of the "Filioque" (without imposing it on the Greeks, as far as the recital of the creed is concerned), the immediate vision of God after death for those who have not committed or have been purified from post-baptismal sin, the primacy of the pope (in somewhat general terms) and the seven sacraments (DS 1305–06, 1330–51). Motivated partly by the fear of Turkish conquest, the unions achieved at Florence did not prove long-lasting. See *Basle, Council of; Conciliarism; Eastern Churches; Filioque; Primacy; Procession; Schism.*

FOOLS FOR CHRIST'S SAKE. A category of saints, who are particularly but not exclusively cherished in eastern Christianity and who have taken seriously St. Paul's words: "We are fools for Christ's sake . . ." (1 Cor 4:10; see 1 Cor 1:18–19, 25; 3:18–19; 2 Cor 6:8; Matt 5:11). This type of sanctity is known to us already in the *Apophthegmata Patrum.* In Greek the fool for Christ's sake is known as *salos* (probably from the Syriac rendering of 1 Corinthians 4:10 as "sakla"). Among the Greeks perhaps the most beloved of such saints is the legendary St. Andrew of Constantinople (tenth century?) whose life is associated with the great eastern feast of the *Pokrov Bogomateri* (Russ. "Protection of the Theotokos"). The land of holy fools par excellence is Russia, where the fool for Christ's sake is called *jurodivij;* examples are St. Isaac Zatvornik (d. 1090) and St. Basil the Blessed (d. 1552). By what can seem to be a mere caricature of real holiness, such fools for Christ's sake prophetically challenge the pseudo-values of society and the superficiality of many Christians. In the west saints known for their holy folly include St. Francis of Assisi (ca. 1181–1226), St. Philip Neri (1515–95) and St. Benedict-Joseph Labré (1748–83). The theme of holy folly has inspired classical literary creations like Ramon Lull's (ca. 1233–ca. 1315) *Blanquerna,* Miguel de Cervantes' (1547–1616) *Don Quixote,* Fyodor Dostoyevsky's (1821–81) *The Idiot,* as well as various figures in the works of Alexander Pushkin (1799–1837) and Leo Tolstoy (1828–1910). See *Apatheia; Apophthegmata Patrum; Cross; Eschatology; Holiness; Saint; Theologia Crucis; Wisdom Literature.*

FOREKNOWLEDGE. God's knowledge of all future events. Since some future events depend partly on human choice, there exists the problem of reconciling the divine foreknowledge with human freedom. See *Freedom; Grace, Systems of; Predestination; Prophecy.*

FORGIVENESS OF SINS. A central belief in the Jewish-Christian understanding of God's merciful dealings with us (Ezek 18:21–28; Mk 1:4; Lk 15). Jesus forgave sins (Mk 2:1–12; Lk 7:36–50) and empowered his Church to do the same (Lk 24:47; Jn 20:22–23). The forgiveness of sins through baptism (Acts 2:38) and in other ways requires repentance from us and the willingness to forgive those who sin against us (Matt 5:23–24; 6:12, 14–15; 18:21–35). See *Baptism; Penance, Sacrament of.*

FORUM INTERNUM (Lat. "internal forum"). The arena of the personal conscience, to which only God has adequate access. Church tribunals deal with the *forum externum* (Lat. "external forum") or the publicly observable arena, and document in writing their proceedings and judgments (CIC 37; see also CIC 74, 130, 144, 1074, 1081–82, 1123, 1126, 1145, 1319, 1340, 1361 and 1732). What penitents say in the sacrament of reconciliation belongs to the internal forum, and is strictly protected by the seal of confession (see CIC 64, 74, 130, 142, 144, 508, 596, 1079, 1082, 1355 and 1357). See *Beatification; Canonization.*

FOUNDER. One who creates a movement or institution, and shapes it by laying down at least some principles or guidelines. Thus Christ is the founder of Christianity and St. Dominic (1170–1221) the founder of the Order of Preachers, popularly known as Dominicans. See *Christianity; Religious Orders.*

FRANKFURT SCHOOL. A group of scholars associated with the University of Frankfurt whose critical theory has uncovered various links between our understanding and interests, and aims to produce a more rational society by freeing knowledge from domination and manipulation. Important members of this school (which has had a considerable influence on contemporary theology) include Theodor Adorno (1903–69), Jürgen Habermas (b. 1929), Max Horkheimer (1895–1973) and Herbert Marcuse (1888–1979). See *Hermeneutics; Liberation Theology; Political Theology.*

FREEDOM. The power of self-determination—that is, of deliberately choosing and following a course of action. Created in the likeness of God, human persons have this capacity which has been impaired but not destroyed by sin (DS 1965–67). Through redemption Christ has set us free (Gal 5:13; 1 Pet 2:16), and this freedom is the foretaste of our future freedom in glory (Rom 8:18–25). See *Anthropology; Concupiscence; Image of God; Liberty, Religious; Sin; Torah.*

FRIENDS, SOCIETY OF. A body of Christians, founded by George Fox (1624–91), which branched off from the Anglican Church. They describe themselves as "friends of truth," but are popularly known as *Quakers,* because when listening to the word of God they were supposed to quake or shiver. Their doctrine stresses the inner light of the living Christ, and a church order based on the priesthood of all the faithful, both men and women, with a consequent rejection of the sacraments and the ordained ministry. There are, however, "elders" to lead the congregation in prayer and "overseers" to watch over the observance of church order. Quakers are also known for their opposition to war. See *Anglican Communion.*

FUNCTIONAL CHRISTOLOGY. A christology which focuses on the saving activity of Christ and thus largely coincides with Soteriology. It necessarily implies, however, an ontological christology which focuses on who and what Christ is in himself. See *Christology; Soteriology*.

FUNDAMENTAL OPTION (Lat. "basic choice"). The general orientation of life or a particular, very serious decision that determines our essential moral and religious situation for good or evil. Reflections on the fundamental option have developed in reaction to a legalism that considered moral acts in isolation from the whole context of one's life and growth. See *Conversion; Freedom; Moral Theology; Person; Sin*.

FUNDAMENTAL THEOLOGY. That branch of theology which studies foundational issues: in particular, the divine revelation in the history of Israel and Jesus Christ; the conditions that open human beings up to this self-communication of God; the signs that make faith in and through Jesus Christ a reasonable option; the transmission (through the church's tradition and the inspired scriptures) of the experience of God's self-communication. See *Apologetics; Dogmatic Theology; Faith; Inspiration, Biblical; Preambles of Faith; Revelation; Tradition*.

FUNDAMENTALISM. A movement in twentieth-century Protestantism, especially in the U.S.A., which generally defends such fundamental beliefs as the divinity of Christ and his bodily resurrection but interprets the Bible with little attention to its historical formation, various literary forms and original meaning. This neglect of good exegesis has led to false problems about such OT stories as creation, the flood and the story of Jonah. See *Biblical Criticism; Evangelicals; Evolution; Inerrancy*.

FUNERAL RITE. Set of liturgical ceremonies for taking leave of deceased Christians from the time of death until the burial or cremation of the body (see CIC 1176–85). Reverence for the body, prayers for the dead and hope of the resurrection characterize the various ceremonies: at the funeral home, in the church and at the graveside. The requiem (Lat. "rest") mass, as well as the homily, is dominated by the resurrection theme; the cemetery (Gr. "sleeping-place") is a sacred place (CIC 1205). In the Byzantine church the rites differ considerably, depending on whether a child of not more than seven years, a lay person or a priest is being buried; bishops are buried with the rite for priests and deacons with that for lay people. See *Death*.

82

G

GALLICANISM. A long-standing movement in France, with parallels in other countries, claiming considerable independence from the papacy. It was classically expressed in the Four Gallican Articles (a) which were drawn up by the Bishop of Meaux, Jacques Bénigne Bossuet (1627–1704) and approved by a Paris assembly of the clergy in 1682 and (b) which, among other things, asserted the authority of general councils over the pope (DS 2281–85). Though revoked by King Louis XIV and the clergy in 1693, the influence of these articles continued into the nineteenth century until a strong papacy and the teaching of Vatican I (1869–70) put an end to Gallicanism. See *Conciliarism; Constance, Council of; Febronianism; Vatican, First Council of.*

GENERATION. The teaching of Nicaea I (325) ("begotten, not made") about the way the Son eternally originates from the Father without being created by the Father (see DS 125). See *Arianism; Homoousios; Nicaea, First Council of.*

GENRE, LITERARY. A particular style or form of writing. It may be shorter (like a psalm of lamentation or a parable within the gospels) or longer (like a gospel or a homily from a father of the church). A literary genre is to be interpreted according to the common norms that govern this style of writing and set it apart from other styles. See *Exegesis; Hermeneutics.*

GIFTS OF THE HOLY SPIRIT. Ways in which the Spirit of God is manifested in human beings. To a list in the Hebrew text of Isaiah 11:2–3 (wisdom, understanding, counsel, fortitude, knowledge and fear of God), the Septuagint and the Vulgate added "piety" to make up a seven-fold gift. Originally meant as a poetic description of God's abundant blessings for the messianic king, the seven gifts were interpreted as graces given to Christians through the indwelling of the Holy Spirit. See *Charisms; Grace; Glossolalia; Messiah; Septuagint; Vulgate.*

GLORIA (Lat. "glory"). Very ancient hymn inspired by the angelic praise when Christ was born (Lk 2:14). In the Latin mass, it is recited or sung on Sunday (except during Advent and Lent) and feastdays. In the east, it is used at morning prayers. See *Advent; Feast; Lent; Sunday.*

GLORY OF GOD. In the OT, the majestic radiance manifesting God's presence (Exod 33:18–23). Through the incarnation the glory of the Son of God was already revealed in this life (Jn 1:14), a glory consummated in his death and resurrection (Jn 17:1, 4–5). Like the angels (Lk 2:14) human beings are called to give glory and praise to God (Lk 17:18; Acts 12:23). See *Doxa; Doxology; Epiphany; Grace.*

GLOSSOLALIA (Gr. "speaking in tongues"). Broken and unintelligible utterances of those gifted by the Spirit in praising and petitioning God (1 Cor 12:10, 28, 30; 13:1, 8; 14:1–27; see Rom 8:26). Prophetic inspiration, a higher and more useful charism, can express for others the meaning of these utterances. While interpreting the phenomenon of tongues as miraculously speaking foreign languages (Acts 2:4; see Mark 16:17), St Luke also refers to glossolalia in a way that resembles what we learn from St. Paul in 1 Corinthians (Acts 10:46; 19:6). See *Charism; Holy Spirit; Pentecost; Pentecostals; Prophet.*

GNOSIS (Gr. "knowledge"). A way of describing eternal life (Jn 17:3). No mere intellectual grasp of things, this life-giving knowledge of Father and Son springs from a deep personal relationship (Jn 10:14–15; 14:9). For St. Paul knowledge is imperfect and even useless, if it is not animated by love (1 Cor 13:2, 9, 12).

GNOSTICISM. A dualistic, religious movement, which (a) drew on Jewish, Christian and pagan sources, (b) clearly emerged in the second century, and (c) presented salvation as spiritual elements being freed from an evil material environment. Christian Gnostics denied Christ's real incarnation and the *salus carnis* (Lat. "salvation of the flesh") he effected. They rejected (or modified) the tradition and scriptures of mainline Christianity, claiming a privileged knowledge (of God and our human destiny) from secret traditions and revelations. Orthodox Christian writers, especially St. Irenaeus (ca. 130–ca. 200) provide much information about gnosticism. Extensive direct knowledge of the movement became available after 1945 when 52 separate Gnostic tractates, written in Coptic and from the fourth century A.D., were found at Nag Hammadi (Egypt). See *Albigensianism; Bogomils; Demiurge; Dualism; Manichaeism; Regula Fidei; Valentinians.*

GOD. The supreme being (a) who is to be worshiped and served (Deut 6:4–5) and (b) who, in the monotheistic tradition, is acknowledged as the personal, eternal, immutable, all-knowing and all-powerful creator. According to the OT, the unique and holy God of Israel transcends our material world and is not to be represented in images (Exod 20:4; Lev 19:4; Deut 4:12, 15–24). At the same time, God is ever close to the chosen people, cherishing them with covenanted love and the merciful fidelity of a parent (Josh 24; Isa 46:1–13; Hos 2:14–23). At the incarnation God's self-communication within history reaches its climax in the revelation of the Trinity. In the Son and through the indwelling Spirit human beings are adopted (Gal 4:4–6) and can come to the Father (Jn 14:6–7). Although the OT had already indicated the divine concern for other nations (e.g., Jonah), God in the NT is revealed as the God of love (1 Jn 4:7–10, 16) for all peoples (Matt 28:19–20; Rom 3:29–30; 9:1–11:36). See *Attributes, Divine; Creation; Covenant; Incarnation; Monotheism; Polytheism; Transcendence; Trinity.*

GOD OF THE GAPS. A phrase used against those who (a) look for God in phenomena that science has not yet been able to explain and (b) forget that God is actively present within all processes of the created world.

GOD'S WRATH. The anger ascribed to God (Exod 4:14; Deut 11:17; 2 Sam 24:1; Rom 1:18; 2:5–8). Besides being anthropomorphic, such talk (like that about creation, incarnation and other mysteries) also raises the question of the divine immutability, as when God threatens to destroy sinful Nineveh and then "repents" (Jonah 3:1–10). God's anger should be interpreted in an analogical way as indicating the utter incompatibility between the divine holiness and human sin. Hans Urs von Balthasar (1905–88) gave God's wrath a place in the drama of salvation to recall that salvation involves both divine and human freedom. See *Analogy; Anthropomorphism; Immutability.*

GOOD WORKS. Actions that are inspired by faith and the Holy Spirit, and that include prayer, fasting, almsgiving, protecting the weak, visiting the sick, building community, teaching and practicing hospitality (Matt 8:12; Rom 12:1–15:13; Jas 1:26–2:17). See *Faith and Works.*

GOSPEL (Old English "good news"). The message or proclamation that the kingdom of God is at hand (Mk 1:14–15) and that Jesus is effectively revealed as God's Son and our Lord through his resurrection from the dead (Rom 1:3–4; 1 Cor 15:1–11). This good news brings salvation to everyone who believes (Rom 1:16), sums up St. Paul's message (Gal 1:11) and calls for personal sacrifice (Mk 8:35; 10:29). In the second century "gospel" became a title for the four NT books dealing with the teaching, activity, death and resurrection of Jesus: the gospels according to Matthew, Mark, Luke and John. See *Apocryphal Gospels; Evangelism.*

GRACE (Lat. "favor"). Any undeserved gift or help freely and lovingly provided by God, but above all the utterly basic gift of being saved in Christ through faith (Rom 3:21–26; 4:13–16, 25; Eph 2:5–8), a grace that God wishes to give all human beings (1 Tim 2:4–6). The fullness of Christ's grace (Jn 1:16–17) brings us new birth (Jn 1:13; 3:3; 1 Pet 1:3–5), and the gift of the Holy Spirit (Rom 5:5), making us adopted children of God (Rom 8:14–16) and members of Christ's body (1 Cor 12:27). The self-communication of God (often called *uncreated grace*) means the deification of human life (2 Pet 1:4) and lifts to a new and undeserved level the relationship of creature to creator, thereby transforming human nature (= *created grace*) and anticipating the future life of heaven. From the beginning Christians have recognized the special role of the sacraments in the life of grace. It is through the grace of baptism, for example, that our sins are forgiven and that we are justified and sanctified (1 Cor 6:9–11). See *Adoption as God's Children; Beatific Vision; Deification; Faith; Gifts of the Holy Spirit; Heaven; Justification; Pelagianism; Sacraments; Sanctification; Supernatural Existential.*

GRACE, EFFICACIOUS. Any grace offered by God which is freely accepted. Where human beings fail to accept such an offer, grace is called (merely) *sufficient.*

GRACE, HABITUAL. A term for the new ongoing life in Christ brought about by (uncreated) grace. It is often called *sanctifying grace* because it is the state of being fundamentally sanctified or made holy by the Holy Spirit. As distinguished from habitual grace, *actual grace* is the effect of the Holy Spirit in meeting a particular need or supporting a specific action. See *Habit; Holiness; Holy Spirit.*

GRACE, SYSTEMS OF. Speculative attempts to explain how God's absolute freedom in granting grace and anticipating human decisions does not rule out human collaboration and responsibility. See *Apophatic Theology; Molinism; Predestination; Semi-Pelagianism; Synergism.*

GREGORIAN CHANT. The music of the Latin rite traditionally attributed to Pope Gregory I, the Great (ca. 540–604), who may have contributed to its development in Rome. Called plainchant or plainsong because it does not have a complicated rhythm, Gregorian chant is characterized by an austere beauty and discipline that favor an atmosphere of prayer. See *Chant.*

GUARDIAN ANGELS. Intelligent, non-material spirits charged by God to care for human beings (see Matt 18:10; Acts 12:15). In the OT angels protect individuals (Tob 5:1–12:21; Ps 91:11–12), small groups of people (Dan 3:24–28), and even whole nations (Dan 10:13–21). See *Angels.*

GUILT. The fact and/or awareness of having done wrong and so being culpable. Legal guilt comes from committing a crime (to which penalties are attached), ethical guilt from violating moral norms, and religious

guilt from offending God through sin. Scrupulous people can feel them-
selves to be guilty even when they have not in fact sinned against God.
At the other extreme, the lax claim to be innocent even when they offend
God and do real harm to their fellow human beings. See *Conscience;
Repentance; Sin.*

GUILT, COLLECTIVE. The guilt attributed to a whole nation, family or
some other group. At times we can truly speak of sins in which the
overwhelming majority or practically a whole society shares. Nevertheless, only a personal decision makes one participate in such collective
guilt, which is not transferred automatically to the innocent (see Deut
24:16; Jer 31:29–30; Ezek 18:2–4). See *Original Sin.*

H

HABIT (Lat. "dress"). The distinctive clothes worn by men and women
who belong to religious orders and congregations. In western philosophy and theology, habits mean modifications within us that produce
regular patterns of good or bad behavior. Virtues like courage are good
habits, while vices like cowardice are bad habits. Western scholasticism
called sanctifying grace a created, *supernatural* habit because (a) it transforms our soul and its merely natural capacities, and (b) supports the
three theological virtues that go beyond our natural powers. See
*Grace, Habitual; Religious Orders; Scholasticism; Supernatural; Vice; Vir-
tue; Virtues, Theological.*

HABIT, INFUSED. A good habit suddenly provided by God, as distinct
from an *acquired* habit that grows and matures gradually.

HAGGADAH (Heb. "narrative"). Jewish interpretation of the scriptures
by narrating legends, folklore, parables and other non-legal material.
Together with *Halachah* it forms the *Talmud.* See *Talmud.*

HAGIOGRAPHY (Gr. "saints," "writing"). Written works on the lives of
saints. While such writing goes back to early Christianity, as a scholarly
enterprise hagiography received a great impulse from John van Bolland,
S.J. (1596–1665), whose work has been continued by the Jesuit
Bollandists. See *Martyrs; Saints.*

HAGIOS (Gr. "holy"). A Greek anthem acclaiming God three times to
show the fullness of the divine holiness (see Isa 6:3), and hence better
known as *Trisagion* (Gr. "threefold holy"): "Holy God, Holy and

Mighty, Holy and Immortal, have mercy on us!" Whereas in the Latin liturgy this refrain is used only on Good Friday, it is regularly chanted in eastern liturgies. See *Good Friday; Holiness; Trisagion.*

HALLEL (Heb. "praise"). The name given by the Jews to Psalms 113–118, which were sung at such festivals as the Passover (see Matt 26:30), Pentecost and the Feast of the Tabernacles (see Jn 7:2). "Hallelujah" (Heb. "praise to the Lord"), a word that occurs frequently in these psalms, is used by all Christian liturgies, especially during the Easter cycle. See *Passover; Pentecost; Liturgy.*

HAMARTOLOGY (Gr. "study of sin"). That section of theology that studies sin and its effects on human beings. See *Sin.*

HANUKKAH. See *Temple, The.*

HEART. For the Bible the innermost place for a human being's knowledge, feelings and decisions (Isa 65:14; Jer 24:7; Lk 2:19). The heart is the principle of good and evil thoughts (Mk 7:21; Lk 6:45) and can be the seat of wisdom (1 Kgs 3:12) and the instrument of faith (Rom 10:10). The Holy Spirit dwells in the hearts of the justified (Rom 5:5)—a theme maintained by the fathers and still a central concept for eastern anthropology. Western scholasticism, while appreciating the biblical worth of the term, found "heart" somewhat too unspecific and preferred to argue in terms of the faculties of the soul (intellect, will, emotions). See *Anthropology; Kardiognosis; Hesychasm; Jesus Prayer; Scholasticism.*

HEART, HARDENING OF. A sinful refusal to see God's hand at work (Exod 11:10) or to help the poor (Deut 15:7). The NT uses similar language of those who refuse to open themselves in faith to Christ and his message (Matt 13:13–15; Mk 16:14). See *Depravity, Total.*

HEART, PRAYER OF THE. See *Hesychasm; Jesus Prayer.*

HEART, SACRED. The wounded heart of Jesus symbolizing his self-sacrificing love for all human beings (see Jn 7:37–39; 19:34). While present in the middle ages, devotion to his wounded heart became much more popular through the visions of St. Margaret Mary Alacoque (1647–90), which encouraged, for example, acts of reparation and the practice of receiving holy communion on the first Friday of every month. See *Devotions; Love; Reparation; Symbol.*

HEAVEN. According to a primitive religious understanding, the place in or beyond the sky where the gods live. The Bible reflects an early cosmology about the vault of heaven resting on pillars (Job 26:11). It speaks of heaven as the place where God is enthroned (Ps 11:4; 115:16) and from which God descends (Exod 19:18–20), but recognizes that "heaven and earth" cannot contain God (see Gen 1:1; 1 Kings 8:27). At the end new heavens and a new earth will be created (Isa 65:17; 2 Peter 3:13; Rev 21:1–22:5), heaven being the "place" or state where the blessed will dwell forever with God through Christ's glorified humanity (see 1 Thess 4:17; Jn 14:3; 1 Pet 1:4). See *Beatific Vision; Eschatology; Life after Death; Paradise; Resurrection.*

HEBREWS (etymology uncertain). The people who under Moses entered the land promised to Abraham and who preferred to call themselves Israelites, or sons of Israel, the name God gave to Jacob (Gen 32:28; 35:10). They were called Hebrews mainly by others, sometimes in contempt (see Gen 43:32). An archaizing term (Gen 14:13), "Hebrew" pointed to the core qualities of an authentic Jew (see 2 Cor 11:22; Phil 3:5). "Hebrew" is also the older, classical language in which almost all the OT books were written. It was supplanted by Aramaic after the Babylonian captivity, and ceased to be commonly spoken around the fourth century B.C. It has been revived as the official language for the modern state of Israel. See *Exodus; Israel; Judaism; Old Testament.*

HEILSGESCHICHTE. See *Salvation History.*

HELL. The place or state where devils and unrepentant sinners suffer forever (DS 1002). This eternal punishment, which varies according to the gravity of the sins committed (see DS 1306), consists in exclusion from God's presence (*poenae damni* = damnation proper), and in suffering from an unextinguishable but unspecified "fire" (*poenae sensus;* see DS 443, 780). Church teaching follows the NT (Matt 13:36–43; 25:31–46) by insisting on the possibility of hell for those who through free malice refuse to love God and their neighbors. But it makes no claims about the number of the damned. God's saving love for all remains a fundamental and effective force (1 Cor 15:28; 1 Tim 2:3–6). See *Apocatastasis; Eschatology; Heart, Hardening of.*

HENOTHEISM. See *Monotheism.*

HERESY (Gr. "choice"). In the NT a sectarian group (Acts 5:17) or a disruptive faction and opinion (1 Cor 11:19; Gal 5:20; 2 Pet 2:1). Heresy came to mean a baptized person's wilful and persistent dissent from orthodox doctrines of faith (see CIC 751, 1364). At times the challenge of heresy has encouraged the solemn definition of church teaching. See *Apostasy; Faith; Orthodoxy; Orthopraxis; Revelation; Schism.*

HERMENEUTICAL CIRCLE. A notion developed, at times differently, by Martin Heidegger (1889–1976), Rudolf Bultmann (1884–1976), Hans Georg Gadamer (b. 1900) and others apropos of the interpreter's search for meaning. In a particular historical situation and with some prior understanding of what a given text is about, the interpreter begins a "dialogue." The text will modify questions put to it, challenge expectations and even radically correct our presuppositions. In the dialogue with the interpreter, the text and its message retain their priority. A 1989 document of the International Theological Commission ("The Interpretation of Dogmas") proposed a "metaphysical hermeneutics" as a solution to the risk of relativism involved in the hermeneutical circle.

HERMENEUTICS (Gr. "interpretation," from Hermes, the messenger of the gods). The theory and practice of understanding and interpreting texts, biblical or otherwise. Hermeneutics, while seeking to (a) establish the original meaning of a text in its historical context and (b) express that meaning today, recognizes that a text can contain and convey meaning that goes beyond the original author's explicit intention. Besides drawing help from such disciplines as philology, history, literary criticism and sociology, interpreters need also to reflect philosophically on the human condition and its role in creating and reading texts. Despite the distance between individual minds and cultures, our common humanity bridges the gap to allow texts to be understood and interpreted. See *Allegory; Analogy of Faith; Biblical Criticism; Dogma; Exegesis; Haggadah; Halachah; Magisterium; Scripture and Tradition; Senses of Scripture.*

HERMIT (from Gr. "desert"). A person who retires from society to spend a solitary life dedicated to prayer and penance. The place where such recluses live is called a hermitage. Although the number of hermits fell after the reformation, much of their tradition has passed into such monastic orders as the Carthusians, Camaldolese and Carmelites. The Latin church still recognizes the life of solitaries as long as they take vows before the local bishops and remain under his ultimate guidance (see CIC 603). In the eastern church, hermits flourish and are known as anchorites. See *Anchorites; Athos, Mount; Monasticism; Religious Life.*

HEROIC VIRTUE. The practice of Christian virtues to an unusual degree. Such heroism is characterized by charity, humility and endurance through long periods of difficulty. Before being beatified and canonized, a candidate's practice of Christian virtues must be shown to be above average in this sense. Martyrs form the only exception, because the heroic nature of their deaths puts their whole life in a new perspective. See *Beatification; Canonization; Holiness; Martyrs; Virtue.*

(813) 472-1541 Local
(800) 282-2831 Florida
(800) 824-0476 National
988749 Telex

West Wind Inn

P.O. Box F
3345 West Gulf Dr.
Sanibel Island, FL 33957

discover — find root .
strong to guide, discover or reveal
valuable for stimulating or conduc-
ting empirical research but
unproved or incapable of
proof — used q arguments or
methods or constructs that
assume or postulate what
remains to be proven or
that lead a person to find
out for himself

making hypotheses more completely
understood

HESED (Heb. "loving kindness"). A word characterizing God that occurs 245 times in the OT, including 127 times in the psalms. God is even addressed as "my *hesed*" (Ps 144:2). *Hesed* indicates God's merciful fidelity in keeping the covenant promises, despite the fickleness of the human partners. See *Berith; Covenant*.

HESYCHASM (Gr. "quiet"). A style of unremitting prayer and ascetical life which is characteristic of eastern Christianity and enables the practioner to remain tranquilly recollected in God. In its inspiration and general approach, hesychasm coincides with the origins of monasticism itself. Its founder is held to be Arsenius the Great (d. ca. 449), who abandoned a brilliant career as imperial preceptor to live in the desert. With St. Simeon the New Theologian (949–1002) the mystical approach of this spirituality was deepened. St. Gregory of Sinai and St. Nicephorus the Hesychast (thirteenth/fourteenth century) both contributed much to its propagation; the latter added an intricate psychosomatic technique involving the repetition of the "Jesus prayer." With St. Gregory Palamas (ca. 1296–1359) hesychasm attained full-fledged dogmatic status. But the claim that one could see the uncreated light of the divinity as the apostles did on Mount Tabor touched off controversy. This light, while held to be truly divine, was considered one of God's energies rather than the divine essence itself. When St. Nicodemus of Mount Athos (ca. 1749–1809) published the anthology of patristic and hesychast spiritual writings known as *Philocalia*, the movement experienced a new popularity. Hesychasm aims at human integration through the constant remembrance of God, which we can attain by "guarding" our hearts. Hesychasm can therefore be summed up as the "prayer of the heart." See *Essence and Energies; Jesus Prayer; Palamism; Philocalia*.

HETERODOX (Gr. "of different belief"). Opinions which deviate from the normative teaching of the church. See *Orthodoxy*.

HETERONOMY (Gr. "alien law"). A term used since Immanuel Kant (1724–1804) to describe the state of those who are not autonomous or self-determining, but live subject to some external law. Since God's supreme authority is mediated through our created consciousness and freedom, *theonomy* (Gr. "divine law"), when rightly understood delivers us from an unreal alternative: either an absolute autonomy or a slavish heteronomy. See *Autonomy; Ethics; Freedom; Theonomy*.

HIERARCHY (Gr. "holy origin," "order"). The principle of order organizing the universe, angels, human society and the church. Pseudo-Dionysius (fifth or sixth century) popularized the notion of a hierarchy among the angels. Through holy orders (*hierarchia ordinis*) the church has the

91

classes of bishops, priests and deacons (see CIC 330–572). In the *hierarchia jurisdictionis* jurisdiction belongs to the pope and bishops, other forms of church government being derivative from them (see CIC 1008–1054). The hierarchical union between pope and bishops and between a bishop and his priests is expressed through collegiality (see DS 1767–1770; LG 18–29). The notion of hierarchy as the three classes of bishops, priests and deacons, who do not derive their authority from the people, distinguishes the Roman Catholic and Orthodox Churches from Protestants (see also DS 2595). In a popular sense, the hierarchy simply refers to the pope and the bishops. See *Bishop; Collegiality; Choirs of Angels; Episcopacy; Holy Orders; Ordination.*

HIERARCHY OF TRUTHS. A principle for interpreting (not selecting!) truths of faith by their nearness to the central mystery of faith, the revelation of the Trinity which Christ brought and through which we are saved in the Spirit. Clearly enunciated by the Second Vatican Council (UR 11), this principle has biblical precedents, in particular when the NT states briefly the essentials of faith (e.g., Rom 1:3–4; 1 Cor 15:3–5). While all truths should be believed, classifying and interpreting these truths according to their relative importance can eliminate false emphases and facilitate ecumenical dialogue (see DS 3016). See *Analogy of Faith; Creed; Dialogue; Dogma; Ecumenism; Faith; Revelation.*

HIGH CHRISTOLOGY. As distinguished from a "low christology," a high christology highlights Christ's divinity. This distinction should not be confused with another distinction, explicit/implicit christology. See *Christology from Above; Christology from Below.*

HINDUISM. One of the world's main religions and the principal religion of the Indian subcontinent. Not founded by one person at a given point in history and not holding a clear-cut ensemble of truths, Hinduism accepts many gods, notably *Brahma* who creates the Universe, *Vishnu* who preserves it and *Siva* who destroys it. Yet these gods are understood to be only different manifestations of One Supreme God (either Siva for Saivism or Vishnu for Vaishnavism) in the theist current, or of an impersonal, divine Absolute (Brahman) in the non-dualist current. The earliest sacred writings of Hinduism are the *Vedas;* later, more mystical treatises are called *Upanishads,* and the most popular religious work is the *Bhagavad-gita.* Hinduism has been transmitted through the tradition of spiritual masters and teachers in different castes and sociocultural contexts. Its ascetical practices and meditation ("dhyana") through yoga aim at freeing people from passion and restlessness in order to be united with God in love and surrender (theist trend) or absorbed into the ultimate divine Absolute (non-dualist trend)—a freedom believed to come normally after a series of reincarnations (see NA 2). See *Religion; World Religions.*

HISTORICAL CRITICISM. See *Biblical Criticism.*

HISTORICAL JESUS. The earthly Jesus as known through "purely" historical research without recourse to faith. Often the "historical Jesus" has been contrasted with the "kerygmatic Christ" or the "Christ of faith" (= the Christ believed in and preached by the church). Nowadays it is generally agreed that it is impossible to write a genuine "life" of Jesus. Nevertheless, a soundly-based consensus maintains many historical conclusions about Jesus: his Jewishness, his proclamation of the kingdom, his miraculous activity, his parables and his crucifixion at Jerusalem under Pontius Pilate. The real challenge to the quest for the historical Jesus comes, however, from the question: Is it really possible to make a merely critical study of Jesus that looks only to "facts" and refuses to evaluate them theologically? See *Christ of Faith; Christology.*

HISTORY (Gr. "inquiry, narrative"). The record and study of important events in human affairs, at the local, national, international or world level. Modern historians, while developing the careful use of evidence from the datable past, have come to recognize how presuppositions, methods and the inevitable role of interpretation show the aim of writing purely "objective," "scientific" history to be a fallacy. Many have also abandoned any hope of producing a coherent system that would describe and explain the meaning, direction and unity of *all* history.

As an historical religion, Christianity is tied to a series of specific events and persons—above all, to Jesus and the events in which he was involved. He came at "the fullness of time" (Gal 4:4), bringing God's self-revelation to its definitive climax (DV 4). The church lives now in the expectation of the end (LG 48–51), when Christ's *parousia* or second coming will terminate and consummate world history (1 Cor 15:20–28; Tit 3:1–7). Like the Israelites (Exod 20:1; Deut 26:5–9), Christians accept a saving revelation of God mediated through human history. They experience their own history as founded in and nourished by Jesus' own history. While not being simply validated by historical inquiry, their faith is supported by historical signs and inspires them to be active protagonists in history. This faith accepts the divinely guided direction, meaning, and unity of all human history, even though we cannot yet recognize very many clear features in this total story. From the individual to the global level it remains true that "God writes straight, but with crooked lines." See *Eschatology; Historical Jesus; Liberation Theology; Parousia; Salvation History.*

HISTORY-OF-RELIGIONS SCHOOL. A largely German group of scholars who included Wilhelm Bousset (1865–1920), Hermann Gunkel (1862–1932) and Richard Reitzenstein (1861–1931). In interpreting Judaism, Christianity and their origins, they argued for many parallels and sources in other religious traditions of the Near East. See *Comparative Religion.*

HOLINESS (Old German "whole"). The attribute of a being which entirely fulfills the purpose of its existence and is thus at one with itself. Strictly speaking, only God is holy, as being "the awesome and fascinating mystery (*mysterium tremendum et fascinans*)," "utterly other" than human beings and indescribably holy (see Isa 6:3, 5) and yet the source of all our spiritual and moral perfection. In the OT a Holiness Code (Lev 17–26) invites the Israelites to be holy because their God is holy (Lev 19:2; 20:26). Paul understands both the whole church and individual Christians to be the temple of the Holy Spirit (1 Cor 3:16–17; 6:19). Things, places, ceremonies, scriptures, law and a covenant may also be said to be holy, inasmuch as they are sanctified and consecrated to God. See *Consecration; Covenant; Doxa; Grace; Hagios; Perfection; Saint; Sanctification; Trisagion.*

HOLINESS OF THE CHURCH. One of the main marks characterizing the church and her members, and an article of faith found in the earliest creeds (DS 1–76). Through Christ's sacrifice, the Holy Spirit and baptism, the whole church has been sanctified (Rom 5:5; 1 Cor 6:11; Eph 5:25–27). Paul addresses Christian communities as the "holy ones" (2 Cor 1:1) or "called to be holy ones" (Rom 1:7; 2 Cor 1:2). At times, Donatists and others have exaggerated the holiness of the church here and now. The truth is rather that, for her present pilgrimage, the church has been made holy by God's Spirit, is always supported by the witness of some heroically dedicated members, and yet (because of the many sins of Christians) constantly needs purification (LG 8). At the end the heavenly church, the new Jerusalem, will shine with radiant holiness (Rev 21:2, 10–11; 22:19). See *Canonization; Communion of Saints; Donatism; Marks (Notes) of the Church; Saint; Sanctification.*

HOLOCAUST (Gr. "something completely burnt up"). An OT sacrifice in which the victim was entirely consumed by fire. God was understood to be manifested in fire (Exod 3:2; 19:18; 1 Kgs 18:36–39). On the human side, burning symbolized that nothing was kept back by those making the offering. Prophets and others insisted that such sacrifices were superficial or even useless unless accompanied by a right relationship to God and neighbor (Isa 1:11; Jer 7:21–26; Ps 51:18–19; Mk 12:33). According to the NT, Christ's self-sacrificing obedience fulfilled and went beyond all holocausts (Heb 10:1–10). Since World War II "holocaust" has been applied to the six million Jews murdered by the Nazis in an attempt to exterminate the whole Jewish race. See *Judaism; Sacrifice.*

HOLY ORDERS. A sacrament imparting a special character and empowering the recipient to share in Christ's priestly ministry by teaching, governing and officiating at worship as bishop, priest or deacon. In each of these cases the rite of ordination shows that the candidate has been called and chosen, invokes the Holy Spirit for the effective exercise of the new ministry and, along with various prayers, includes an imposition of hands by the ordaining bishop. The Anglican, Roman Catholic and Orthodox Churches hold that holy orders are of divine institution, and qualify those ordained to represent Christ in certain ministries that the non-ordained cannot perform. See *Anointing; Bishop; Character; Clergy; Deacon; Ministry; Ordination; Priest; Sacraments.*

HOLY SEE (Lat. "holy seat"). The government of the pope, whose authority is symbolized by his throne as bishop of Rome. In canon law "Holy See" and "Apostolic See" refer not only to the pope himself but also, when the context so indicates, to his Secretariat of State and other offices in the papal government (CIC 361). See *Cathedra; Enthronement; Pope.*

HOLY SPIRIT. The third person of the Trinity, adored and glorified together with the Father and the Son as one in nature and equal in personal dignity with the Father and the Son. The Council of Braga (675), or possibly the third Synod of Toledo (589), added to the creed by saying that the Spirit proceeded from the Father "and the Son" (= *Filioque*). The earlier eastern formulations agreed that the Spirit was not begotten like the Son, but proceeded from the Father "through the Son (= *per Filium*). The work of sanctification, common to all three persons, is appropriated to the Spirit, because it entails the self-gift of the Spirit (Jn 20:22; Rom 5:5). Both St. Athanasius of Alexandria (ca. 296–373) and St. Cyril of Alexandria (d. 444) argued for the divinity of the Spirit precisely because the Spirit makes us similar to God by divinizing or sanctifying us. The divinity of the Spirit was proclaimed at the First Council of Constantinople in 381. See *Appropriation; Constantinople, First Council of; Filioque; Florence, Council of; Pneumatology; Trinity.*

HOLY WEEK. The most important week in the church's calendar, which starts with the blessing of the palms and the procession on Palm Sunday, recalls the institution of the eucharist on Holy Thursday, also known as Maundy Thursday (Lat. "command" for the Lord's injunction to love one another as He loved us Jn 13:34), and culminates in the Easter Vigil on Holy Saturday. In the east it is known as "The Week of Salvation";

the Greeks call it "The Great Week." The *Festal Letters* of St. Athanasius of Alexandria (ca. 296–373) offer the first clear documentary evidence of Holy Week celebrations. When Egeria made her pilgrimage from Spain to Jerusalem in the late fourth century, she found a highly developed Holy Week liturgy in the city where Christ spent the last few days of his earthly life. See *Easter Triduum; Mass of the Presanctified.*

HOMILETICS. The branch of pastoral theology dedicated to the art and science of effective preaching. See *Pastoral Theology.*

HOMILY (Gr. "company," "conversation"). Originally a reflection on scripture during Christian worship—a custom derived from a similar practice in Jewish synagogues (see Lk 4:16–22; Acts 13:15). The term came to mean the sermons which bishops preach to their flocks. *Homiliaries* were collections of homilies from the fathers to be used during the Liturgy of the Hours. In current usage, a homily is the sermon which is given during the eucharist after the gospel and which aims to develop Christian faith and life by explaining the texts of scripture that have just been read. On Sundays and important feastdays the homily should not be omitted; it is recommended for weekday masses, especially during Advent and Lent (SC 24, 52; CIC 767). The homilist at mass is normally a bishop, priest or deacon. Since Christ is present not only in the sacraments but also in the word of God (DV 24), Vatican II encouraged homilies. They require a deep familiarity with scripture and should encourage listening to the word of God. See *Bible; Pastoral Theology; Preaching.*

HOMOEANS (Gr. "similar"). A group of Arians led by Bishop Acacius of Caesarea (d. ca. 366) who tried to mediate between the Semi-Arians and those who accepted Nicaea I. With Emperor Constance's support, their formula ("the Son was similar in all things to the Father, according to the scripture") was endorsed at the Council of Sirmio (359). Subsequently weakened to "similar to the Father," the formula of the Homoeans failed as soon as the emperor died. See *Arianism; Homoousios; Semi-Arians; Nicaea, First Council of.*

HOMOOUSIOS (Gr. "of the same substance," "consubstantial"). Word referring to Christ and inserted into the creed by the Council of Nicaea (325) to combat Arianism. Although previously used in a doubtful or even heretical sense by Gnostics and others, at Nicaea the term expressed the identity of nature between the Father and the Son, implying a corresponding equality in dignity. Fifty years of dispute followed. St. Athanasius (ca. 296–373) in the east and St. Hilary of Poitiers (ca. 315–67) in the west championed *homoousios*, whereas such opponents as Basil of Ancyra (now Ankara) and George of Laodicea added an "i" to the term and called Christ "homo-i-ousios," i.e., "similar in substance" to the Father. See *Arianism; Constantinople, First Council of; Nicaea, First Council of.*

HOPE. The active expectation of future blessings (1 Cor 15), based on faith and expressing itself through love (1 Cor 13:13). Hope responds to God's promises communicated through the history of the OT and NT— in particular, through the exodus from Egypt, Christ's resurrection from the dead (1 Pet 1:3; 2 Cor 1:9–11; Heb 6:19–20) and the gift of the Holy Spirit. In hope we go beyond our present incomplete existence to antici- pate the full future of God's final kingdom and the liberating resurrec- tion of all creation (Rom 8:18–25). Far from encouraging mere passive waiting for God's definitive intervention, authentic hope obliges Chris- tians to be responsible for the world and work for more justice and peace here and now (GS 21, 34, 39, 43). See *Eschatology; Virtues, Theological.*

HOUSE CHURCHES. A post-Second World War movement to relive the early Christians' experience of common prayers and eucharist in their homes (see Acts 1:12–14; 2:42, 46). In some cases the movement has led to groups breaking away from institutional churches. This has hardly happened in the Catholic Church, where many regular or spontaneous groups enjoy the mass celebrated at home. See *Charismatic; Pentecostals; Worship.*

HUMANISM. Any movement that values the intellect, freedom and dig- nity of human beings and their capacity to learn and improve their whole cultural situation. The rediscovery of classical culture inspired the Renaissance humanism. Its typical leaders, while often critical of church and society, could be devout and religious: Lorenzo Valla (ca. 1406–57), Pico della Mirandola (1463–94), Erasmus of Rotterdam (1469–1536) and St. Thomas More (1478–1535). Recent humanists have often been non- believers (GS 7, 56), who regard human beings as the absolutely auton- omous "measure of all things." Nevertheless, a new humanism that responsibly seeks to build a better world based on truth and justice (GS 55) is quite compatible with Christian faith. See *Anthropology; Atheism; Autonomy; Reformation.*

HUSSITES. Followers of Jan Huss (ca. 1369–1415), a priest from Bohemia who taught philosophy and theology at the University of Prague. He came to know and spread the reforming ideas of John Wycliffe (ca. 1330–84). He was tried and burned at the stake during the Council of Constance (see DS 1201–30; 1247–79), thus becoming a national Czech hero. The Hussites adopted his positions, which included predestination and scripture as the only norm of faith. Their legacy is continued somewhat in various Moravian churches around the world. In 1920 the Czechoslovak Hussite Church, which claimed to represent this legacy, broke off from the Catholic Church, after its demands for a vernacular liturgy, optional celibacy for the clergy and lay participation in church government were not met. Huss himself wrongly rejected the validity of sacraments administered by a simoniacal priest. The primacy he accorded to scripture as the sole norm of faith made him a precursor of the reformers (see DS 1480). His view that the laity should receive from the chalice was accepted at the Second Vatican Council (see DS 1725; SC 55). See *Constance, Council of; Donatism; Predestination; Reformation; Simony; Sola Scriptura; Vernacular.*

HYLOMORPHISM. See *Matter and Form.*

HYPERDOULIA (Gr. "more than just veneration"). The special devotion paid to Mary as the Mother of God. It is more than the *doulia* (Gr. "servitude") or honor shown to other saints, but less than the *latria* (Gr. "worship") or adoration due to God alone. See *Adoration; Theotokos; Veneration of Saints.*

HYPOPANTE (Gr. "encounter"). The Greek name for the feast of our Lord's presentation in the temple and the meeting that followed with Simeon and Anna (Lk 2:22–38). In the west during the middle ages, the feast was known as *occursus Domini* (Lat. "the Lord's encounter"). Celebrated in Jerusalem from at least the fourth century, the feast became universal in the seventh century.

HYPOSTASIS (Gr. "substance," "that which stands or is set under"). The substantial nature or reality underlying something (see Heb 1:3). The term created problems in christological and Trinitarian controversies of the fourth and fifth centuries, when it came to mean "concrete, individual reality" or "distinct personal existence." Eventually official church teaching spoke of God as three "hypostaseis," sharing one substance or nature, and of Christ as two natures in one "hypostasis" or person (see DS 125–26; 300–03; 421). See *Chalcedon, Council of; Monophysitism; Neo-Chalcedonianism; Nicaea, First Council of.*

HYPOSTATIC UNION. The union between full divinity and humanity in the one (divine) person of Jesus Christ, which occurred when "the Word became flesh" (Jn 1:14; see DS 252–63; 301–02). See *Arianism; Apollinarianism; Nestorianism; Monophysitisim.*

I

I AND THOU. The name of a short work by a Jewish religious thinker, Martin Buber (1878–1965). Published first in 1923 in Germany, it exercised a great influence on subsequent philosophy and theology. Buber argued for a qualitative difference between relating to and using a thing (I–it) and relating to a person. In dealing with persons who address me and respond, authentic I–Thou interrelationships are possible. I–Thou interreaction is the way to become one with onself—a self-identity ultimately made possible through an integrating relationship to God. See *Mysticism.*

ICON (Gr. "image"). A sacred image, painted on wood or formed by a mosaic. Icons are flat pictures, even if sometimes the outlines of clothes may be portrayed on a protective shield. Rather than realistically representing persons and scenes, icons present them symbolically and have an integral function for public and private worship in eastern churches. Makers of icons frequently remain anonymous because devout faithfulness to tradition rather than originality is central. Artists create these works as a religious activity, preparing themselves for it by prayer and fasting. The reverence shown to icons does not refer to the images in themselves but to the sacred persons they represent: the living God, Our Lady, the angels or the saints. See *Adoration; Eastern Theology; Veneration of Saints; Worship.*

ICONOCLASM (Gr. "smashing of images"). A movement which opposed the use of images in Christian worship and disturbed the Byzantine Empire from ca. 725 to 843. In a first phase, icons were destroyed as being pagan idols that were incompatible with Christian faith and a scandal to Jews and Moslems. From the monastery of St. Sabas near Jerusalem, St. John Damascene (ca. 675–ca. 749) argued that using images to represent Christ and other sacred persons was a necessary consequence of the incarnation. After iconoclasm was accepted by the heretical synod of Hieria (753), the ecumenical council of Nicaea II (787) restored images and their veneration (DS 600–03; 2532). In a second phase of the crisis (814–43) icons, while tolerated for teaching purposes, were considered unsuitable for public worship and so removed from churches. From the beginning monks were persecuted and sometimes killed by the iconoclasts. Another great monastic defense of images came from St. Theodore the Studite (759–826). To mark the end of the controversy the Feast of Orthodoxy was established, and it is still celebrated on the first Sunday in Lent by the eastern churches. See *Image of God; Islam; Nicaea, Second Council of; Orthodoxy.*

ICONOSTASIS (Gr. "image wall"). In Oriental churches, a screen or wall that is covered with icons and separates the nave from the sanctuary. The sanctuary symbolizes heaven and the nave earth. However, both are found under the same roof, to show that in the liturgy we on earth are united with heaven. The iconostasis has three doors: the royal door, in the center, is reserved for the main celebrant, bishop or priest, and leads directly to the altar; the door on the right leads to the *diakonikon*, a kind of sacristy for the deacons who assist the celebrant; the door on the left leads to the *prothesis* or chamber reserved for the preparation of gifts.

IDEALISM. Any comprehensive interpretation of reality and history in which ideas and ideals predominate over concrete experience and the objects of external perception. More specifically, idealism refers to any philosophical system which subsumes everything under consciousness, mind and reason. In this sense, idealism is opposed to common sense realism, as well as to naturalism and materialism, which interpret the real as being constituted, respectively, by nature and matter. Idealism has varied from Plato (427–347 B.C.), who considered the world of changing sense experience unreliable and found true knowledge in the higher realm of eternal ideas, to Georg Wilhelm Friedrich Hegel (1770–1831), for whom all history is the evolutionary manifestation of the Absolute. In between are such variants as René Descartes (1596–1650), who anchored certainty in the individual's act of knowing, and Immanuel Kant (1724–1804), who showed to what extent the human mind constructs what we call external reality. Church teaching has condemned idealism in those extreme forms (DS 3878, 3882) which exclude God's absolute freedom and our limited freedom, rejecting, in particular, the rationalistic attempt by Anton Günther (1783–1863) to adapt theology to Hegelianism (see DS 2828–31, 2914, 3025). See *Philosophy; Rationalism.*

IDOLATRY (Gr. "adoration of images"). The worship of false, nonexistent gods. The OT rigorously condemns adoring idols or the images of false gods (Exod 20:3–4; Deut 5:7–9; Ps 115:4–8). The NT not only denounces idolatry (1 Cor 5:10; Rev 21:8; 22:15), but also, developing an extension of the notion (see Isa 2:6–11), it rejects the cult of money as idolatry (Eph 5:5; Col 3:5). See *Adoration; Icon; Iconoclasm; Judaism; Worship.*

IMAGE OF GOD. The doctrine according to which human beings, male and female, were created in the divine image and likeness (Gen 1:26–27). Some fathers of the church and later theologians distinguished between (a) the "image" of God which belongs to human beings as creatures of reason and free will and which can only be obscured by sin, and (b) the "likeness" to God which, if lost by sin, can be restored through grace by baptism and a life of faith. The NT recognizes Christ as God's true image (Col 1:15), the model according to whom men and women are to be shaped (Rom 8:29). See Creation; Deification; Depravity, Total; Fall, The; Grace; Original Sin.

IMAGINATION. The creative capacity to go beyond the immediate data, so as to form, recall and relate ideas and objects presented here and now by the senses. Although some major philosophers and theologians have rejected the imagination for its dangerous and distorting influence, more and more contemporaries have seen the positive role of the imagination in religious life, thought and worship. It is essential for the communication of faith. The disciplined exercise of the imagination leads to knowledge, and helps us to perceive, interpret and integrate the truth. See Aesthetics; Beauty, Theology of; Icons.

"IMITATION OF CHRIST." A very influential manual on seeking spiritual perfection through following Christ as model. Usually ascribed to Thomas a Kempis (ca. 1380–1471), the book classically expresses the devotio moderna (Lat. "modern devotion"), a form of deeply prayerful and personal piety which in the late fourteenth century spread from Holland to the rest of Europe. See Devotion.

IMITATION OF CHRIST. The ideal and practice of following Jesus Christ which is found in the earliest Christian document (1 Thess 1:6) and in Paul's letters is also associated with imitating the apostle himself (1 Cor 4:16; 11:1; 2 Thess 3:7). For Paul the imitation of Christ means a deliverance from sin and a self-abnegation that conform believers to the pattern of the crucifixion and resurrection (Rom 6:1–11), a readiness to be shaped by the indwelling Holy Spirit (see Rom 8:4, 11), and a self-giving service of love toward others (1 Cor 13; Gal 5:13). The gospels characteristically speak of a personal discipleship that is ready to serve the neighbor in need (Lk 10:29–37) and to follow the Son of man on the road through suffering to glory (Mk 8:31–38). Instead of the "imitation" of Christ, the Christian east prefers to speak of "life in Christ" (see Jn 15:1–17; 1 Jn 2:1–6), a theme found in many eastern treatises on the spiritual life; see The Life in Christ by Nicholas Cabasilas (b. ca. 1332) and Fr. John of Cronstadt's (1829–1908) My Life in Christ.

IMMACULATE CONCEPTION. A western feast held on December 8 and celebrating the fact that, by a unique privilege and in view of her Son's merits, Mary of Nazareth was free of all sin, even original sin, from her very conception (see DS 2800–04). Several passages from scripture have been constantly understood to point in this direction (Gen 3:15; Lk 1:28). Although the dogma itself was defined by Pius IX only in 1854, the feast is known to go back at least to the seventh century. Partly because of differences over the notion of original sin, the Orthodox do not honor the Mother of God as "immaculately conceived," but as *achrantos* (Gr. "immaculate") and *Panagia* (Gr. "all-holy"). See *Original Sin; Theotokos.*

IMMANENCE, DIVINE (Lat. "remaining in"). God's presence everywhere and in everything (see Ps 139). Unless complemented by a sense of the divine transcendence, which means that God also exists apart from and beyond the whole universe, the notion of immanence can lapse into pantheism. See *Omnipresence; Panentheism; Pantheism; Transcendence.*

IMMANENT TRINITY. The absolute mystery of the three divine persons in their eternal life. Through the "economy" or history of salvation, initiated in the OT and fulfilled in the NT with the incarnation of the Son and sending of the Spirit, the triune God has been revealed. Thus from the "economic" Trinity we come to know the "immanent" Trinity. See *Economy; Trinity, Theology of.*

IMMENSITY OF GOD. The divine attribute of being unmeasured and unmeasurable. Being beyond measure, God is the measure for everyone and everything else. This theme is developed in a particularly dramatic way in Job 38–42 (see DS 800; 3001). See *Attributes, Divine; God.*

IMMOLATION (Lat. "sprinkling the sacrificial victim with meal"). A sacrifice involving victim, priest and people in an offering to God. In the eucharist Christ's sacrifice, which was ritually expressed at the last supper and consummated on Calvary, is represented (not repeated) and its effects made available today (see 1 Cor 11:23–26; DS 1740–41). See *Eucharist; Sacrifice.*

IMMORTALITY. See *Death; Life after Death; Resurrection; Soul.*

IMMUTABILITY. Freedom from change and the possibility of change. Strictly speaking, only the all-perfect God is completely immutable (see Mal 3:6; Ps 102:27; DS 285; 294; 800; 3001). As man, Christ was subject to change and death. See *Incarnation.*

IMPASSIBILITY (Lat. for *apatheia*). Freedom from the possibility of pain and being changed by an outside cause. Only the all-perfect and immutable God is impassible (see DS 16, 166, 293, 300, 358–59). But this does not mean that God is indifferent and unconcerned. The divine love brought about the incarnation (Jn 3:16), through which the Son of God came to suffer and die by reason of his human nature. See *Apatheia; Immutability; Passion; Theopaschite Controversy.*

IMPETRATORY PRAYER (Lat. "obtain by asking"). Praying to God for our own needs and those of others. Such prayer is legitimate so long as we ask God to bring about what is according to the divine will and for our own real good (Gen 18:22–33; Matt 6:9–13; 7:7–11; Lk 11:1–13; see DS 957–59). See *Intercession; Prayer.*

IMPOSITION OF HANDS. A way of blessing found in the OT (Gen 48), adopted by Jesus in working miracles (e.g., Mk 1:41; 5:41) and used by his followers (Acts 13:3; 1 Tim 4:14; 5:22), in particular to communicate the Holy Spirit (Acts 8:17f; 19:6). The laying on of hands became the chief rite in conferring the sacrament of orders (see DS 3858–60). By not insisting that the Greeks accept the Latin rite and its own ceremony of ordination (DS 1326) the Council of Florence (1439) approved of the way the Greeks ordained—by the imposition of hands. The rites of baptism and confirmation include a laying on of hands, which is also recommended in the new rite of confession. See *Florence, Council of; Holy Orders.*

IMPUTATION. Legally ascribing to someone the guilt or righteousness of another. This notion is central to the Protestant view of justification as Christ's righteousness being ascribed (rather than imparted) to us sinners. Recent discussions, however, have tended to mitigate any sharp distinction between the Protestant view (God merely declares sinners to be just) and the Catholic view (God truly makes sinners just). See *Deification; Justification; Lutheranism; Protestant.*

INCARNATION (Lat. "enfleshing"). The belief that for the salvation of the world, the Son of God, while remaining fully divine, became truly and fully human (Jn 1:14; Gal 4:4–5). At a particular place and time in history he was born of the Virgin Mary, died on a cross under Pontius Pilate and rose from the dead with a glorified humanity (Rom 1:3–4). From Nicaea I (325) to Constantinople III (680), church councils have rejected various attempts to tamper with or deny the full humanity and the full divinity of Jesus Christ. See *Chalcedon, Council of; Constantinople, Third Council of; Docetism; Nicaea, First Council of.*

INCOMPREHENSIBILITY. That which puts God as the absolute mystery quite beyond the reach of human understanding. What we know through revelation enables us to realize even more deeply that we do not really know God (see DS 800, 3001). See *Apophatic Theology; Mystery; Negative Theology.*

INCULTURATION. A new term for the old obligation to contextualize and indigenize the Christian message and way of life in the various cultures and peoples of our world. St. Paul and other early missionaries met the challenge of adapting to the masses of non-Jewish believers (see Acts 15:1–29; 17:16–34; Gal 2:1–10). After Christianity struck deep roots in Europe, it became too closely identified with European culture. Vatican II (1962–65) taught that the gospel does not make one culture normative but should be incarnated in every culture for the salvation of all peoples (see LG 13, 17, 23; GS 39, 55, 58; AG 9–11, 21–22). See *Catholicity; Evangelization; Mission, Theology of.*

INDEFECTIBILITY (Lat. "freedom from being liable to failure, decay and death"). The gift Christ gave to his church whereby she will last till the end of the world (see Matt 16:18; 28:18–20; Jn 14:16–17). Through the risen Lord's presence and the guidance of the Spirit, the church taken as a whole cannot fail in her central qualities and witness to revealed truth (see DS 3050–52; LG 12). Infallibility is one aspect of this general guidance by the Holy Spirit. See *Infallibility; Marks (Notes) of the Church.*

INDIFFERENCE. The lack of interest in religious matters which comes from secularism, the absence of a proper religious education or a personal failure to practice one's faith in God (see DS 2915–18). "Indifference" can also mean a detachment from all creatures and experiences which allows the divine will to guide our choices. In this sense indifference characterizes the spirituality of St. Ignatius of Loyola (1491–1556). See *Apatheia; Hesychasm; Secularism.*

INDULGENCES. The remittance of temporal punishment due to sin for which sorrow has already been expressed and forgiveness received. This cancelling of punishment comes from the treasury of Christ's infinite merits and the saints' participation in his passion and glory. In the early church the intercession of those awaiting martyrdom could reduce the severe penance imposed on repentant sinners. In the sixteenth century the scandalous misuse of indulgences helped to trigger the reformation. The right to grant indulgences is in principle reserved to the Holy See. Unlike partial indulgences, plenary indulgences are held to remove the whole debt of punishment, if the full conditions for their reception are met. Both kinds may be applied to the dead in purgatory. In his Apostolic Constitution *Indulgentiarum Doctrina* (1967), Paul VI restricted plenary indulgences and emphasized the need for personal conversion of heart (see DS 1467; CIC 929–97). See *Merit; Penance, Sacrament of; Purgatory; Sin.*

INEFFABILITY (Lat. "being inexpressible or indescribable"). God's being unutterably mysterious and despite the divine names, ultimately unnamable (Exod 3:14; Jn 1:18; 1 Tim 1:17; Rom 11:33–36). While known, God remains indescribable or, at least, can be described only negatively (see DS 800, 3001). In the Synagogue, when the name of God occurs in the reading, it is not pronounced but replaced by *Adonai* (Heb. "Lord"). See *Incomprehensibility; Yahweh.*

INERRANCY. A term which refers primarily to a major consequence of biblical inspiration: the saving truth of the scriptures (DV 11). This truth emerges progressively from the inspired record, is centered on Christ and is to be found in the whole of the Bible. To appreciate the truth conveyed by particular books of the Bible, we need to examine the intentions, presuppositions, context and modes of expression of the authors and the traditions behind them (DV 12). Inerrancy also characterizes the sensitivity to the truth displayed by the whole people of God. Guided by the Spirit, the church cannot err in matters of belief (see 1 Jn 2:20, 27; LG 12). See *Bible; Exegesis; Inspiration; Senses of Scripture; Sensus Fidelium; Truth.*

INFALLIBILITY. That freedom from the possibility of error in matters of revealed faith and morals, which Christ bestowed on the whole church through the Spirit (Jn 16:12–15; LG 12) and in particular on the whole college of bishops in union with Peter's successor, the pope (see Acts 15:1–29; 1 Cor 15:3–11; LG 25). Infallible definitions have come normally from ecumenical councils (see DS 265, 363–64) and rarely from the pope. Vatican I (1869–70) taught that the pope is infallible when, as pastor of all Christians and successor of Peter (see Matt 16:18–19; Lk 22:31–32), he solemnly teaches some revealed truth concerning faith and morals *ex cathedra* (DS 3065–75). In their ordinary magisterium the whole college of bishops in union with the Pope teaches infallibly when they agree about some revealed truth "to be held definitively and absolutely" (LG 25). In interpreting infallible statements one must distinguish the point of the definition from its formulation which will be conditioned by the historical circumstances of the time. See *Collegiality; Council, Ecumenical; Ex Cathedra Definition; Magisterium; Truth; Vatican Council, First.*

INFANCY GOSPELS. Such apocryphal works as the *Book of James* (or *Protoevangelium*) and the *Infancy Gospel of Thomas,* which invent miracles and further material in order to relate, often in a fantastic way, the story of Jesus' birth and childhood. These non-canonical works are to be distinguished from the infancy narratives of the gospels according to Matthew (1:1–2:23) and Luke (1:5–2:52). Although they are not to be harmonized in detail, Matthew and Luke agree that after being virginally conceived through the power of the Holy Spirit, Jesus was born of Mary in Bethlehem. His coming fulfilled the OT preparation and was to bring saving revelation to all the peoples on earth (Matt 2:1–12; Lk 2:30–32). See *Apocrypha; Protoevangelium; Virginal Conception of Jesus.*

INFANT BAPTISM. The baptism of babies born to Christian parents. The NT hints at the practice of infant baptism, when reporting that whole families embraced the faith and were baptized (see Acts 10:1–48; 16:15, 33; 18:8; 1 Cor 1:16). By the third century we find St. Cyprian (d. 258) and Origen (ca. 185–ca. 254) explicitly referring to infant baptism and Tertullian (ca. 160–ca. 225) polemicizing against it. By the early fifth century infant baptism seems to have become a widespread, even universal practice. With the arrival of the Reformation, first Anabaptists and later Baptists and other groups abolished infant baptism as opposed to the conscious and personal choice for Christ which they always require from the one being baptized. However, since all human beings are called to eternal salvation, the church asserts her right and duty to baptize the children of Christians (see DS 2552–62; 3296), provided that at least one of the parents agrees and there is hope that the child will be educated in a Christian manner (see CIC 867–68). The baptism of infants may be postponed if this will prepare the parents to fulfill better their Christian responsibilities. In the eastern church, infant baptism is followed at once by confirmation and the eucharist. The new Catholic rite for adult baptism follows this practice. In the case of infants, however, they receive baptism alone. Communion and confirmation (in this order) are postponed until they reach at least the age of reason. See *Anabaptists; Baptism; Baptists; Pelagianism; Sacraments.*

INFINITY (Lat. "boundlessness"). The quality of being unlimited and endless. Strictly speaking, only God is fully and perfectly infinite, being unlimited by space and time and immeasurably superior to all creatures. In Aristotelian philosophy prime matter, or pure potency "prior" to any determination, is indefinite in the sense of lacking any specification or quality that would make it concrete and limited. See *Aristotelianism; Eternity; Immensity.*

INFUSED KNOWLEDGE. Knowledge freely given through the Holy Spirit for some special task in the church, and also given, according to a long tradition, to Christ and the OT prophets. It is opposed to acquired knowledge, which is the result of normal study and effort. See *Charism.*

INITIATION. Introduction in stages to the mysteries of a religion. When Christianity began, it faced competition from Middle-Eastern religions that were characterized by esoteric doctrines and cults to which the

106

neophytes were gradually introduced. Like these religions Christian initiation practiced a *disciplina arcani*. The creed was fully explained only shortly before the reception of baptism. Detailed instruction in the faith usually followed baptism. See *Baptism; Catechumenate; Disciplina Arcani; RCIA.*

INQUISITION (Lat. "investigation"). A special ecclesiastical tribunal for tracking down, examining and punishing heretics. This procedure spread from the time of Pope Innocent III (1160–1216) and fed on the conviction that as a threat to the social order, heresy had to be suppressed. In 1479, with the approval of Pope Sixtus IV, Ferdinand V and Isabella introduced the Spanish Inquisition against relapsed converts from Judaism and Islam, known respectively as Marranos and Moriscos. Those found guilty by inquisitors were usually handed over to the state for punishment. In 1542 Pope Paul III founded the Holy Office as the final court of appeal in heresy trials. In 1967 Paul VI not only changed its name to the Congregation for the Doctrine of Faith, but also gave it the more positive role of encouraging as well as safeguarding sound doctrine in faith and morals. See *Heresy.*

INSPIRATION, BIBLICAL. The special impulse and guidance of the Holy Spirit through which the books of scripture were composed and so can be called the word of God (see Jn 20:31; 2 Tim 3:16; 2 Pet 1:19–21; 3:15–16; and also Jer 18:18; Neh 8:1). What God had to say is found in what was said by the human writers, who were genuine authors and not mere stenographers copying down what God dictated (see DV 11; DS 3006, 3629). The inspiration of the 72 books of the OT and NT was part of God's action in bringing the church into full existence. Hence the Bible can also be called the Book of the Church. See *Bible; Biblical Criticism; Hermeneutics; Inerrancy; Senses of Scripture.*

INTENTION. The purpose for which one acts. "Purity" of intention comes from acting from completely worthy motives. The valid administration of the sacraments requires from the minister at least the intention to do what the church does (DS 1611). Besides expressing our willed purpose, "intention" (and intentionality) also refer in various ways to human concepts, knowledge and consciousness. See *Epistemology; Ethics; Moral Theology.*

INTERCESSION (Lat. "passing between"). Prayer of petition for others. Primarily intercession refers to the risen Christ's continuing mediation on our behalf in heaven (see 1 Tim 2:5; Heb 7:25; 9:24; DS 1523). His mother, Mary, also intercedes for us (DS 1400; 3274–75; 3370; 3916), as do the angels and saints (DS 3320–21). Intercession forms an integral part of all Christian worship. See *Impetratory Prayer; Liturgy; Mediation; Prayer.*

INTERCOMMUNION. See *Communicatio In Sacris.*

INTERDICT (Lat. "prohibition by decree"). A rarely used ecclesiastical punishment which for a time deprives the offenders of certain spiritual rights and functions but without their being cut off from the church. Generally interdiction suspends the right to celebrate the sacraments (in the case of the clergy) and to receive them (in the case of the laity)—a prohibition which is automatically lifted in danger of death. An interdict may affect an individual person, a place (like a church, a cemetery or a convent), a group of people, a city or even a whole country (see CIC 915, 1109, 1331–32, 1370, 1373). See *Excommunication.*

INTER-FAITH AND INTERRELIGIOUS. See *Dialogue; World Religions.*

INTERPRETATION. See *Hermeneutics.*

INTINCTION (Lat. "dip in"). The dipping of the consecrated bread in the consecrated wine at the distribution of communion. One of the main ways in which communion under both kinds is administered, this is the standard practice in the eastern churches. See *Communion.*

INTROIT (Lat. "entry"). Known also as "the entrance antiphon," the verse which is sung or recited as the priest enters to say mass. Often taken from a psalm, it sets the tone for the day. Its opening words sometimes provide the name for the feast: e.g., "Gaudete" for the third Sunday in Advent and "Laetare" for the fourth Sunday in Lent. See *Chant.*

INTUITION (Lat. "looking at attentively"). An immediate grasp of reality by the mind or the senses. Immediate intellectual apprehension is usually attributed to angels; as pure spirits they do not need to reason by inference. In a lesser sense the power of intuition also belongs to human beings. In theology, Thomism denies that we can enjoy here on earth an immediate insight into ourselves or God without this being mediated by the senses—a possibility accepted by Augustinianism. This latter view runs the risk of claiming a kind of *illuminism* or direct access to God free from the mediation of creatures and of the church herself. Our intuitive vision of God in heaven, however, has been officially taught (see DS 990–91, 1000). See *Augustinianism; Beatific Vision; Thomism.*

INVINCIBLE IGNORANCE. A lack of knowledge which remains even after serious efforts to be appropriately informed and which excuses from any guilt before God. Thus, despite their conscientious concern and through no fault of their own, people may be unable to accept the church and her teachings. They can be prevented from doing so by their upbringing, social prejudices or sheer lack of contact with the message of Christianity (see DS 2865–67; LG 16; GS 16). Invincible ignorance is physical, as in the case of children and the mentally sick; it is moral, in other cases. See *Error; Tolerance.*

IRENECISM (from Gr. "peace"). A peaceful or conciliatory approach to problems of church unity, which may try to water down real differences between Christians or promote understanding at the expense of truth, an attitude which has rightly been condemned (see DS 3880; UR 11). But irenecism may also mean the serenity with which controversial issues are analyzed with a hope to further unity, in which case it is practically indistinguishable from true ecumenism. See *Dialogue; Ecumenism.*

ISLAM (Arab. "submission," namely to God's will). The world religion which recognizes Mohammed (ca. 570–632) as God's last prophet in a line that started with Abraham and continued through Jesus. Mohammed blamed the Jews for refusing to accept Jesus and the Christians for relapsing into polytheism by their teaching on the Trinity. Islam's absolute monotheism denies the possibility of God or *Allah* having a Son. Jesus is revered as a prophet; his death on the cross is denied and held to be only apparent. It is absolutely forbidden to represent God in images. Islamic art in general does not portray even human beings, since they are made in the image of God. Mohammed is believed to have received the revelation that later was written down in the *Koran* (Arab. "recital"), which reflects some OT and NT traditions and is divided in 114 sections or *suras*, all accepted as divinely inspired word by word.

Islam involves five chief obligations: (1) the confession of God's unity and of Mohammed as God's last messenger or prophet; (2) ritual prayer five times a day, Friday being the special day for common noon-prayer at the mosque; (3) almsgiving to support the poor; (4) fasting during the whole month of Ramadan, which entails complete abstention from food, drink or sex from sunrise to sunset; (5) the pilgrimage to Mecca, at least once in a lifetime. Besides the *shariah* (Arab. "path of law"), Islam developed a mystical tradition, *sufism* (Arab. "ascetic woollen garment"), which through self-renunciation seeks unity with God. While professing the same faith, Muslims have divided into various groups, above all the *Sunnites* (the orthodox) and the *Shiites*. The former follow the *sunna* or authoritative traditions which were established by Mohammed and his first four successors or caliphs but not written down in the Koran. The Shiites, found chiefly in Iran, held that Mohammed

109

named only his cousin Ali to be his successor and rejected the other three caliphs. While granting freedom of religion to the "people of the Scripture" (= the Jews and Christians), Islam aims at winning the whole world to its message. Muslims consider themselves to be the heirs of Abraham's faith (see Gen 16:1–16; 21:1–21). The Second Vatican Council stressed Abraham's faith and the expectation of the judgment as elements which Christians have in common with Muslims (see LG 16; NA 3). See *Docetism; Monotheism; Polytheism; Prophet; Religion; Trinity; World Religions.*

ISRAEL (Heb. "God rules"). The Hebrew or Jewish nation, descended from Jacob, who received this new name as "he that struggles with God" (Gen 32:28–29). The twelve tribes of Israel (Gen 49:1–28) split after the death of Solomon (ca. 933 B.C.) into a Southern kingdom (Judah) with Jerusalem as capital and a Northern kingdom with Samaria as capital. The latter was known as Israel because of its closer connections with the Jacob heritage (e.g., Jacob's well at Shechem). After this kingdom fell in 722 B.C., the Southern kingdom was at times called Israel (e.g., Isa 1:3–4; 30:11–12; Ezek 2:3; 6:2–3). The NT applies the term to descendants of Jacob (Matt 10:6; 15:24; Lk 1:16) and the Jewish nation (Mk 12:29; Lk 1:54). The church understands herself as the new or true Israel (Gal 6:16). In the late eighteenth century hopes for emancipation led many Jews to speak of "Israel" rather than of "Judaism." See *Hebrews; Jew; Judaism.*

J

JACOBITES. See *Syrian Orthodox Church.*

JANSENISM. A theological and spiritual movement, characterized by moral rigidity and pessimism about the human condition. It is named after Cornelius Otto Jansen (1585–1638), who in 1636 was consecrated bishop of Ypres, Belgium. With his friend Jean Duvergier de Hauranne, abbot of Saint-Cyran (1581–1643), Jansen wanted to encourage a true reformation of Catholic doctrine and morals. Since Protestantism frequently appealed to St. Augustine of Hippo (354–430), Jansen studied thoroughly his writings, especially those directed against Pelagius. In his posthumous *Augustinus* (1640), among other points Jansen argued that God's grace irresistibly determines our free choices and that without special grace we cannot keep the commandments. Five propositions taken from Jansen's *Augustinus* were officially condemned in 1653 (DS 2001–05), in 1656 (DS 2010–13) and 1690 (DS 2301–32). Despite their stress on the power of God's grace, Jansenists preached and practiced a strict morality and a scrupulous approach to the reception of the sacraments. See *Augustinianism; Determinism; Freedom; Grace; Pelagianism; Reformation.*

JEHOVAH. A hybrid name for God created at the time of the Renaissance. It was formed by fusing two Hebrew words for God, the consonants coming from the sacred name JHVH or YHWH, and vowels from *Adonai* ("Lord"), with the initial "a" being changed for euphonic reasons into an "e." See *Yahweh.*

JEHOVAH'S WITNESSES. A sect which started in the U.S.A. with Charles Taze Russell (1852–1916) and was first called the "International Bible Students Association." He held Christ's second coming to be imminent and propagated his ideas in "The Watch Tower." Hostile toward the mainline churches and subversive of civil authority, his followers often clashed with the law and were defended by Joseph Franklin Rutherford (1869–1941). He became the second head of the sect which came to be called "Jehovah Witnesses." They have become less aggressive in their missionary methods but continue to interpret the Bible and world history in a fanciful way. See *Fundamentalism; Millenarianism; Parousia.*

JERUSALEM (Hebr. "city of peace"). The city of the king and priest Melchisedek who blessed Abraham (Gen 14:18–20). Strategically placed on Mount Zion and adjacent hills, Jerusalem was a stronghold of Jebusite resistance against the invading Israelites. Around 1000 B.C. David conquered the city and made it the capital of Judah (2 Sam 5:6–7). Solomon built there a "magnificent temple" (1 Kgs 6:1–38), and Jerusalem was praised as the city of God (Pss 48; 87). But Solomon possibly did no more than to transform an already existing Jebusite sanctuary into a kind of royal chapel. After its fall in 586 B.C. (2 Kgs 24–25), Jerusalem became the home the exiles yearned for (Ps 137). When they returned, the temple was rebuilt (see Ezra 3:1–13; 4:24–6:22). After the Romans captured the city in 64 B.C., Herod the Great (who ruled 37–4 B.C.) built a more majestic temple. From childhood Jesus visited Jerusalem and its temple (Lk 2:22–38, 41–50). He wept over the city (Lk 19:41–44) where he died by crucifixion. The Romans destroyed Jerusalem in A.D. 70. At the time of the Bar-Cochba revolt (A.D. 132–35) they rebuilt the city, naming it Aelia Capitolina and under pain of death forbidding Jews to return there. The mother church and most special place of pilgrimage for all Christians, Jerusalem was recognized as a patriarchate with the Council of Chalcedon (451). In Jerusalem the church of the Holy Sepulcre, which covers both the tomb of Christ and the site of Calvary, expresses the present divisions between Christians, as it has six separate groups of

Christian occupants: Latin Catholics, Greek Orthodox, Armenians, Syrians, Copts and Ethiopians. There are at present three patriarchs in Jerusalem: the Greek Orthodox, the Armenian Apostolic (= Oriental Orthodox) and the Latin. The "new" and "holy" city of Jerusalem will be the final home of all the blessed (Gal 4:25–26; Rev 3:12; 21:2, 10). See *Chalcedon, Council of; Eastern Churches; Pentarchy; Temple, The.*

JESUS CHRIST (Heb. "God saves" and Gr. "the anointed one"). Born ca. 7/6 B.C. and crucified ca. A.D. 30, Founder of Christianity, and confessed as one divine person (the Son of God) in two natures (being truly and fully both divine and human). A basic history of Jesus would include at least the following items. He was a Galilean Jew of the house of David, the son of a woman called Mary who was married to Joseph, a carpenter. After being baptized by John, Jesus proclaimed the kingdom of God, associated in a special way with public sinners and other outcasts, called disciples to follow him, chose a core group of twelve, worked miracles and taught some memorable parables. His challenge to given forms of piety (Matt 6:1–18), his desire to correct certain traditions (Mk 7:1–23), his violation of some sabbath observances (Mk 2:23–27), his attitude toward the temple in Jerusalem (Mk 14:58; 15:29), his claim to divine authority in changing the law (Mk 10:2–12; Matt 5:21–48) and forgiving sins (Mk 2:17; Lk 7:48) and his attitude of extraordinary familiarity with God aroused the antagonism of some Jewish leaders and teachers. In Jerusalem (where he instituted a new covenant with God in the context of the Passover celebration) he was betrayed, arrested, interrogated by members of the Sanhedrin, condemned by Pontius Pilate, executed on a cross (which bore an inscription giving the charge against Jesus as a messianic pretender), and buried later the same day.

Shortly thereafter he appeared gloriously alive to a number of individuals and groups. Mary Magdalene (Jn 20:1–2), probably accompanied by other women (Mk 16:1–8), found his tomb to be open and empty. Empowered by his Spirit, a community of disciples gathered around Peter and the twelve to acknowledge and proclaim the risen and exalted Jesus as Christ (or messiah), savior, divine Lord and Son of God. See *Abba; Chalcedon, Council of; Christology; Communicatio Idiomatum; Enhypostasis; Hypostatic Union; Kyrios; Logos; Messiah; Passover; Soteriology; Trinity.*

JESUS PRAYER. A popular eastern prayer which consists in the repetition of the name of Jesus within a short formula, "Lord Jesus Christ, Son of God, have mercy on me." There are several variants, including the Russian addition of "sinner" at the end. The Jesus prayer, which echoes appeals (Mk 10:47–48; Lk 23:42) and acclamations (1 Cor 12:30) already found in the NT, came from a monastic spirituality with its desire to pray

112

always (see Lk 18:1; Eph 6:18; 1 Thess 5:17). Since the thirteenth century, it has often been accompanied by a breathing technique. See *Hesychasm; Philocalia.*

JEW, JEWISH. Those of Hebrew descent and/or whose religion is Judaism. According to a law passed in 1962 by the State of Israel, a Jew is someone who is born of a Jewish mother or is a convert to Judaism. See *Hebrews; Judaism.*

JOHANNINE THEOLOGY. The theology drawn from the fourth gospel and 1 John and, to a lesser degree, from 2 and 3 John and Revelation. John's gospel uses symbols (e.g., bread, water and shepherd), contrasting images (e.g., truth/lies and love/hatred) and, in general, a prayerful, experiential and Trinitarian language to encourage faith in Jesus as the Christ and Son of God (John 20:31). This Gospel is rich in the language of revelation (e.g., glory, signs, truth and witness), without, however, neglecting what Christ, the true vine to whom we are to be joined (Jn 15:1–8), does in sharing life (*passim*) and empowering believers to become children of God (Jn 1:12–13). The prologue to the gospel (Jn 1:1–18) announces a struggle between light and darkness. An initial favorable reaction to Jesus who comes as the divine "light of the world" (Jn 8:12; 9:5; 12:46) leads to a division between (a) those who remain spiritually blind, hate the light (Jn 1:5; 3:19; 9:39–41) and go into the night (Jn 13:30), and (b) those who are healed and see the truth (Jn 1:39; 9:1–38; 20:29). After Jesus' final words to his closest followers, the promise of the Holy Spirit and high-priestly prayer (Jn 13:1–17:26), the powers of darkness seem to prevail during the passion but give way to the dazzling victory of the resurrection. To offset docetic misunderstandings of the truth that the Logos did become flesh (Jn 1:14), 1 Jn insists again on the reality of the incarnation (1 Jn 4:2–3) which revealed God as love (1 Jn 4:7–12). The eastern church reveres St. John as *the* theologian. Patmos, the place where he is supposed to have written the book of Revelation, is a place of pilgrimage. See *Docetism; Doxa; Revelation; Three Theologians, The.*

JOSEPHINISM. An attempt of the state to become sovereign in church matters, inspired by the Enlightenment and adopted by Joseph II of Austria (Holy Roman Emperor 1765–90) who, for his interference in ecclesiastical matters, was nicknamed "the Emperor Sacristan." By his Edict of Toleration in 1781, contemplative religious orders were suppressed, pilgrimages were curtailed, and jurisdiction over church benefices and property were transferred from the Pope to the state. Although Joseph II repealed part of the legislation on his deathbed, Josephinism was officially abolished only in 1850. See *Church and State; Enlightenment; Febronianism; Gallicanism.*

JUDAISM. Religion of the Jews, a people descended from Abraham, delivered from Egypt and uniquely chosen by God (Rom 9–11) who became strictly and clearly monotheistic at the time of the Babylonian exile (587–538 B.C.). After surviving centuries of foreign domination and the destruction of Jerusalem in A.D. 70, they lost their land with the revolt of Bar Cochba (132–35) and regained it only in 1948 with the foundation of the State of Israel. The religious and cultural identity of Judaism has been maintained through the Jewish Bible, the sabbath, circumcision and faithful observance of the Mosaic law and traditional teaching. The Second Vatican Council stressed the common religious history which binds Jews and Christians together and which is recorded in the OT (see NA 4; LG 9). See *Diaspora; Haggadah; Halachah; Hebrews; Holocaust; Monotheism; Old Testament; Sabbath; Shema; Synagogue.*

JURISDICTION (Lat. "judgment concerning what is lawful"). The legal authority to judge what is right and wrong and to act accordingly. In canon law jurisdiction means the right and duty to govern within the church, an authority understood as being properly pastoral and to be exercised with loving humility (Jn 21:15–17; 1 Pet 5:1–4). Although ordained, clerics generally need to receive jurisdiction before exercising their ministry: e.g., before hearing confessions (see CIC 966). Parish priests have ordinary delegated authority from their bishop and may delegate the right to baptize and officiate at marriages to other priests and deacons. Only those in holy orders may receive real jurisdiction (CIC 274, 129). See *Clergy; Holy Orders.*

JUST WAR. A war which might be considered morally right. Although building on ideas coming from Cicero (106–43 B.C.), St. Augustine of Hippo (354–430) came to be considered the author of the just war theory. He understood war to be a lesser evil when compared with the raw cruelty of some barbarian hordes for whom might could be right. By the twentieth century the conditions justifying a war were established as follows: (a) the war must be defensive and a response to unjust aggression; (b) there must be a realistic chance of success to justify all the wartime sacrifices; (c) there must be some proportion between the moral and physical costs of the hostilities and the peace and better social order sought after; (d) only military targets, not unarmed civilians, can be the targets of military strikes; (e) force may never be used as a means in itself or to brutalize the social order and the military personnel. Since some of these conditions can hardly be met in a nuclear war, that kind of war is ruled out by most moralists, but the problem of nuclear deterrence is still debated (GS 79–82). See *Peace*.

JUSTICE. The fairness and uprightness characteristic of a good judge. In the OT God's justice is often synonymous with the divine fidelity and steadfast love (Mic 7:8–20), and is closely linked with mercy (Sir 35:11–24). The messianic king will show justice and wisdom (Isa 11:3–5; Acts 7:52). God's justice is revealed in the salvation bestowed on those who believe in Jesus Christ (Rom 3:21–26) and who dedicate themselves to a blameless life (Matt 5:6). The Christian tradition calls justice, along with prudence, temperance and fortitude, one of the four *cardinal* (Lat. "hinge") *virtues*, because right human conduct revolves on them. Pope John Paul II in his encyclical *Sollicitudo Rei Socialis* (1987) highlighted the collective evil and structures of sin that hinder the realization of social justice, both nationally and internationally. See *Liberation Theology; Option for the Poor; Social Teaching; Virtues, Cardinal*.

JUSTIFICATION. The saving gift of righteousness which makes human beings acceptable to God. Righteousness comes through faith in Christ (Rom 1:17; 9:30–31) and not through the works of the law (Rom 3:28; Gal 2:16). Lutherans have stressed the justifying verdict passed by God on those who have sinned (Rom 3:9–12, 23), whereas Catholics (and Orthodox) have highlighted the grace received which actually transforms sinners through the Holy Spirit (Rom 5:5; 6:4; 2 Cor 5:17; DS 1580–81). Although often seen as mutually exclusive, the two approaches can be interpreted as complementing rather than contradicting each other. See *Deification; Faith and Works; Good Works; Grace; Imputation; Lutheranism; Sanctification*.

JUSTINIAN CODE. See *Canon Law, Sources of Oriental; Nomocanon*.

K

KAIROS (Gr. "right time"). A word used not only like *chronos* (Gr. "time") to indicate the historical sequence of events (2 Tim 4:3), but also to point to God's special interventions at turning points in the history of salvation (Mk 1:15). In particular, *kairos* (in the singular and plural) denotes God's final dealings with human beings through Christ in the fullness of time (Eph 1:10; 1 Thess 5:1–2; Rev 1:3; 22:10). See *Eschatology; Parousia; Salvation History; Time*.

KARDIOGNOSIS OR **CARDIOGNOSIS** (Gr. "knowledge of the heart"). A word from eastern Christianity for the insights of and into the human heart in its yearning for God, who sees the heart and does not judge on outward appearances (see 1 Sam 16:7; Jer 20:12). Jesus himself knew the secrets of the human heart (Mk 2:6–8; Jn 2:25). Insight into the "hidden person of the heart" (1 Pet 3:4) is what one expects from a spiritual director, known in Russian as *staretz* and in Greek as *geron*. See *Discernment of Spirits; Heart*.

KENOSIS (Gr. "emptying"). The self-abasement that the second person of the Trinity underwent in the incarnation (Phil 2:5–11; see 2 Cor 8:9). This did not (and could not) mean abandoning the divine nature or substance. Rather it entailed accepting the limitations of a human existence that in fact ended with the utter humiliation of death by crucifixion. See *Cross; Glory; Incarnation; Pre-existence; Suffering of God*.

KERYGMA (Gr. "the act of proclaiming" or "the message proclaimed"). The core message which announces God's decisive act and offer of salvation in the death and resurrection of Jesus (Rom 16:25; 1 Cor 1:21; 15:3–5), and which precedes detailed instruction about Christ and Christianity. In the Septuagint *kerygma* can be an official announcement by a priest (see Exod 32:5) or the inspired word of a prophet (see Isa 61:1). The gospels are eminently kerygmatic, because they set out to announce the good news (e.g., Mk 1:1, 14). See *Homily; Preaching; Septuagint*.

KERYGMATIC THEOLOGY. A theology oriented toward proclaiming the decisive events of salvation history. In the 1930's at the theology faculty in Innsbruck Franz Lakner developed a kerygmatic theology centered on Christ as he is to be preached. This experiment did not fully succeed. Nevertheless, through the work of Hugo Rahner, Joseph Jungmann and others, a more kerygmatic approach to theology has widely replaced the abstract speculations of scholasticism. See *Scholasticism; Schools of Theology; Theology*.

KIDDISH (Heb. "holy"). A Jewish doxology used for daily prayer in the synagogue. It glorifies God's name for its grandeur and holiness, and echoes Ezek 38:23: "And so I shall be magnified and sanctified and be known among the multitude of pagan nations and they, for their part, will soon realize that I am the Lord." See *Doxa; Doxology; Synagogue*.

KIDDUSH. The name given to the very old way Jews observe the Sabbath and other feasts of obligation. At supper on the eve of the feast (e.g., for the sabbath, on Friday evening), the head of the family offers a cup of wine to all present and pronounces a blessing.

KINGDOM OF GOD. Jesus' central message about the climactic reign of God (Mk 1:15), that divine act of salvation which is coming not as a reward for human merits but as sheer gift from God's kindness. Jesus invited his hearers to "enter" this kingdom or receive it as a child does a gift. Jesus gave himself totally in the service of the present (Matt 12:28; Lk 11:20; 17:21) and future (Matt 8:11) divine rule. This final saving intervention of God was already operative through Jesus' preaching, teaching and miracles (Matt 4:23; 9:35). His parables, in particular, indicated how the kingdom of God was an eschatological reality that began to take shape in the present. For Jesus to proclaim that "the reign of God is near" was to say "God and divine salvation are near." While the NT did not identify God's kingdom with the church, from the time of St. Augustine of Hippo (354–430) this has often been done. See *Church; Eschatology; Heaven; Parousia; Salvation.*

KOINONIA (Gr. "communion," "fellowship"). A term used in the NT for sharing in Christ's sufferings (Phil 3:10), subsidizing those in need (Rom 15:26), participation in the eucharist (1 Cor 10:16), the fellowship with (or brought about by) the Holy Spirit (2 Cor 13:13) and (as an adjective) of believers sharing in the very life of God (2 Pet 1:3–4). Nowadays *koinonia* often expresses the union which exists and should exist between churches, linked by the love of Jesus Christ present through his Spirit. See *Conciliarity; Deification; Sobornost.*

KONDAKION (from Gr. "short"). One of the oldest and most important forms of liturgical hymns in the eastern church, going back to the fifth or sixth century and probably so named because of the short wooden stick around which the text was wrapped. The name, however, may have come from the fact that the composition succintly sets the tone for the liturgical celebration that follows. A *kondakion* may contain from 18 to 30 (or more) strophes. The composition has a title, followed by a poignant "proiomion" or introduction that summarizes the spirit of the feast and climaxes in the "ephymnion" or refrain. Then follows a series of "oikoi" (houses) or stanzas, the first of which is called "hirmos," each ending with the refrain. The *oikoi* are often linked acrostically, each strophe beginning with a different letter of the alphabet. St. Romanos the Melodian, who was born in Homs near Edessa toward the end of the fifth century and served as deacon in Constantinople, is the most famous composer of *kondakia.* The best-known *kondakion* is the hymn *Akathistos.* See *Akathistos; Chant.*

KYRIE ELEISON (Gr. "Lord have mercy"). The triple prayer for mercy, originally addressed to Christ the Lord (though subsequently interpreted as addressed to the three persons of the Trinity), intoned by the celebrant (or the choir) and repeated by the congregation. In the Latin mass, it comes after the introit and the penitential rite (if not incorporated in the latter) and before the Gloria and the Collect. In eastern liturgies, it is the commonest response in the litanies. The *Kyrie* is found in the Antioch-Jerusalem liturgy at least as early as 350. See *Collect; Gloria; Jesus Prayer.*

KYRIOS (Gr. "Lord," "Sir"). (a). One who has sovereign rights and full control over someone or something, and (b) a polite form of address. In the OT God is called "Lord" and (especially in the prophetic books) "Lord of hosts." When Jesus receives the title of "Lord" (Mk 12:36; Lk 19:31; Jn 20:18; 1 Cor 12:3; Phil 2:11; 2 Pet 2:20; Rev 22:20–21), he is clearly acknowledged as more than merely human. Whether this christological title has an OT and Jewish origin or a Hellenistic-pagan origin (where the emperor, considered to be divine, was so addressed) is still a matter of debate. See *Christology; Jehovah.*

L

LAICIZATION. The legal process whereby a cleric is dispensed from his obligations and returns to the lay state. This change of status is relative because sacred orders, once validly received, can never be cancelled. The process of laicization is reserved to the Holy See, whose sentence does not allow for any appeal. Laicization can be granted to deacons for grave reasons and to priests only on very serious grounds (CIC 290–93). Except when the cleric's ordination is proved to have been invalid, laicization merely as such does not dispense from celibacy. A laicized cleric may not exercize his ministry except when somebody is in danger of death (see CIC 976). See *Annulment; Cleric; Clergy; Laity; Validity.*

LAITY (Gr. "people"). The faithful who have been fully incorporated into the church through baptism, confirmation and communion (1 Pet 2:9–10), but who have not received holy orders and become clerics. To designate Israel as God's chosen people, the Hebrew OT uses "'am," a word translated in the Septuagint by "laos" (see Exod 19:3–7; Deut 7:6; 14:2). The same Hebrew and Greek words can also refer to the people as contrasted with their leaders: priests, prophets or princes (see Isa 24:2; Jer 26:11). The NT recognizes different offices, ministries and gifts of the Spirit as given to be exercised in harmonious collaboration for the good of the whole church (see 1 Cor 12:4–31; Rom 12:3–8). A later sharp distinction between clergy and laity sometimes involved an emphasis on the former as if they alone were the real church (see DS 3050–75). This one-sidedness was counterbalanced by the Second Vatican Council, which not only insisted that "the church" consists of the entire people of God and not just the hierarchy (see LG 9), but also reminded the laity of their common call to holiness and wide responsibility in the life of the church and the world (LG 30–38; 39–42; AG 41; also: CIC 224–231). See *Basic Communities; Clergy; Cleric; Hierarchy; Holy Orders; Ministry; Office; Priest.*

LAMBETH CONFERENCES. The assemblies of Anglican bishops which began in 1867 and are now held about every ten years generally at the London residence of the Archbishop of Canterbury. The resolutions of these conferences as such are not binding but have enjoyed a worldwide influence, particularly within the Anglican community. See *Anglican Communion.*

LAST JUDGMENT. The belief that Christ will come again at the end of time to judge the living and the dead (see DS 10, 13–14, 76, 150). The OT prophets announce the coming of "day of the Lord," when God's will will be manifested, the nations judged and an abundance of blessings granted (Isa 2:6–22; Jer 17:16–18; Joel 2:28–3:21; Amos 5:18–20). Often developing OT images of judgment, the synoptic gospels speak of the wheat and chaff being separated at the end (Lk 3:17), the weeds being burned when the wheat is harvested (Matt 13:24–30, 36–43), the sorting out of the good and bad fish (Matt 13:47–50). While retaining a future judgment (Jn 5:28–29), John's gospel also points to the present occurrence of judgment when people here and now believe or refuse to believe in Christ (Jn 3:18–19). The Council of Florence taught that, besides a general judgment at the end of time, there is also a particular judgment for the individual immediately after death (see DS 1304–06). Nevertheless, given the social nature of human beings and their redemption, the collective general judgment at the end remains paramount. See *Advent; Eschata; Johannine Theology; Parousia.*

LATAE SENTENTIAE (Lat. "by imposed sentence"). An ecclesiastical penalty automatically incurred by somebody who commits a particular offence (see CIC 1314, 1318). The 1983 code reduced the number of such penalties. Examples that remain are the excommunications automatically incurred for desecrating the Blessed Sacrament (CIC 1367) or bringing about an abortion (CIC 1398). See *Ferendae Sententiae.*

LATERAN COUNCIL(S). A series of synods and councils held in the Lateran palace, which adjoins St. John Lateran, the cathedral of the Bishop of Rome. In the first millennium all the ecumenical councils met in the east, yet some synods at the Lateran enjoyed a certain importance. The first was convoked by Constantine the Great against the Donatists and held in 313 under Pope Miltiades. To combat Monotheletism, another famous synod met in 649 under Pope St. Martin I, who was supported by a great eastern theologian, St. Maximus the Confessor. Five councils held at the Lateran in the middle ages came to be considered ecumenical by the Latin church. See *Council, Ecumenical; Donatists; Monotheletism; Synod.*

LATERAN COUNCIL, FIRST (1123). Convoked by Pope Callistus II to ratify the Concordat of Worms, which settled the long-standing *investiture* conflict between church and state. The question at issue was the right of emperors and princes to deliver to bishops the insignia of office and receive from them a pledge of loyalty. The council ruled against investiture by lay authorities, and through twenty canons tried to reform the clergy (see DS 710–12). It is considered the ninth ecumenical council by the Catholic Church.

LATERAN COUNCIL, SECOND (1139). Called by Pope Innocent II, whose election had provoked a schism, to condemn the anti-Pope Anacletus II (d. 1138) and his followers. This council also promulgated canons against usury and simony (see DS 715–16), and condemned those who tamper with the sacraments or reject them outright (see DS 717–18). There was some representation from the east. By Catholics it is considered the tenth ecumenical council.

LATERAN COUNCIL, THIRD (1179). A council summoned by Pope Alexander II to secure freedom in the church after Emperor Frederick I (Barbarossa) had supported three anti-popes. Its most significant decree required from the cardinals a two-thirds majority for the election of the pope. This council also issued decrees on the bond of marriage and the form of baptism (see DS 751–58). Catholics count it as the eleventh ecumenical council.

LATERAN COUNCIL, FOURTH (1215). The most important medieval council in the west, called by Pope Innocent III at the height of the temporal power of the church. Its legislation aimed to secure a universal Christian society, a dream fed by the recent foundation of a Latin empire and patriarchate in Constantinople (1204–63). Presupposing that the schism between east and west had ended, Lateran IV ranked the patriarchates as follows: Constantinople, Alexandria, Antioch and Jerusalem. Adopting measures against the Albigensians, Cathars and the Waldensians, the council also condemned some of the views of Joachim of Fiore (d. 1202). Preachers were required to have a special license or *missio canonica* from their bishop. The word "transubstantiation" was used to describe the change effected by the consecration during the eucharist. The council prohibited new religious orders, forcing the Dominicans to adopt an existing rule. Yearly confessions were required from those who had fallen into mortal sin (see DS 800–20). Catholics consider Lateran IV to be the twelfth ecumenical council. See *Albigensians; Crusades; Inquisition; Jurisdiction; Transubstantiation; Waldensianism.*

LATERAN COUNCIL, FIFTH (1512–17). Convened by Pope Julius II (1443–1513) to combat resurgent forms of conciliarism and some views which seemed to deny the individuality and immortality of the soul. After Julius' death Leo X (1475–1521) took over. Some very useful reforms were agreed upon but little was done to implement them. The church was thus caught unprepared for the real challenge that emerged in the year it closed: the 95 theses published by Martin Luther in 1517 (see DS 1440–49). Catholics consider Lateran V the eighteenth ecumenical council. See *Conciliarism; Lutheranism; Reformation.*

LATRIA (Gr. "adoration," "worship"). See *Hyperdoulia; Worship.*

LAUDS (Lat. "praise"). The ancient and official morning prayer of the western church, called "laudes matutinae" or "dawn praises." "Matins" referred to the early morning prayer in monasteries, whereas the cathedral services were called "lauds." The two have coalesced into the morning prayer which, in the reform after the Second Vatican Council, has the following structure: an invitatory prayer, a hymn, three psalms (one of which may be a canticle), a reading from scripture, a short responsory, the *Benedictus*, the intercessions, the Our Father, the collect for the day and a final blessing. In the Byzantine rite the *Orthros* (Gr. "dawn") or morning prayer is longer. See *Collect; Liturgy of the Hours.*

LAW. A recurrent pattern in the way human beings and other creatures operate (as seen, e.g., in the laws of history and physical laws). In a normative sense law recognizes and regulates the rights and duties of citizens or believers, so as to make possible and enhance the common good in human society and the church. "The law" could designate the Jewish religion (Acts 23:29), just as "the holy commandment" was a way of referring to Christianity (2 Pet 2:21). The law of love (Matt 22:36, 38) was taken from the OT but given new force by being personified in Christ (Jn 13:34; 15:12–13). See *Antinomianism; Autonomy; Canon Law; Decalogue; Heteronomy; Law and Gospel; Natural Law; Torah.*

LAW AND GOSPEL. The contrast stressed by Martin Luther (1483–1546) between (a) fruitless attempts to be redeemed through one's own religious achievements and (b) the justification that comes by faith alone, the gospel which is "the saving power of God for all who believe" (Rom 1:16). In this scheme law, even the God-given law of Moses, increases our consciousness of a radical bondage to sin. The word of God announces that we are set free through the merits of Christ being graciously imputed to us and that we thus participate by faith in Christ's justice. Although intended as a principle for interpreting the whole of scripture and life itself, at times the notion of "Law and Gospel" has led to an exaggerated contrast between the OT and the NT. See *Faith and Works; Imputation; Justification; Law; Lutheranism; Reformation; Torah; Trent, Council of.*

LAWS OF THE CHURCH. Particular commandments binding on all members of the Catholic Church. They include attending mass on Sundays and feasts of obligation (CIC 1246), confessing mortal sins and receiving holy communion at least once a year (CIC 920, 989), keeping the laws of fast and abstinence, and contributing to the work of the church and the welfare of the poor (CIC 222). See *Canon Law; Marriage.*

LAXISM (Lat. "slackness"). A seventeenth-century development in moral theology which excused Christians from their obligations on slight and insufficient grounds. In his *Lettres Provinciales* (1657) Blaise Pascal attacked Jesuit casuistry, wrongly interpreting it as a form of laxism. Laxism was condemned by Alexander VII in 1665 (DS 2021–65) and by Innocent XI in 1679 (DS 2101–65). See *Casuistry; Probabilism.*

LECTERN (from Lat. "read"). A stand or raised platform from which to read or sing. For a long time the lectern had practically disappeared as an official piece of liturgical furniture—the available space being monopolized by the altar, the pulpit and, in the case of the cathedral, the bishop's throne. The Second Vatican Council helped to bring back the lectern, by teaching that it is Christ who speaks when scriptures are read in church (SC 7).

LECTIONARY. A liturgical book containing the official readings for the various feasts and seasons of the year. See *Calendar, Liturgical; Feast.*

LECTOR (Lat. "reader"). Somebody who reads the scriptures during church services. The eastern churches have retained this ancient office as one of the minor orders. A 1972 reform in the Catholic Church preserved as two ministries the office of acolyte and that of lector. During the mass, laypersons may read the scriptures, except for the gospel, which is reserved for clerics. See *Cleric; Holy Orders; Liturgy.*

LENT. The forty days before Easter which through prayer, fasting, almsgiving and conversion prepare Christians for the greatest feast of the year. Obviously imitating the forty-day fasts of Moses (Exod 24:18), Elijah (1 Kgs 19:8) and above all Jesus himself (Mk 1:13), the present length of Lent was established in the seventh century, when in Rome the fast began on Ash Wednesday instead of after the first Sunday of Lent. In the Ambrosian rite of Milan these extra days have never been added. The same holds true of the east, where the Lenten period extends over seven weeks, but as no fast is observed on Saturday or Sunday, the total number of fasting days is thirty-six. Originally the Lenten fast was very strict and allowed for only one meal toward evening, with meat, fish and generally also dairy products being forbidden. Eastern Christians have maintained something of this severe discipline. Lent is the special season for catechumens to be prepared for baptism. It is forbidden to celebrate marriage during this time. In Rome, special masses are celebrated each day in a particular church or "station." In the Byzantine tradition the first Sunday of Lent is the Feast of Orthodoxy, marking the victory over iconoclasts and other heretics; the second Sunday is the feast of St. Gregory Palamas (1296–1359), on the third the cross is venerated, and on the Friday of the fifth week the *Akathistos* is sung. See *Abstinence; Akathistos; Catechumenate; Fasting; Holy Week; Palamism.*

LESSON (Lat. "read"). The passages chosen (primarily from the Bible) for reading during liturgical services—a practice that goes back to the synagogue readings from the law and the prophets. At the eucharist, the OT reading precedes the epistle and the gospel. For the divine office or liturgy of the hours, the lessons are taken not only from the Bible but also from the fathers, saints and other spiritual authors. See *Epistle; Gospel.*

LEX ORANDI—LEX CREDENDI (Lat. "the law of prayer is the law of belief"). An axiom whose fuller form is: "legem credendi lex statuat supplicandi" ("let the law of prayer establish the law of belief"), and which goes back to St. Prosper of Aquitaine (ca. 390–ca. 463). A secretary to Pope Celestine I, he composed the *Indiculus*, a dossier on grace drawn from St. Augustine of Hippo (354–430) (DS 246). From the need to pray for everybody (1 Tim 2:1–4) Prosper concluded to the universal need for grace. Prayer, especially liturgical prayer, plays an essential role in the interpretation of Christian faith, as eastern theology has always recognized. Western theology has often paid mere lip-service to this principle, and at times not even that. In his classic work on theological sources and arguments Melchior Cano (1509–60) did not list liturgy as a *locus theologicus* (Lat. "theological place"), and many have followed him in that omission. See *Development of Doctrine; Liturgy; Theology, Methods in.*

LIBERAL PROTESTANTISM. A movement in nineteenth- and twentieth-century Protestant theology, heavily influenced by the philosophy of the Enlightenment, often opposed to church dogmas, and intent on developing a scientific approach to the Bible. Generally considered the founder of this movement, Friedrich Schleiermacher (1768–1834) took religious experience and inner awareness of God to be normative in matters of faith. Various successors aimed to strip away from the scriptures legendary and mythical accretions, so as to lay bare the original history. A strong ethical concern (that downplayed eschatology) highlighted the religion of the historical Jesus expressed through the sermon of the mount and summarized as human solidarity under God. Some, like Ernst Troeltsch (1865–1923), underplayed the uniqueness of Christian revelation and understood Christianity as little more than a striking phenomenon in the history of religion. Faith in modern science, philosophy and progress encouraged theologians to ally themselves deeply with European bourgeois culture and its political leaders, a stance strikingly exemplified by Adolf von Harnack (1851–1930). World War I and the emergence of dialectical theology checked for a time Liberal Protestantism. It has enjoyed a certain revival since the 1960's. See *Dialectical Theology; Enlightenment; Eschatology; Historical Jesus; Modernism; Protestant.*

LIBERALISM. A broad tendency in politics and religion which followed the Enlightenment in supporting freedom and progress and in welcoming new ideas from the science and culture of the day. At its best liberalism has promoted open-minded education and social justice. At its worst it has become a form of secular humanism that rejects religious authority, judges Christianity by the spirit of the age, and is incompatible with orthodox belief. See *Enlightenment; Humanism; Liberal Protestantism; Modernism.*

LIBERATION THEOLOGY. A largely Latin-American movement which (a) is inspired by the exodus, prophetic calls for justice and Jesus' proclamation of the kingdom, (b) reads the Bible in the key of integral liberation, and (c) has struck deep roots where structures of injustice and economic dependence oppress great masses of poor people. Its better exponents include Juan Luis Segundo (b. 1925), Jon Sobrino (b. 1938) and, above all, Gustavo Gutierrez (b. 1928), whose book *A Theology of Liberation* (original edition 1972) launched the movement. Deeply concerned with the public function of theology in encouraging social change, the leaders of this movement have always been developing a spirituality of liberation. In his 1987 encyclical *Sollicitudo Rei Socialis* Pope John Paul II called for a worldwide process of "development and liberation" which expresses itself in a "love and service" of our neighbors, "especially the poorest" (nr 46). See *Black Theology; Feminist Theology; Option for the Poor; Political Theology; Theology, Methods in.*

LIBERTY, RELIGIOUS. The right of every human person and group to practice their religion without interference from other groups. After centuries of persecution, the church gained her freedom with the so-called Edict of Milan in 313, enjoying toleration and support from Constantine the Great (d. 337), who is revered as a saint by the Orthodox. At a time when Christianity dominated European life, St. Thomas Aquinas (ca. 1225–74) maintained that, as their defection threatened the social fabric, lapsed Catholics should be regained even by force, but held that such interference with non-Christians sinned against natural justice. Centuries of religious wars, persecution and discrimination in the name of established religions have illustrated repeatedly the evil of such intolerance. Provided the adherents of a particular religion do not infringe on the right of others, their freedom should be respected and protected. The Second Vatican Council emphasized the right to freedom in religious practice, in particular for minority groups (see DH 2–8, 15; NA 4–5). The world remembers with gratitude such modern defenders of religious freedom as Roger Williams (ca. 1604–84), Thomas Jefferson (1743–1826), Mohandas Gandhi (1869–1948) and John Courtney Murray (1904–67). See *Church and State; Freedom; Rights, Human; Tolerance.*

LIFE AFTER DEATH. The conscious, personal existence of human beings that through God's power continues after they die biologically. While teaching that the definitive fate of all men and women is either heaven or hell, official Christian faith cannot specify in detail what life after death will be like. Reports from those revived after being thought to be dead cannot provide reliable information about life after death. Such persons were close to death, but did not return to life *after* being truly dead and genuinely experiencing the life to come. See *Beatific Vision; Eternity; Heaven; Hell; Last Judgment; Limbo; Purgatory; Resurrection; Soul.*

LIGHT OF GLORY. The light needed by those in heaven to see God in the beatific vision. Psalm 36:10 says that in God's light we see light, and Revelation speaks of the divine light replacing normal light in the new Jerusalem (Rev 21:23; 22:5). Against errors attributed to the Beghards and the Beghins, official teaching defined that without the special light of glory the human intellect cannot see God (see DS 895). The west has tended to interpret this light as a created, supernatural habit which transforms our intellect. The east has identified the light with God, while allowing for a distinction between the inaccessible divine essence and the transforming energy of God. See *Beatific Vision; Essence and Energies; Habit; Hesychasm; Palamism.*

LIMBO (Lat. "hem of garment"). The supposed abode for unbaptized infants who die in original sin but with no personal guilt (*limbus puerorum* or children's limbo). The souls of righteous persons who died before Christ were held to have waited for his coming in the *limbus patrum* or limbo of the fathers. Theologians have normally believed that limbo involves no punishment but a natural happiness which, however, falls short of the full blessedness of the beatific vision. See *Beatific Vision; Descent into Hell; Life after Death; Original Sin.*

LITANY (Gr. "petition," "religious procession"). Prayer in dialogue during which a priest, deacon or cantor recites a series of petitions or, in the west, titles of Jesus or names of saints, and the congregation repeats a fixed response. Rooted in the repeated acclamations found in some psalms (e.g., Pss 118; 136), Christian litanies, at first associated with processions, seem to have originated in late fourth-century Antioch. The Byzantine church frequently uses such litanies as the *ektenai* and the *synapté*. The most frequent response is "*Kyrie eleison*" (Gr. "Lord, have mercy"). In the west litanies have a significant place in the Easter vigil, at the canonization of saints and during the ordination of bishops, priests and deacons. The litany to Our Lady, which has a special link with the shrine of Loreto in Italy, may have been modelled on the *Akathistos*. See *Akathistos; Kyrie Eleison.*

LITURGICAL MOVEMENT. A modern movement which started among Catholics but soon spread to other denominations, and which encourages all members of the church to participate actively in official worship and let the eucharist become the real center of their community life. The movement was initiated by Abbot Prosper Guéranger (1805–75) and the Benedictine Abbey of Solesmes. Official encouragement came in 1903 when Pius X legislated measures encouraging frequent communion and effecting the reform of church music. Across Europe, Benedictines like Lambert Beauduin (1873–1960) and Odo Casel (1896–1948) with others like Pius Parsch (1884–1954), Romano Guardini (1885–1968) and Joseph Jungmann (1889–1975) promoted not only scholarly studies of the liturgy but also its pastoral development. Pius XII's 1947 encyclical *Mediator Dei* brought some reforms, which culminated in the restoration of the Holy Week ceremonies and the work of the Second Vatican Council which introduced the full use of the vernacular and reformed the rites. For the Orthodox, liturgy has always remained central. Such minor reforms as the adoption of the Gregorian calendar have at times led to protests and even schisms. Protestantism was born as a reform movement which included a change to the vernacular and a stress on the liturgy of the word at the expense of the eucharist. In the last century many Anglicans and some Protestant churches began to reform and

126

encourage sacramental worship. In recent decades the ecumenical movement has helped to promote the reform of the liturgy in many denominations. See *Holy Week; Old Believers; Oxford Movement; Rite; Vernacular; Worship.*

LITURGY (Gr. "public service"). In the NT, cultic priestly activity (Lk 1:23; Heb 8:6) or wider acts of Christian service (Phil 2:17, 30). In Byzantine Christianity since the ninth century "liturgy" refers to community worship, above all the eucharistic liturgy or mass. Originally the Latin church spoke of *divina officia* or divine offices, but from the sixteenth century adopted the Byzantine term. The first document promulgated by the Second Vatican Council was dedicated to the liturgy (see SC 5–13). See *Eucharist; Lex Orandi—Lex Credendi; Sacraments; Worship.*

LITURGY OF ST. JOHN CHRYSOSTOM. A liturgy ascribed to the Patriarch of Constantinople, St. John Chrysostom (ca. 347–407). This is the normal liturgy in the Byzantine rite, that of St. Basil taking its place on January 1, on the Sundays of Lent (except Palm Sunday), on Holy Thursday, Holy Saturday, on the vigil of Christmas and Epiphany (unless they fall on a Saturday or a Sunday), and on both feasts themselves if they fall on a Sunday or a Monday. The liturgies of St. Chrysostom and St. Basil both have the following structure: *prothesis* or the private preparation of bread and wine; *enarxis* or the opening service of three antiphons; *synaxis* or the readings from scripture (= liturgy of the word); and liturgy of the eucharist (= preanaphora, anaphora, communion, thanksgiving and dismissal). See *Eastern Churches; Eucharist; Mass; Rite.*

LITURGY OF THE EUCHARIST. Term for the second part of the mass which follows the liturgy of the word. It consists in the offering of the bread and wine which are changed into the body and blood of Christ. This celebration re-presents the sacrificial death and resurrection of Christ, and ends with the participation in the sacrificial meal at communion. See *Communion; Eucharist; Liturgy of the Word; Mass; Sacrifice; Transubstantiation.*

LITURGY OF THE HOURS. The official worship of the community, gathered at different times of day or night to hear passages from scripture (and other sources), and recite or sing together psalms and other prayers. The participants give praise to God, fulfill Christ's priestly office, and intercede for the salvation of the whole world (CIC 1173). The Jews recalled the divine blessings through morning and evening sacrifice in the temple (see Exod 29:38–42; Num 28:3–8), while those in exile practiced fixed times of prayer (Dan 6:10). Christian communities, both secular and monastic, developed a daily program of common prayer. When clerics often could not be present for the common services, the west developed the *breviary* (Lat. "abridgment") or short version of the canonical hours for private recital. In the west the canonical hours of the divine office became: matins (or night prayer), lauds, prime (or first prayer), terce (or prayer at nine o'clock), sext (or prayer at twelve o'clock), none (or prayer at three o'clock), vespers and compline (or final prayer at night). See *Breviary; Lauds; Monasticism; Secularism; Vespers.*

LITURGY OF THE WORD. The first part of the eucharist, which consists in: the opening prayers of the assembly gathered to worship, and readings from the Bible, with the last reading always from the gospels and followed ideally by a homily, and on some days by the creed and the prayers of the faithful. See *Collect; Creed; Epistle; Eucharist; Gospel; Catechumens, Mass of the; Homily; Word of God.*

LOCAL CHURCH. The community gathered around its bishop may be called "church" in the full sense, as long as it is in communion with the other local churches. The NT applies "church" both to the local congregations (Acts 8:1; 11:2; Rom 16:1; 1 Cor 1:2) and to the whole body of Christians (Matt 16:18; Eph 1:22). The Second Vatican Council teaches that through the bishop of the diocese presiding at the liturgy, the people of God are more visibly manifested (see SC 41–42; LG 26; AG 19–22). See *Catholicity; Church; Eucharist; Rite.*

LOCUS THEOLOGICUS (Lat. "place of theology"). The main themes of Christian faith (= *loci communes* or common topics), or else fundamental principles and sources for medieval, baroque and neoscholastic theology (and renaissance humanism) in systematically presenting doctrines. In a posthumous work *De locis theologicis* (1563) Melchior Cano displayed the impact of the new humanism. He enumerated seven *loci* which depend, directly or indirectly, on divine authority and revelation: (a) God's word in scripture; (b) the tradition of the apostles; (c) the universal church; (d) councils; (e) papal teaching; (f) the Fathers of the Church; and (g) theologians and canonists. As additional helps Cano named: (h) natural reason; (i) philosophers and jurists; and (j) history and tradition. Cano's method has exercised a great influence, but needs to allow more for mystery and to incorporate the themes of salvation history and liturgy. See *Deposit of Faith; Dogma; Doxology; Lex Orandi–Lex Credendi; Liturgy; Neoscholasticism; Revelation; Theology, Methods in; Tradition.*

LOGOS (Gr. "word," "message," "discourse," "reason"). In Greek philosophy the reason that permeates and rules the cosmos. The OT wisdom books spoke of the Logos as the personified wisdom which God showed in forming the universe (Prov 8:1–36; Wis 7:22–30; 9:1–2). The Jewish philosopher Philo (ca. 20 B.C.–ca. A.D. 50) linked Greek philosophy and OT wisdom literature to represent the Logos as the divine pattern and purpose active in creation. In Johannine thought the Logos is the preexistent divine Word through whom "all things were made" and who "became flesh and dwelt among us" (Jn 1:1–14; 1 Jn 1:1–2; Rev 19:11–16). The "verbal" character of this christological title suggests how the divine self-revelation reached its climax with the historical incarnation of the Logos. After Nicaea "Logos" and "Son of God" were used interchangeably for the second person of the Trinity. See *Apollinarianism; Appropriation; Arianism; Christological Titles; Johannine Theology; Nicaea, First Council of; Word of God.*

LOGOS-ANTHROPOS CHRISTOLOGY (Gr. "Word-man"). A christology "from below," characteristic of Theodore of Mopsuestia (ca. 350–428) and the school of Antioch, and concerned to maintain the full humanity of Jesus Christ. Since the Antiochenes began with the duality of natures (the full human nature of Christ and his divine nature), they had to face the question: How are Christ's divinity and humanity united in one acting subject? Their christology could go astray by abandoning the real unity of Christ and ending up with two subjects: the assuming Word and the man Jesus who is assumed. See *Alexandrian Theology; Antiochene Theology; Chalcedon, Council of; Christology From Below; Nestorianism.*

LOGOS-SARX CHRISTOLOGY (Gr. "Word-flesh"). A christology "from above," characteristic of Origen (ca. 185–ca. 254) and St. Cyril of Alexandria (d. 444) and centered on the eternally preexistent *Logos* who descends into the world. The Alexandrian school normally did well in maintaining the genuine divinity and true unity of Christ as an acting subject. For some Alexandrians the most serious challenge came in showing his real humanity and facing the question: How could the eternal Word of God take on a genuinely and fully human way of acting? As for Logos-Sarx christology in its relationship to Logos-Anthropos, Aloys Grillmeier (b. 1910) has pointed out that they cannot simply be identified with Alexandria and Antioch respectively, since there are important counter-examples. See *Ephesus, Council of; Neo-Chalcedonianism.*

LORD'S SUPPER, THE. A name used by some church fathers and current among Protestants for the eucharistic meal instituted by Christ at the last supper. In its one NT appearance (1 Cor 11:20), "the Lord's Supper" includes both the eucharistic sacrifice and the *agape* or fraternal meal which followed. See *Agape; Eucharist; Holy Week; Liturgy; Mass.*

LOVE. That free, self-transcending, life-giving and unifying approval which has its source and standard within the life of the blessed Trinity.

129

The OT repeatedly acknowledges God as the faithful and tender covenant-partner of the chosen people, who are called to respond by loving God (Deut 6:5) and neighbor (Lev 19:18). Jesus joined together these two basic commandments (Mk 12:29–31) and taught that our love should reach out in a particular way to enemies and those in special need (Matt 5:43–48; 25:31–46; Lk 10:29–37). As the greatest and "new" commandment (Jn 13:13, 34; see 1 Cor 12:31–13:13), love can even entail dying for others as Jesus did (Jn 15:13; 1 Jn 3:16). It is God's initiative of love towards us sinners that makes possible our response of love (Lk 15:3–32; Jn 3:16; Rom 5:6–8; 8:31–39; 1 Jn 4:19). We are given the Spirit of love (Rom 5:5), called into the new community of love (Eph 5:25–26, 29) and invited to share in the divine love which is the inner life of the Trinity (Jn 17:26). See *Agape; Charity; Covenant; Virtues, Theological.*

LUMEN GLORIAE. See *Light of Glory.*

LUTHERANISM. That form of Christianity inspired by Martin Luther (1483–1546), initiator of the German reformation. After joining the Augustinian Hermits in 1505, he eventually became professor of scripture at Wittenberg, where in 1517 he produced his famous 95 theses in protest against the scandalous sale of indulgences. He was excommunicated by Pope Leo X in 1521. Lutheranism spread over a large part of Germany, as well as over the Scandinavian countries and Finland. Along with communities in the United States and elsewhere, nearly all these churches now form the Lutheran World Federation. The typical doctrines of Lutheranism can be found in the Lutheran confessional writings, especially the *Augsburg Confession* (1530), the *Apology of the Augsburg Confession* (1531), the *Smalkald Articles* (1536) and Luther's catechisms. They may be summarized as follows: *sola fides* or justification by faith alone (not by good works); *sola gratia* or justification through God's grace alone; and *sola scriptura* or the Bible (not human traditions) as the only authoritative rule of faith. Lutheranism emphasizes Christ's cross and human bondage to the rule of sin. It accepts only baptism and the eucharist as sacraments truly instituted by the Lord. See *Augsburg Confession; Law and Gospel; Faith and Works; Imputation; Indulgences; Protestant; Reformation, The; Sola Fides; Sola Gratia; Sola Scriptura; Tradition; Trent, Council of.*

LYONS, FIRST COUNCIL OF (1245). Convoked by Pope Innocent IV to deal with what he called in his opening homily "the five wounds of the Church": the scandalous life-style of many clerics and laypersons; the capture of Jerusalem by the Saracens; the Greek threat to the Latin Empire in Constantinople; the invasion of Hungary by the Mongols; the conflict between the church and the German Emperor Frederick II. Besides ordering the Greeks to conform more to the Latin rite and clarifying some points concerning the sacraments and purgatory (see DS 830–39), the council deposed the emperor for heresy and encroaching on the rights of the church. Catholics consider it to be the thirteenth ecumenical Council. See *Crusades; Lateran Council, Fourth.*

LYONS, SECOND COUNCIL OF (1274). Convoked by Pope Gregory X who wanted a crusade (to free the Holy Land from the Saracens), an agreement with the Greeks and a reformation of the church. It was attended by great theologians like St. Bonaventure and St. Albert the Great. St. Thomas Aquinas had been invited, but he died on the way, after having finished a preliminary study, "Concerning the Errors of the Greeks." In spite of a tax imposed on clerics' income, the crusade never materialized. The legates of the Greek Emperor Michael VIII Paleologus signed an agreement of union, which was celebrated on July 6 with the *Filioque* being sung three times. The union, which partly aimed at calming fears that Charles of Anjou would try to restore the Latin Empire in Constantinople, proved ephemeral. Legislation for the reform of the church included suppression of some new orders and strict rules to be followed when cardinals gather to elect a new pope. Catholics have normally considered Lyons II to be the fourteenth ecumenical council, but in 1974 Paul VI spoke of it as "a general council of the West." See *Conclave; Crusades; Filioque.*

M

MACEDONIANS. A sect which took its name from Macedonius, bishop of Constantinople from 342 until he was deposed by the Arian Council of Constantinople in 360. He himself had Semi-Arian tendencies (see DS 156, 2527). At Constantinople I (381) he was condemned with those who denied the divinity of the Holy Spirit (see DS 151), but it is doubtful whether he really subscribed to that heresy. See *Arianism; Constantinople, First Council of; Holy Spirit; Semi-Arianism; Pneumatomachians.*

MAGISTERIUM (Lat. "office of teacher"). The office of authoritatively teaching the gospel in the name of Jesus Christ. All baptized believers are anointed and guided by the Spirit (Jn 14:26; 16:13; Rom 8:14; 1 Jn 2:27), and in some degree have a prophetic responsibility for announcing the good news about Christ. Those who have the authority to proclaim and teach officially share in the church's magisterium. Catholics believe that this magisterial authority belongs to the whole college of bishops (as successors to the college of apostolic witnesses) and to individual bishops united with the Bishop of Rome (LG 20–25; DV 10). The bishops generally fulfil this magisterium on a day-to-day basis (various kinds of "ordinary" magisterium). When assembled in an ecumenical council or represented by the pope, they may teach some revealed truth to be held absolutely and definitely (the "extraordinary" magisterium). As a specific service on behalf of the whole community, the magisterium recalls Christ's saving truth to clarify and apply it in the face of the new challenges of each age and situation. The office of the magisterium comes from Christ himself, is guided by (and does not supplant) the Holy Spirit, and is exercised within the whole community of the faithful, who were and remain the primary recipients of God's self-revelation. The intersubjective nature of truth lends credibility to the existence of such a magisterium. Truth, including revealed truth, is experienced and maintained by human beings in community. This makes it more plausible that the church should be equipped with an institution (the magisterium) which functions to help people experience and abide in the truth of revelation. In the middle ages theologians and the theological faculties of great universities were also credited with exercising a certain magisterium. Such authority derived from the quality of their personal gifts, just as apparently there was a similar "charismatic" basis for the role of "teachers" in the NT church (1 Cor 12:28; Acts 13:1). See *Apostolic Succession; Authority; Bishop; Collegiality; Council, Ecumenical; Deposit of Faith; Ex Cathedra Definition; Hierarchy; Infallibility; Pope.*

MALABAR CHRISTIANS. Three groups of eastern-rite Christians who reside in Kerala (South-West India). They are also known as St. Thomas Christians, for they claim that St. Thomas the Apostle converted them and that his tomb is found near Madras. At an early date they belonged to what is now called the (Assyrian) Church of the East, but what was often known as the Nestorian or Chaldean Church, or as the East Syrian Church (= East of the Byzantine Empire). When the Portuguese came to India in the sixteenth century, the Malabar Christians renounced their allegiance to the Mesopotamian Patriarch and abjured their Nestorian errors at the Synod of Diamper in 1599. But the Latinization of their rite led to many breaking away from Rome and forming three communities:
(a) The group which broke with Rome in 1653 and joined the Syrian Orthodox Church, which is still known to many as the Jacobite Church and uses the West-Syrian Antiochene liturgy;
(b) The group which broke away from Rome in 1652 but returned in 1662. With slight changes, they were allowed to use the Nestorian *Liturgy of Addai and Mari*, characterized by the full words of epiclesis and the absence of the words of institution;
(c) The group of Jacobites who joined Rome in 1930 and formed the *Malankarese (Union) Church*, Malankara being another word for Kerala.

They have retained their ancient Syrian liturgy as translated into Malayalam.
See *Church of the East; Epiclesis; Jacobites; Liturgy; Monophysitism; Rite.*

MANDATE. An attestation from the competent ecclesiastical authority recognizing that someone who teaches a theological discipline at a Catholic university or similar institute of higher learning is in good standing with the church and is teaching Catholic doctrine in communion with the bishops (CIC 812; see 810, 818). In this context "mandate" replaces the term previously used, "canonical mission." See *Magisterium; Missio Canonica; Theology.*

MANICHAEISM. The doctrine of Mani, born in Persia ca. A.D. 215 and skinned alive by order of the Persian emperor in 275. Borrowing elements from Zoroastrianism, Buddhism, Gnosticism and Christianity, Mani saw himself as following the OT prophets, Zarathustra, Buddha and Jesus to free the spark of light in human beings and so deliver them from matter and darkness. A strict asceticism and vigorous missionary activity spread this teaching to India, China, Italy, North Africa and other parts of the Roman Empire. For nine years prior to his conversion St. Augustine of Hippo (354–430) subscribed to Manichaeism. "Manichee" was often used synonymously with "heretic," especially in the context of similar dualistic movements (see DS 435, 444–45, 457, 461–64, 718, 1336, 1340, 3246). See *Albigensianism; Cathars; Dualism; Gnosticism; Priscillianism.*

MANNA (Gr. "small grain"). Food which through God's special providence (Ps 78:24–25) the Jews ate on their flight from Egypt and for forty years before they entered the promised land (Exod 16:12–36). The popular etymology of Exodus 16:15, according to which the word derives from the Hebrew "what is this?," is meant to underline God's intervention. Manna seems to have been a resinous, white substance which some desert trees and shrubs produce and which falls on the ground like frost. The plain taste of manna (Num 11:4–9) was one reason for the people complaining in the desert and incurring the divine displeasure (Num 11:1–35). John's gospel presents Jesus as the bread of eternal life, incomparably superior to the manna eaten in the desert (Jn 6:25–58; see Rev 2:17). See *Eucharist; Israel; Typology.*

MARANATHA. An Aramaic word used in 1 Corinthians 16:22 which as *maranatha* means "O Lord, come!" and as *maran-atha* means "The Lord has come." Most probably the first meaning is the one intended (see Rev 22:20). See *Advent; Eschatology; Kyrios; Lord; Parousia.*

MARCIONISM. A dualistic, ascetic movement founded by Marcion, a native of Pontus in Asia Minor, who came to Rome around 140 and was excommunicated in 144. In his *Antitheses* he maintained that the creator (or demiurge) and OT law were quite incompatible with the God of love and grace preached by Jesus. Hence, he rejected completely the Hebrew scriptures, retaining only the Pauline letters and a truncated version of Luke's gospel. He interpreted the person and work of Christ along docetic lines. For some time Marcion had many followers, and major theologians like St. Irenaeus of Lyons (ca. 130–ca. 200) and Tertullian (ca. 160–ca. 220) felt obliged to refute him. The formation of the canon came in part as a response to his erroneous teaching. By the end of the third century his followers had largely become Manichees. But a Marcionite rejection or downplaying of the OT remains a recurrent temptation for Christians. See *Canon of Scripture; Demiurge; Docetism; Dualism; Manichaeism.*

MARIOLOGY. The systematic study of the person of Mary and her role in salvation history. Luke's infancy narrative (Lk 1–2) presents her as model believer, representative of the church and mother of the savior whom she has conceived virginally. In John's gospel she stands by the cross (Jn 19:25–27), and Acts reports that she was present with the community before Pentecost (Acts 1:14). For centuries theological, pastoral and popular reflection on these and other scriptural passages rightly associated Mary with Christ, the Holy Spirit, the church and human redemption. When the Council of Ephesus (431), for example, declared Mary to be the Mother of God, it did so to defend the personal unity of Christ and reject the false teaching that in Christ there were two different persons, one divine and the other a merely human person born of Mary. In the west devotion to Mary at times presented her apart from the proper christological, pneumatological, ecclesiological or anthropological context, and indulged in exaggerations summarized by the adage, *"de Maria nunquam satis"* (Lat. "one can never say enough about Mary"). The Second Vatican Council, while warning against abuses and purposely avoiding the title "co-redemptrix," was the first ecumenical council to offer a systematic treatment of the role and importance of Mary (LG 52–69). See *Assumption of the Blessed Virgin; Co-Redemptrix; Ephesus, Council of; Immaculate Conception; Nestorianism; New Eve; Theotokos.*

MARKS (NOTES) OF THE CHURCH. The essential qualities of Christ's Church: unity, holiness, catholicity and apostolicity (Nicene-Constantinopolitan Creed). After John Wycliffe (ca. 1330–84) and Jan Huss (ca. 1372–1415) stressed the "spiritual" side of the church, in 1431 the Dominican Cardinal Juan de Torquemada (an uncle of the future Grand

Inquisitor) wrote a treatise about the church based on her four visible marks. During the reformation such Catholic apologists as Cardinal Stanislaus Hosius (1504–79) and St. Robert Bellarmine (1542–1621) emphasized these marks, in response to those like Martin Luther (1483–1546) who held that the unadulterated teaching of the gospel characterized the true church of Jesus Christ. In recent years prophetic denunciation of and action against injustice has assumed a larger role as a visible sign of the church's holiness in the world; see John Paul II, *Sollicitudo Rei Socialis* (1987). See *Apostolicity; Catholicity; Church; Holiness; Holiness of the Church; Hussites; Reformation; Unity.*

MARONITES. Members of an eastern Catholic Church who trace their origin back to St. Maron, friend of St. John Chrysostom (ca. 347–407). The Maronite Church, which remained faithful to the Council of Chalcedon, probably achieved its organizational independence in the seventh century, at the time of the Monothelite dispute. Whether the Maronites endorsed this teaching at least verbally, is a matter of controversy. In the eighth century, at a time when the patriarchal see of Antioch was empty, the title of patriarch was given to the superior of the Maronite monastery on the Orontes in Syria. With the arrival of the crusaders, communion with the Catholic Church, never renounced, was resumed without formality and there have been only Catholic Maronites ever since. The Maronite Jeremias II attended the Fourth Lateran Council and was recognized as Patriarch of Antioch a year later (1216). In 1584 Pope Gregory XIII founded a Maronite college in Rome, where important liturgical and other texts were published during the eighteenth century. The Maronite rite, one of the seven major extant rites, once considered simply a Latinized variant of the west-Syrian rite, is now recognized to be an independent tradition related to both the west and east Syrian liturgies. It underwent superficial Latinization in the seventeenth and eighteenth centuries, much of which has been purged in recent reforms. Maronites are found in Lebanon, Syria, Israel, Cyprus, the United States and elsewhere. See *Crusades; Eastern Churches; Rite.*

MARRIAGE. A covenanted communion for life between one man and one woman through which they become husband and wife, mutually share their complete selves, promote each other's fullest welfare and in love beget and raise children (GS 47–52). The OT speaks of man and woman as both being created in the image of God to rule over the earth, procreate children and complete each other's being (Gen 1:27–28; 2:18–25). Jesus emphasized the dignity of married life in various ways—for instance, by comparing the divine kingdom to a wedding feast (Matt 22:1–14; 25:1–13). His love for the church is compared to the marriage bond (Eph 5:22–33) which is a sacrament for baptized Christians (LG 11,

135

35). The two partners are themselves the ministers of this sacrament, the priest (or deacon) serving only as official witness. The bond of marriage is indissoluble as long as both partners remain alive. See *Sacrament*.

MARRIAGE FORM. The way of performing the marriage ceremony established by the Council of Trent in 1563 and prescribed in canon law (CIC 1108–23). For a marriage to be valid, it must be celebrated before the local bishop, the parish priest, or a priest or deacon legitimately delegated for the celebrations. Where priests or deacons are not available, lay persons may be delegated, if this is granted by the episcopal conference. Two other witnesses must be present. For just reasons the local bishop may dispense from the form prescribed by the law. See *Validity*.

MARRIAGE IMPEDIMENTS. Qualities or personal circumstances which stand in the way of contracting a marriage, are called *diriment impediments* and rule out a valid marriage. Diriment impediments include insufficient age, impotency, an already existing marriage, holy orders, public perpetual religious vows and close blood-relationships (see CIC 1073–94). See *Ratum et Consummatum; Validity*.

MARTYR (Gr. "witness"). Somebody who, because of his or her faith in and love for Christ, undergoes suffering and death (LG 50; PG 14). In St. John's gospel the term is used of the Father's witness in favor of the Son (Jn 5:37), and the witness given by Jesus (Jn 3:1–12) or by John the Baptist (Jn 1:6–8, 15, 19–36; 3:22–30; 5:33). The apostles and other Christians witnessed to the truth (Lk 24:48; Acts 1:8, 22). In due course "martyrs" designated those who suffered and died for their testimony (Acts 22:20; Rev 12:11), the death of Jesus himself being considered the prime example of martyrdom (see Acts 1:5; 3:14). Isolated episodes of persecution became large-scale and systematic under the Emperors Septimius Severus (202–203), Decius (249–50) and Valerian (257–58). The Roman persecution reached its climax under Diocletian and Galerius from 303 onwards, ending with the victory of Constantine the Great in 312. The first Christians to be venerated as saints were the martyrs. A chapel built on their tombs was known as a *martyrion*, being visited particularly on the *dies natalis* (Lat. "birthday, anniversary") or the day of their heavenly birth through martyrdom. From the beginning the church has considered martyrdom as a "baptism of blood" that can replace sacramental baptism. The *martyrology* is a liturgical book containing the names of martyrs and other saints, listed according to the day of their death. In modern times there have been numerous martyrs in and outside Europe—in Africa, the Americas, Asia and Oceania. In this century many Christians have endured suffering and martyrdom be-

136

cause of their commitment to and solidarity with those who suffer (see Jn 15:13). See *Baptism; Holiness; Veneration of Saints*.

MARXISM. The social, economic, political and philosophical doctrine developed by Karl Marx (1818–83) and his collaborator Friedrich Engels (1820–95), and actualized in its most powerful way by Vladimir Ilyich Lenin (1870–1924) and Mao Tse-Tung (1893–1976). Outraged by massive social injustices, they argued that private property and capitalistic society had alienated human beings from themselves, their work, their products and each other. A class struggle, led by the industrial proletariat, was expected to end this radical alienation, go beyond capitalism and bring in a classless society of self-emancipated people. In that future society the question of God would simply disappear. The atheistic materialism of official Marxism has opposed all religions, which were dismissed as ideologies favoring the prosperous and powerful and encouraging the poor to suffer patiently and look for rewards after death. While condemning atheistic Marxism, church teaching has also criticized capitalistic materialism (DS 2786, 3773, 3865, 3930, 3939; John Paul II, *Sollicitudo Rei Socialis* 20–21). Hardline Marxism has not achieved either the true emancipation of humanity or economic prosperity for all. In a dramatic way the governments of nearly all Communist countries have allowed and even initiated reforms that make the old, official Marxism a thing of the past. See *Atheism; Frankfurt School; Materialism; Political Theology; Social Teaching*.

MARY, MOTHER OF GOD. See *Mariology; Theotokos*.

MASS (Lat. perhaps "dismissal"). A word commonly used in the Roman Church, where the regular form of *dismissal* at the end of the liturgy is *"Ite missa est"* (Lat. "Go, the mass is ended"). See *Eucharist; Liturgy*.

MASS OF THE PRESANCTIFIED. Liturgy in which there is no consecration of bread and wine but hosts, consecrated at a previous mass, are distributed: hence the name mass of the "presanctified." In the Byzantine rite such a mass of the presanctified is celebrated on Wednesdays and Fridays during Lent, the normal eucharist being limited to Saturdays, Sundays and the feast of the Annunciation (= the festive days free from fasting and abstinence). In the Latin rite the mass of the presanctified is celebrated only on Good Friday. See *Abstinence; Fasting; Lent; Rite; Trisagion*.

MATERIALISM. Any belief that denies such spiritual entities as God and the human soul and accepts the existence only of perceptible, extended reality. A classical form of materialism was articulated by the Greek philosopher Epicurus (341–270 B.C.) and expressed in verse by the Roman poet Lucretius (ca. 99–55 B.C.). Modern versions of materialism have come from Ludwig Feuerbach (1804–72), Karl Marx (1818–83) and Friedrich Engels (1820–95). See *Atheism; Marxism; Pantheism.*

MATTER AND FORM. The Aristotelian analysis of all material reality into two complementary principles: the underlying stuff or pure potentiality which is actualized by the form that determines the nature of things. This theory of *hylomorphism* (Gr. "matter," "form") enjoyed great popularity among scholastic philosophers and theologians. See *Aristotelianism; Causality; Scholasticism.*

MEDIATION (Lat. "going between"). The intervention of a third party to reconcile two parties in conflict with each other and so promote, through a new understanding, some common goal or good. In the OT, Abraham (Gen 18:16–33), Moses (Exod 32:7–14) and various prophets, priests, judges and kings mediated between the people and God. Being both divine and human, Jesus Christ is, fully and finally, *the* Mediator, that is, the only ultimate Mediator between God and sinful humanity (1 Tim 2:5; Heb 8:6; 9:15; 12:24)—a central Christian belief thematized by Pius XII in such encyclicals as *Mystici Corporis* (1943) and *Mediator Dei* (1947) (see DS 1526; 3370; 3820). See *Redeemer; Redemption; Salvation.*

MEDIATRIX. A title for Our Lady which originated in the east and for which the first certain documentary evidence comes from St. Andrew of Crete (d. 740). Being so close to her Son, Mary can intercede for her other children (Jn 19:26), an intercession that relies on her Son's infinite merits. Angels, saints and human beings alive today also intercede for others (1 Tim 2:1) and, in their own way, mediate God's blessings. Such subordinate mediators are sometimes called "mediators in a relative sense," relative, that is, to the merits of Jesus Christ (see DS 3320s; 3370; 3916). See *Guardian Angels; Intercession; Mariology; Veneration of Saints.*

MEDITATION (Lat. "reflection"). Mental prayer which aims at union with God and insight into the divine will by reflecting on biblical and other spiritual themes. As a form of prayer for beginners, the exercise of step-by-step meditation should lead to the higher and simpler stage of contemplation. See *Contemplation.*

MELKITES (more commonly nowadays) or *Melchites* (Syrian "king"). Those Christians in the Byzantine Empire, especially in Egypt and Syria, who supported the emperor and orthodox faith against the "Monophysites" or those who dissented from the Council of Chalcedon (451). When Constantinople broke with Rome in 1054, the Melkites sided with

Constantinople, but after 1724 a Melkite Church united with Rome came into being. Today "Melkite" most often refers to Catholics of the Byzantine rite who belong to the patriarchates of Alexandria, Antioch and Jerusalem. See *Chalcedon, Council of; Eastern Churches; Monophysitism; Rite; Schism.*

MERCY. God's loving care for all creatures, especially human beings, which invites us in turn to empathize with and alleviate the misery of others. The OT employs three words for mercy. *Hesed* (Heb. "goodness") or faithful kindness is founded on a bond or covenant like marriage (Gen 20:13) or close relationship (1 Sam 20:8, 14–15). *Rahamin* (Heb. "womb") is visceral sympathy or compassion, like that of a mother for her child (Isa 49:15). *Hen* (Heb. "grace") expresses the way God's favor is bestowed gratuitously and independently of the recipient's merits (Exod 33:12–17). Human beings call for mercy and God is more than willing to grant it (see Pss 51; 113; 117). The NT celebrates God's mercy (Lk 1:50, 54, 72, 78), revealed and expressed above all through Jesus' words and deeds (Matt 9:10–13; 18:21–35; Lk 10:29–37). The blind man's plea to Jesus for mercy (Mk 10:47–48) has become part of Christian prayer-life, especially in the east. One should aim at imitating the heavenly Father in one's mercy, and, in turn, God will be merciful with those who exercise mercy (see Matt 6:12; 25:31–46; Lk 11:4). See *Grace; Hesed; Jesus Prayer; Love.*

MERIT (Lat. "reward, recompense"). The goodness of some deed that entitles one to a reward. After Tertullian (ca. 160–ca. 220) introduced the term, medieval theologians distinguished between *meritum de condigno,* or merit based on a strict claim in justice, and our situation before God, *meritum de congruo,* where it is appropriate to reward good actions of the justified (or the not yet justified). Behind this teaching were many scriptural passages indicating that God rewards good deeds and punishes evil ones (Exod 23:20–22; Matt 5:3–12; 6:4; 19:21; 25:31–46; 1 Cor 3:8; Rev 22:12). At the same time, St. Augustine of Hippo (354–430) pointed out that any "claims" before God are based only on what God has previously given freely: "God does not crown your merits as your merits, but as his own gifts" (see DS 248, 388). The Council of Trent, with reference to Romans 11:6, taught that we cannot merit the initial grace of justification and the eternal reward accompanying it (DS 1532). Nevertheless, justification through Christ's infinite merits brings an intrinsic change through which the justified can produce the fruits of the Spirit (Gal 5:22–23). The reformation controversy over merit hardly touched the eastern churches. Their liturgies not only pray to the angels and saints, but also *for* them, indicating that the grandeur of any creature is always due to God's mercy. See *Deification; Good Works; Grace; Imputation; Justification; Sanctification; Trent, Council of.*

MESSALIANS (Syrian "praying people"). A sect which was found in the Middle East, Greece and Egypt and which was condemned at the Council of Ephesus (431). They held that through Adam's sin a devil was united to every soul and could be expelled only by sustained prayer and asceticism. Such prayer and asceticism would also automatically bring a vision of the Trinity. In the ancient world their emphasis on prayer led them to be called *Euchites* (Gr. "praying people"). The Jesuit scholar Irenaeus Hausherr (1891–1978) wrote of Messalianism as the "Pelagianism of the East," since it taught that sustained human effort was all that was needed to attain the highest spiritual gifts. Much of the sect's literature was apparently attributed to St. Macarius of Egypt (ca. 300–ca. 390). See *Asceticism; Pelagianism; Prayer.*

MESSIAH (Heb. "anointed one"). God's promised deliverer for a suffering people. The Hebrew adjective *mashiach* ("anointed") was used of an anointed king (1 Sam 10:1; 24:7; 2 Sam 2:4) and anointed priest (Lev 4:3, 5), in both cases indicating a person invested by God with special powers and functions. Through Nathan's promise to David (2 Sam 7:12–16) and other influences (Isa 9:5–7; Ezek 34:23–24; 37:24–25; and the "Messianic" psalms [Pss 2; 17, 22; 45; 49; 72; 89; 110]) "the Messiah" (or in Greek "the Christ") eventually came to indicate the promised king from the line of David who would finally deliver the people. The NT recognizes Jesus as the kingly messiah now reigning in heaven (Acts 2:36; 5:31) and to come in power and glory (Acts 3:20–21). But he was already invested with such functions during his ministry (Lk 4:17–21; Mk 8:29) and even in his infancy (Lk 1:32–33; 2:11; Matt 1:23; 2:6). As a comprehensive designation for Jesus, his powers and identity, "Messiah" or "Christ" (Jn 1:41; 4:25) was so frequent that by the time of Paul's first letter it had already become a (second) proper name (1 Thess 1:1), as is usually the case today when people speak of "Jesus Christ." See *Anointing; Christological Titles.*

METANOIA (Gr. "change of mind"). The biblical term for that repentance or complete change of heart which turns one away from sin to serve the living God. OT prophets called for a conversion that would turn people away from idolatry and from a merely superficial practice of religion to live in fidelity to God's law and their social responsibilities (Isa 1:10–20; Ezek 18:1–32). John the Baptist and then Jesus preached a radical change of heart as demanded by the coming of God's kingdom (Matt 3:1–12; Mk 1:15). John's baptism was for repentance (Mk 1:4; Acts 13:24; 19:4). In the name of Jesus the apostles invited people to be converted and baptized and so begin a new life in the Spirit (Acts 2:38). The gift of authentic *metanoia* (see Ps 50:14) is so special that whoever jeopardizes it by subsequent sin may lose it forever (see Heb 6:4–6). See *Conversion; Faith; Penance, Virtue of.*

METAPHYSICS (Gr. "after the physics"). The study of the ultimate causes and constituents of reality. In the order in which his works were edited, Aristotle's *Metaphysics* came after the *Physics* (which studied natural things subject to change, as opposed to the permanent and all-pervasive features of reality examined by metaphysics). Since René Descartes (1596–1650) and Immanuel Kant (1724–1804), the tradition of Aristotelian metaphysics has been modified by an awareness of the extent to which "objective" reality is constructed by the knowing subject. Joseph Maréchal (1878–1944), Karl Rahner (1904–84) and Bernard Lonergan (1904–84) developed a moderate realism which allows for the role of subjectivity. Classical metaphysics has been opposed by those who reject as meaningless any statements that are not empirically verifiable. However, as that principle itself is empirically unverifiable, its challenge to classical metaphysics has had to be substantially modified. See *Analogy; Aristotelianism; Augustinianism; Causality; Philosophy; Positivism; Thomism.*

METEMPSYCHOSIS. See *Reincarnation.*

METHOD, THEOLOGICAL (Gr. "on the way towards"; "pursuit of"). Way of examining, classifying and coherently teaching Christian doctrines. Theology finds its subject matter in the divine revelation narrated and communicated by scripture and tradition (DV 24; OT 16). Method covers (a) one's presuppositions, (b) use of biblical and historical data, (c) approaches to questions of meaning and truth, (d) reflection on the ecclesial, social and cultural context in which one operates as a theologian, (e) one's particular aim and audience and (f) the degree of systematic generalization desired. In the east, proper recognition of the divine mystery is guaranteed by the method of apophatic theology. The centrality of the liturgy accounts for the doxological character of eastern theology. See *Analogy; Analogy of Faith; Apophatic Theology; Deposit of Faith; Dogmatic Theology; Doxology; Exegesis; Fundamental Theology; Hermeneutics; Kerygmatic Theology; Liberation Theology; Locus Theologicus; Mystery; Negative Theology; Orthopraxis; Theology, Methods in; Tradition.*

METHODISM (Gr. "following a way"). That form of Christian practice which started as a revival movement in Great Britain under the leadership of John Wesley (1703–93) and his brother Charles (1707–88). It led to the establishment in 1784 of free associations (later churches), independent from the episcopal structure of the Church of England, but in communion among themselves and now members of the World Federation of Methodist Churches. Methodism imitated German Pietism and has cherished the conversion experience of the Wesley brothers in preferring a theology of the heart over a rigid and rationalist orthodoxy. Methodists stress evangelism, the priesthood of all the faithful and social welfare. Their theology has tended to be largely Arminian; that is, it favors the anti-Calvinistic teaching of the Dutch Reformed theologian Jacob Arminius (1560–1609), who taught that Christ did not die just for the predestined few but for all, and that God's sovereign freedom does not exclude true freedom in human beings. See *Calvinism; Evangelism; Protestant*.

MIDRASH (Heb. "investigation, research"). A method of Jewish exegesis developed after the return from the Babylonian Captivity. It aimed to edify by eliciting from a scriptural text associations and applications which went beyond its literal meaning. The Jews distinguished two kinds of midrash: *midrash halachah* (Heb. "conduct"), which was concerned with the oral law, and *midrash haggadah* (Heb. "narrative"), which aimed to elucidate non-legal sections of the Bible. See *Haggadah; Halachah*.

MIGNE. The summary title for the publications of Jacques Paul Migne (1800–75), who after nine years as a parish priest in the country moved to Paris and edited an immense number of theological texts. His main work was the *Patrologia Cursus Completus*. The 217 volumes of its *Patrologia Latina* (PL) include all Latin ecclesiastical authors up to Pope Innocent III (1160–1216). The 161 volumes of the *Patrologia Graeca* (PG) include the Greek writers (with a Latin translation) up to 1439. Where recent and more critical editions are not available, Migne's patrology is invaluable and remains a standard work of reference. See *Patrology*.

MILLENARIANISM (Lat. "thousand"). The belief, influenced by apocalyptic writings and based on a literalistic interpretation of Revelation 20:1–7, that Christ will reign on earth for a thousand years with his saints until the final defeat of Satan and a definitive entry in glory. In the early centuries even some mainline Christians like St. Justin Martyr (ca. 100–ca. 165) and St. Irenaeus of Lyon (ca. 130–ca. 200) accepted this belief. After St. Augustine of Hippo (354–430) only some sectarian groups (e.g., around the year A.D. 1000) have at times revived Millenarianism. See *Chiliasm; Eschatology; Fundamentalism; Jehovah's Witnesses*.

MINISTER (Lat. "servant"). A person authorized to exercise spiritual functions in the church. A term for the clergy in nonepiscopal communities, it is increasingly used in the Catholic Church. *Sacred Ministers* are clerics ordained to administer the sacraments (CIC 276). *Ministers of the Word* (see Acts 6:4; Col 1:23) preach the gospel, a responsibility not only of the pope and bishops (CIC 756), but also of priests, deacons and others commissioned to preach and teach (CIC 757–61). Ordinary *ministers of Holy Communion* are bishops, priests and deacons; extraordinary ministers of communion are those laypersons commissioned to do so (CIC 910). In case of necessity lay persons may be authorized to minister by baptizing, distributing communion, preaching and presiding at the liturgy of the word (CIC 290). See *Bishop; Clergy; Cleric; Deacon; Laity; Priest.*

MINISTRY. A sharing in Christ's roles as prophet, priest and king. All the faithful participate in these functions in virtue of their baptism and confirmation, clerics in a particular way through the sacrament of orders (see DS 1326; PO 1; AA 10). Particular and special gifts should be exercized through ministries that help the whole church (Rom 12:6–8; 1 Cor 12:1–31; 1 Pet 4:10–11). See *Charism; Holy Orders; Ordination.*

MIRACLE. An event which is caused by a special divine intervention, does not follow the normal laws of nature and carries a religious message for people now and later. Far from being mere astonishing prodigies, miracles are saving and revealing signs from God (Jn 2:11, 18, 23; 12:18, 37). The synoptic gospels (Matt 4:23; 8:5–17; 11:5, 21; Mk 8:22–26; Lk 13:32) and Acts (e.g., Acts 2:22–23) witness to Jesus' miracles, which were tied in with his powerful proclamation of God's final kingdom. Acts reports various miraculous deeds of Peter and Paul. Without going into detail, Paul testifies to the same gift from God (Rom 15:19; 2 Cor 12:12). Miracles are normally required for the beatification and canonization of servants of God (see CIC 1403). See *Determinism; Doxa; Johannine Theology; Kingdom of God; Nature.*

MISHNAH (Heb. "repetition"). Jewish collection of tractates interpreting and teaching scripture and law. This work was probably compiled by Rabbi Judah ha-Nasi (ca. 135–ca. 220) and served as the basis for both the Palestinian and the Babylonian versions of the *Talmud*. The *Mishnah* still determines how a pious Jew ought to behave in many circumstances. See *Halachah; Judaism; Talmud.*

MISSIO CANONICA. Official authorization to participate in some way in the church's teaching, sanctifying and pastoral ministry to the world. See *Cleric; Deacon; Lateran Council, Fourth; Mandate; Preaching.*

MISSION, THEOLOGY OF. Systematic reflection on the way the whole

143

church and individual Christians are sent by Christ. Prior to the Second Vatican Council, four papal encyclicals took missionary activity as their theme: Benedict XV's *Maximum Illud* (1919), Pius XI's *Rerum Ecclesiae* (1926), Pius XII's *Evangelii Praecones* (1951) and John XXIII's *Princeps Pastorum* (1959). While confirming the church's commitment to spread the gospel everywhere, these popes indicated the need to build up the local churches (Benedict XV), to develop an indigenous clergy (Pius XI), to encourage the laity in renewing the social fabric (Pius XII) and to adapt to the local culture (John XXIII), as Matteo Ricci (1552–1610) did in China. Vatican II saw the church's mission to be rooted in Christ's sending the apostles just as he himself had been sent by the Father (LG 17; GS 91). By her very nature the church is on mission to the whole world (AG 2, 10). In the past some missionary activity suffered from the scandal of Christian divisions, tolerated much political, economic, racial and cultural injustice, and could be partly a form of spiritual colonialism. Almost all mission theology nowadays recognizes that integral development and liberation belong to the full missionary task of the church. For Catholics Pope Paul VI's *Evangelii Nuntiandi* (1975) offers excellent guidelines on the nature of evangelization in the modern world. See *Anonymous Christians; Inculturation; Local Church; Proselyte.*

MISSIONS, CHURCH. The church's response to her being sent by Christ to continue his work for the whole world. The prophetic books of the OT indicate how Jerusalem, the chosen people and her representatives have a missionary role for the salvation of the nations (see Isa 2:1–5; 42:6–7; 49:6, 22–23; 56:1–8; 60:1–22; Jonah). Of universal significance (Lk 2:29–32), the good news of Christ was to be preached everywhere and to everyone (Matt 28:18–20; Mk 16:15–20; Lk 24:47; Jn 20:21; Acts 1:8). Led by Peter, Paul and others (Gal 2:7–8; Rom 1:5; 16:3), the apostolic church spread the Christian faith through the Roman Empire. In the early centuries Christianity reached Abyssinia, India and (through the Nestorian Church of the East) even China. Great missionaries and their followers, at times supported by powerful rulers, had converted practically all Europe to Christianity by the year 1000. St. Patrick (ca. 390–ca. 460) helped to evangelize Ireland, St. Augustine of Canterbury (d. 604) England, St. Boniface (680–754) Germany, St. Anskar (801–65) the Scandinavian countries, and Sts. Cyril (826–69) and Methodius (ca. 805–85) the Slavic countries. With the discovery of America in 1492 and the opening up of new routes to Asia, a heroic missionary activity began in the Americas, China, India, Japan and elsewhere. The foundation of the Congregation for the Propagation of the Faith by Pope Gregory XV in 1622 encouraged and helped to organize this development. From the early nineteenth century Anglican and Protestant missionary societies, led and inpired by figures like David Livingstone (1813–73), became very active outside Europe. In the late twentieth century the need for Europe itself to be re-evangelized has become more and more apparent. See *Apostle; Evangelization*.

MISSIONS, DIVINE. The sending (or "procession") of the second and third persons of the Trinity by the Father in eternity and time (see Jn 14:26; 20:21; Gal 4:4–6). See *Appropriation; Filioque; Processions; Trinity, Theology of*.

MODALISM (Lat. "aspect, facet"). The heresy that so stressed the divine unity as to deny that "Father," "Son" and "Spirit" are personally distinct. They are only three manifestations or ways in which the one God is revealed and acts in creation and redemption. Starting in Asia Minor with Noetus (ca. 200), the heresy was propagated in the West by Praxeas (ca. 200), Sabellius (early third century), Photinus (fourth century) and, to a certain degree, by Marcellus of Ancyra (= Ankara) (d. ca 374) (see DS 151, 284). See *Patripassianism; Trinity, Theology of*.

MODERNISM. An umbrella term for a rather diffuse Catholic theological movement of the late nineteenth and early twentieth century, found in England, France, Italy and, to some extent, Germany. Among its main representatives were Alfred Loisy (1857–1940), George Tyrrell (1861–1909) and perhaps Baron Friedrich von Hügel (1852–1925). Modernists endorsed contemporary biblical criticism, accepted historical developments in Christianity, strongly opposed Neoscholasticism and were thoroughly receptive to progress in science and philosophy. At times they went astray, for example, by overemphasizing religious experience and reducing the value of common statements of faith. In 1907 through the decree *Lamentabili* and the encyclical *Pascendi* the Holy See condemned modernism in a way that failed to make careful distinctions. There was a subsequent campaign against those suspected of modernist tendencies. Pius XII (on biblical criticism), the Second Vatican Council and later developments in church teaching and theology have vindicated some, but not all, of the concerns and insights of the modernists. See *Biblical Criticism; Development of Doctrine; Doctrine; Experience, Religious; Immanence; Neo-Scholasticism*.

MOLINISM. The doctrine developed by the Spanish Jesuit Louis de Molina (1535–1600) about the relationship between free will and grace. God gives grace, arranges circumstances to bring about the proper result and foresees our future actions. But since this foresight "depends" upon our free decisions, Molina called it *scientia conditionata* or *scientia media*: knowledge relative to future human decisions and actions. This system was opposed by the Dominicans, especially by Domingo Bañez (1528–

1604). In emphasizing God's sovereign freedom, Bañez spoke of the divine concurrence in human action as *praemotio physica* (Lat. "physical pre-motion"), an idea which does not seem to do full justice to human freedom. Between 1598 and 1607 a commission, *"De Auxiliis"* met in Rome but failed to resolve the issue. It ended by forbidding Jesuits to brand the Dominicans as "Calvinists" and the Dominicans to call Jesuits "Pelagians" (see DS 1997, 2008). This debate indicates how the deepest theological questions cannot finally be answered adequately. The divine mystery has the first and the last word. See *Calvinism; Foreknowledge; Freedom; Grace; Mystery; Pelagianism; Semi-Pelagianism.*

MONARCHIANISM (Gr. "of one principle"). A term coined by Tertullian (ca. 160–ca. 220) for the heretical belief that so stressed the unity of God as to deny a truly divine Son with a distinct personal existence. Some Monarchians held that Jesus was divine only in the sense of God's *dynamis* (Gr. "power") coming upon him and adopting him. Modalist Monarchians reduced the Trinity to the different ways in which God is manifested and acts. See *Adoptionism; Modalism; Patripassianism; Trinity.*

MONASTICISM (Gr. "life alone"). A movement among baptized believers who respond to Christ's call for perfection (Matt 5:48; 19:16–26) by giving themselves through poverty, celibacy and obedience to a life of prayer, common worship and service. Toward the end of the Roman persecution, an ascetic existence in the deserts of Egypt, Palestine and Syria began to provide an heroic alternative to real martyrdom. In Egypt St. Antony the Abbot (ca. 251–356) and St. Pachomius (ca. 290–346) helped to organize their followers around a rule of life and spiritual guides, thus preparing the way for the two standard forms of monasticism: *anachoretism* or the life of hermits and *cenobitism* or life in common. Deeply influenced by St. Basil the Great (ca. 330–379), eastern monasticism helped to promote western monasticism through such writings as the *Life of St. Antony* by St. Athanasius of Alexandria (ca. 296–373) and the *Conferences* of John Cassian (ca. 360–435). After St. Martin of Tours (d. 397) and St. Augustine of Hippo (354–430), St. Benedict of Nursia (ca. 480–ca. 550) and his rule essentially shaped the future of monasticism in the west. Dominicans, Franciscans and other active religious orders have offered an alternative to a strictly contemplative monastic life (see UR 15; PC 9). In the east, however, all religious are still monks. See *Acoemetae; Anachoretism; Athos, Mount; Cenobites; Hesychasm; Liturgy of the Hours; Religious Life.*

MONISM (Gr. "one"). A term coined by Christian Wolff (1679–1754) for all attempts to interpret reality by eliminating diversity and distinctions (e.g., between body and soul or between the visible created world and

146

the invisible God) and reducing everything to a single principle. Thus *solipsism* allows only for the existence of oneself and denies the ideas, experiences and existence of other subjects. Or else the difference between mind and matter is denied by asserting that everything is only a modality of mind (idealism) or of matter (materialism). Pantheism rejects any real distinction between God and the created world. Greek philosophers prior to Socrates tended to interpret all reality through one primordial principle: e.g., Thales of Miletus considered water to be the primeval stuff of the universe. Other monists include Plotinus (ca. 205–270), Benedict Spinoza (1632–77) and idealist philosophers like Johann Gottlieb Fichte (1762–1814) who reduced everything to the "I." Both the OT (see Gen 1–3; Job 38:1–40:5) and the NT (see Jn 1:18; Rom 11:33–35) indicate the radical differences between God and creatures. Catholic teaching has insisted on this fundamental "dualism" (see DS 3022–23), as does the Protestant theme of the *Deus totaliter aliter* (Lat. "God as completely other") and Orthodoxy's *apophaticism* (Gr. "negative theology"). See *Apophatic Theology; Dualism; Idealism; Materialism; Pantheism.*

MONOENERGISM (Gr. "sole activity"). A seventh-century attempt to reconcile the so-called "monophysites" with the teaching accepted by the Council of Chalcedon (451) and developed by Constantinople II (553). According to the compromise formula of *monoenergism*, proposed by Patriarch Cyrus of Alexandria in 633 and supported by Patriarch Sergius of Constantinople, there is only one form of activity in Jesus Christ, namely the divine energy. Through the opposition of the monk St. Sophronius, who became Patriarch of Jerusalem in 634, *monoenergism* was abandoned. See *Chalcedon, Council of; Constantinople, Second Council of; Essence and Energies; Monophysitism; Monotheletism.*

MONOGAMY (Gr. "one marriage"). The ideal of being married to only one person (see Matt 5:31–32; 19:1–9; Mk 10:2–12; Lk 16:18). Many societies have allowed *polygamy* (Gr. "many marriages") or the practice of having more than one wife, either simultaneously or successively. Some societies have accepted *polyandry* (Gr. "many husbands"), the practice of a woman having more than one husband. The OT patriarchs were initially polygamous, while the law of Moses allowed for divorce and remarriage. Christ ascribed this custom to "the hardness" of the human heart, and aimed at restoring God's initial monogamous plan for marriage. In the Catholic Church, a previous valid marriage rules out a second marriage so long as the other partner is still alive (see DS 777–79, 1798, 1802, 3706–09). See *Marriage; Marriage Impediments; Polygamy.*

MONOPHYSITISM (Gr. "one nature"). The heresy attributed to those who refused to accept the teaching of the Council of Chalcedon (415) that in Christ there are "two natures in one person" (DS 300–03), and broke away from the patriarchate of Constantinople. None of the parties, however, clearly defended a full-blown version of Monophysitism: namely, that the incarnation meant either the fusion of Christ's divinity and humanity into a third "nature" or the absorption of his human nature into his divine nature like a drop into an ocean. The difference over Chalcedon seems to have been partly terminological. Among the dissidents Timothy Aerulus (d. 477) became "Monophysite" Patriarch of Alexandria, and Peter the Fuller (d. 488) Patriarch of Antioch. "Monophysite" Churches were eventually organized by Severus of Antioch (ca. 465–538), deposed from being Patriarch of Antioch in 518. The "Monophysite" churches are now generally called Oriental Orthodox. See *Chalcedon, Council of; Constantinople, Second Council of; Eutychianism; Hypostatic Union; Oriental Orthodox Churches.*

MONOTHEISM (Gr. "one God"). The belief in one (and only one), personal, all-powerful, all-knowing and all-loving God, who is the creator and Lord of everyone and everything and yet exists distinct from and beyond the whole universe. Initially Israel may have worshiped only one God, without necessarily denying the existence of (lesser) heathen deities. By the sixth century, however, Israel's monotheism clearly entailed rejecting the reality of any other gods (Isa 41:21–24; 43:10–13; 44:8). The NT revelation that in the one God there are three persons is not opposed to genuine monotheism. Judaism and Islam, however, reject belief in the Trinity as incompatible with their monotheistic faith. In the field of comparative religion some have argued either that monotheism evolved from an earlier polytheism (belief in many gods) or that a primitive, pure monotheism often lapsed into later polytheism. However, the actual development of various religions does not seem to correspond easily and clearly to either of these master theories. See *God; Islam; Judaism; Mystery; Pantheism; Polytheism; Revelation; Transcendence; Trinity, Theology of.*

MONOTHELETISM (Gr. "one will"). The heresy which maintained that Christ, despite his having a human nature, lacked a human will and possessed only one (divine) will. After the Council of Chalcedon (451) taught the personal unity but duality of natures in Christ, various attempts were made to reconcile the "Monophysite" dissidents who stressed the unity of Christ. After a compromise notion of two natures but only one "energy" (= monoenergism) was tried and found wanting, Patriarch Sergius of Constantinople encouraged Honorius I (Pope, 625–38) to propose the unfortunate formula of "two natures but only one will" in Christ, a formula for which Honorius was later censured (DS

487–88; 496–98; 550–52; 561, 563). The *Ekthesis* (Gr. "exposition of faith") promulgated by Emperor Heraclius in 638 was based on the one-(divine)-will formula. In 638 and 639 synods held in Constantinople upheld the formula, but the Lateran Synod of 649 under Pope St. Martin I, assisted by St. Maximus the Confessor, condemned it as contrary to the full humanity of Christ. The sixth ecumenical council, Constantinople III (680/81) solemnly defined that in Christ there are not only two natures but also two wills, which, nonetheless, operate harmoniously in his one person (see DS 550–64). See *Chalcedon, Council of; Constantinople, Third Council of; Dyotheletism; Monophysitism; Monoenergism.*

MONTANISM. An enthusiastic, revival movement which was initiated by Montanus, a converted pagan priest, in second-century Phrygia (in modern-day Turkey) and won many adherents including even Tertullian (ca. 160–ca. 220). Announcing the consummation of the world, Montanus saw the activities of ecstatic prophets and prophetesses (such as his associates, Priscilla and Maximilla) as signs of the end. Ascetic in its demands, the movement forbade remarriage after the death of one's partner and imposed severe rules of fasting. Montanus came to regard himself as the incarnation of the Holy Spirit. The movement's contempt for institutional structures, expressed by its free-lance way of administering the sacraments, met with church condemnation (see DS 211, 478). See *Parousia.*

MORAL DEVELOPMENT. Growth in awareness of one's responsibilities and a corresponding maturation in personal freedom. Official church teaching spoke of children reaching "the age of reason" at around seven years of age and beginning then to act as responsible human beings. Modern psychology, however, has illustrated how children often behave under constraint and only slowly interiorize moral principles to start acting freely as responsible persons. Christian communities should foster conditions which encourage development toward moral responsibility in full freedom. See *Faith Development; Moral Theology.*

MORAL THEOLOGY. That field of theology which studies and teaches how Christians (and others) ought to live. This systematic reflection on Christian conduct draws from the Bible (e.g., the decalogue, the sermon on the mount and the parenesis of Paul), philosophical reason, and the traditional experience and teaching of the church. It should be based on a full vision of what is entailed by the original creation (Gen 1:26–27) and the refashioning of humanity in Christ (Rom 6:4; 8:28–30; 1 Cor 15:49; 2 Cor 5:17; Eph 4:24; Col 3:10). After St. Thomas Aquinas (ca. 1225–74) moral theology often became isolated from its dogmatic and scriptural roots, and at times a healthy casuistry lapsed into empty legalism. The moral teaching of St. Alphonsus Liguori (1696–1787) was marked by great learning and deep pastoral concern. Johannes Baptist Hirscher (1788–1865) of Tübingen systematically presented morality in terms of the kingdom of God. In the late twentieth century biblical studies, the human sciences, philosophical developments and, most of all, a renewal in christology, ecclesiology and anthropology have challenged and enriched moral theology. Since Leo XIII (1810–1903) papal teaching has more and more encouraged moral theologians not only to study questions of individual morality but also to take up once again wider questions of social justice, Church-state relations and international peace. See *Anthropology; Casuistry; Church and State; Decalogue; Ethics; Fundamental Option; Holiness; Jansenism; Justice; Parenesis; Perfection; Probabilism; Rigorism; Social Teaching; Tübingen and its Schools.*

MORMONISM. The teaching of the "Church of Jesus Christ of Latter-Day Saints," founded in New York State by Joseph Smith (1805–44) in 1830. The *Book of Mormon*, which he claimed to have discovered through revelation, tells of a prophet Mormon and of Jewish refugees—in a story that runs from the time of the Tower of Babel till the establishment of Mormonism in the United States. An 1843 revelation led Smith to endorse polygamy. When he was murdered, Brigham Young (1801–77) established the sect in the desert where they founded Salt Lake City, Utah. Mormons expect Christ to return and establish a kingdom on earth for his saints. See *Millenarianism; Polygamy.*

MORNING PRAYER. See *Lauds.*

MORTAL SIN. See *Sin.*

MORTIFICATION (Lat. "putting to death"). The discipline and self-denial required for growth in the new life given through faith and baptism (Rom 8:13; Gal 5:24). Jesus stressed the cost of discipleship (Matt 10:34–39). Paul describes vividly the struggle with sin and deadly forces which faces those who live with God in Christ (Rom 6:1–19). See *Asceticism; Cross; Fasting.*

MOTU PROPRIO (Lat. "of one's own accord"). A personal letter written by the pope to the whole church, a local church or some particular group. When Pope John XXIII set up a commission to prepare for Vatican II, he sent out a *motu proprio* (*Acta Apostolicae Sedis* 52 [1962] 433–37). If an episcopal conference wishes to enact laws for its territory, it should request from the Holy See a special mandate unless the pope grants it *motu proprio* (CIC 415). See *Holy See.*

MURATORIAN FRAGMENT. The oldest list of NT books, named after Ludovico Antonio Muratori (1672–1750), priest, librarian and archivist, who discovered it in the Ambrosian Library (Milan) and published it in 1740. Mutilated at the beginning and at the end, this 85-line, Latin manuscript has been generally dated to the end of the second century AD. Four books later officially recognized as part of the NT (Hebrews, James and 1 and 2 Peter) are missing from the list. See *Canon of Scripture; Marcionism.*

MUSLIM. Adherent of Islam. See *Islam.*

MYSTAGOGY (Gr. "leading to the secrets"). Instruction into the secret rites and mysteries of a religion. In his mystagogical *Catecheses* given during Lent and Eastertide St. Cyril of Jerusalem (ca. 315–86) prepared catechumens for baptism on Holy Saturday and further instructed them afterwards. St. Maximus the Confessor (ca. 580–662) called his mystical interpretation of the liturgy "mystagogy." Currently some use the term for a catechesis and theology drawn from and aimed at promoting a deeper experience of God. See *Catechesis; Catechumenate; Disciplina Arcani; Experience, Religious; Mystery; RCIA.*

MYSTERY (Gr. "secret"). Not a merely obscure or inexplicable matter (as in a "murder mystery") but God's loving plan for human salvation now disclosed through Christ (Rom 16:25; Eph 1:9; 3:9; Col 1:26–27; 2:2; 4:3). While definitively revealed in Christ, the mysterious reality of God transcends human reason and comprehension. It is not the human mind that grasps God; the divine majesty grasps us. Protestant theology has followed Luther's theme of *Deus revelatus sed absconditus* (Lat. "God revealed but still hidden"). Orthodoxy has cultivated its apophatic theology which stresses the divine inaccessibility. In the nineteenth century the First Vatican Council (DS 3015–20), Matthias Scheeben (1835–88) and others spoke of the revealed mysteries or truths about God (in the plural). Recent theology and official teaching has stressed the unity of God's self-revelation. Karl Rahner (1904–84), the Second Vatican Council and encyclicals by John Paul II favor the language of the Mystery rather than the divine mysteries. See *Apophatic Theology; Mystagogy; Paschal Mystery; Salvation History.*

MYSTERY RELIGIONS. Religions of Greek origin (like Orphism) or of Oriental origin (like Mithraism), where rites were often secret and reserved for the initiates. Unlike Judaism and Christianity, which are based on God's intervention in history, these religions were based on a mythic interpretation of natural phenomena like the seasons, vegetation and, especially, fertility. Key roles were assigned to female and male deities, whose heroic deeds were celebrated in such cultic acts as a bath of purification or a sacrificial meal—acts that superficially resembled Christian sacraments. The mystery religions were much in vogue from the first century B.C. to the fourth century A.D. See *History-of-Religions School; Mystery; Myth; Religion.*

MYSTICAL BODY OF CHRIST. See *Body of Christ.*

MYSTICISM. A special, deep experience of union with and knowledge of the divine reality, freely granted by God. Mystical experiences, which may be accompanied by ecstasy, visions and other such phenomena, are usually preceded by the serious practice of contemplation and asceticism. While found in all the great world religions, mysticism in Christian experience has a highly personal quality, enhancing rather than suppressing the sense of distinction between the mystic and God. Genuine mysticism always produces more generous love toward others, and seems to be found frequently among Christians who are dedicated to prayer and sensitive to God's presence in their lives. See *Contemplation; Mystery; Visions.*

MYTH (Gr. "fable," "story"). A symbolic story about ultimate realities. "Myth" has often been understood to be a story about purely fictitious persons, events and things. While *logos* offers a rational and true account of reality and its causes, an imaginative *mythos* (e.g., about the scandalous activities of gods) may be entertaining but is essentially false. The NT also reflects this negative view of the term "myth" (1 Tim 1:4; 4:7; Tit 1:14; 2 Pet 1:16). The human mind, however, does not operate merely on the basis of abstract concepts alone. It needs symbolic-imaginative language to find and express the truth about our existence. In his dialogues Plato (427–347 B.C.) at times skillfully uses myths to guide his reader toward the truth. See *Analogy; Demythologization; Narrative Theology; Symbol.*

N

NARRATIVE THEOLOGY. A modern attempt to renew Christian theology as the theology of a historical religion which not only has something to say but also a story to tell. Breaking away from abstract doctrinal statements, narrative theology finds its home in biblical and other religious stories. While usefully correcting tendencies to cut off theology from life and worship, narrative theology needs critical criteria to establish meaning and truth. Among eastern Christians the narrative element in theology is safeguarded by the liturgy and icons. See *Icon; Liturgy; Theology.*

NATURAL LAW. The universal, moral law given by God in the very act of creating human beings and open to being known by the light of reason (see GS 79, DH 2). Pagan literature, as in the Antigone passage of Sophocles (ca. 497–406 B.C.), the western legal tradition, the Bible (e.g., Rom 2:14–15) and other voices witness to the natural law, which points to the right way of acting freely and responsibly as a human being. Sin makes it harder to discern and obey the natural law (see Matt 19:1–9), the main principles of which are enumerated in the decalogue. In the light of the natural law *alone,* it is often difficult to reach moral certainty on *specific* issues in such areas as international relations, social justice and sexual behavior. See *Decalogue; Freedom; Law; Moral Theology; Sin.*

NATURAL THEOLOGY. The discipline dealing with the knowledge of God available through reason alone (see Ps 19:1–4; Wis 13:1–9; Acts 14:17; 17:22–31; Rom 1:18–23; 2:14–15). Developed by St. Thomas Aquinas (ca. 1225–74), natural theology was challenged from the time of the Enlightenment when the validity of the arguments of God's existence came under fire. The First Vatican Council (1869–70) taught that "from the things that were created, God can be known with certainty through the natural light of human reason" (DS 3004; see DV 6). The council affirmed a possibility ("can be known"), did not indicate ways of knowing God (by logical proofs? intuition? mystical experience?), and did not claim that anyone had ever actualized this possibility without the hidden help of grace. Karl Barth (1886–1968) and other exponents of dialectical theology, arguing that sin has made human reason by itself simply incapable of knowing God, vigorously excluded any kind of natural theology. Mostly natural theology has been practiced by Christian believers. Even if they prescind from what they know through revelation, nevertheless, they raise questions about God that presuppose a prior familiarity with the answers. Finally, a purely natural theology approach presents an abstract, philosophical view of humanity—quite different from the concrete view of sinful humanity found in salvation-history theologies. The Second Vatican Council set the knowledge of God through creation (and hence natural theology) within the context of the history of revelation and salvation (DV 2–6). See *Arguments for the Existence of God; Dialectical Theology; Enlightenment; Five Ways, The; Salvation History; Theodicy; Theology.*

NATURE (Lat. "that which is born"). The entire cosmos which is good because created by God (Gen 1–2), or else something developing and acting according to its own essential characteristics. In the latter sense

153

Christian doctrine refers to the one nature of God and the two natures (divine and human) in Christ. Catholic theology has distinguished grace (= what comes to us through God's redeeming activity in Christ) from nature (= that which belongs to human beings as human beings). A classical axiom states that grace does not destroy but presupposes and elevates nature. Here it is important to recall that a purely natural order is an abstraction. The order of grace has existed right from the beginning, in that God has freely called all men and women to the supernatural destiny of eternal life. Calvinists and some other Protestants have pessimistically stressed the way sin has thoroughly corrupted human nature (see DS 1521, 1555; GS 13). See *Concupiscence; Cosmos; Creation; Creature; Ecology; Entelechy; Grace; Original Sin; Potentia Oboedentialis; Supernatural.*

NEGATIVE THEOLOGY. Like apophatic theology an approach to the divine mystery which insists that we can say more what God is not than what God really is. It is a way of doing theology that may put more stress on *sapientia* (Lat. "wisdom") than *scientia* (Lat. "science"). See *Apophatic Theology; Cataphatic Theology; Mystery; Theology; Wisdom.*

NEOCATECHUMENATE. A post-Vatican II itinerary of Christian initiation, started by Kiko Arguello (b. 1939) and Carmen Hernandez, which aimed at helping baptized Christians to discover or rediscover what faith and baptism really entail. This "way" of formation for the baptized, which follows the structures of the catechumenate in the early church, reinitiates believers into their Christian life, and aims either at reevangelizing traditionally Christian countries or at helping to root the gospel more deeply in recently evangelized areas. Lay persons, priests and families, formed through the neocatechumenate, go out as itinerant missionaries to all parts of the world. In 1987 a large diocesan seminary ("Redemptoris Mater") was opened in Rome for members of the neocatechumenal "way" who have a priestly vocation. See *Baptism; Catechumenate; RCIA.*

NEO-CHALCEDONIANISM. An attempt to mediate between the Council of Chalcedon (451), which taught that there are two natures in the one person of Jesus Christ, and the so-called "Monophysites." They maintained the pre-Chalcedonian formula of St. Cyril of Alexandria (d. 444), "the one incarnate nature of Jesus Christ." The controversy hinged on the word *physis* (Gr. "nature"), which was still being used to mean both a concrete subsisting individual (= a person) and the nature of that individual. Those Cyrillian theologians who considered Chalcedon a surrender to Nestorian theologians (guilty, in their eyes, of having divided Christ into two individuals) sought to reinterpret Chalcedon in terms of Cyril's condemnation of Nestorianism. In his "third letter to Nestorius" (DS 252–63) Cyril stressed Christ's one divine person, anathematizing anyone who failed to proclaim that God, in Christ, had suffered on the cross. At Chalcedon this letter had been read, recorded but not acclaimed. Neo-Chalcedonianism or the interpretation of Chalcedon in terms of Cyril's theology of God's suffering, was officially endorsed at the Second Council of Constantinople in 553 (DS 421–38). See *Chalcedon, Council of; Ephesus, Council of; Constantinople, Second Council of; Monophysitism; Suffering of God.*

NEOORTHODOXY. A post-World War I movement inspired by Karl Barth (1886–1968) and developed in various ways by such other theologians as Emil Brunner (1889–1966), Reinhold Niebuhr (1892–1971) and Helmut Richard Niebuhr (1894–1962). Dissatisfied with the optimistic humanism of Liberal Protestantism, they sought to recover the essential insights of the reformation and stressed the revealing and judging word of God. In a prophetic way they insisted on God's sovereign transcendence over against a sinful world. "Neoorthodoxy" has been applied to the work of others like Karl Rahner (1904–84). But in the strict sense the term applies only to the movement initiated and led by Barth. See *Dialectical Theology; Liberal Protestantism.*

NEO-PALAMISM. An attempt launched at the First Panorthodox Conference (Athens, 1936) to develop an Orthodox theological synthesis by retrieving the thought of St. Gregory Palamas (1296–1359). Palamite theology highlights both (a) human transformation into the divine image and (b) the real distinction between the essence and energies in God, who always remains transcendent and radically different from creatures. Some of the most famous Orthodox theologians of this century may be classified as Neo-Palamite: George Florovsky (1893–1979), Vladimir Lossky (1903–58), Paul Evdokimov (1900–71) and John Meyendorff (b. 1925). See *Palamism; Thomism.*

NEOPLATONISM. A revival and religious interpretation of the philosophy of Plato (427–347 B.C.) which flourished from the third to the sixth century A.D. Plotinus (205–70) was the most important representative of this movement, other exponents being Porphyry (ca. 232–ca. 303), Iamblichus (ca. 250–330) and Proclus (410–85). Plotinus argued for the soul or *psyche*, the mind or *nous* and the One or *hen*, from which the world of matter has come about through a system of emanations. Behind and beyond all experience is the One from which we have come and to which we should return through purification, knowledge and love. Highly mystical, Neoplatonism has often been interpreted as pantheistic. It had a considerable influence on St. Augustine of Hippo

(354–430) and other fathers of the church. See *Fathers of the Church; Pantheism; Platonism.*

NEOSCHOLASTICISM. A revival of medieval Christian philosophy and theology, often considered synonymous with Neo-Thomism, but in fact somewhat wider in its content and method. At the Roman College (later the Gregorian University) Jesuits like Aloisius D'Azeglio Tapparelli (1793–1862), Matteo Liberatore (1810–92) and Joseph Kleutgen (1811–93) began to restore scholasticism. One of Tapparelli's former students, Gioacchino Pecci (1810–1903), as bishop of Perugia and later as Pope Leo XIII, decisively encouraged the movement. His encyclical *Aeterni Patris* (1879) prescribed the teaching of Thomism in Catholic faculties (see DS 3135–40). Up until Vatican II (1962–65) neoscholasticism helped to give a structure and clarity to Catholic theological thought. But progress in biblical, historical, liturgical and patristic studies showed this clarity to be at times merely formal, verbal and lacking in substance. On the philosophical side, such new currents as existentialism, linguistic analysis, personalism and process thought have created a situation of pluralism. See *Neo-Thomism; Scholasticism; Thomism.*

NEO-THOMISM. A modern retrieval of the thought of St. Thomas Aquinas (ca. 1225–1274), generally considered the greatest medieval philosopher and theologian. The most important Neo-Thomists include Louis Billot (1846–1931), Mercier (Cardinal) Désiré (1851–1926), Ambrose Gardeil (1859–1931), Antonin Gilbert Sertillanges (1863–1948), Maurice de Wulf (1867–1947), Maurice de la Taille (1872–1933), Réginald Garrigou-Lagrange (1877–1964), Jacques Maritain (1882–1973), Étienne Gilson (1884–1978), Marie-Dominique Chenu (1895–1990) and Yves Congar (b. 1904). See *Neo-Scholasticism; Scholasticism; Thomism.*

NESTORIANISM. The heresy (condemned in 431 at the Council of Ephesus) that in Christ there are two different persons, one human and the other divine. It was attributed to Nestorius (d. ca. 451), a monk from Antioch who became Patriarch of Constantinople (428–31), but it seems as if he did not genuinely endorse this view. One should rather distinguish between Nestorianism itself as a heresy, rightly condemned at Ephesus (431), and Nestorius' own views, whose orthodoxy has continued to be debated right up until our times, but whose intention seems to have been orthodox. Nestorius opposed a popular Marian title *Theotokos* (Gr. "Mother of God"), apparently fearing that it threatened the full and distinct divinity *and* humanity of Christ, but was willing to accept the title if interpreted correctly. See *Antiochene Theology; Arianism; Apollinarianism; Chalcedon, Council of; Church of the East (Assyrian); Ephesus, Council of; Eutychianism; Monophysitism; Theotokos.*

NEW EVE. A title for Mary, the physical mother of Christ and spiritual mother of all human beings. The parallel and contrast between the first Eve, "the mother of all the living" (Gen 3:20), and Mary as the new Eve goes back to St. Justin Martyr (d. 165). The contrast builds not only on language about Jesus as the "last" or new Adam (Rom 5:14; 1 Cor 15:22, 45–49; see DS 901), but also on the faith shown by Mary. As the fathers of the church reflected, where Eve's disobedience brought death, Mary's obedient love brought life to all humanity through the redemptive activity of her Son (LG 56, 63). See *Adam; Co-Redemptrix; Eve; Mariology.*

NEW TESTAMENT. The 27 books in the Bible which follow the 45 books most of which are shared in common with Jews (= the Old Testament). Christians recognize these books (the four gospels, Acts of the Apostles, twenty-one letters, and the book of Revelation) as written under the special inspiration of the Holy Spirit, normative for faith and belonging to the canon of scripture. "In a most excellent way" the church finds in the NT, and in particular the gospels, a "perpetual and divine witness" to the reality of Jesus Christ (DV 17–20). See *Bible; Covenant; Canon of Scripture; Infancy Gospels; Inspiration; Marcionism; Old Testament.*

NICAEA, FIRST COUNCIL OF (325). The first ecumenical council, which was convoked by Emperor Constantine the Great (d. 337) and met at Nicaea (now Iznik in Turkey) to deal with the Arian heresy that threatened to disrupt the unity of the church and the Roman Empire. Arius, an Alexandrian priest, had been claiming that, so far from being fully and truly divine, Christ was merely the first among God's creatures. In answer the council taught that Christ was the "only-begotten" Son of the Father and *homoousios* (Gr. "of the same being" or "consubstantial") with the Father (see DS 125–30). It also recognized the patriarchal rights of Alexandria, Antioch and Rome, and prescribed for all the Alexandrian solution for the date of Easter. A rising star at the council was St. Athanasius, later Bishop of Alexandria (d. 373), who came as an archdeacon to accompany his bishop, Alexander of Alexandria. See *Arianism; Council, Ecumenical; Creed, Nicene; Homoosios; Patriarch.*

NICAEA, SECOND COUNCIL OF (787). A council convoked by the Empress-regent Irene, Patriarch Tarasius of Constantinople and attended by about 350 bishops, including a delegation from the west. Being under Moslem domination, the patriarchates of Alexandria, Antioch and Jerusalem could send only two monks each. In condemning the heresy of *iconoclasm* (Gr. "image-smashing"), the council endorsed a letter sent by Pope Hadrian I and distinguished between *proskynesis* (Gr. "veneration") or the devotion shown to images insofar as they represent God and saints, and *latria* (Gr. "adoration") or the absolute cult due to

God alone. The council also condemned simony and declared the elections of bishops by secular authorities to be null and void (see DS 600–09). This council is regarded by Greek Orthodox as the seventh—and last—ecumenical council. It forms a summary and epilogue of the previous six. See *Icon; Iconoclasm; Seven Councils, The; Veneration of Saints.*

NIHILISM (Lat. "accepting nothing"). A general term for philosophies which claim that in itself reality is ultimately meaningless. Such an essentially atheistic attitude may assert life and impose meaning by exercising one's will—as was the case with Friedrich Nietzsche (1844–1900). By professing the absurdity of the universe, the philosophy of Albert Camus (1913–60) and some other existentialists contains elements of nihilism. See *Atheism; Existentialism.*

NOMINALISM. A philosophy which developed during the middle ages and claims that names (Lat. *nomina*) for things, while useful for purposes of classification, do not validly describe reality. Every substance is irreducibly individual; there are no common natures; and universal concepts exist only in the mind. William of Occam (ca. 1285–1347) was the most famous of the nominalists. This philosophy affected theology, especially the doctrines of God, justification and sacraments. Through Martin Luther's (1483–1546) teacher, Gabriel Biel (ca. 1420–95), nominalism exercised an influence on the reformation. Elements of nominalism are found in some forms of modern language philosophy and existentialism. See *Existentialism; Philosophy; Platonism; Reformation; Universals.*

NOMOCANON (Gr. "law" and "rule"). A term used in eastern Christianity for collections of ecclesiastical canons and civil law that affected to the church. The earliest example is attributed to John III, Patriarch of Constantinople (d. 577), called *Scholasticus* (Gr. "lawyer"), because he practiced law as a young man in Antioch. See *Canon Law, Sources of Oriental; Symphony.*

NON-CHALCEDONIAN CHURCHES. Those churches which did not accept the Council of Chalcedon (451). See *Oriental Orthodox.*

NONVIOLENCE. The theory and practice of those who, like Mahatma Gandhi (1869–1948) and Martin Luther King (1929–68), work to remedy political and religious injustice without having recourse to physical attacks on people and straight-out war. Such contemporary, nonviolent movements have drawn on Hindu thought, the endorsement of civil disobedience toward unjust laws by Henry David Thoreau (1817–62) and, above all, Christ's example and teaching—in particular, the beatitudes and the sermon on the mount (Matt 5:1–7:29; see GS 78). See *Beatitudes; Law; Peace; War.*

NOTES OF THE CHURCH. See *Marks of the Church.*

NOUS (Gr. "mind"). Reason or the human faculty of understanding. In what has been called a *"Nous-Logos"* ("Mind-Word") christology Evagrius Ponticus (346–99) proposed that Christ's soul was preexistent and that the mind was the point of union between the eternal Logos and Christ's humanity. See *Christology; Origenism.*

NOVATIANISM. A schism which arose over the treatment of those who lapsed from Christian faith during the persecution (249–50) of Emperor Decius. Novatian, a Roman priest and the author of a thoroughly orthodox work on the Trinity, at first went along with the policy of reconciliation, but later advocated a rigorous treatment of the apostates. The catalyst of this *volte-face* may have been his disappointment over the election in 250 of Pope Cornelius. Novatian had himself consecrated as the rival bishop of Rome, and died a martyr in the persecution (257–58) under Emperor Valerian. His community continued until the fifth century (see DS 109). At the First Council of Nicaea (325) they were mildly condemned for pretending to be *catharoi* (Gr. "pure") and form an all-holy church that excluded sinners (DS 127). Later they were criticized for rebaptizing heretics (DS 183, 211–12, 214; see also 705, 1670). See *Donatism; Penance, Sacrament of; Rigorism; Schism.*

NOVICE (Lat. "new"). A probationary member of a religious institute. Novices live together in a special residence called noviciate, may wear the religious dress of their institute and must follow a course of formation for at least a whole year (see CIC 641–53; 1196) before being admitted to their first vows. See *Monasticism; Religious Life; Vows.*

NUMINOUS (Lat. "appertaining to the deity"). The awe-inspiring divine presence. In *The Idea of the Holy* (German original 1917) Rudolf Otto (1869–1937) argued that religion originates with the numinous experience of the *"mysterium tremendum et fascinans"* (Lat. "the mystery which is both awe-inspiring and fascinating"). See *Experience, Religious; Holiness.*

O

OBEDIENCE. The willingness to comply with laws and commands or accept as true statements coming from authority. Only God has supreme and absolute authority. Human beings (e.g., parents toward their children, the state toward its citizens and church leaders toward believers) share in various, limited degrees in that divine authority. In fulfilling his Father's will, Christ became "obedient unto death" (Phil 2:8; see Heb 5:8), leaving us the perfect example of loving obedience (Jn 15:10). Radically opposed to the disobedience which is sin, faith means obedience to God and the divine commands (Matt 7:21; Rom 1:5; 16:26). Within the church all owe respectful obedience to the pope and bishops—the nature of submission involved being affected by the degree of authority exercised (LG 25, 27). Those who have a vow of religious obedience in religious life owe a particular obedience to their superiors and the rule of their religious institute (PC 14; CIC 573, 590, 598, 601, 618). Diocesan priests owe a special obedience to their bishops (PO 15; CIC 273). See *Authority; Magisterium; Religious Life.*

OBEDIENTIAL POTENCY. See *Potentia Oboedientialis.*

OCCASIONALISM. A philosophy that denies the causal activity of all created things. God is the sole cause of everything that happens; there are no real secondary causes. While anticipated by some Muslim and other medieval thinkers, classical occasionalism emerged as a response to the problem raised by the dualism of René Descartes (1596–1650): How can mind have a causal influence on matter? The occasionalism of Arnold Geulincx (1624–69) and, especially, that of Nicolas Malebranche (1638–1715) simply denied any such causality. Created things, including the human mind, do not act; they simply provide the "occasion" for God's innumerable interventions. In theology, occasionalist trends have at times denied genuine sacramental causality, reducing the sacraments to mere "excuses" for the gift of God's grace. See *Causality; Creation.*

OCTOECHOS (Gr. "eight tones"). Liturgical book used in the Greek church for the offices of propers for the movable cycle from the first Sunday after Pentecost (which in the Greek church is All Saints' Day) to the first Sunday of the pre-Lenten period. It covers what the Latin liturgy calls "the ordinary time" of the year, and is used with the *Triodion* until it is replaced entirely by the latter for Palm Sunday and Holy Week. The name *Octoechos* refers to the eight-scale character of its tones: in the first week after Pentecost, the first tone is used, followed by the second tone in the second week, and so forth. Through this repetition an eight-week cycle of fifty-six propers, one for each weekday in each of the eight tones, is reenacted during most of the liturgical year. Originally used only on Sundays, the *Octoechos* was later extended to include weekdays in what was called the "great *Octoechos*" or *Parakletike.* See *Menaion; Pentecostarion; Triodion.*

OFFICE, THE DIVINE (Lat. "duty," "service"). The Liturgy of the Hours or official prayers (mainly the psalms), used by priests, religious and others (SC 83–101). In this Christian practice, derived from the Jewish custom of praying at fixed hours of the day or night, the church praises God and intercedes for the salvation of the world. The Divine Office was called *"opus Dei"* (Lat. "work of God") by St. Benedict of Nursia (ca. 480–ca. 550). See *Acoemetae; Breviary; Liturgy of the Hours.*

OIKOUMENE OR OIKUMENE (Gr. "the inhabited earth"). The inhabited world or the Roman Empire which was (exaggeratedly) said to correspond to the whole world (see Lk 2:1). Those who spoke of the Mediterranean (Lat. "middle of the world") as the world center saw the countries sharing the Greek culture as the *oikumene* or whole civilized world. Thus "ecumenical" came to mean "universal" in such terms as an "ecumenical council." From the sixth century the Patriarch of Constantinople was called "Ecumenical Patriarch," in the sense of enjoying a primacy for Byzantine Christianity. See *Autocephalous; Councils, Ecumenical; Ecumenism.*

OLD BELIEVERS. Those Russians, especially peasants, who rejected the reforms (mainly liturgical) of Nikon, Patriarch of Moscow (1605–81). Excommunicated in 1667 as *Raskolniki* (= schismatics), they were persecuted by the state, especially under Peter the Great (1672–1725); their leader, archpriest Avvakum, was burnt at the stake (1682). When no bishop joined them, the Old Believers divided into two groups: those who sought to have priests and those who tried to survive without them. In 1846, a deposed bishop, Ambrose of Bosnia, joined them and state recognition followed in 1881. See *Gregorian Calendar.*

OLD CATHOLICS. Catholics who have left the Roman Catholic Church over various issues while retaining much of the same tradition. The most important of them is the German-speaking group which left in protest over the dogmas of the infallibility and the universal jurisdiction of the pope proclaimed at Vatican I in 1870 (DS 3050–75). This group felt encouraged to do so by a Bavarian priest and church historian, Johann Joseph Ignaz von Döllinger (1799–1890). In 1889 the Jansenist Church of Utrecht, which had broken with Rome in 1724, joined the Old Catholics. In 1932 the Old Catholics entered into full communion with the Church of England. See *Infallibility; Jansenism; Jurisdiction; Pope; Vatican Council, First.*

OLD TESTAMENT. Those sacred books accepted by Jews and Christians as inspired and canonical (NA 4). The Jews have a threefold division: a) the Law or the Pentateuch (Genesis, Exodus, Leviticus, Numbers and

Deuteronomy); b) the Prophets, which include most of the historical books plus the major and minor prophets (excluding Daniel); and c) the Writings, which include such books as Psalms, Proverbs, Job and Daniel. The church recognizes some other books like the Wisdom of Solomon and Judith, making an Old Testament of 45 books (or 46 if the Letter of Baruch is counted separately from Jeremiah) that are divided as follows: the Pentateuch, the historical books, the wisdom literature and the prophets. Against Marcion (d. ca. 160) and others, the Church has always held that the OT books are divinely inspired and belong to the canon of scripture. Vatican II underlined the permanent value of the OT scriptures (DV 11, 14–15), which record and interpret the history of preparation for the coming of Christ and his church (DV 16; LG 2, 6; SC 5). See *Bible; Canon of Scripture; Inspiration; Marcionism; New Testament.*

OMEGA POINT (Gr. last letter of the alphabet). The final goal (see Rev 1:8; 21:6; 22:13) of the evolving and converging universe in the thought of Pierre Teilhard de Chardin, a French Jesuit and paleontologist (1881–1955). Synthesizing Christian faith with the data of science in his *Phenomenology of Man, Le Milieu Divin* and other (posthumous) works, he pictured a world of growing complexity being progressively humanized and "christified" or evolving toward its culmination in the cosmic Christ (see 1 Cor 15:28; Eph 1:3–10; Col 1:15–20). See *Christocentrism; Entelechy; Eschatology; Parousia.*

OMNIPOTENCE (Lat. "being all-powerful"). The divine attribute of being infinitely powerful (2 Cor 6:18; Rev 1:8; 4:8). In the creeds omnipotence is usually "appropriated" or assigned to God the Father, but the other persons of the Trinity are also confessed to be omnipotent (see DS 29, 75, 164, 169, 173, 441 and 449). The mystery of evil has often been invoked as an objection against the existence of a God who is all-powerful, all-good and all-wise. Omnipotence does not mean that God can do what is logically impossible (e.g., make a square circle) or do what is opposed to other divine attributes. See *Albigensianism; Appropriation; Attributes, Divine; Dualism; Evil, Mystery of; Pantocrator; Theodicy.*

OMNIPRESENCE (Lat. "presence everywhere"). The divine attribute of being present everywhere (Ps 139:7–12; Acts 17:24–28). While present everywhere as the creative source of all things, God is present in various other ways: e.g., through human persons, the Bible, community worship and the sacraments (SC 7). See *Creation; Pantheism; Transubstantiation.*

ONTOLOGICAL ARGUMENT. A way of "demonstrating" God's existence developed by St. Anselm of Canterbury (ca. 1033–1109). Since what we mean by "God" is *id quo nihil majus cogitari possit* (Lat. "that than which nothing greater can be conceived"), the very idea of God demands the objective existence of God. Otherwise we would be involved in a contradiction, being able to imagine something greater than "God"—namely, a God who exists. St. Thomas Aquinas (ca. 1225–74), Immanuel Kant (1724–1804) and others have rejected the argument for moving fallaciously from the level of mere thought to that of actual existence. Other philosophers, however, in various ways have defended the argument: René Descartes (1596–1650), Baruch Spinoza (1632–77), Gottfried Wilhelm Leibniz (1646–1716) and Georg Wilhelm Friedrich Hegel (1770–1831). More recently some have claimed that, instead of being a "proof," the ontological argument simply explicates the implicit knowledge of God we already possess. See *Five Ways, The; Ontologism.*

ONTOLOGISM. A nineteenth-century epistemology endorsed by many Catholic thinkers in Belgium, France and Italy which argued that we have an immediate, innate knowledge of God. The term was first used in *Introduction to the Study of Philosophy* (1840) by Vincenzo Gioberti (1801–52), who was followed by Antonio Rosmini-Serbati (1799–1855). With some justification the ontologists claimed to stand in the line of Plato (427–347 B.C.), St. Augustine of Hippo (354–430), St. Anselm of Canterbury (ca. 1033–1109) and St. Bonaventure (1221–74). Nevertheless, they dealt inadequately with the role of sense-perception and the limited nature of our knowledge of God in this life (see Jn 1:18; 1 Jn 3:2). In 1861, the Vatican condemned several propositions from ontologism as ambiguous (see DS 2841–47). In arguing that some prior presence of God in our knowledge is the logical condition for any further knowing, transcendental Thomists like Bernard Lonergan (1904–84) and Karl Rahner (1904–84) have preserved, in a modified form, a central insight from ontologism. See *Augustinianism; Beatific Vision; Epistemology; Ontological Argument.*

ONTOLOGY (Gr. "study of being"). The study of the necessary truths of beings as existent beings. Brought into common use by Christian Wolff (1679–1754), "ontology" is often synonymous with "metaphysics." See *Causality; Metaphysics; Philosophy.*

OPTION FOR THE POOR. A policy for church life popularized by the theologians of liberation and urging Christians to work in a special way to effect social justice for those many millions who are deprived of proper food, housing, medical services, education, employment and other basic human rights. This has been a theme of the Latin American bishops since their Second General Council held at Medellin in 1968. In his 1987 encyclical, *Sollicitudo Rei Socialis,* John Paul II called for a solidarity with and preferential love for the poor that would be expressed in

163

concrete activity at the local level (42, 43, 47). This special concern for the exploited, defenseless, and marginalized draws its inspiration from the OT prophets (e.g., Isa 1:10–20) and from the message and practice of Jesus (Lk 6:20; 16:19–31; 17:11–19). In both the OT and the NT God is revealed as having a preferential, although not exclusive, love for the poor. In a special way God's presence and activity are revealed in the poor. The Second Vatican Council called on all Christians, especially those of rich nations, to exercise greater justice and love in promoting the cause of the poor (GS 69, 88). See *Anawim; Beatitudes; Liberation Theology; Poverty; Social Teaching.*

ORDINARY. The bishop of a diocese (= the "local ordinary"), his vicar general and episcopal vicars that he may also appoint, all of whom exercise normal jurisdiction in the diocese and have the chief responsibility for this particular church (CIC 134, 368). In the case of institutes of clerical religious, the major superiors (e.g., the provincial or head of a province) exercise "ordinary" jurisdiction over those under their charge. See *Bishop; Clergy; Cleric; Diocese; Jurisdiction; Local Church.*

ORDINATION. The liturgical ceremony through which candidates become deacons, presbyters (priests) or bishops. At the end of the liturgy of the word and before the liturgy of the eucharist begins, the sacrament is conferred by the imposition of hands and the recital of the prescribed formula. Following ordination the deacon is vested with the stole and the priest with the chasuble. Both are presented with a book of gospels, while the priest receives as well the chalice and paten. After ordination the bishop receives his ring, mitre and crozier or pastoral staff, and is seated on his throne as the symbol of his teaching authority. See *Bishop; Deacon; Enthronement; Holy Orders; Presbyter; Priests.*

ORIENTAL ORTHODOX. A modern term for those eastern churches which rejected the Council of Chalcedon (451) as betraying St. Cyril of Alexandria (d. 444) and capitulating to a Nestorian *dyophysism* (Gr. "two natures"). These churches accept the first three ecumenical councils— unlike the eastern Orthodox who accept the first seven. Whereas the eastern Orthodox autocephalous churches recognize the Patriarch of Constantinople as a symbol of unity, the Oriental Orthodox autocephalous churches have no such point of unity. See *Autocephalous; Chalcedon, Council of; Constantinople, First Council of; Eastern Churches; Ephesus, Council of; Monophysitism; Nestorianism; Nicaea, First Council of; Seven Ecumenical Councils, The.*

ORIGENISM. The doctrines and school of thought inspired by Origen of Alexandria (ca. 185–ca. 254). He developed a biblical hermeneutic in terms of the literal, moral and allegorical senses of scripture. As the first great systematic theologian of Christianity, he stressed images (with sensible reality symbolizing the invisible spiritual world) and our deification through grace. His liking for allegory and, much more, his theses about the ultimate salvation of all (= *apocatastasis*), the preexistence of human souls (including Christ's) and an apparent subordination of the Son to the Father met with repeated criticism and opposition. Eventually Emperor Justinian II had Origenism condemned at a synod in 543 and then at the Second Council of Constantinople in 553 (see DS 298, 353, 403–11, 433, 519). Nevertheless, it is still not clear how far Origen himself was at fault, how far he was simply exploring a variety of views and how far false views were ascribed to him after his death. It is difficult to decide, since his works were to a large extent destroyed. Any fair judgment on Origen should also take into account such fathers of the church who greatly admired him as St. Athanasius of Alexandria (ca. 296–373), St. Basil the Great (ca. 330–79) and St. Gregory of Nazianzus (329–89). See *Alexandrian Theology; Allegory; Apocatastasis; Exegesis; Hermeneutics; Platonism; Senses of Scripture.*

ORIGINAL JUSTICE. The graced state of the first human beings before they fell into sin. Interpreted for centuries as an historical period of time, this original righteousness is better understood to be a way of speaking of our goodness as created and sanctified by God (Gen 1:26–31). Up to recent times theologians elaborated on a whole range of "preternatural" or special gifts which Adam and Eve were supposed to have received. See *Adam; Concupiscence; Eve; Fall, The; Grace; Original Sin; Preternatural Gifts.*

ORIGINAL SIN. Traditionally understood as the loss of grace and wounding of nature suffered by our first parents, which affected all later generations, the notion was developed on the basis of scripture (above all, Gen 3:1–24; Ps 51:7 and Rom 5:12–21) and the ancient practice of baptizing infants for the forgiveness of sins. St. Augustine of Hippo (354–430) argued against the Pelagians that, since infants are not able to commit personal sins, the "sin" from which they are delivered in baptism must be an inherited sinfulness. The doctrine of original sin (DS 496, 621, 1510–16) expresses not only the sinful condition into which all human beings are born, but also the fact that the new life of grace coming through baptism is no "natural" right but the free gift of God. Thus original sin refers to our human solidarity in sin and common call to the supernatural life in Christ. Eastern Christianity, while maintaining infant baptism, has developed no theology of original sin. Protestants have often over-stressed original sin and its evil effects. See *Concupi-*

scence; Depravity, Total; Fall, The; Immaculate Conception; Infant Baptism; Lutheranism; Natural Theology; Pelagianism; Supernatural.

ORTHODOXY (Gr. "right belief"). Belief and teaching recognized by the church as truly based on the divine self-revelation in Jesus Christ. The OT used various criteria to distinguish between true and false prophets (Deut 13:1–7; 18:21–22; Jer 23:9–40; 28:9, 15–17; see Matt 7:15–20). His letters show St. Paul deeply concerned to maintain the genuine revelation and doctrine he and others have transmitted (Rom 16:17; 1 Cor 11:2; 15:1–11; Gal 1:6–9). Later books of the NT reflect a similar commitment to a teaching that is sound and faithful to the original revelation (1 Tim 1:3–11; 6:2–5; 2 Tim 1:13–14; 4:3; Titus 1:9; 2:1; Jude 3). "Orthodoxy" entered the church's terminological repertoire during the great christological and Trinitarian controversies of the third, fourth and fifth centuries. In the east it came to be used of the churches united to Constantinople and Rome, as opposed to the dissident Nestorian and Monophysite churches. When the crisis of iconoclasm finally ended in 842, a Feast of Orthodoxy was established in the east for the first Sunday of Lent. In the *Synodikon,* or summary of synods which is read on that day, a litany of orthodox teachers and saints is contrasted with a list of anathematized heretics. The popular etymology linking "orthodoxy" with "right worship" indicates how the liturgy guarantees the truth and vitality of teaching in the eastern churches. See *Creed; Deposit of Faith; Dogma; Eastern Churches; Heresy; Heterodox; Iconoclasm; Monophysitism; Nestorianism; Oriental Orthodox Churches; Tradition.*

ORTHODOXY, OLD PROTESTANT. That fidelity to Christian beliefs that are derived from scripture and the early church which was championed by the mainline churches of the reformation in the sixteenth and seventeenth centuries. See *Calvinism; Lutheranism; Neo-Orthodoxy; Protestant; Reformation.*

ORTHOPRAXIS (Gr. "right conduct"). Self-critical activity which aims to "do the truth" (Jn 3:21; see Gal 5:6), practice Christian discipleship and transform human society. From the early 1960's this term was popularized by Johann Baptist Metz (b. 1928), Nikos Nissiotis (d. 1986), the World Council of Churches and liberation theology. Orthopraxis draws its inspiration from Jesus' preaching of the kingdom and his praxis, which led to his death. Orthopraxis leads to and is nurtured by prayer and public worship. Authentic orthopraxis lends credibility to orthodoxy, while true orthodoxy is manifested in orthopraxis. On the one hand, a purely formal orthodoxy is no better than verbal conformity to a set of doctrinal statements. On the other hand, a one-sided emphasis on orthopraxis can deteriorate into mere activism divorced from Christian faith and worship. See *Basic Communities; Black Theology; Feminist Theology; Frankfurt School; Liberation Theology; Orthodoxy; Pluralism; Political Theology; Praxis.*

OUSIA (Gr. "substance," "essence"). The term used at Nicaea I (325) for one divine nature shared by God the Father and the Son (DS 125–126). Constantinople I (381) taught the divinity of the Holy Spirit (DS 150–51). That all three divine persons share the same "ousia" was made explicit at Constantinople III (553) (DS 421). In Latin, *ousia* is translated not only by *"essentia"* ("essence") but also by *"substantia"* ("substance"), a term which is too easily associated with a Greek word for "person" (*"hypostasis"*). See *Constantinople, First Council of; Constantinople, Second Council of; Constantinople, Third Council of; Homoousios; Hypostasis; Nicaea, First Council of; Person.*

OXFORD MOVEMENT. An Anglican movement (1833–45) centered on Oxford University, led by John Keble (1792–1866), John Henry (later Cardinal) Newman (1801–90) and Edward Bouverie Pusey (1800–82) and forming the first period of Anglo-Catholicism. Inspired by the High Church (rather than the Low Church or Evangelical) tradition, it aimed to reform Anglicanism, stressed the apostolic and sacramental character of the church and her priesthood, resisted the inroads of Liberalism, promoted a Catholic tradition of worship, worked for the poor, and encouraged the formation of male and female communities of religious. To further its cause the Oxford Movement produced *Tracts for the Times* (1833–41), Newman's *Tract 90* (1841) rousing much debate by its pro-Catholic tendency. From 1836, Keble, Newman and Pusey started publishing the *Library of the Fathers*, a series that revealed the inspiration they found in a return to the fathers of the church. Keble's sermon on "National Apostasy" (1833) marked the start of the movement. Its end is generally considered to be Newman's entry into the Catholic Church (1845). See *Anglican Communion; Anglo-Catholicism; Evangelicals; Fathers of the Church; Liberalism; Religious Life.*

P

PAGANS (Lat. "country dwellers"). A term initially used for those in the Roman Empire who lived out in country villages and, being evangelized after the urban population, became Christians later. In the OT the *goyim* (Heb. "nations") or Gentiles were those who did not acknowledge the one true God (Deut 7:1; Ps 147:20). While denouncing their idolatry, the OT also witnessed to God's saving concern for the pagans (Isa 2:1–4;

49:6; 60:1–3; Amos 9:7; Jonah). Abraham was called to mediate divine blessings to the whole human race (Gen 12:1–3). The OT introduces such "holy pagans" as Melchisedek, the Queen of Sheba, Job and Ruth. St. Paul proclaims God's desire to justify both Jews and Gentiles (Rom 3:29; 9:24; 15:8–12; see Luke 2:29–32). The followers of some non-Christian religions have been called (in a derogatory sense) "pagans" or "heathens." Superstitions still found among those converted to Christianity have been labelled "pagan." The Second Vatican Council avoided altogether the terms "pagan" and "paganism," speaking rather of the "nations (*gentes*)" to be evangelized. See *Animism; Anonymous Christians; Evangelization; Idolatry; Polytheism.*

PALAMISM. The theological synthesis of Gregory Palamas (1296–1359), a monk of Mount Athos and a defender of the method of prayer called hesychasm, practised on the Holy Mountain. Palamas is a saint of the Greek Orthodox Church and is considered the greatest Byzantine theologian of medieval times. To maintain that human beings genuinely become like God through deification without jeopardizing God's transcendence, he distinguished between the inaccessible divine essence and the energies through which God becomes known to us and makes us share in the divine life. After a controversy with Barlaam (ca. 1290–1348), a monk from Calabria and an expert on Pseudo-Dionysius (fifth century), a synod held in Constantinople (June 1341) censured Barlaam, but another synod (August 1341) imposed silence on both. In 1344, Palamas was even excommunicated for heresy. In 1347, however, a synod in Constantinople upheld his orthodoxy and he was consecrated Archbishop of Thessalonica. But he had to cope with criticisms coming from the monk Gregorios Akindynos (ca. 1300–49), a one-time friend turned enemy. A third attack came from the humanist philosopher Nikephoros Gregorios (ca. 1294–ca. 1359). A synod held in Constantinople in 1351 condemned Gregorios Akindynos posthumously and silenced Nikephoros Gregorios, while recognizing the full orthodoxy of Palamas. In 1368, nine years after his death, Palamas was canonized. His feast is celebrated both on the second Sunday in Lent and on November 14. See *Athos, Mount; Deification; Essence and Energies; Hesychasm; Neo-Palamism.*

PALLIUM (Lat. "cloak"). A circular band of white wool adorned with six violet crosses and supporting two strips. As a symbol of his apostolic authority, it is worn by the pope, who since early times has granted it to archbishops as a sign of communion and to certain bishops as a sign of honor. Nowadays, within three months of his appointment a metropolitan (= archbishop) must ask for the pallium, and should request a new pallium if subsequently transferred to another metropolitan diocese. He wears it within his ecclesiastical province and then only on occasions prescribed by the liturgy. During the liturgy in the eastern church, bishops wear an *omophorion,* an embroidered scarf that corresponds to the pallium. See *Archbishop; Metropolitan; Pope.*

PANENTHEISM (Gr. "everything in God"). A system developed in various ways by such philosophers as Christian Kranse (1781–1832), Friedrich Heinrich Jacobi (1743–1819) and Charles Hartshorne (b. 1897) according to which God so penetrates the universe that everything is in God. Unlike pantheism which holds that the universe and God are so identical that everything is God, panentheism maintains that, while including the universe, God's being goes beyond it. See *Pantheism; Process Theology; Theism.*

PANORTHODOX CONFERENCES (Gr. "all Orthodox"). A movement aimed at fostering unity of action within the various autocephalous churches which make up the Orthodox Church and at promoting relations with other churches. The first Panorthodox consultation took place in Constantinople in 1923. The second, which met on Mount Athos in 1930, discussed the agenda for a future Panorthodox pre-council which was to prepare for a Holy and Great Panorthodox Council. The first Panorthodox Conference was held in 1961; the second on the island of Rhodes in 1963 discussed sending observers to Vatican II; the third took place on Rhodes in 1964 and officially expressed commitment to dialogue with the Roman Catholic Church. The fourth met in 1968 at Chambésy, near Geneva, and it was decided to open there a secretariat to prepare for a future Great Council and revise its agenda. Themes like marriage impediments, calendar reform, fasting and the position of Orthodox churches outside their traditional territories figured prominently. A preparatory meeting took place in 1971 at Chambésy. This led to three Panorthodox preconciliar conferences (in 1976, 1982 and 1986) held at the same place for discussion in depth of these themes and also of the ecumenical relations with other churches. See *Dialogue; Ecumenism; Eastern Churches; Vatican Council, Second.*

PANTHEISM (Gr. "all [is] God"). Doctrine which identifies God with the universe. Although the word appears for the first time in 1709, pantheistic systems of thought are at least as old as Hinduism. Some interpret the divine in natural terms (*naturalistic pantheism*), as does Benedict Spinoza (1632–77); others interpret nature in divine terms (*emanationistic pantheism*), a temptation for mystical and Neoplatonic thinkers. Dionysius the Pseudo-Areopagite (ca. 500), John Scotus Erigena (ca. 810–ca. 877), Cardinal Nicholas of Cusa (1401–64), Meister Eckhart (ca. 1260–1327), Giordano Bruno (1548–1600) and Jacob Boehme (1575–

1624) have all been accused, justly or unjustly, of including elements of pantheism in their thought. A modern form of pantheism interprets God as the big "I," a view at least closely approached by such idealists as Georg Wilhelm Friedrich Hegel (1770–1831), Friedrich Wilhelm Joseph von Schelling (1775–1854) and Francis Herbert Bradley (1846–1924). While often described as a form of atheism, pantheism can also be seen as a form of imprisoned theism. The First Vatican Council condemned pantheism (DS 3023; see also DS 285, 722, 976–77, 1043, 2843, 2901, 3201–3216. See *Atheism; Emanation; Hinduism; Idealism; Immanence; Monism; Nature; Neoplatonism; Panentheism; Theism; Transcendence.*

PANTOCRATOR (Gr. "ruler of all"). A majestic representation of Christ as sovereign ruler of the universe, usually with his hands raised in blessing. Two famous examples are those in the Church of the Apostles in Constantinople and in St. Sophia in Kiev. See *Icon; Kingdom of God; Omnipotence; Theocracy.*

PAPALISM. An attitude toward church teaching and life which exaggerates the Petrine ministry of the pope, while ignoring the role of other bishops and what can be learned from the whole People of God. See *Collegiality; Petrine Ministry; Pope; Sensus Fidelium; Ultramontanism.*

PARABLE (Gr. "comparison"). A comparison drawn from nature (e.g., the mustard seed in Mark 4:30–32) or from human life (e.g., the marriage feast in Matt 22:1–14) and told as a story to embody and evoke some moral or religious insight. While already found in the OT (2 Sam 12:1–14; and perhaps Isa 5:1–7), parables characterize in a special way the preaching and teaching of Jesus. The synoptic gospels report many parables used by Jesus in challenging his hearers to recognize God's final rule and decide accordingly. Strictly speaking, John's gospel contains no parables, although the language about the good shepherd (Jn 10:1–19) and the vine and the branches (Jn 15:1–8) show clear parabolic elements. Adolf Jülicher (1857–1938), Charles Harold Dodd (1884–1973), and Joachim Jeremias (1900–1979) have enriched our understanding of Jesus' parables. They are not, for example, allegories in which every detail carries an intended meaning. Parables convey one point, although long parables (e.g., the Prodigal Son [better called the Merciful Father] in Luke 15:11–32) can also yield meaning through their subordinate details. See *Allegory; Exegesis; Biblical Criticism; Hermeneutics; Senses of Scripture.*

PARACLESIS (Gr. "supplication"). The little office of Our Lady used in the Byzantine rite for fifteen days immediately preceding the feast of the *koimesis* or dormition of the Mother of God (celebrated on August 15). See *Assumption of the Blessed Virgin; Liturgy of the Hours.*

PARACLETE (Gr. "helper" or "attorney"). A term used of Jesus himself who intercedes with the Father on behalf of sinners (1 Jn 2:1–2). In St. John's gospel, the word is applied to the Holy Spirit as the Helper (14:16; 14:26; 15:26; 16:7), the Spirit of truth who will be sent to dwell in the disciples and guide them by witnessing to Jesus and his teaching. See *Holy Spirit.*

PARADISE (Persian "enclosed garden"). A walled park containing exotic plants, trees and animals and attached to a palace. In the Septuagint (LXX) this is the "garden of Eden," where Adam and Eve once lived and from which they were expelled after falling into sin (Gen 2:8–10, 15; 3:23–24; Ezek 28:13; 31:8; 36:35). "Paradise" came to designate the place of blessedness after death (Lk 23:43), the "third heaven" above the earth to which St. Paul was once carried in ecstasy (2 Cor 12:2–4). Revelation promises life in God's "paradise," where the blessed will eat from "the tree of life" (Rev 2:7; 22:1–2, 14). See *Eschatology; Heaven; Septuagint.*

PARADOSIS (Gr. "handing on, tradition"). In the NT some tradition handed on within a community. It can be a question of Jewish religious traditions (Gal 1:14), even wrong-headed and reformable ones (Mk 7:1–13). *Paradosis* can be generic Christian teaching that is handed on (2 Thess 3:6), or else specific traditions of great importance (1 Cor 11:2, 23; 15:3–5). See *Bible; Tradition.*

PARENESIS (Gr. "exhortation, advice"). Preaching aimed at building up community by practical recommendations or warnings. St. Paul "advises" the crew of a storm-battered ship on its way to Malta (Acts 27:9, 22), while he, St. Peter and St. Barnabas "exhort" different audiences (Acts 2:40; 11:23; 14:22). Parenetical passages turn up in the Pauline letters (see Rom 6:1–4; 1 Cor 5:7f; Col 3:1–4), sometimes as lists of virtuous actions (e.g., Rom 12:1–21) or of vices (Rom 13:13). The parenesis can be rather general (as is the case toward the end of most Pauline letters), or can be aimed at particular problems (1 Cor 11:17–22, 27–34). See *Moral Theology.*

PARISH (Gr. "neighborhood"). A subdivision of a diocese which has its own priest, and enjoys a certain degree of autonomy under the jurisdiction of the local bishop (see CIC 374, 515). Since a bishop cannot preside everywhere in his diocese, he appoints parish priests and sets up parishes (SC 42; CD 32). There people are incorporated into the church through baptism (CIC 858), the young receive religious education, mission work takes place (AA 10; AG 37) and care is given to the sick, the needy and the aged. The center of parish life is the celebration of the eucharist and the proclamation of the word of God (see CD 30). See *Bishop; Chaplain; Diocese; Ordinary; Pastor.*

PAROUSIA (Gr. "presence," "arrival"). The official visit of a ruler. From the earliest Christian documents (1 Thess 4:15; 1 Cor 15:23) the *parousia* designated the return of Christ in glory at the end of history to judge the world (Matt 24:29–31; 25:31–46). This will be "the day of the Lord" (1 Cor 1:8) when Christ "will appear a second time" (Heb 9:28)—an appearance for which Christians wait with patience (Jas 5:7, 8; 2 Pet 1:16; 3:4, 12; 1 Jn 2:28). The synoptics link the expectation of the end with a warning to keep on the watch (Matt 24:36–25:13; Mk 13:1–37; Lk 21:5–36). John's gospel speaks of the resurrection to come on the "last day" (Jn 6:39, 40, 44, 54; 11:24). Christ's future coming in glory to judge the living and the dead is confessed by various creeds (see DS 6, 10, 13–17, 19, 76 and 150). More than western Christianity, the east highlights the collective dimension of that future consummation. Some modern theologians prefer not to speak of the "second" coming, since the *parousia* is only the ultimate consequence of Christ's first coming in the incarnation. With Karl Rahner (1904–84) we might say that it is the world which will come to God in the *parousia* rather than Christ to the world. See *Eschatology; Heaven; Hell; Last Judgment; Resurrection.*

PARRHESIA (Gr. "boldness in speaking"). The fearless openness with which the apostles publicly proclaimed the message of the crucified and risen Christ despite imprisonment and the threat of punishment and death (see Acts 2:29; 4:13, 29, 31; 28:31). Paul shows this frankness in dealing with his communities (2 Cor 7:4). Christians should have a similar boldness as they relate to God (see 1 Jn 3:21; 5:14) and wait for the day of judgment (1 Jn 2:28; 4:17). Christian *parrhesia* finds its model in the way Jesus openly proclaimed his message to a hostile world (Jn 7:26; 18:20). See *Virtues, Cardinal.*

PARTHENOGENESIS (Gr. "virgin birth"). The generation of a child without the intervention of a human father. It has sometimes been alleged that the story of Jesus' conception was derived from pagan legends about women producing remarkable children through the intervention of male gods. But such legends are quite different from the account of the virginal conception found in the infancy narratives of Matthew and Luke. See *Virginal Conception of Jesus.*

PASCH (Gr. "passover"). A term previously used for the Passover of the Jews and the Christian Easter. See *Easter; Passover.*

PASCHAL MYSTERY. The redemption effected by Christ above all through his death, resurrection and ascension (SC 5; GS 22) in which Christians participate through baptism, the eucharist, the other sacraments and their whole life (SC 6–10; see Rom 6:3–4; 12:1; 1 Cor 11:23–26). See *Easter; Redemption; Resurrection.*

PASSION (Lat. "suffering"). In Aristotelian philosophy, as applied to a contingent being and contrasted with action, passion means being changed. In Christian terminology, the passion refers to the suffering and crucifixion Jesus endured for our salvation (see 1 Pet 2:21–25). All four gospels end with a detailed account of his passion (Matt 26–27; Mk 14–15; Lk 22–23; Jn 18–19). On Palm Sunday the story of the passion is read from one of the synoptics, and on Good Friday from the gospel of John. See *Atonement; Holy Week; Redemption; Salvation.*

PASSOVER. The Jewish family feast celebrated in the spring at the time of the full moon and commemorating the exodus from Egypt (Exod 12:1–28; Deut 16:1–8). On the afternoon of Nisan 14 the paschal lambs were sacrificed; that evening at the Passover meal unleavened bread was eaten with roast lambs. Whether it was a Passover meal (the synoptic gospels) or not (John), the last supper, followed by Jesus' crucifixion and resurrection, coincided with the Passover and its associated week-long feast of unleavened bread (Mk 14:1–2, 12–16). Hence, Christians quickly understood Jesus' dying and rising to have fulfilled the original exodus and its commemoration in the Passover festival. He was seen as *the* paschal lamb whose sacrifice of deliverance took away the sin of the world (Jn 1:29; 1 Cor 5:7). See *Easter; Holy Week; Pasch; Resurrection.*

PASTOR (Lat. "shepherd"). Term used of rulers in the OT (Jer 2:8; 3:15) and of God as the good shepherd (Ezek 34:1–31; Ps 23:1–4). Christ was sent to the lost sheep of Israel (Matt 10:6; 15:24; see Lk 15:3–7). As the good shepherd he lays down his life for the sheep (Jn 10:11–16; see Heb 13:20; 1 Pet 2:25). He calls others to be pastors in the church, but the people remain his sheep (Jn 21:15–17; 1 Pet 5:1–4). Among Protestants the ordained minister serving a local church is often called "pastor," as is the case with Catholics in certain parts of Germany (see CIC 519). See *Bishop; Ministers; Parish; People of God; Priest.*

PASTORAL OFFICE. The ministry of clergy, as pastors serving the People of God. The term may be applied to those whom the bishop has put in charge of particular ministries like religious education and family welfare. See *Clergy; Jurisdiction; Laity; Ministry.*

PASTORAL THEOLOGY. Theology inasmuch as it is concerned with and

173

reflects on (a) the passage to preaching and catechetics from the study of scripture and systematic theology, (b) the practice of liturgical and sacramental life, (c) moral and spiritual counselling, (d) the care of people facing special problems (e.g., refugees, drug addicts, the sick, the very old and the dying), (e) struggles for justice and peace and (f) the care of people of different ages and in different life-situations. Many see pastoral theology as synonymous with practical theology or critical reflection on the church's manifold mission in the world. Over the centuries outstanding contributions to pastoral theology have come from such figures as St. Gregory the Great (ca. 540–604) and Karl Rahner (1904–84). See *Catechesis; Evangelization; Homiletics; Ministry; Mission, Theology of; Pastoral Office; Theology.*

PATRIARCH (Gr. "father who rules"). Name given to Abraham, Isaac, Jacob, the twelve sons of Jacob, and David (Gen 12–50; Acts 2:29; 7:8–9; Heb 7:4). From the sixth century onward the title was given to the bishops of Rome, Constantinople, Alexandria, Antioch and Jerusalem. These patriarchs exercised wide authority in such ways as appointing bishops to major dioceses and judging appeals to their jurisdiction. The First Council of Nicaea (325) recognized this role of Rome and acknowledged Alexandria to take precedence over Antioch. The First Council of Constantinople (381) gave Constantinople a "primacy of honor after Rome, because it is a second Rome" (canon 3) which the Council of Chalcedon (451) in its twenty-eighth canon (that Pope Leo I never approved) extended to make Constantinople second only to Rome in jurisdiction. The Fourth Council of Constantinople (869–70), usually considered by Catholics to be the eighth ecumenical council, recognized the primacy of Rome and listed the patriarchates in this order of dignity: Rome, Constantinople, Alexandria, Antioch and Jerusalem (recognized as a patriarchate at the Council of Chalcedon) (see DS 661). The Fourth Lateran Council (1215) and the Council of Florence (1438–45) repeated that same list of patriarchates and in the same order (DS 811; 1307–08). In the case of those eastern churches united with Rome, the Second Vatican Council recognized their traditions, rights, privileges and jurisdiction (OE 7–10). It indicated that, where necessary, an ecumenical council or the pope could set up new patriarchates (OE 11)—a suggestion made by many theologians for future unions between sister churches and Rome. Vatican II also proposed general guidelines toward a reunion with the eastern churches separated from Rome (UR 13–18), among which "the Patriarchal Churches hold first place" (UR 14). See *Autocephalous; Eastern Churches; Orthodoxy; Primacy; Orthodox, Eastern; Orthodox, Oriental; Pentarchy.*

PATRIARCH, ECUMENICAL (Gr. "universal patriarch"). A title used by the Patriarchs of Constantinople since the sixth century. See *Oikoumene; Primacy.*

PATRIPASSIANISM (Lat. "suffering of the Father"). A term coined by Tertullian (ca. 160–ca. 220) for that form of Monarchianism which we call Modalism, in his campaign against Praxeas (lived ca. 200) whom he mocked as having driven out the Spirit and crucified the Father. Another Modalist, Noetus (lived ca. 200) asserted that it was the Father who had been born and had suffered on the cross. See *Monarchianism; Modalism; Suffering of God.*

PATRISTICS (Lat. "study of the Fathers"). The study of the theology of the church fathers. The term has often been used inaccurately as a synonym for patrology. See *Fathers of the Church; Patrology.*

PATROLOGY (Gr. "study of the Fathers"). A term coined in the seventeenth century for the study of the fathers of the church. A 1989 instruction on the study of the fathers (issued by the Vatican's Congregation for Catholic Education) distinguishes "patrology" as the historical and literary study of the fathers from "patristics," the study of their theological thought. See *Fathers of the Church; Patristics.*

PAULINE PRIVILEGE. The right to remarry of persons who are already married, convert to Christianity and find that their non-Christian marriage partners either wish to separate or will not let them practice their religion in peace (CIC 1143). St. Paul first laid down this privilege (1 Cor 7:12–15). See *Marriage; Marriage Impediments.*

PAULINE THEOLOGY. The theology developed by St. Paul (d. ca. 67), whose call/conversion around 34 (1 Cor 9:1; 15:8–11; Acts 9:3–9) changed him from a zealous Pharisee (Phil 3:5–8; Acts 22:3–5) persecuting Christians (1 Cor 15:9; Gal 1:13–14; Acts 7:58–8:3; 9:1–2) to the great apostle of the Gentiles (Gal 1:12; 15–16; 2:7; Acts 9:15). Radically centered on the resurrection of the crucified Jesus (Rom 4:25; 1 Cor 1:17–25; 15:14–15; Phil 2:6–11), Paul taught that our justification comes by faith and Christ's reconciling grace (Rom 5:6–11) and not through the works of the law (Gal 2:16–4:31). By baptism believers exist "in" Christ (Rom 8:1; 16:7; 1 Cor 15:22; Phil 3:8–9) and through the Holy Spirit live a new life (Rom 5:1–8:39), being progressively changed into the image of Christ (Rom 8:29) and forming together the Temple of the Spirit (1 Cor 3:16–17) and the body of Christ (1 Cor 12:12–27). In the new "Israel of God" (Gal 6:16) all the baptized enjoy a basic unity (Gal 3:26–28), and are called to use their different charisms (1 Cor 12:1–31) to build up the community in love (Rom 5:5; 1 Cor 12:31–13:13) and show in their lives the fruits of the Spirit (Gal 5:16–26). Along with Johannine theology Pauline theology is the primary NT theology and has had the greatest influence in the history of Christianity. See *Appearances of the Risen Lord; Body of Christ; Charism; Grace; Holy Spirit; Justification; Law.*

PEACE. Called by St. Augustine of Hippo (354–430) "the tranquility of order." For both the OT and NT peace is more than freedom from war (see Isa 2:4; Mic 4:3; Mk 9:50; Lk 14:34). *Shalom* (Heb. "health," "peace") is the comprehensive welfare given through union with God— in particular, the saving peace associated with the messianic age (Isa 9:1–7; 11:1–9; 32:15–20). Jesus blessed the peace-makers (Matt 5:9). Risen from the dead he brought that peace "the world cannot give" (Jn 14:27; 20:19, 21; Col 3:15), which entails a new solidarity (Gal 3:28; Eph 2:13–18) effected by his death and resurrection (Col 1:20). His followers are to proclaim peace, the message of eschatological salvation (Acts 10:36; Rom 10:15; see Matt 10:12–13). In his 1963 encyclical *Pacem in Terris* (Lat. "Peace on Earth") Pope John XXIII placed his hopes for international peace in a social order based on freedom, justice, love and truth. Pope Paul VI's 1967 encyclical *Populorum Progressio* (Lat. "Development of the Peoples") called development "the new name for peace" (14). The Second Vatican Council pleaded for greater effort in fostering peace and community among the nations (GS 77–90). Through its Peace and Justice Commission and in many other ways the Holy See has constantly tried to promote international peace. In the USA the National Conference of Catholic Bishops has spoken out prophetically in its *The Challenge of Peace: God's Promise and Our Response* (1983). But in this world "peace comes dropping slow" (William Butler Yeats [1865–1939]). See *Justice; Just War Theory; Kingdom of God; Messiah; Non-Violence; Salvation; Tolerance.*

PELAGIANISM. A heresy concerning grace initiated by Pelagius (lived ca. 400), a monk from Britain or Ireland, who, first in Rome and then in North Africa, taught that human beings can achieve salvation through their own sustained efforts. Original sin amounted to no more than Adam's bad example which did not harm interiorly his descendants and, in particular, left intact the natural use of free will. Reducing grace to the good example provided by Christ, Pelagius encouraged a strongly ascetical life and the emergence of a Church for the morally elite. Strongly opposed by St Augustine of Hippo (354–430), Pelagianism was condemned by various councils in North Africa (DS 222–30), by two popes and in 431 by the Council of Ephesus (DS 267–68). See *Augustinianism; Messalianism; Original Sin; Semi-Pelagianism.*

PENANCE, SACRAMENT OF. One of the seven sacraments instituted by

Christ for the forgiveness of sins after baptism. This sacrament answers a deep need to confess sin, receive pardon from God and be reconciled with the community harmed by our sins (2 Sam 12:1–25; Ps 51; Mk 1:4–5; Lk 7:36–50; 15:11–32; 18:9–14). That reconciling role is suggested by some words from St. Augustine of Hippo (354–430): *"pax cum ecclesia dimittit peccata"* (Lat. "it is peace with the church which forgives sins") (see PO 5). The gospels present Christ as forgiving sins (Mk 2:5–11; Lk 7:36–50) and giving his disciples the power to forgive sins (Jn 20:19–23). In the early church baptized Christians who committed murder, apostasy or adultery and then repented had to undergo a long, severe and public period of penance before they were readmitted by the bishop to holy communion. From the sixth century Irish and other missionaries spread the practice of repeated private confession to priests; the penances imposed on penitents became less rigorous. The Fourth Lateran Council (1215) prescribed confession at least once a year for those who had fallen into mortal sin (see DS 812). The Council of Florence (1438–45) declared that the sinner's confession is the matter of the sacrament, whereas the words of absolution are the form (see DS 1323). Martin Luther (1483–1546) recognized penance as a sacrament, but subsequent reformers considered only baptism and the eucharist to be sacraments. The Council of Trent (1545–63) reaffirmed the sacramentality of penance (DS 1667–93). In the east, there is a "medicinal" approach to the sacrament, which aims at healing human beings from their wounds and evil inclinations. Conditions for the fruitful reception of the sacrament are: a real contrition for sin; the confession of at least all mortal sins; a genuine intention not to sin again and to avoid all occasions of sin; the willingness to do the penance imposed by the priest. This penance, which can take various forms (e.g., prayer, fasting, almsgiving or some other good work), should facilitate the conversion from sin to God. See *Attrition; Confession; Contrition; Forgiveness; Reconciliation; Sacraments; Sin.*

PENANCE, VIRTUE OF (Lat. "repentance"). The real desire to turn from sin and be once again oriented towards God. See *Attrition; Contrition; Conversion; Metanoia.*

PENTARCHY (Gr. "rule of five"). A theory, especially popular in the first millennium, that the one and undivided Christian church was to be governed by the patriarchs of Rome, Constantinople, Alexandria, Antioch and Jerusalem. With the schism between east and west (definitive only with the rejection of the Council of Florence), Greek Orthodox churches spoke of the *tetrarchy* (Gr. "rule of four"). But the idea of a pentarchy has never been completely abandoned and suggests some ecumenical possibilities. See *Code of Canon Law for the Oriental Churches; Florence, Council of; Patriarch; Primacy; Schism.*

PENTATEUCH (Gr. "five books"). The usual Catholic and Orthodox name for the first five books of the Bible (= Genesis, Exodus, Leviticus, Numbers and Deuteronomy), which Jews call "the Torah" and some Protestants call "the first five books of Moses." The tradition about Moses as the author of these books should be understood in the sense of his having inspired much of the story and legislation recorded in the Pentateuch. Following on some insights of Jean Astruc (1684–1766), Johann Gottfried Eichhorn (1752–1827) postulated as sources for the Pentateuch the Yahwist Document (J) and the Elohist Document (E). Julius Wellhausen (1844–1918) claimed a further source, the Priestly Code (P), to which a Deuteronomistic Source (D) was later added to complete the four-source theory. Nowadays, more attention to oral traditions and other factors has modified any neat theory about four preexisting documents (J, E, P and D), from which the books of the Pentateuch were simply written. See *Bible; Old Testament; Torah.*

PENTECOST (Gr. "the fiftieth day"). Along with the Passover (fifty days before) and the subsequent (autumn) Feast of the Tabernacles, the third major Jewish feast which celebrated initially the harvesting of the grain and later the giving of the Law to Moses on Mount Sinai. As a Christian feast, Pentecost recalls the day when the Holy Spirit descended upon the disciples, Peter preached to the people and pilgrims in Jerusalem, and around three thousand accepted his message and were baptized (Acts 2:1–42). From the *Apostolic Constitutions* and the pilgrim Egeria we have evidence that in the Holy Land Christians already celebrated this feast in the fourth century. The twentieth canon of the First Council of Nicaea (325) speaks of "Pentecost" as the time from Easter till the first Sunday after Pentecost, a period when fasting was prohibited and prayers, including many Allelujas, were said standing. The Feast of Pentecost is also called Whitsunday (Old English "White Sunday"), probably because that was a day (the last day?) when the newly baptized wore their white garments. In the Byzantine liturgy Pentecost is celebrated on two consecutive days: on Sunday is celebrated the completion of the revelation of the Trinity (a feast celebrated in the Latin rite on the Sunday following Pentecost, known as Trinity Sunday) and on Monday the descent of the Spirit on the apostles. See *Holy Spirit; Passover; Pentecostarion.*

PENTECOSTALS. Certain Christian communities who stress baptism in the Spirit and special gifts like healing, prophecy and speaking in tongues (1 Cor 14:1–40). These assemblies originated in Kansas and

California during the first years of the twentieth century. Since the 1960's many charismatic prayer groups have appeared in the Catholic Church and other mainline Christian churches. They are open to renewal in the Spirit and use their charisms (1 Cor 12:4–11) to serve the whole people of God. Unlike the Pentecostals, this renewal does not set up distinct assemblies, but aims to help all baptized Christians experience their new life in the Spirit. See *Charisms; Glossolalia; Holy Spirit; Miracle; Prophecy.*

PENTECOSTARION. The book of seasonal liturgical propers used in the Byzantine liturgy for the divine services from Easter Sunday till Pentecost Sunday inclusive. See *Easter; Octoechos; Pentecost.*

PEOPLE OF GOD. Israel as God's chosen people, set apart from other nations and cherished by God through a special covenant (Exod 5:1; 19:3–6; Deut 4:20; 7:6–8; Isa 43:20–21; Jer 31:33; Ps 100:3). For the NT those who believe in Christ form the new people of God (Rom 9:25–26; 1 Pet 2:9–10; Apoc 21:3). The Second Vatican Council used "the People of God" as a central designation for the church (LG 9–17), and the theme has been subsequently developed by some exponents of liberation theology. See *Berith; Church; Covenant; Ecclesiology; Exodus; Liberation Theology.*

PERENNIAL PHILOSOPHY. A theme which has been popularized by Neoscholasticism and which goes back to a book written by Augustinus Steuchus (1496–1548), bishop of Kissamos in Crete who in his *De perenni philosophia* (1540) argued for an essential harmony between (a) the thought of Christian Platonists like Marsilio Ficino (1433–99) and Giovanni Pico della Mirandola (1463–94) and (b) the philosophy of classical antiquity. Subsequently other writers like Gottfried Wilhelm Leibniz (1646–1716) developed this thesis and maintained a basic unity in the whole history of western thought. Aldous Huxley (1894–1963) and others have used "perennial philosophy" in a broader sense, claiming that all great religious traditions share the same ancient wisdom. See *Neo-Aristotelianism; Neoscholasticism; Neo-Thomism; Platonism; Scholasticism; Thomism.*

PERFECTION. The condition of those who are mature, complete and blameless (Job 1:1). The sermon on the mount names God as the standard of our perfection (Matt 5:48), an aim that is closely connected with total commitment to the law of love (Mk 12:28–34; Col 3:14) and constitutes a lifelong quest (Phil 3:12). All the baptized are called to perfection, and some to the practice of the "three counsels of perfection": voluntary poverty (Matt 19:21), complete abstention from sexual relationships (see

Matt 19:10–12) and obedience to a religious superior. See *Holiness; Love; Religious Life*.

PERICHORESIS, CHRISTOLOGICAL (Gr. "going around"). The interpenetration of the divine and human natures of Christ. While remaining intact and not confused one with the other, they coinhere without separation or division (see DS 112, 113, 115, 1301, 1331). See *Chalcedon, Council of; Hypostatic Union; Incarnation*.

PERICHORESIS, TRINITARIAN. The reciprocal presence and interpenetration or coinherence of the three persons of the Trinity. St. Gregory of Nazianzus (329–89) used the term which acquired its full technical meaning with St. John Damascene (ca. 675–ca. 749). See *Immanent Trinity; Relations, Divine*.

PERSON (Lat. "actor's mask"). Word originally employed to designate the role someone plays on the stage or in life. Boethius (ca. 480–ca. 524) classically defined "person" as *"rationalis naturae individua substantia"* (Lat. "an individual substance of rational nature"). Over the centuries various aspects of what is to be a person were explicitated or added: relationship, incommunicability, self-consciousness, freedom, duties, inalienable rights and dignity. For Immanuel Kant (1724–1804) the human person is an absolute that may never be used as a means but must always be respected as a moral end-in-itself. Nowadays much stress is laid on the way persons are always persons-in-relationship, constituted through relations with other persons and the environment. See *Hypostasis; I and Thou; Immanent Trinity; Personalism; Persons of the Trinity*.

PERSONALISM. A philosophy centered on the unique value of human persons. On the one hand, it opposes totalitarian ideologies (which subordinate the welfare of individuals to that of the collectivity), behaviorism and any psychology which understands human beings as case studies to be interpreted simply in terms of their functions and reactions. On the other hand, true personalism excludes any selfish individualism bent on furthering one's own "interests" at the expense of others. Many (rather diverse) thinkers can be called personalists: for instance, Nicholas Berdyaev (1874–1948), E. S. Brightman (1884–1953), Martin Buber (1878–1965), Ferdinand Ebner (1882–1931), Emmanuel Mounier (1905–50) and Michael Polanyi (1891–1976). See *Person*.

PERSONS OF THE TRINITY. The Father, Son and Holy Spirit who share *in* the one divine nature and subsist in relationship *to* each other. In speaking of the divine persons the Greek fathers often preferred the word *hypostasis* (Gr. "subsisting individual") over *prosopon* (Gr. "face"), with its suggestion of mere modalism ("three faces of God"). They had their difficulties also with the Latin *persona*, even though Tertullian (ca. 160–ca. 225) had introduced the term precisely to combat the modalism of Praxeas. For their part, western theologians feared and fought again tritheistic tendencies ("three Gods") when speaking of the Trinity. See *Hypostasis; Modalism; Ousia; Patripassianism; Person; Relations, Divine; Tritheism.*

PESSIMISM (Lat. "tendency to expect the worst"). A view of the world that underlines the presence of evil and expects its victory, at least in the short run. Over against the optimism of Gottfried Wilhelm Leibniz (1646–1716) and his claim that "this is the best of all possible worlds," Voltaire (1694–1778), moved by the disastrous earthquake in Lisbon, wrote his play *Candide* (1759). While recognizing how sin and other evils overshadow and harm our human condition, Christians find hope through their life of grace and expect the ultimate victory of the general resurrection (Rom 8:18–25; Rev 21:1–4). See *Eschatology; Evil, Mystery of; Grace; Original Sin.*

PETRINE MINISTRY. The special service for Christian faith, life and unity performed by St. Peter and handed on to his successor, the Bishop of Rome, the city where Sts. Peter and Paul died as martyrs. The Petrine office meant witnessing to Christ's resurrection (Lk 22:31–32; 24:34; Acts 2:22–36) and exercising pastoral authority with love (Matt 16:17–19; Jn 21:15–19; 1 Pet 5:1–4). St. Ignatius of Antioch (ca. 35–ca. 107) called the church of Rome "the president of charity," a phrase repeated by Patriarch Demetrios when Pope John Paul II visited Constantinople in 1979. St. Irenaeus of Lyons (ca. 130–ca. 200) appealed to apostolic succession in general and that of the Bishop of Rome in particular as a criterion for recognizing Christian truth. When the "Tome" (his letter to the Patriarch of Constantinople, St. Flavian) of St. Leo I (Pope 440–461) was read at the Council of Chalcedon (451), the members of the council exclaimed, "Peter has spoken through the mouth of Leo." The First Vatican Council (1869–70) expressed this Petrine office in terms of universal jurisdiction and infallibility (DS 3050–75). The Second Vatican Council spelled out the collegial character of this office, exercised together with all the bishops who with and under Peter's successor share responsibility for the whole church (LG 22). Recent ecumenical dialogues with Anglicans, Orthodox and Protestants have shown a growing sensibility to the need for a central church office as a visible sign and agent of Christian unity in faith, but no agreement is yet in sight on the concrete exercise of the Petrine ministry. See *Apostle; Apostolic Succession; Catholicism; Collegiality; Conciliarism; Febronianism; Gallicanism; Infallibility; Jurisdiction; Pope; Protestant; Reformation; Pentarchy.*

PHARISEES (Heb. "separated ones"). A pious Jewish group who formed in the second century B.C., accepted both the oral and the written law and scrupulously observed many practices (guided by 366 positive norms and 250 negative ones). They criticized Jesus for forgiving sins, breaking the sabbath and associating with sinners. In his turn he objected to their external legalism and self-righteous formalism (Mk 7:1–23; Lk 18:9–14). Nevertheless, the gospels also record how he was defended and entertained by some Pharisees (Lk 7:36; 13:31; Jn 7:50–51; 19:39). St. Paul's teacher, the Pharisee Gamaliel, urged restraint in dealing with the apostles (Acts 5:34–40). Not only Paul, but also other Pharisees (Acts 15:5) became Christians. After the revolt of Bar-Cochba (A.D. 135) the traditions of the Pharisees were preserved by the rabbis and the Mishnah. See *Mishnah; Sadducees; Talmud.*

PHENOMENOLOGY (Gr. "study of appearances"). The study of phenomena as opposed to *noumena* (Gr. "things that are apprehended") or things as they are in themselves and not simply as they appear to be. After Immanuel Kant (1724–1804) had drawn a sharp distinction between the noumenal and the phenomenal world, Georg Wilhelm Friedrich Hegel (1770–1831) in his *Phenomenology of the Spirit* (1807) claimed to trace various phases the mind passes through from naive consciousness, sensible certitude of phenomena and on to the absolute knowledge of the Spirit. By studying the contents of human consciousness, the phenomenology of Edmund Husserl (1859–1938) aimed at describing the way that things, as they really are, actually manifest themselves. Max Scheler's (1874–1928) work on feelings and values took phenomenology in a somewhat Augustinian direction, as did that of Husserl's assistant, Blessed Edith Stein (1891–1942). Phenomenology may also be existential, as with Maurice Merleau-Ponty (1908–61), who aimed at describing "my" world rather than the world as it is in itself. With Martin Heidegger (1889–1976) phenomenology became a philosophy of existence, based on historicity and time. See *Existentialism; Experience, Religious; Philosophy.*

PHILOCALIA (Gr. "love of what is beautiful"). (a) An anthology drawn from the writings of Origen (ca. 185–ca. 253) by St. Basil the Great (ca. 330–79) and St. Gregory of Nazianzus (329–89). (b) The same title was chosen for an anthology on asceticism, solitude and the prayer of the heart called *hesychasm,* drawn from thirty-eight fathers of the church and published in 1782 by St. Macarius Notaras, Bishop of Corinth (1731–1805) and St. Nicodemus Hagiorita of Mount Athos (ca. 1749–1809). Inspired by this anthology, Paisy Velichovsky (1722–94) translated into Slavonic his own selection from the Greek fathers and published it in 1793 as *Dobrotoliubie* (Slav. "love of what is good"). Bishop

Theophan Zatvornik (Russ. "the Recluse") (1815–94) made a free translation into Russian from the 1782 anthology, considerably enlarging it and giving it the title of Paisy's collection. Both editions of the *Dobrotoliubie* have greatly influenced Russian spirituality and affected a wide public, as evidenced by the anonymous *The Way of a Pilgrim* (ed. Kazan' 1870). In the last decades the rediscovery of the *Philocalia* has greatly contributed to make Orthodox spirituality (and the spirituality of the fathers generally) known in the west. See *Cappadocian Fathers; Fathers of the Church; Hesychasm; Jesus Prayer.*

PHILOSOPHY (Gr. "love of wisdom"). The study of the most general principles of things and our knowledge of them. After Socrates (ca. 469–399 B.C.) and Plato (ca. 428–ca. 348 B.C.), Greek philosophy reached its climax with Aristotle (384–22 B.C.). He set philosophy within a unified scheme for learning that for centuries had a massive influence both in the east and the west. An introductory study of *logic* or the science of reasoning was to serve as the *organon* (Gr. "instrument") for further knowledge. Then followed (a) *theoria* (Gr. "contemplation") which was divided into first philosophy (= metaphysics), mathematics and physics; (b) *praxis* (Gr. "action," "behavior") which was divided into ethics and politics; and (c) *poiesis* (Gr. "making," "production") which was divided into rhetoric, poetics and economics. After René Descartes (1596–1650) and Immanuel Kant (1724–1804) the problem of the nature, conditions and limits of human knowledge has often occupied center-stage in philosophy. In the twentieth century various forms of existentialism, linguistic analysis, various forms of Marxism, process philosophy, various forms of Thomism and other philosophies have produced a situation of pluralism—at least in the western world. Theology needs help from some well-based philosophy if it is to clarify critically its concepts, questions and method. See *Aristotelianism; Epistemology; Ethics; Existentialism; Hermeneutics; Idealism; Materialism; Metaphysics; Neoplatonism; Nominalism; Perennial Philosophy; Personalism; Phenomenology; Platonism; Pragmatism; Process Theology; Scholasticism; Structuralism; Theology.*

PHILOSOPHY OF RELIGION. The philosophical study of religious language, beliefs, experience and practice. This rather vaguely focused discipline was created by David Hume (1711–76), Immanuel Kant (1724–1804), Georg Wilhelm Friedrich Hegel (1770–1831) and other figures of the Enlightenment who often played down the significance of revelation and wished to develop a religion within the limits of reason alone. Nowadays some use this discipline to elaborate grounds for religious belief or else to study the relations between philosophical reason and religious faith. In philosophizing *about* religion, this discipline normally prescinds from the standpoint of personal faith and reflects on all world religions, without endorsing the preeminence, let alone uniqueness, of any one religion. Hence it is usually to be distinguished from philosophical theology, which does not prescind from Christian faith and largely coincides with fundamental theology. See *Fundamental Theology; Natural Theology; Philosophy; Religion; Revelation.*

PIETISM. A revival movement in Protestantism that was shaped by Philipp Jakob Spener (1635–1705) and that (over against the prevailing, formal orthodoxy of the official church) stressed prayer, reading of the Bible, religious experience and committed Christian life in small communities. Other notable names in the movement include the hymn-writer Paul Gerhardt (ca. 1607–76), Nikolaus Ludwig Graf von Zinzendorf (1700–60), and the mystic Gerhard Tersteegen (1697–1769). Pietism helped the rise of Methodism as well as influencing theologians like Friedrich Daniel Ernst Schleiermacher (1768–1834). See *Liberal Protestantism; Lutheranism; Methodism; Protestant.*

PILGRIMAGE. Journey of devotion to holy places—a practice common to Christianity and other world religions. After the conversion of Emperor Constantine in A.D. 312, pilgrimages to the Holy Land and to the tombs of the martyrs in Rome increased. Other traditional and modern places of Christian pilgrimage include Santiago de Compostella (Spain), the Marian shrines of Lourdes (France), Fatima (Portugal) and the island of Tinos (Greece) where the Orthodox celebrate in a special way the dormition of Our Lady. See *Assumption of the Blessed Virgin; Martyrs.*

PLATONISM. The philosophy inspired by Plato (427–347 B.C.), whose Academy remained a center of learning, though not necessarily of Platonism itself, until closed by the Emperor Justinian (483–565) in A.D. 529. The famous *Dialogues*, in which Plato presents Socrates (ca. 469–399 B.C.) debating with Sophists and others, converge on a central theme: statements about justice, truth, goodness, beauty and other things in our changing and visible world are valid if they can be "universalized," and this points to a higher world of eternal, changeless, universal Ideas. Our souls preexisted in that world and enjoy an innate knowledge which derives from their previous vision of the Ideas. Clement of Alexandria (ca. 150–ca. 215) and Origen (ca. 185–ca. 254) drew much from Plato, and Origen accepted the preexistence of human souls (see DS 403–04). Initially it was "middle" Platonism, with its stress on God's absolute transcendence, that influenced the fathers. In a sense, the crisis of Arianism was a crisis of this form of Platonism. Neoplatonism had its impact on St. Augustine of Hippo (354–430), his followers and Renaissance Platonists like Marsilio Ficino (1433–99). Unlike the west, where

Aristotelianism eventually more or less prevailed, in the east Platonism dominated with humanists like Michael Psellus (ca. 1019–ca. 1078) and theologians who clarified deification through the Platonic notion of participation. Matthew Arnold (1822–88) suggested that everyone is born either a Platonist or an Aristotelian. Alfred North Whitehead (1861–1947), however, gave the precedence to Aristotle's teacher by claiming that all philosophy is only a series of footnotes to Plato. See *Alexandrian Theology; Arianism; Aristotelianism; Augustinianism; Deification; Fathers of the Church; Idealism; Neoplatonism; Origenism; Universals.*

PLEROMA (Gr. "plenitude"). In the Pauline letters the term refers to the fullness of God (Eph 3:19), the full measure of Christ's divinity (Col 1:19; 2:9), the church as the complement of Christ (Eph 1:23) and the fullness of time when the Son of God was sent (Gal 4:4). Gnostics applied *pleroma* to the Son's attributes, which through a series of emanations prepare the transition to the *kenoma* (Gr. "emptiness, void"). See *Emanation; Gnostics; Kenosis.*

PLURALISM. Any philosophical outlook that does not attempt to reduce everything to one ultimate principle. According to whether it accepts a variety of cultures, political parties or religious confessions, pluralism takes a cultural, political or religious form. Over against a rigid uniformity, the Second Vatican Council endorsed a proper diversity in Christian traditions and worship (SC 37; UR 14–17). A few months after announcing on January 25, 1959, his plan to convoke the Second Vatican Council, John XXIII recalled the traditional maxim, *"in essentialibus unitas, in dubiis libertas, in omnibus caritas"* (Lat. "unity in essentials, freedom in debatable matters, charity in everything"). Some distinguish "pluralism" as fracturing the true unity of faith and theology from a legitimate "pluriformity," through which the Christian faith is variously expressed. See *Church and State; Classical Consciousness; Dualism; Eastern Churches; Liberty, Religious; Monism; Rite.*

PNEUMATOLOGY (Gr. "study of the Spirit"). The branch of theology that studies the Holy Spirit. St. Paul's letters testify to the role of the Spirit in revealing God, enabling faith, inspiring prayer, dwelling in the church, blessing the community with various charisms and working toward the final consummation of all things in Christ (Rom 8:1–27; 1 Cor 2:10–16; 12:1–11; Gal 4:6). Often the Holy Spirit has not been studied alone but in the context of such other main themes of theology as Trinity, church, grace and sacraments. This "neglect" corresponds to what St. Basil the Great (ca. 330–379) called the *"kenotic"* (Gr. "emptied") character of the Spirit, who comes anonymously to confirm in us the image of the Son. To borrow from Gustave Flaubert (1821–80), the Holy Spirit functions somewhat like an author in his or her works: being everywhere and nowhere in particular. In a sense the study of the Spirit belongs everywhere in theology rather than being limited to one particular sector. The Second Vatican Council, for example, in its teaching in the church (LG 3–4, 9–17), illustrates how christological and pneumatological reflections require and complement each other. See *Christology; Grace; Holy Spirit; Trinity.*

PNEUMATOMACHIANS (Gr. "Spirit-fighters"). A late fourth-century sect which denied the full divinity of the Holy Spirit. They are also called Macedonians, possibly because they were joined after his death by followers of Bishop Macedonius of Constantinople (d. ca. 362). They were condemned at Constantinople I (381), which defined the divinity of the Spirit, but without calling the Spirit consubstantial with the Father and the Son (see DS 150–51). See *Constantinople, First Council of; Holy Spirit; Macedonians; Nicaea, First Council of.*

POLITICAL THEOLOGY. A theology which protests against the privatization of religion and insists on the social responsibility of Christians. After the *perestroika* of Constantine the Great (ca. 280–337) brought them religious liberty, Christians like Eusebius of Caesarea (ca. 260–ca. 340), at times used their beliefs to legitimate the imperial claims, policies and practices. A new, false association of the political order and religion led to war and persecution. The Enlightenment went to the other extreme by encouraging the view that religion and politics should be kept apart and that faith is a private matter for the individual's conscience. Far from seeking to politicize religion, the political theology of Johann Baptist Metz (b. 1928) and others aims rather to express the implications of Christian faith for the social and political order—above all by protesting against the massive injustice in our world and emphasizing solidarity with the crucified Jesus and countless victims of the world's past and present history. This theology of praxis has found a kind of official counterpart in John Paul II's 1987 encyclical, *Sollicitudo Rei Socialis.* See *Black Theology; Church and State; Enlightenment; Feminist Theology; Liberation Theology; Option for the Poor; Praxis; Symphony.*

POLYGAMY (Gr. "many marriages"). Having more than one wife (or husband) at the same time. In the period of the OT patriarchs and later (Deut 21:15–17) polygamy was accepted. Appealing to God's original plan (Gen 2:24), Jesus supported monogamy (Gr. "one marriage") and rejected divorce and remarriage, which amounts to subsequent polygamy (Mk 10:2–12). The Second Vatican Council condemned polygamy as against the true dignity of marriage (GS 47). See *Marriage.*

POLYGENISM (Gr. "many origins"). The view that the human race has not come from an original pair of ancestors, as *monogenism* asserts, but from many. Pius XII's encyclical *Humani Generis* (1950) warned against polygenism as not being clearly reconcilable with the doctrine of original sin and its transmission to all the descendants of Adam and Eve (DS 3897). Since 1950 reputable and orthodox theologians, supported by an improved exegesis and a more accurate interpretation of Romans 5:12–19, have proposed ways of reconciling belief in original sin with polygenism. At the same time, however, biologists today are holding that our race derives not from many families, but from one. See *Creation; Evolution; Original Sin.*

POLYTHEISM (Gr. "belief in many gods"). The belief that there are many gods, who are often grouped around a supreme deity in a *pantheon* (Gr. "all gods") of hierarchical importance, and personify various experiences and functions of life. Polytheistic religions were and are found in African, Asian, Greek, Roman and other ancient and modern cultures. Some writers have argued that in the religious history of the human race polytheism led to the higher stage of monotheism or that a primitive monotheism declined into polytheism. The historical and anthropological data seems to be too complex to support such simple theories. See *Monotheism; Theism.*

POPE (Gr. "father"). Title originally reserved in the east for the Bishop of Alexandria, but now applied also to priests because of their spiritual parentage. In the west the title was originally used of important bishops, but by the eleventh century had come to be limited to the Bishop of Rome alone. The head of the Catholic Church, the Pope of Rome is also called Vicar of Jesus Christ and Patriarch of the West. See *Bishop; Collegiality; Infallibility; Jurisdiction; Petrine Ministry; Priest; Primacy.*

POSITIVE THEOLOGY. A branch of theology which deals with historical data and particular facts (drawn from the Bible and tradition to determine the doctrines Christians believe), as opposed to natural theology which treats of universal religious principles known from reason. Nowadays "positive theology" hardly ever appears among the schemes for dividing the whole field of theology; its place has often been taken by "historical theology." See *Biblical Theology; Dogmatic Theology; Fundamental Theology; Moral Theology; Patristics; Systematic Theology.*

POSITIVISM. The philosophy popularized by Auguste Comte (1798–1857) who held that we know only what we can percieve through the senses, rejected theological and metaphysical claims, and wished to reorganize society on scientific lines. Between the two World Wars logical positivists like Alfred Jules Ayer (1910–89) argued that only statements which are either tautological or can be tested by empirical observation are meaningful—a principle that is itself neither tautological nor open to be verified by such observation. See *Materialism; Metaphysics; Science and Religion.*

POSSESSION, DIABOLICAL. The frenzied, violent or obscene state of persons controlled by demonic forces. The NT, but not John's gospel, speaks of such possession and deliverance from it through Christ's saving power (Mk 1:23–28; 5:1–20; Lk 11:14–20; Acts 19:13–16). The Christian tradition has accepted the real possibility of diabolical possession. At the same time, many alleged causes can be explained as psychological disturbance rather than literal enslavement by the devil. A famous case involved the Jesuit Jean Joseph Surin (1600–65), who set out to exorcize an Ursuline convent and wound up in a pathological state interpreted by many as diabolical possession. See *Demons; Devil; Exorcism.*

POTENTIA OBOEDIENTIALIS (Lat. "potency under obedience"). Human nature, insofar as it is open to divine grace. The term goes back to St. Thomas Aquinas (ca. 1225–74) and Blessed Peter of Tarantaise (ca. 1224–76), who is also known as Pope Innocent V. In post-Tridentine theology this human openness to God was often interpreted in a static way. Henri de Lubac (b. 1896) and others have used the term to indicate how human beings are dynamically open to God's initiatives. See *Grace.*

POTENTIA JURISDICTIONIS. See *Hierarchy; Jurisdiction; Ordination.*

POTESTAS ORDINIS. See *Hierarchy; Jurisdiction; Ordination.*

POVERTY. (a) The state of being without such essential goods and services as food, clothing and shelter, and, by analogy, the state of those who in various ways are spiritually poor. Down to John Paul II's 1987 encyclical *Sollicitudo Rei Socialis* (see 14–19) and beyond, like many other Christians, church leaders have prophetically denounced the subhuman conditions of life to which war, military expenditure, the greed of rich nations and other factors have condemned millions of people. (b) As an evangelical counsel poverty means the voluntary renunciation of private property, so as to follow Christ more closely (see Mk 10:17–22; 2 Cor 8:9), serve others more freely and witness more clearly to the absolute value of God's final kingdom (PC 13). The CIC sums up what is essentially involved in the practice of the evangelical counsel of poverty in institutes of consecrated, religious life. See *Anawim; Beatitudes; Evangelical Counsels; Justice; Liberation Theology; Option for the Poor; Religious Life; Rights, Human; Social Teaching; Vow.*

PRACTICAL THEOLOGY. See *Pastoral Theology.*

PRAGMATISM (Gr. "belief in things"). An American philosophical movement initiated by Charles Sanders Peirce (1839–1914) and developed by William James (1842–1910) and John Dewey (1859–1952). Highlighting the reality of experience, this school tested the truth of assertions by their practical results. Dewey, in particular, had a profound influence on American thought and education. Pragmatism also influenced George Tyrrell (1861–1909) and other Modernists. See *Modernism; Philosophy.*

PRAXIS (Gr. "doing, performing"). Self-critical activity which is not satisfied with a merely theoretical vindication of truth but aims to verify truth by transforming society. Christian discipleship requires a praxis which is centered on Jesus and, far from denigrating the church's public worship, leads to it and issues from it. See *Frankfurt School; Orthodoxy; Orthopraxis; Political Theology.*

PRAYER. Traditionally defined, with Evagrius Ponticus (346–99), as "the dialogue of the mind with God" or, with St. John of Damascus (ca. 675–ca. 749), as the "elevation of the mind to God." "Mind" should not be understood here in a merely intellectual way, as prayer involves also our freedom and emotions. God is present in a way that goes far beyond the presence of human partners in dialogue. To pray is to invoke, adore, praise, thank, express sorrow to and ask blessings from our personal creator and Lord. Prayer may be uttered aloud or occur silently in the heart, can take place alone or with others, within the official liturgy of the church or beyond it. Jesus prayed publicly and in private (e.g., Mk 1:35; 6:46; 14:12–26; 32–42), taught his disciples to pray (Matt 6:9–13; 7:7–11; Lk 11:1–4) and with them inherited the OT tradition of prayer represented classically by the psalms. The richest collection of NT prayers occur in the opening chapters of Luke's gospel (Lk 1:46–55, 68–79; 2:14, 29–32). Christians know how the Holy Spirit makes possible their life of prayer (Rom 8:15, 26–27; Gal 4:6). See *Acoemetae; Apophatic Theology; Asceticism; Cataphatic Theology; Contemplation; Hesychasm; Impetratory Prayer; Intercession; Jesus Prayer; Liturgy; Liturgy of the Hours; Meditation; Mysticism; Philocalia; Worship.*

PREACHING. Proclaiming the word of God within Christian worship, or as an invitation to conversion and worship. Preceded by John the Baptist (Mk 1:1–8), Jesus proclaimed the good news of God (Mk 1:14–15) and sent the twelve to preach (Mk 6:7–13). Peter (Gal 2:7–8), Paul and other Christian missionaries proclaimed the gospel of Jesus crucified and risen from the dead as Christ, Lord and Son of God (Rom 1:1–6, 15–16; 10:14–18; Gal 1:15–16). Great Christian preachers have included St. John Chrysostom (ca. 347–407), St. Augustine of Hippo (354–430), Bishop Jacques Bénigne Bossuet (1627–1704), Louis Bourdaloue (1632–1704), John Wesley (1703–91) and John Henry Newman (1801–90). The "Order of Preachers" was the name given to the religious institute founded by St. Dominic Guzman (1170–1221). Faced with the modern revolution in social communications, styles of preaching have been changing to serve better the challenge of evangelization. See *Catechesis; Evangelization; Homiletics; Kerygma; Proclamation; Word of God; Worship.*

PREAMBLES OF FAITH. Those presuppositions of Christian faith that can be made explicit to show how the act of faith is also a reasonable human act. On the one hand, human experience, especially in its deepest aspects, can make people open to hear and believe the word of revelation. On the other hand, accepting God's self-communication in Christ presupposes some knowledge of God, human destiny (see Rom 1:19–20; 2:15; Heb 11:6) and of Jesus' earthly history. See *Analysis of Faith; Faith.*

PRECIOUS BLOOD. See *Blood of Christ.*

PREDESTINATION (Lat. "being fore-ordained"). Being elected for salvation through the eternal foreknowledge and will of God (see Matt 20:23; Jn 10:29; Rom 8:28–30; Eph 1:3–14). The Pelagian controversy provoked from St. Augustine of Hippo (354–430) some extreme assertions about God electing (from the "mass of sin" which is the human race) only some for eternal salvation. Disallowing the universal saving will of God, John Calvin (1509–64) held a double predestination: some human beings are elected by God for eternal salvation and others for eternal damnation. This view had been held by the monk Gottschalk (ca. 804–ca. 869), and condemned at synods in Mainz and Quiercy (see DS 621, 685, 1567). While properly vindicating the primacy of the divine grace on which we depend utterly, predestination should not be pushed to the point of denying either God's universal saving will (1 Tim 2:3–6) or human freedom. See *Apocatastasis; Calvinism; Foreknowledge; Freedom; Grace; Merit; Molinism; Pelagianism; Providence; Salvation.*

PREEXISTENCE. The belief that Jesus of Nazareth was/is personally identical with the Son of God, who has existed from all eternity and who entered the world to be revealed in human history (Jn 1:14; 1 Cor 8:6; 2 Cor 8:9; Phil 2:5–11; Col 1:15–17; Heb 1:2–3). Although pre-Christian Jewish thought envisaged intermediaries between God and the world, there are no demonstrable antecedents for the notion of Christ's fully personal preexistence as the Son of God and Logos who "descends" to earth. In pre-Christian Judaism, Wisdom and the Logos are only vivid metaphors for God's attributes and activities. Plato (427–347 B.C.) argued for preexisting ideas that provided the pattern for the demiurge in fashioning the world. His philosophy encouraged Origen (ca. 185–ca. 254) to propose that God created spirits whose use or misuse of free will either made them angels or devils, or else turned them into souls inhabiting human bodies. See *Christology from Above; Demiurge; Eternity; Incarnation; Logos; Wisdom.*

PREFACE (Lat. "spoken before"). Originally, in the Latin rite, any prayer "spoken before" the people. It now refers only to the prayer which introduces the canon in the Latin mass and enumerates reasons for giving praise to God. Prefaces vary with the time of the year (e.g., Advent, Lent, Easter and Pentecost) as well as for the various feasts (e.g., those of Our Lady, apostles and martyrs). See *Eucharist; Eucharistic Prayer; Liturgy.*

PRESBYTER (Gr. "elder"). Term used for officials of a synagogue, members of the Jewish Sanhedrin or supreme council in Jerusalem, and those who led early Christian communities (see Acts 11:30; 14:23). Originally the "presbyters" seem to have been synonymous with the *episkopoi* (Gr. "overseers") (see Phil 1:1; Titus 1:5,7). In the Jerusalem church the "presbyters" were associated with the apostles (Acts 15:2, 4, 6, 22–23; 16:4). By the time of St. Ignatius of Antioch (ca. 35–ca. 107) the presbyters (or priests) were a group coming after the overseers (or bishops) and before the deacons. The decree of the Second Vatican Council on priests is entitled *Presbyterorum Ordinis* (1965). See *Bishop; Deacon; Elders; Priest.*

PRESBYTERIANISM. A form of church government distinguished, on the one hand, from episcopalianism or the rule of bishops and, on the other, from congregationalism or the rule of the community. It involves rule through a series of courts, up to the General Assembly—with the representative ministers and elders participating after being elected. Presbyterians stand in the tradition of John Calvin (1509–64) and the Scottish reformer John Knox (ca. 1505–72). The Church of Scotland is the only Presbyterian Church which is also a state-church. See *Calvinism; Congregational Theology; Elders; Episcopalians.*

PRETERNATURAL GIFTS. Special endowments that enhanced the human nature of Adam and Eve apart from the basic, supernatural gift of grace. Official church teaching spoke of integrity (or freedom from concupiscence) and immortality (DS 222, 370–96, 1515–16, 1926, 1955, 1978, 2616–17, 3514), while theological speculation suggested further privileges. See *Concupiscence; Original Justice; Original Sin; Paradise; Polygenism; Supernatural.*

PRIESTS. Members of the community set apart to offer sacrifice and mediate between God and human beings—in a cultic way like the OT Levitical priesthood (Exod 28:1; 32:25–29; Lev 8:1–9:24), as priest-kings like Melchisedek (Gen 14:18–20) or in a prophetic way. The one supreme mediator between God and humanity (1 Tim 2:5), Jesus is called the "great high priest" by Hebrews (Heb 4:14–5:10) which expounds the nature of his sacrifice, mediation of the new covenant and priesthood as being superior to the Levitical priesthood (Heb 6:20–10:18). (a) Through baptism all believers share in Christ's royal priesthood (1 Pet 2:4–10; SC 14; AA 3); this is called the "priesthood of all the faithful." (b) Through the sacrament of holy orders priests are consecrated, by the Holy Spirit and for the good of the whole church, to a special ministry of word, sacraments and pastoral leadership (PO 2, 4–6)—often called the "ministerial priesthood," for which some prefer the name "presbyterate," to underline the essential difference from the priesthood of all the faithful. Besides being confessors, anointing the sick and administering other sacraments, the ministry of ordained priests means offering the sacrifice of the mass "in the person of Christ and as representing the church" (LG 10, 28). There is one priesthood, that of Jesus Christ, in which in their own different ways the baptized and ordained ministers share. See *Baptism; Bishop; Celibacy; Clergy; Deacon; Holy Orders; Initiation; Mediation; Ministry; Ordination; Pastor; Presbyter; Prophet; Protestant.*

PRIMACY (Lat. "first seat"). The office of the leading bishop or *primate* in a church and the respect due to his rank. A *primacy of honor* means presiding at synods and conferences but does not entail special authority beyond his own diocese, as is the case with the Archbishop of Canterbury in the Anglican Communion. The pope's *primacy of jurisdiction* means real authority in the pastoral government of the whole church (see DS 875, 3059–60, 3063–64 and 3074). Many Orthodox recognize the pope's primacy of honor, but not his real jurisdiction. However, when John Paul II visited Constantinople in 1979, Patriarch Demetrios I greeted him with the words of St. Ignatius of Antioch (ca. 35–ca. 107) describing the Roman see as "presiding in charity," a venerable title that indicates a pastoral service for the whole church. In the Armenian and Syrian churches, the primate is called *catholicos* (Gr. "general superior"). See *Armenian Christianity; Authority; Bishop; Church of the East; Diocese; Jurisdiction; Pope; Synod.*

PRISCILLIANISM. A fourth-century heresy associated with the Spaniard Priscillian, preacher and one-time Bishop of Avila. This dualistic heresy borrowed from Gnosticism and Manichaeism, and followed Sabellian tendencies by interpreting "Father," "Son" and "Holy Spirit" as merely three modes or facets, i.e., only ways of considering the same God. Reaction against this heresy accelerated developments in Trinitarian doctrine, and Spain became the first Catholic land to use the "Filioque" in its creed. In 386, despite the protests of St. Martin of Tours (d. 397), Priscillian was executed by state authorities in Trier (see DS 188–208, 283–86 and 451–64). See *Dualism; Gnosticism; Manichaeism; Modalism; Patripassianism.*

PROBABILISM. System of moral theology characterized by the principle that, if after seeking to arrive at certainty, an objective doubt remains about a law's existence or application, it is lawful to act on a merely probable opinion, even when the opposite opinion favoring a stricter interpretation may seem more probable. This system, supported by Jesuits and others, was challenged by *probabiliorism*, a system adopted by the Dominicans in 1656, which allowed one to follow only those opinions that have more evidence in their favor. St. Alphonsus Liguori (1696–1787), the founder of the Redemptorists, through his mediating position lent support to probabilism, the system commonly accepted today (see DS 2725–27). See *Jansenism; Laxism; Moral Theology; Rigorism.*

PROCESS THEOLOGY. The theological movement inspired by Alfred North Whitehead (1861–1947), whose philosophy, like some other philosophies, stresses the priority of becoming over being, but goes beyond them in trying to synthesize this approach to reality with the results of the natural sciences. Whitehead understands the ultimate constituents of reality to be "actual entities" rather than substances, and makes his point of departure "actual occasions" or entities in interaction with the whole universe. Through love God is at work non-coercively, being "the great companion—the fellow-sufferer who understands." Whitehead's translation of traditional metaphysics into dynamic terms has attracted followers in the United States, the British Isles and elsewhere. Some, like Charles Hartshorne (b. 1897), have developed process thought in a somewhat different way. Although recognizing his valuable stress on personal categories, commentators have criticized Whitehead's philosophy over such matters as his notion of a "finite God." See *Panentheism.*

PROCESSIONS. A theological term for the way in which the second and third persons of the Trinity originate from the Father. The derivation of the Son from the Father is also called "generation" or "filiation," whereas that of the Spirit from the Father and the Son is also called "spiration" (see DS 150, 804). St. Augustine of Hippo (354–430), followed by the medieval scholastics, interpreted the generation of the Son as the act of self-knowledge by the Father, with the Spirit proceeding through the mutual love of Father and Son. See *Filioque; Immanent Trinity; Scholasticism; Trinity, Theology of.*

PROCLAMATION. Announcing Christ (Col 1:28) and the gospel (1 Cor 9:14) with praise and thanksgiving. This may take place through the evangelization of "outsiders," or else within the liturgy—as in the *Exsultet* or Easter proclamation and the eucharist which "proclaims the death of the Lord until he comes" (1 Cor 11:26). See *Anamnesis; Doxology; Evangelization; Homily; Kerygma; Preaching; Prophet.*

PROLEPSIS (Gr. "anticipation"). The principle of real anticipation which comes from the way in which Christ's resurrection represents in advance what will happen at the end of history (1 Cor 15:20, 28) and illuminates the nature of grace and sacraments as the real beginning of our life in glory (Jn 6:54; Rom 6:3–8; 1 Cor 11:26). Munich theologian Wolfhart Pannenberg (b. 1928) appeals to the principle of prolepsis in facing a wide range of theological and philosophical questions. See *Eschatology; History.*

PROPHECY. See *Prophet.*

PROPHET. Someone inspired by the Spirit of God to speak and/or act in a certain way. Interpreting past and present events and announcing coming events, the OT prophets spoke from a deep knowledge of God, preached fidelity to the covenant and opposed a mere external observance of the law. Called by God (Isa 6:1–13; Jer 1:4–19; Ezek 1:1–3:27), they delivered God's word to the people. Conflicts between prophets highlighted the challenge of identifying those who were genuinely authorized to speak in God's name (1 Kings 22; Jer 27–28). The NT witnesses to similar problems in testing and discerning prophecy (1 Cor 14:37–40; 1 Thess 5:19–21). Acknowledged as a prophet (Mk 6:15; 8:28) or *the* prophet (Jn 6:14; 7:40; see Deut 18:15, 18), Jesus spoke and acted prophetically (Mk 11:15–18; 13:1–2; Lk 11:29). While placing himself in the prophetic line (Matt 13:57; Lk 13:34), Jesus claimed that he was "more than" the prophetic, royal and sacred persons and places of the OT (e.g., Matt 12:15–21, 41–42). The NT repeatedly notes how the OT prophetic expectations were fulfilled in Jesus. The prophetic charism continued in the NT communities (Rom 12:6; 1 Cor 12:28–30; 14:29, 32) and the later church. The Second Vatican Council emphasized how all the baptized share in Christ's prophetic office (LG 12, 35). See *Charism; Islam; Jesus Christ; Old Testament; Priests.*

PROPITIATION. An explanation of redemption in terms of God's anger being appeased through Christ's sacrificial death. This explanation rests on a misinterpretation of some NT passages (e.g., Rom 3:25; 8:3; 2 Cor 5:21; Gal 3:13). The appropriate terms for the atonement (e.g., expiation and sacrifice) should be sharply distinguished from the language of propitiation which a number of Catholic and Protestant authors have unfortunately used down to the twentieth century. See *Atonement; Expiation; Redemption; Sacrifice; Satisfaction.*

PROSELYTES (Gr. "those who have come over"). Gentile converts to Judaism (see Matt 23:15; Acts 2:11) or else "God-fearers" who observed only part of the Jewish law (see Acts 10:2; 13:43).

PROSELYTISM. In the past proselytism was often synonymous with evangelization. In fact, the Second Vatican Council affirmed the church's right to evangelize and make converts (AG 7; DH 13–15). However, proselytism almost always now has the negative meaning of forcing or otherwise manipulating people into accepting a particular faith. Religious and civil societies have often condemned this type of proselytism, which was also decried by Vatican II (AG 13; DH 4). In ecumenical dialogue with the eastern Orthodox churches proselytism is one of the questions for the official agenda. See *Conversion; Evangelization; Liberty, Religious; Uniates.*

PROSOPON (Gr. "face," "mask," "role"). Initially a mask worn on stage and later a term for person. Some fathers of the church wrote of the three *prosopa* of the Trinity and the one *prosopon* in Jesus Christ (see DS 250, 302). But *hypostasis* was their commoner term for person. See *Hypostasis; Person.*

PROTESTANT. Person, church, theology or institution related in some way to the "protestant," sixteenth-century reformation. The beginning of Protestantism is symbolically dated to October 31, 1517, when Martin Luther published his ninety-five theses on indulgences, in which he attacked various abuses regarding the doctrine, preaching and practice of penance. The term "protestant" comes from the non-Catholic minority at the Imperial Diet held at Speyer in 1529, who presented a "protest" against the religious policies of the Catholic Emperor Charles V. Often identical with "evangelical," "protestant" sometimes expresses an antagonism to Catholicism. The common theological principles of Protestantism include: the doctrine of justification by faith alone and not by works, the sole authority of holy scripture, and the universal priesthood of all believers. See *Baptists; Calvinism; Congregational Theology; Depravity, Total; Dialectical Theology; Evangelicals; Faith and Works; Hus-*

sites; Imputation; Law and Gospel; Liberal Protestantism; Puritans; Reformation, The; Lutheranism; Methodism; Neo-Orthodoxy; Penance, Sacrament of; Presbyterianism; Sola Fides; Sola Gratia; Sola Scriptura; Theologia Crucis; Theologia Gloriae; Zwinglianism.

PROTOCANONICAL (Gr. "first-time members of the canon"). Term applied to (many) OT books accepted by all as inspired and canonical. See *Apocrypha; Canon; Deuterocanical Books.*

PROTOEVANGELIUM (Gr. "first gospel"). The story of the infancy of Jesus in the apocryphal book of James. The term also refers to a traditional interpretation of the woman crushing the serpent's head (Gen 3:15) as the first promise of salvation and Our Lady's role in it. See *Apocryphal Gospels; Eschatology; Infancy Gospels; Senses of Scripture.*

PROTOLOGY (Gr. "study of first things"). Doctrine about the origin of the world and human beings. Protology corresponds to eschatology, since God's plan at the beginning is best illuminated by its full unfolding at the end. See *Adam; Creation; Eve; Fall, The; Original Justice; Original Sin.*

PROVIDENCE (Lat. "foresight"). God's all-wise, all-loving and all-encompassing guidance of nature, history and the course of individual lives (see Matt 6:25–34; 10:29–31). The Christian doctrine of providence allows for both human freedom and the mysterious ways of God who can "write straight but with crooked lines." See *Deism; Foreknowledge; Freedom; Predestination; Theism.*

PRUDENCE (Lat. "foresight"). The first of the cardinal virtues, entailing the capacity to translate general norms and ideals into practice. Christian prudence is more than a mere shrewdness that foresees difficulties and avoids undesirable consequences. It involves the exercise of a practical imagination that makes a coherent whole of one's moral life. See *Virtues, Cardinal.*

PSALMS (Gr. "songs"). OT religious songs that express to the all-holy God the adoration, thanksgiving, complaints, sorrow, trust and other feelings of individuals and the whole people. Though traditionally attributed to King David (d. ca. 970), perhaps only a few of the 150 psalms go back to him. This Jewish liturgical book is used by Christians everywhere for their public worship and private prayer. A landmark of OT scholarship was the study by Hermann Gunkel (1862–1932) of the psalms according to their literary forms (see DS 3521–28). See *Biblical Criticism.*

196

PSEUDEPIGRAPHA (Gr. "false title"). Books attributed to someone other than their real author, presumably to enhance their authority. Examples are the noncanonical book of Enoch and the Assumption of Moses. Catholics use the term "apocrypha" in referring to such pseudonymous Jewish works. See *Apocrypha*.

PURGATORY (Lat. "purification"). State of those who die in God's friendship but who still need their personal sins to be expiated (through the merits of Christ) and should grow spiritually before enjoying the beatific vision. The scriptural passages that have been adduced (2 Macc 12:38–46; Matt 5:25–26; 12:31–32 and 1 Cor 3:11–15) do not as such establish the existence of purgatory. It can be validated in the light of divine justice and by the fact of Christians praying (attested at least since the second century) and celebrating the eucharist (attested at least since the third century) for their dead. In line with this practice, Greek authors like St. Clement of Alexandria (ca. 150–ca. 215), Origen (ca. 185–ca. 254) and St. John Chrysostom (ca. 347–407) and Latin authors like Tertullian (ca. 160–ca. 225), St. Cyprian (d. 258) and St. Augustine of Hippo (354–430) wrote in various ways of purification after death and our communion through prayer with our dear departed. Praying for the dead has remained a typical feature of eastern and western liturgies. The Second Council of Lyons (1274) and the Council of Florence (1438–45) taught the cleansing suffering endured after death (by those not yet fit for the beatific vision) and the value of prayers and pious works offered on their behalf (DS 856–57, 859, 1304–05)—avoiding, however, the language of "fire" which the Orthodox oppose. Martin Luther (1483–1546) rejected first the value of indulgences for the dead and then the very existence of purgatory. The Council of Trent (1545–63) maintained the doctrine of purgatory, said nothing about the nature and duration of purgatory, and reiterated the value of offering prayers and the eucharist for those in purgatory (DS 1580, 1820). The Second Vatican Council briefly recalled our communion with those being purified after death and endorsed the teaching of Florence and Trent (LG 49, 51). The state of purgatory can be understood as a final process of loving but painful maturation before we see God face-to-face. With the last judgment purgatory will come to an end (DS 1067). See *Beatific Vision; Communion of Saints; Death; Eschata; Indulgences.*

PURITANS. An umbrella term for those influential groups within the Church of England who opposed the religious settlement of Queen Elizabeth I (1533–1603), and following a Calvinist theology aimed to purify the church of nonbiblical elements. They insisted on preaching a strict observance of the Sunday and an austere moral code. Many Puritans came to reject the episcopal government of the church. Leading

English Puritans included Thomas Cartwright (1535–1603), the Lord Protector Oliver Cromwell (1599–1658) and the poet John Milton (1599–1658). In the early seventeenth century Puritan refugees established the Massachusetts Bay Colony. The most notable theologian to emerge among the New England Puritans was Jonathan Edwards (1703–58). In the British Isles "Low Church" Anglicans, Baptists, Congregationalists, Presbyterians and Quakers have all inherited elements from the original Puritans. See *Anglican Communion; Baptists; Calvinism; Congregational Theology; Episcopacy; Presbyterianism; Protestant; Quakers; Reformation.*

Q

QUAKERS. See *Friends, Society of.*

QUALIFICATION, THEOLOGICAL. An evaluation of a particular theological proposition in its relationship to revealed truth and church doctrine. If found in the sources of revelation, a statement can be qualified as *de fide divina* (Lat. "of divine faith"). If it has been solemnly defined by the extraordinary magisterium, it becomes *de fide definita* (Lat. "of defined faith"). Other theological notes include such qualifications as *de fide ecclesiastica* (Lat. "of the church's faith"), *fidei proximum* (Lat. "close to faith") and *theologice certum* ("theological certain") (see DS 2269, 2374). Once a constant feature of Catholic theological remarks, the use of theological notes has been already largely dropped. A 1989 document of the International Theological Commission ("The Interpretation of Dogma") called for their revival. See *Council, Ecumenical; Heresy; Infallibility; Magisterium; Theology.*

QUELLE OR Q (German "source"). A hypothetical lost document composed largely of sayings or *logia* of Jesus and used as a major source by Matthew and Luke. Very many scholars accept this hypothesis which explains numerous close similarities between Matthew and Luke. See *Synoptic Gospels; Two-Source Theory.*

QUIETISM. School of spirituality developed by Miguel de Molinos (ca. 1640–97), who preached a total abandonment to God that reduced human responsibility and dismissed outward acts of religion as superfluous. In 1687 he was condemned by his former friend, Pope Innocent XI (see DS 2201–69). Charges of quietism were also made against Madame Guyon (1648–1717) and François de Salignac Fénelon, Archbishop of

198

Cambrai (1651–1715), who was condemned by Innocent XII in 1699 (DS 2340–74). See *Spirituality*.

QUMRAN SCROLLS. Manuscripts written in Hebrew and Aramaic between 20 B.C. and A.D. 70 and discovered in 1947 and later in caves at Qumran, eight miles south of Jericho and close to the Dead Sea. Hence the manuscripts are also known as the Dead Sea Scrolls. The manuscripts, which seem to have belonged to a nearby Jewish community, include fragments, sometimes extensive ones, from nearly all of the books of the OT and other religious works. This discovery has proved of major importance for biblical studies, in particular, for research into the OT and the environment in which Christianity was born. See *Bible; Essenes; Old Testament*.

R

RATIONALISM. Any system which privileges reason in the search for truth, including religious truth. A strongly rationalist strain characterizes the Enlightenment. Some of its figures used reason to reject revelation; others went on to reject all religious belief. While acknowledging (against the fideists) the capacity of human reason to know God from the created world, against rationalists Vatican I (1869–70) asserted the "supernatural," divine revelation to which we owe the assent of faith (DS 3004–05, 3008). As a synonym for atheism or agnosticism, rationalism is no longer used so much nowadays. See *Enlightenment; Fideism; Liberalism; Revelation; Vatican Council, First*.

RATUM ET CONSUMMATUM (Lat. "ratified and consummated"). A term in canon law for a marriage that has been validly contracted and sexually consummated in a way that is humanly dignified and open to the procreation of children (see CIC 1061). A marriage is indissoluble if it is both ratified and consummated; if it is only *ratum*, it may be dissolved for good reasons. See *Marriage; Validity*.

RCIA (THE RITE OF CHRISTIAN INITIATION OF ADULTS). A recently introduced (1972) course of preparation for adults who wish to be baptized and enter the Church. Once enrolled as catechumens, the candidates are instructed in the faith and obligations of Christians—normally during Lent. At the Easter vigil they receive the sacraments of baptism, confirmation and communion—thus following as adults the order the Eastern Church follows for the Christian initiation of children, who in one ceremony are baptized, confirmed and receive communion. See *Catechumenate; Easter Triduum; Holy Week.*

REAL PRESENCE. Among the various presences of the risen Christ in our world, *the* presence *par excellence* (SC 7). After the consecration at mass he is present with his body, blood, soul and divinity under the appearances of bread and wine (see DS 1637, 1640–41, 1651–53). See *Consecration; Eucharist; Transubstantiation.*

RECAPITULATION. See *Anakephalaiosis.*

RECEPTION. The process by which official teachings and decisions are accepted, assimilated and interpreted by the whole church. It has often taken time before the pronouncements of an ecumenical council have been known, understood and received by the local churches and their leaders. In a broader sense "reception" refers to the whole process by which each generation accepts the revelation transmitted through scripture and tradition (DV 8–9). See *Council, Ecumenical; Deposit of Faith; Magisterium; Sensus Fidelium; Sobornost.*

RECONCILIATION. Re-establishing friendship after a situation of conflict and alienation has been overcome. (a) A term with an ordinary, "secular" meaning (see 1 Cor 7:11), "reconciliation" is applied by St. Paul to God's loving initiative in redeeming us and to our need to accept this new situation of being reconciled through Christ (Rom 5:8–11; 2 Cor 5:18–20). In an extended fashion "reconciliation" is applied to the effect of redemption on the whole world (Col 1:19–20). (b) As it brings reconciliation with God and the church, the sacrament of penance is now often called "the sacrament of reconciliation" (see LG 11; PO 5). See *Penance, Sacrament of; Redemption; Salvation.*

REDAKTIONSGESCHICHTE (German "story of editing"). The name given by Willi Marxsen (b. 1919) to the work of the final editors or writers of our biblical texts. Redaction criticism, as it is often called, studies the motivation of these authors in editing earlier material, the changes they introduced and the message they wished to communicate to their particular audience (see DV 19). See *Biblical Criticism; Exegesis.*

REDEEMER (Lat. "one who pays to liberate somebody"). The title given to Jesus for delivering us from sin and evil through his incarnation, life, death, resurrection and sending of the Holy Spirit. While having a different origin, in actual usage the title is synonymous with "Savior." See *Salvation.*

200

REDEMPTION (Lat. "buying back"). God's activity in delivering us from the bondage of sin and evil. The liberation from oppression in Egypt was the paradigmatic case in the OT of the divine redemptive activity (Exod 15:1–21; Deut 7:8; 13:5; 24:18). The deliverance from the Babylonian exile also revealed God's loving fidelity as redeemer (Isa 41:14; 43:14; 44:24; 54:8). Through his death and resurrection (Mk 10:45; Rom 4:25; Eph 1:7; 1 Pet 1:18–21) Christ delivered us from the power of sin and evil (Col 1:13–14) in a redemption that is appropriated by faith (Rom 3:24–30) and will be completed in the resurrection to come (Rom 8:23; Eph 4:30). From the time of the NT, redemption has been understood not only as deliverance from oppression (1 Cor 15:20–28, 54, 56–57) but also as purification from guilt (1 Cor 6:11; Eph 5:25–26; Heb 2:17–18) and a love that changes the human heart (Mk 7:21–23; Rom 5:5; 1 Jn 4:9–10) and brings a new covenant of friendship with God (Mk 14:24; 1 Cor 11:25). See *Atonement; Cross; Covenant; Expiation; Justification; Reconciliation; Salvation; Satisfaction.*

REDUCTIONISM. Any attempt to explain or explain away the complex data of reality by appealing to only one of its aspects. Thus a philosopher may identify reality at large with the immediately available sense-data. Rejection of faith in God usually takes the form of reductionism. In his *Essence of Christianity* (German original, 1841) Ludwig Feuerbach (1804–72) argued that belief in God was "nothing but" the projection of human desires and aspirations. A concern to speak to the culture of their age has often led deists, liberal protestants and rationalists to over-simplify and dilute the full Christian revelation. See *Deism; Liberal Protestantism; Rationalism.*

REFORMATION, THE. At least since the Council of Vienne (1311–12) a cry for "reform in head and members" was heard in the church, whose life at all levels had become marked by many grave abuses. They were aggravated by the "Babylonian Captivity" of the papacy in Avignon (1305–74), the Great Western Schism when there were two or three popes (1378–1417), the Conciliarist Movement and the scandals associated with the renaissance papacy. Various attempts at reform within the Catholic Church gained strength and finally broke through at the time of the Council of Trent (1545–63). The Protestant reformation, often improperly called "The Reformation," must be seen in the same perspective. At the center of this movement stood Martin Luther (1583–1546) and, for a second generation, John Calvin (1509–64). Other leading figures were Ulrich Zwingli (1484–1531), reformer of Zurich, and Philipp Melanchthon (1497–1560), collaborator of Luther in Wittenberg. The English reformation began over the marital problems of Henry VIII (1491–1547) and the failure of Cardinal Thomas Wolsey (ca. 1474–

1530) to secure him a divorce. Papal authority was rejected and the monasteries suppressed. The leading reformers in England included Archbishop Thomas Cranmer (1489–1556), Bishop Hugh Latimer (ca. 1485–1555) and Bishop Nicholas Ridley (ca. 1500–55). Undoubtedly nationalism and economic interests helped the cause of the reformation. But it was often a deeply-felt religious movement that aimed to purify the church life and base Christian living on the scriptures (UR 21). The Second Vatican Council acknowledged "that continued reformation" to which Christ always calls his Church (UR 6). See *Anabaptists; Anglican Communion; Augsburg, Confession of; Baptists; Calvinism; Conciliarism; Counter-Reformation; Hussites; Lutheranism; Nominalism; Protestant; Puritans; Presbyterianism; Trent, Council of; Vernacular; Vienne, Council of; Waldensianism; Zwinglianism.*

REGENERATION (Lat. "new birth"). The spiritual rebirth brought by baptism (Jn 3:5; Titus 3:5; 1 Pet 1:3). St. Paul speaks equivalently of baptism as death to the old state of sin and new life in the risen Christ (Rom 6:1–11). See *Baptism.*

REGULA FIDEI (Lat. "rule of faith"). Norm of faith as a public, ecclesial criterion for discerning the true revelation communicated by Christ to the Church. St Irenaeus of Lyons (ca. 130–ca. 200) developed this idea against Gnostic claims to special revelations accessible only to the elite. See *Creed; Gnosticism; Revelation.*

REIGN OF GOD. See *Kingdom of God.*

RE-INCARNATION. The belief, also called *metempsychosis* (Gr. "animate afterwards"), that souls inhabit a series of bodies and can live many lives on this earth before being completely purified and so released from the need to migrate to another body. According to this belief the soul pre-exists its embodiment, and after death exists in a disembodied state before animating once again a body of the same or a different species. In various forms, reincarnation has been accepted by Buddhists, Hindus, Neoplatonists and others. Belief in resurrection and official rejection of the preexistence of souls (see DS 403, 854, 1440) rule out reincarnation. By maintaining an indefinite series of chances, the doctrine of reincarnation reduces the seriousness of God's grace and human liberty exercised in one life that is terminated by a once-and-for-all death (1 Cor 15:20–28; 2 Cor 5:10; Heb 9:27). See *Death; Resurrection; Soul.*

RELATIONS, DIVINE. The ordering of the Divine Persons among themselves in a way that constitutes them three Persons in one God. There are four such relations: paternity, filiation, active and passive spiration. Paternity constitutes the Father, filiation the Son and passive spiration the Spirit. Active spiration is common to the Father and the Son and does not form a new person. See *Filioque; Immanent Trinity; Trinity, Theology of.*

RELATIVISM. The view that there are no absolute truths or values but they are all *determined* by particular periods, cultures, societies and persons. Pure relativism ("all claims and truths are relative") is self-contradictory. Milder forms of relativism stress the way that historical, cultural and religious presuppositions condition one's grasp of meaning and truth. The relativizing approach of Ernst Troeltsch (1865–1923) left contemporary theology with the major challenge of elucidating Christ's absoluteness, so as to show how in a definitive and unsurpassable manner he is the fullness of divine revelation for all peoples of all times. In the area of dogmatic definitions historically conditioned formulations should be distinguished from the lasting truths being taught. See *Biblical Criticism; Christology; Classical Consciousness; Dogma; Idealism; Modernism; Pluralism.*

RELICS (Lat. "remains"). The bodily remains of saints or else objects closely connected with them (such as their clothing and letters). From early centuries the tombs and remains of martyrs and other saints were venerated. The Crusades brought a traffic in relics, but those taken back to Europe were often spurious. Since Trent (DS 1821–23) official Church teaching has tried to correct abuses connected with relics (see CIC 1190) and, in general, to relate the veneration of saints, their images and their relics to the central worship of God (SC 111, LG 51). In the west relics of martyrs and other saints are normally inserted under fixed altars (CIC 1237; see Rev 6:9). See *Crusades; Icon; Iconoclasm; Nicaea, Second Council of; Saint; Trent, Council of; Veneration of Saints.*

RELIGION (Lat. "being bound"). The basic attitude human beings should take up toward God, their creator and redeemer. The moral virtue of religion expresses itself in adoration and wholehearted service of our loving God. Karl Barth (1886–1968) opposed faith (as founded in the Word of God and utterly dependent on divine grace) to "religion," which he dismissed as the worthless product of merely human aspirations. See *Adoration; Creation; Love; Redemption; Worship.*

RELIGIONS. Systems of belief in and response to the divine, including the sacred books, cultic rituals and ethical practices of the adherents. Christians in general and Catholics in particular are called to live the tension between evangelization and dialogue represented, respectively, by the Decree on the Church's Missionary Activity (*Ad Gentes*) and the

Declaration on the Relationship of the Church to Non-Christian Religions (*Nostra Aetate*) of the Second Vatican Council. See *Animism; Anonymous Christians; Buddhism; Christianity; Dialogue; Evangelization; Hinduism; Islam; Judaism; Mission, Theology of.*

RELIGIOUS LIFE. A form of Christian existence which practices the evangelical counsels of chastity, poverty and obedience and involves a common life under a superior. A period of novitiate comes at the beginning and vows regulate the life-style. In the west the approved forms of religious life include the monastic orders (like the Benedictines, Carthusians and Cistercians), the canons regular (like the Premonstratensians, founded by St. Norbert in the twelfth century), the mendicants (like the Franciscans and the Dominicans, founded in the thirteenth century) and the clerics regular (like the Jesuits and the Theatines, founded in the sixteenth century). Institutes of consecrated life founded in more recent times are called congregations if their members pronounce only simple vows (unlike orders whose vows are solemn). Religious life is followed by both non-ordained lay-persons and ordained clergy. The Second Vatican Council taught (a) that all the baptized are called to the fullness of Christian life and the perfection of love (LG 39–42); and (b) that religious follow their way of life in order to be consecrated with greater liberty to the love and service of God and others (LG 43–47; PC 1). The council also called for an *aggiornamento* of religious institutes by a return to the original spirit of their founders (see PC 2; CIC 573–709). "Secular institutes," associations of laypersons, priests or both, which have come into existence since World War II, are a form of consecrated Christian life but as such not a form of religious life (CIC 710–30). Among the enduring results of the Oxford Movement has been the revival of religious life in the Anglican community. Similar revivals of religious life have come among Protestants, such as the *Christusbruderschaft* in Germany and the ecumenical community at Taizé. See *Anachoretism; Celibacy; Cenobites; Chastity; Evangelical Counsels; Hermit; Monasticism; Obedience; Oxford Movement; Perfection; Poverty; Vow.*

REPARATION. Making amends for the offense committed against or the damage done to another. Reparation can refer to the compensation to be made when, for instance, someone's property or good reputation has been unjustly damaged. In the area of devotion to the Sacred Heart, reparation refers to prayers and good works undertaken to make amends for sins against Jesus' love expressed in the gift of the Blessed Sacrament and the suffering through which he redeemed us. See *Atonement; Blessed Sacrament; Expiation; Heart, Sacred; Penance, Sacrament of; Satisfaction.*

REPENTANCE. See *Metanoia.*

REPROBATION. Act whereby God excludes those in the state of unrepented mortal sin from final salvation and condemns them to eternal punishment (see Matt 25:41–46). See *Calvinism; Hell; Jansenism; Predestination; Sin, Mortal.*

RES ET SACRAMENTUM (Lat. "thing signified and its sign"). To be distinguished (a) from *sacramentum tantum* (Lat. "only a sign") such as bread and wine destined for use in the eucharist, and (b) from *res sacramenti (tantum)* (Lat. "the thing signified [taken by itself]") or the grace signified and produced by a sacrament. *Res et sacramentum* goes beyond the immediate grace effected by a sacrament, and refers to such enduring realities as the real presence of Christ in the eucharist (and not merely the grace of holy communion), and the indelible character imparted by baptism, confirmation and holy orders. See *Character; Communion; Grace; Sacraments; Sphragis; Symbol.*

RESERVATION OF THE BLESSED SACRAMENT. The practice of keeping in a tabernacle consecrated hosts to serve for the communion of the sick and the adoration of the faithful (CIC 934–44). A lighted lamp near the tabernacle indicates the presence of the Blessed Sacrament. See *Adoration; Blessed Sacrament.*

RESURRECTION (Lat. "rising," "being raised"). Not a mere return to earthly life like the resuscitation of the daughter of Jairus (Mk 5:22–24, 35–43), but the passage of Jesus through death to his definitive, transformed life (Rom 1:3–4; 1 Cor 15:42–50) which has inaugurated the final resurrection of human beings and their world (1 Cor 15:20–28). This central truth of faith formed the initial proclamation of Christians (Acts 2:22–24, 32–33, 36; 1 Cor 15:1–11), who practically defined God (the Father) in terms of having raised Jesus from the dead (Rom 10:9; 1 Cor 6:14; Gal 1:1; 1 Thess 1:10; see 1 Cor 15:15). Later NT traditions, church teaching and creeds (Jn 10:17–18; DS 359, 539) spoke of Christ (as divine) rising by his own power. Through his appearances (1 Cor 15:5–8; Mk 16:7; Matt 28:9–10, 16–20 etc.) the first disciples came to know that Jesus was risen from the dead. The discovery of the empty tomb by Mary Magdalene (probably with one or more women companions) served as a secondary, negative sign confirming the event of the resurrection (Mk 16:1–8; Jn 20:1–2). As the climax of divine revelation (DV 4, 17) the resurrection of the crucified Jesus, together with the sending of the Holy Spirit, contains implicitly all the basic Christian truths. Hence the paschal mystery needs to be explored not only in its factuality but also as the mystery of revelation, redemption, faith, hope and love. See *Appear-*

205

ances of the Risen Lord; Ascension; Descent into Hell; Easter; Eschatology; Paschal Mystery; Passover.

RESURRECTION OF THE DEAD. Final life after death effected by the divine power for the whole human being (= "body and soul"). Although as such it surfaced late in the OT, hope for a general resurrection emerged from ancient Jewish faith in God as the faithful, just and all-powerful Lord of life. Interpretations of the nature of resurrection varied from images of a physical reanimation (2 Macc 7:1–42; 12:44–45; 14:46) to hopes for a glorious, transformed existence (Dan 12:1–4), similar to but not identical with St. Paul's expectations of a "spiritual" body (1 Cor 15:35–54). Jesus' preaching of the final reign of God presupposed a general resurrection (Matt 8:11; Mk 9:43–48; Lk 11:31–32). His refutation of the Sadducees showed that he understood the resurrection of the dead to involve a new form of human existence (Mk 12:18–27; see Rom 14:9; 1 Cor 15:22–23; Col 1:18; Rev 1:5) in a world renewed and transformed (see LG 48–49, 51; GS 14, 22). See *Apocalyptic Literature; Communion of Saints; Eschatology; Eternity; Heaven; Parousia; Soul.*

REVELATION (Lat. "taking away the veil"). The disclosure by God of what was previously unknown. The OT records the divine revelation communicated primarily through words (Jer 23:18, 22) and events of history (Exod 15:1–21) and secondarily through the created world (Ps 19:2; Wis 13:1–9). As major mediators of God's revelation, the classical prophets also spoke of the saving revelation to come (Isa 40:1–11; Jer 31:31–34). In his incarnation, life, death, resurrection and sending of the Holy Spirit (DV 4, 17) Christ was the climax of the divine self-revelation (Jn 1:14, 18; Heb 1:1–2), being simultaneously the Revealer (= agent), the revelation (= the active process of disclosure) and the content of revelation. For the doctrine of revelation John's gospel (with its language of glory, light, signs, truth, witness, the "I am" sayings and, above all, the incarnation of the Word) is the richest NT book. With Christ and the apostolic age foundational revelation is completed, and we await only the final, glorious revelation of the *parousia* (Titus 2:13; 1 Jn 3:2; DV 4). Since the Middle Ages and especially since the Enlightenment, the truths of revelation have been contrasted with those of reason, accessible to us without any special communication from God being strictly necessary. This propositional view of revelation characterized the teaching of the First Vatican Council (DS 3004–07, 3026–29). The Second Vatican Council understood revelation as primarily God's personal self-manifestation that invites our personal response of faith (DV 2, 6) and secondarily as the communication of divine truths (DV 7, 9, 10, 11, 26). Vatican II recognized the essentially salvific and sacramental nature of God's self-revelation, mediated through events (deeds) and words (DV

2, 4, 14, 17). Salvation history and the history of revelation are insepara-
ble, but two sides of the same reality. Since the council some scholars
have been advancing the theology of revelation by reflecting on God's
symbolic self-communication which human beings *experience* in faith.
Both Catholic theology and official teaching have become more aware of
the Holy Spirit mediating revelation and salvation beyond institutional
Christianity. See *Creed; Deposit of Faith; Dogma; Enlightenment; Experience, Religious; Grace; Johannine Theology; Logos; Mystery; Natural Theology; Parousia; Salvation History; Scripture and Tradition; Symbol; Word
of God.*

REVIVALISM. Systematic attempts to rouse new life among lax or nomi-
nal believers by enthusiastic preaching and spontaneous praying aimed
at evoking a mass religious response. From the eighteenth century there
have been recurrent revivalist movements in the United States, the British Isles and elsewhere. A revivalist style of worship characterizes the
Salvation Army, founded by William Booth (1829–1912) in 1865. See
Baptists; Charismatic; Methodism; Pentecostals; Pietism.

RIGHTEOUSNESS. See *Justification.*

RIGHTS, HUMAN. The things to which human beings are entitled in
justice because they are created in the divine image and likeness and
called to eternal life with God. These include freedom of conscience and
the right to life, work, marriage, education and property. The third commandment of the decalogue (Exod 20:2–17; Deut 5:6–21) ensured regular recreation for poor workers and slaves. Many laws of the OT and
prophetic denunciations of injustice (2 Sam 11:1–12:14; Isa 5:23) are
concerned with basic human rights. The OT repeatedly demands protection for orphans, widows and strangers (Deut 24:17–22; 27:19). Despite the basic equality of all persons in Christ (Gal 3:28), slavery, oppression of women, antisemitism and other offenses against human
rights continued to disfigure Christian life. At the same time, for many
centuries monks and other church groups often stood almost alone in
providing education and in caring for the sick, the destitute and the
dying. The Magna Carta (1215), the American Declaration of Independen-
dence (1776) and the United Nations' Declaration of Human Rights
(1948) figure among the major statements expressing and encouraging a
general awareness of basic human rights. Among the many Christians
who have championed human rights we should recall Bartolomé de las
Casas (1484–1566), William Wilberforce (1759–1833), Daniel O'Connell
(1775–1847), Bishop Wilhelm Emmanuel Ketteler (1811–77), Cardinal
Henry Edward Manning (1808–92), Martin Luther King, Jr. (1929–68)
and popes since Leo XIII (1810–1903). The Second Vatican Council en-

dorsed a full range of human rights (GS 27, 29, 66). In particular a whole document (*Dignitatis Humanae*) was dedicated to the right of persons and communities to social and civil liberty in religious matters—a development in church teaching prepared for and encouraged by the American theologian John Courtney Murray (1904–67). See *Anthropology; Black Theology; Decalogue; Feminist Theology; Image of God; Liberty, Religious.*

RIGORISM. A moral system which in cases open to doubt insists on law over liberty, even when the case for liberty enjoys a high degree of probability. Such thinking stifles freedom for the sake of safety and was condemned in 1690 (see DS 2303). See *Laxism; Moral Theology; Probabilism.*

RITE. Way of celebrating a religious ceremony or celebrating a sacrament. The term may also refer to the complex of ceremonies observed by a particular church. In the west such rites as the Ambrosian in Milan differ from the normal Latin rite only through relatively minor liturgical features. Among Eastern Catholics, however, "rite" means not only considerable differences in liturgy, but also the whole style of life for a particular church with its specific spirituality and discipline. Rite in this sense is synonymous with church tradition. In the east there are now seven such major rites left: the Armenian, the Byzantine, the Coptic, the East-Syrian (sometimes called Assyro-Chaldean), the Ethiopian, the Maronite (or Syro-Maronite) and West-Syrian (or Antiochene). These seven rites are found in both the Catholic and Orthodox traditions, except for the Maronite rite which is Catholic. See *Episcopal Conferences.*

RITUAL. An official book containing the prayers and actions prescribed for the celebration of the sacraments, funerals, the public pronouncing of vows, the consecration of a church and other religious ceremonies.

ROMAN CATHOLICISM. See *Catholicism.*

ROSARY (Lat. "rose-garden"). A popular prayer said out of devotion to Our Lady. It consists of fifteen decades, each commemorating a mystery concerning Christ or Mary and including the Lord's Prayer, the Hail Mary (ten times) and "Glory be to the Father." The five joyful mysteries center on Christ's birth and childhood. The five sorrowful mysteries begin with Christ's agony in the garden and end with his death on the cross. The five glorious mysteries begin with Christ's resurrection and end with Mary's sharing in her Son's victory. Although popular tradition says otherwise, the rosary was probably not introduced by St. Dominic (1170–1221). Dominican preachers popularized it, and a Dominican pope, St. Pius V, officially endorsed the rosary in 1569. Because of its repetitions the rosary has sometimes been called the "Jesus prayer" of western Catholicism. See *Devotions; Jesus Prayer.*

RUBRIC (Lat. "red"). Directive printed in red alongside the main text (in black), that is read or chanted at liturgical assemblies. Rubrics indicate how some ceremony can or should be performed. See *Liturgy.*

RULE. The written and approved order of life for men or women with vows who belong to a particular religious institute. The Second Vatican Council invited religious institutes to update their various rules (PC 3–4; see CIC 578, 587). Laypersons associated with a religious order sometimes follow a simplified form of that order's rule. See *Religious Life.*

RUTHENIAN (Lat. "Russian"). A Catholic who belongs to one of the churches which originally depended on the Bishop of Kiev. The metropolitan Isidore of Kiev accepted union with Rome immediately after the Council of Florence (1438–45), which eventually led to very many Slavs returning to Catholicism through the Union of Brest-Litovsk (1596). The Ruthenian churches were signatories to this union and used to be described as the Slav-speaking Catholics of Byzantine rite in Poland, Hungary and Bohemia. Nowadays, "Ruthenians" refers broadly to Byelorussians, Slovaks and Ukrainians. These Catholics were never grouped together under one jurisdiction. The term is also used to refer specifically to Byzantine Catholics who originated in an area known as Carpatho-Ukraine, Transcarpathia and so forth. See *Eastern Churches.*

S

SABBATH (Heb. "rest"). Saturday or the last day of the Jewish week, kept holy through worship of God and abstinence from work (Exod 20:10; 31:13–17). That day recalls how God "rested" from the work of creation (Gen 2:2–3; Exod 20:11; 31:17) and how the people were delivered from Egypt (Deut 5:15). Protesting against a sabbath observance that had become narrowly legalistic (Matt 12:9–14; Mk 2:23–28; Lk 13:10–17), Christ roused opposition by claiming that the "Son of Man is lord even of the Sabbath" (Mk 2:28; see Jn 5:2–18). The Seventh-Day Adventists observe Saturday as their holy day, as does the Ethiopian (non-Chalcedonian) Church. See *Ethiopian Christianity; Seventh-Day Adventists; Sunday.*

SABELLIANISM. See *Modalism; Monarchianism; Patripassianism.*

SACRAMENT (Lat. "public pledge of fidelity"). A visible sign instituted by Christ which reveals and communicates grace. The Catholic Church and the Orthodox accept seven such sacraments: baptism, confirmation, eucharist, marriage, holy orders, anointing of the sick and penance (see CIC 840–1165). Eastern Christians speak of a "sacrament" as *mysterion* (Gr. "hidden reality"), a term that lends itself to a more general use (see DS 860, 1310). Protestants generally recognize only two sacraments, baptism and the eucharist. Three sacraments (baptism, confirmation and priesthood) confer a permanent "character" and cannot be repeated (see DS 781, 1313, 1767 and 1774). Since the middle ages sacraments have been analyzed according to their "form" or words and "matter" or elements like water, bread, wine or oil used for their administration. The confession of sins by the penitent and the exchange of consent during marriage are considered the quasi-matter of those two sacraments (see DS 1601–1816). Outstanding contributions to sacramental theology have come from St. Augustine of Hippo (354–430), Dionysius the Pseudo-Areopagite (ca. 500), Peter Lombard (ca. 1100–60), Hugh of St. Victor (ca. 1096–1142), whose symbolic interpretation of reality brings him closer to eastern theology, St. Thomas Aquinas (ca. 1225–1274), Matthias Joseph Scheeben (1835–88) and Odo Casel (1886–1948). Modern theology speaks of (a) Christ as the primordial sacrament or the efficacious sign of God's grace and (b) the church he established as the foundational sacrament, which is realized concretely in the life of the seven sacraments—a vision of sacramental life developed by Otto Semmelroth (1912–79), Karl Rahner (1904–84) and Edward Schillebeeckx (b. 1914) (see SC 27; LG 7, 11). See *Anointing of the Sick; Baptism; Character; Confirmation; Donatism; Eucharist; Ex Opere Operantis; Ex Opere Operato; Grace; Holy Orders; Marriage; Minister; Penance, Sacrament of; Res et Sacramentum; Sphragis; Symbol, Theology of; Validity.*

SACRAMENTAL. A sacred sign instituted by the church, which resembles the sacraments and which signifies and obtains spiritual effects through the church's intercession (SC 60; CIC 1166). By expanding the definition of sacramentals from things (e.g., the palms distributed on Palm Sunday) or practices (e.g., the rosary) to speak of all-inclusive signs, the Second Vatican Council indicated that every event of life can be sanctified. Formerly only clerics could be legitimate ministers of sacramentals. Now lay persons can administer some of them in accord with the judgment of the local bishop and the norms of the liturgical books (SC 79; CIC 1168). Examples of lay persons administering sacramentals include the distribution of ashes on Ash Wednesday and parents leading their children in saying the rosary. See *Holy Week; Ordinary; Rosary; Sacrament.*

SACRIFICE (Lat. "making holy"). The offering of a gift to God in worship

(Gen 4:2–5). Sacrifices can express praise, thanksgiving and repentance toward God, expiate sin (Heb 9:22), support prayers of intercession, seal a covenant (Exod 24:4–8) and strengthen communion between God and the worshipers. Both within the Jewish-Christian tradition and beyond, the nature and reality of sacrifice usually involve a priest offering a victim in a cultic setting. The OT, especially the prophets, insisted on the proper intention and just life of those worshiping God through sacrifices (Isa 1:2–31; Hos 6:6; Amos 5:21–24; Ps 51:15–17). Jesus echoed Hosea in stressing the priority of "mercy" over sacrifice (Matt 9:13; 12:7). He understood his own coming death as a sacrifice that would atone for sins and bring a new and enduring covenant (Mk 14:22–24; 1 Cor 11:23–26). See *Blood of Christ; Covenant; Eucharist; Expiation; Holocaust; Passover; Priest; Worship; Yom Kippur.*

SACRIFICE OF THE MASS. The re-presentation in the eucharist of the perfect sacrifice of Christ's death and resurrection (Rom 3:25; 4:25; Heb 10:12, 14). So far from being another sacrifice, the mass is the daily offering "in memory of" (Luke 22:19; 1 Cor 11:24–25) and re-presenting what happened once and for all on the first Holy Thursday, Good Friday and Easter Sunday. There are many masses but only one sacrifice. The Council of Trent (1545–63) insisted on the sacrificial nature of the mass, which in a bloodless way reenacts for the benefit of all the one sacrifice of Calvary (see DS 1733–62). The Second Vatican Council gave a richer teaching on the mass (PO 2; SC 7; LG 3, 28), noting, for instance, how it is a "paschal banquet" or sacrificial meal (SC 47). The Byzantine tradition highlights the uniqueness of Christ's sacrifice by not celebrating more than one mass a day in any church. See *Anamnesis; Eucharist; Mass.*

SACRILEGE (Lat. "bringing the sacred under one's control"). Violating sacred persons, events, places and things. Examples would be: profaning a church, stealing chalices and doing violence to persons leading a consecrated life. See *Consecration.*

SADDUCEES. Traditionally considered descendants of the priest Zadok (2 Sam 8:17; 1 Kings 1:8). From the second century this priestly aristocratic group exercised strong economic and political influence. Basing themselves on the Torah, they rejected oral traditions, the resurrection of the dead and the existence of angels (Mk 12:18–27; Acts 23:6–8). The high priest Caiaphas and other Sadducees had their political and religious reasons for helping to bring about Jesus' execution by Pontius Pilate (see also Acts 4:1; 5:17). After the fall of Jerusalem in A.D. 70 the Sadducees disappeared as a group. See *Angels; Pharisees; Resurrection; Torah.*

211

SAINT (Lat. "one who is holy or set apart"). One called to full personal perfection or already enjoying that condition in eternal life with God. All baptized Christians receive a vocation to holiness (LG 39–42). After their death some are officially recognized for their outstanding sanctity (SC 8, 104, 111; LG 50–51). As Léon Bloy (1846–1917) summed up life, "the only sadness is not to love God, not to be a saint." See *Beatification; Canonization; Holiness; Holiness of the Church; Perfection; Trisagion; Veneration of Saints.*

SAINT THOMAS CHRISTIANS. See *Malabar Christians.*

SALVATION (Lat. "making safe," "rescuing"). A comprehensive term for being delivered from personal or collective suffering and evil. The Passover recalls the deliverance through the water (Exod 12:1–28; 14:15–31) of a people threatened with genocide (Exod 1:8–22). Human deliverers often play a part, but in salvation God's role alone is decisive (Exod 15:1–21; Psalms 46, 48, 76, 87). The OT may highlight the this-worldly nature of salvation (Deut 33:28–29; Isa 2:1–5), but the Sinai covenant and its aftermath always include spiritual, other-worldly elements (Ezek 36:22–32). Prophetic (Jer 31:3–34; Ezek 37:1–14), eschatological (Isa 43:5–44:5) and clearly apocalyptic (Dan 12:1–3) promises pointed to a future salvation to come from God. The NT stresses liberation from the bondage to sin and death (Mark 1:5; Rom 5:12–7:25; Heb 2:14–18). Mary's Son is called "Jesus" (= "God is salvation") because "he will save his people from their sins" (Matt 1:21; see Acts 4:12). The "rule of God" and the "kingdom of heaven" are reverent circumlocutions for the divine salvation that will reach its climax at the *eschaton* (Rom 5:8–10; 13:11; Heb 9:28; 1 Pet 1:5). Practically every page of the Bible has something to say, directly or indirectly, about salvation, its nature and its mediation. The *Benedictus* is perhaps the finest biblical prayer of thanksgiving for God's saving interventions (Lk 1:67–79). See *Apocalyptic Literature; Atonement; Covenant; Eschaton; Grace; Holy Spirit; Justification; Kingdom of God; Messiah; Parousia; Passover; Reconciliation; Redemption; Resurrection of the Dead; Sin; Soteriology.*

SALVATION HISTORY. The whole story of human beings and their world seen as a drama of redemption running from creation to the *parousia* and finding its center in Christ (Eph 1:3–14; Col 1:15–20). Developed by Protestant scholars like Johann Christian Konrad von Hofmann (1810–77), the theme of salvation history provided the key to OT theology for Gerhard von Rad (1901–71). He presented Israel's history as first confessed in ancient creeds (Deut 26:5–9; Josh 24:2–13). That history of salvation is marked by ever-increasing expectations as divine promises point to future fulfillment. For Oskar Cullmann (b. 1902) the reality of external events is central to God's saving acts that reach their climax in Christ. Luke's scheme of salvation history, which presents Christ as the center of time, is for Cullmann the heart of NT theology. The Second Vatican Council used the theme of salvation history, understanding it as practically synonymous with the history of revelation (DV 2–4; 14–15; AG 3). See *Creed; Hope; Salvation; Prophet; Parousia; Redemption; Revelation.*

SANCTIFICATION (Lat. "being made holy," "making holy"). God's action in enabling human beings, whose sins have been forgiven, to participate more fully in the divine holiness and perfection. Through the Holy Spirit (1 Pet 1:2) sanctification continues and completes a process that begins with justification (see 1 Cor 1:30; 6:11). Sanctification consists in charity, and comes through frequenting the sacraments (see DS 225–30). Whereas Protestants tend to emphasize how sanctification in this life is radically incomplete, the Council of Trent insists that it is possible through God's abundant grace (see DS 1530–33). Eastern Christians prefer to speak of deification (2 Pet 1:4). See *Deification; Grace; Holiness; Justification.*

SARDICA, COUNCIL OF (ca. 343). A council held in Sardica (= Sofia, capital of Bulgaria) and convoked by the western Emperor Constantius and the eastern Emperor, his brother Constans, to heal a rift between east and west occasioned by Arianism and the question of the orthodoxy of St. Athanasius of Alexandria (ca. 296–373). After arriving, most of the eastern bishops pretended to have heard that their emperor had won a victory and retired to celebrate in nearby Philippopolis. The westerners, under the presidency of Hosius of Cordoba, affirmed the orthodoxy of Athanasius and even of Marcellus of Ancyra (= Ankara; he died ca. 374). This council is also important because of its disciplinary canons which allowed for appeals to the pope (see DS 133–36). See *Arianism; Modalism; Primacy.*

SARX (Gr. "flesh"). The flesh of animals and human beings (1 Cor 15:39), the human body (Acts 2:31), the human condition (Jn 1:14), earthly descent (Rom 1:3), merely natural standards of life (1 Cor 1:26) and the force of bodily existence that leads to sin, as opposed to living by the Spirit (Gal 5:16–26). See *Logos-Sarx Christology; Nature; Soma; Spirit.*

SATAN (Heb. "opponent"). Understood at first as an adversary who plots against someone (Job 1:6–2:10) and later as the devil or supremely evil leader of the fallen angels who seeks to disrupt God's plan of salvation for humanity (Matt 13:39; Mk 1:13; 4:15; Lk 10:18; 13:16; Jn 13:2,

213

27). For opposing his suffering destiny, Jesus rebukes St. Peter and calls him "Satan" (Mk 8:33). See *Angels; Demons; Devil.*

SATISFACTION (Lat. "making amends"). (a) An interpretation of the incarnation and redemption in terms of Christ, by his freely accepted death, vicariously making amends for the offense to the divine honor caused by sin. St. Anselm of Canterbury (ca. 1033–1109) developed the classical version of this view and won a wide following in the middle ages, the reformation period and later. Through his sinlessness, humanity and divinity, Christ (and only Christ) could sufficiently satisfy on our behalf for the infinite dishonor to God which is sin. Anselm's theory has been falsely criticized for highlighting legalistic and punitive elements. One of its real weaknesses, however, is that it interprets the redemption without taking into account the resurrection (see Rom 4:25). (b) "Satisfaction" also refers to the third stage (after contrition and confession) in the sacrament of reconciliation: the penance imposed by the priest to repair in some small way the harm caused by sin and receive further healing grace from God. See *Atonement; Confession; Contrition; Expiation; Incarnation; Penance, Sacrament of; Redemption; Reparation.*

SCANDAL (Gr. "stumbling-block"). Some deed or word that tempts others to sin (Rom 14:13; 16:17). Christ warns against scandalizing others (Matt 16:23; Mk 9:42) or allowing oneself to be "scandalized" (Mk 9:43–47). The 1983 Code of Canon Law both alerts us to ways of avoiding or causing scandal and imposes penalties on those who cause serious scandal (see CIC 277, 326, 695–96, 703, 903, 990, 1132, 1184, 1211, 1455, 1560, 1722 and 1727). In the NT "scandal" can also refer to something good which, nevertheless, arouses disapproval and opposition (Jn 6:61–62; 1 Cor 1:23). See *Canon Law; Sin.*

SCEPTICISM (Gr. "inquiring, doubting"). Doubting the possibility of knowing anything for certain. Gorgias (fifth century B.C.) and Pyrrho of Elis (ca. 360–270 B.C.) held that the human race cannot reach certainty about anything whatsoever. Such absolute scepticism, sometimes called Pyrrhonism, is obviously self-contradictory. Relative scepticism limits itself to some areas of knowledge: for instance, religious and moral truth. See *Relativism.*

SCHISM (Gr. "division"). Separation into opposed groups (Jn 7:43; 1 Cor 1:10; 11:18; 12:25). Prefigured by the OT division between the Northern and Southern Kingdoms that followed Solomon's death (931 B.C.), schisms have harmed the life and unity of the church. Heresy and schism are not always clearly distinguishable, but one can say this: whereas real heresy means sinning against faith by wilfully rejecting revealed truths, schismatics offend against love by breaking off communion with other members of the church. Schisms are not primarily provoked by doctrinal matters but by differences over authority and church order. The most serious schism in Christianity has been that between the Catholic west and the Orthodox east. Although conventionally dated to 1054, on the one hand, this schism had been preceded by many earlier tensions and, on the other hand, was not fully felt by rank and file Christians on both sides for a long time afterwards. Despite the reconciliation between Rome and Constantinople which occurred at the end of the Second Vatican Council, this schism is not yet fully healed today. Vatican II acknowledges separations and divisions (UR 3, 13), but never uses the terms "schism" or "schismatics"; nor for that matter does it ever speak of "heresy" and "heretics." See *Dialogue; Ecumenism; Filioque; Florence, Council of; Heresy; Vatican Council, Second.*

SCHOLASTICISM (Gr. "leisure;" Lat. "study," "teaching"). An academic and monastic tradition that used Aristotelian and Platonic philosophy to understand, interpret systematically and speculate about the truths of faith. Building on St. Augustine of Hippo (354–430), Boethius (ca. 480–ca. 524) and others, scholasticism really began with St. Anselm of Canterbury (ca. 1033–1109) and his program of *fides quaerens intellectum* (Lat. "faith seeking understanding"). After Peter Abelard (1079–1142) and Peter Lombard (ca. 1100–60) it found its greatest exponents in St. Thomas Aquinas (ca. 1225–74), St. Bonaventure (ca. 1217–74) and Duns Scotus (ca. 1265–1308). With William of Occam (ca. 1285–1347) scholasticism declined into empty nominalism. See *Aristotelianism; Neoscholasticism; Neo-Thomism; Nominalism; Perennial Philosophy; Philosophy; Platonism; Schools of Theology; Summa; Thomism.*

SCHOOLS OF THEOLOGY. Various groups of theologians who investigate and systematically present the data of scripture and tradition in their own characteristic ways. Their methods and standards have been affected by their setting (e.g., a university, a monastery or a seminary), their audiences (e.g., seminarians, the general public or the church at large) and their philosophical differences (e.g., Aristotelianism, existentialism, Platonism or process thought). In the middle ages the great schools of theology (Augustinianism, Dominican and Franciscan) were mostly associated with such new universities as Bologna, Cambridge, Cologne, Naples, Oxford and Paris and/or with such great teachers as the Franciscan St. Bonaventure (1221–74), the Dominicans St. Albert the Great (ca. 1200–80) and St. Thomas Aquinas (ca. 1225–74) and, a little later, the Franciscans Duns Scotus (ca. 1265–1308) and William of Occam (ca. 1285–ca. 1347). In the nineteenth and twentieth centuries schools of theology have likewise been associated with particular institutions (e.g., the University of Tübingen, the University of Chicago and the Gregorian University in Rome), and/or with figures like Karl Barth (1886–1968), Karl Rahner (1904–84), Bernard Lonergan (1904–84) Hans Urs von Balthasar (1905–88) and Paul Tillich (1886–1965). See *Augustinianism; Neoscholasticism; Neo-Thomism; Nominalism; Scholasticism; Scotism; Thomism; Tübingen and Its Schools.*

SCIENCE AND RELIGION. The tension that from the seventeenth century emerged between (a) scientific discoveries, laws and methods and (b) religious beliefs. Difficulties have come from such disciplines as astronomy, biology, paleontology, physics, psychology and sociology. Ironically it can be argued that the Jewish-Christian faith in God the creator made possible the very rise of western science. The trial of Galileo Galilei (1564–1642) created the enduring image of an official church refusing to accept new discoveries and trying to limit proper scientific freedom. That case, like the debate over the theory of evolution developed by Charles Darwin (1809–82), also highlighted the issue of the proper interpretation of biblical texts. In the twentieth century scientific and technological growth has been spectacular. Along with that has come the now widely-held conviction that science cannot answer by itself ultimate questions about meaning and values, may prove dehumanizing and extremely dangerous (e.g., nuclear weapons), and should respect the different methods employed in philosophy and theology. Progress in theories of knowledge has shown that even in the natural sciences broad claims to pure, impartial "objectivity" should be abandoned. For many the French priest-paleontologist Pierre Teilhard de Chardin (1881–1955) has symbolized the new dialogue that has replaced the old antagonism between science and religion. Whether found in religion or in science, all truth is based in God and can never be opposed to itself (see GS 36). See *Autonomy; Biblical Criticism; Creationism; Evolution; Fundamentalism; God of the Gaps; Positivism; Truth.*

SCIENTIA MEDIA (Lat. "intermediate knowledge"). Concept developed by the Jesuit Luis de Molina (1535–1600) to reconcile real human freedom with the divine foreknowledge of everything that will happen. He suggested a knowledge with which God knows future possibilities, a knowledge that is more than a knowledge of mere possibilities but less than a vision of actual future events. See *Foreknowledge; Molinism.*

SCOTISM. The system developed by the Franciscan Duns Scotus (ca. 1265–1308), who came from Scotland, taught in Cambridge, Oxford, Paris and Cologne, and for his great speculative capacity was called "*doctor subtilis*" (Lat. "subtle doctor"). Unlike St. Thomas Aquinas (ca. 1225–74) he gave the primacy to love and will (instead of knowledge and reason) and hence argued that our heavenly happiness will consist primarily in our love for (rather than our vision of) God. Scotus also differed from Aquinas by championing the doctrine of the Immaculate Conception. He held that the incarnation was no mere rescue operation mounted because of the Fall but would have happened anyway. Scotus' notion that particular beings are individuated through a *haecceitas* (Lat. "this-ness") which is somehow intelligible and his speculations about *possibilia* (Lat. "possibilities") exercised an influence on Martin Heidegger (1889–1976). See *Beatific Vision; Fall, The; Immaculate Conception; Incarnation; Scholasticism; Schools of Theology; Thomism.*

SCRIBES. Originally copiers and keepers of records whose further skills could lead to their official advancement (Ps 45:2 Ezra 7:6; Sir 39:1–11; see Jer 8:8). At the time of Jesus they came mainly, but not exclusively, from the Pharisees, and with the chief priests and the elders made up the 71 members of the Sanhedrin or supreme Jewish council in Jerusalem. Because of their work in interpreting and applying scripture, they were called "doctors of the law" or "lawyers" (Lk 7:30). See *Bible; Torah.*

SCRIPTURE. See *Bible.*

SCRIPTURE AND TRADITION. The relationship between the written and inspired Word of God and the wider reality of the church in her "doctrine, life and worship" handing on "to every generation all that she herself is, all that she believes" (DV 8). Against the reformers' principle of "sola scriptura" (Lat. "scripture alone"), the Council of Trent (1545–63) taught that the "gospel" was "the source of all saving truth and rule of conduct." It was "contained" not only in the "written books" but also in the "unwritten traditions which have come down to us" (DS 1501). Although the council had spoken of one source ("the gospel"), this teaching led many Catholics to develop the "two-source" theory, according to which some revealed truths could be contained in tradition and not in scripture. The Second Vatican Council understood revelation as being primarily the living self-communication of God (DV 2–6) rather than a body of revealed propositions "contained" in the Bible or other sources. The council stressed the process of tradition (singular!) rather than individual traditions (= particular teachings or practices), insisted on the way tradition and scripture are united in their origin (= revelation), function and goal (DV 9) and, while speaking only of the scripture as the word of God, recognized the role of tradition in clarifying and actualizing revelation (DV 8). Thanks to a 1963 meeting of the Faith and Order Commission of the World Council of Churches and the influence of Yves Congar (b. 1904), Gerhard Ebeling (b. 1912), Hans Georg Gadamer (b. 1900) and others, more and more Protestants have accepted that an exclusive appeal to the scripture alone is not possible. Tradition is an essential means for understanding revelation, while scripture has its special role in judging and reforming traditions. See *Bible; Holy Spirit; Lutheranism; Magisterium; Protestant; Reformation, The; Sola Scriptura; Sufficiency of Scripture; Tradition; Word of God.*

SECOND COMING. See *Parousia.*

SECULARISM (Lat. "belief in the world"). (a) An atheist or agnostic ideology which rules out religious beliefs and values, and which explains everything exclusively in this-worldly terms. (b) This is to be distinguished from "secularity," or the attitude of being concerned with this world and its affairs but not necessarily in an anti-religious way. (c) "Secularization" refers to any social and historical process which brings a change away from ecclesial control and sacred purposes: e.g., the suppression of the monasteries in sixteenth-century England, the impact of the French Revolution in France itself and the policy of Napoleon Bonaparte (1769–1821) in Germany. Land and buildings, originally used for religious life, were appropriated by nobles, merchants and others for thoroughly mundane, this-worldly purposes. (d) The "secular" clergy are priests under obedience to the bishop of their diocese, as distinguished from priests who belong to religious orders or congregations. See *Autonomy; Clergy; Diocese; Ordinary; Religious Life.*

SELF-COMMUNICATION. Term used by German idealists like Georg Wilhelm Friedrich Hegel (1770–1831), and then adopted by theologians like Karl Rahner (1904–84) and the Second Vatican Council (DV 6) to designate the self-manifestation and self-giving of God in the process of revelation and grace. See *Deification; Grace; Idealism; Revelation.*

SEMI-ARIANISM. The teaching of Bishop Basil of Ancyra (= Ankara) and others after Nicea I (325). They did not follow the Arian view of Christ being only the first among creatures but did not yet endorse the orthodox doctrine of his being *homoousios* (Gr. "of one substance") with the Father. They called the Son *homo-i-ousios* (Gr. "of a similar nature") to the Father. Although their term was heretical, the difference of only an "i" created a platform of dialogue which helped many Semi-Arians towards full orthodoxy. See *Arianism; Homoousios; Nicaea, First Council of.*

SEMI-PELAGIANISM. The view which derives from St. John Cassian of Marseilles (ca. 360–435), St. Vincent of Lérins (d. before 450) and other monks in southern France, and according to which human beings can make their first step toward God without the help of divine grace. While accepting that grace is indispensable for salvation and so rejecting Pelagianism, those who developed Semi-Pelagianism (as it came to be called in the late sixteenth century) did so at least partly because of their opposition to the extreme version of predestination advanced by St. Augustine of Hippo (354–430). Eventually Semi-Pelagianism was condemned at the Second Council of Orange (529). Official church teaching, while following Augustine's teaching on grace (see DS 370–97; 2004–05; 2618; 2620), has never endorsed his interpretation on predestination. See *Anthropology; Grace; Pelagianism; Predestination.*

SENSE OF FAITH. See *Sensus Fidelium.*

SENSES OF SCRIPTURE. The various meanings that biblical texts can convey. The *literal* sense is the meaning intended by the original author writing for a particular audience, in given historical circumstances and using specific literary forms. Once written, however, a biblical text, like other texts, begins to have a life of its own. It will be read and interpreted in contexts very different from that in which it was originally composed. It will communicate and evoke meanings that go beyond what the original author intended. Over the centuries those who hear, read and use biblical texts for prayer bring to this dialogue their own questions and interests; they can thus discover fresh ranges of meaning. By looking for and often establishing, at least in part, the literal sense, biblical criticism remains essential; among other things it can check wild flights of subjective interpretation. At the same time, the Holy Spirit who first inspired the writing of the biblical texts enlightens individuals and the whole community to find meaning and life in those texts today (see DV 12, 21–25). From Origen (ca. 185–ca. 234) to Pope Benedict XV (1854–1922) and beyond, believers have witnessed to their conviction that the whole Bible is centered on Christ and finds its meaning in him. See *Alexandrian Theology; Antiochene Theology; Allegory; Biblical Criticism; Exegesis; Fundamentalism; Hermeneutics; Inspiration; Origenism; Sensus Plenior; Typology.*

SENSUS FIDELIUM (Lat. "sense of the faithful"). The instinctive sensitivity in matters of faith exercised by the whole body of believers (LG 12, DV 8), whose appreciation and discernment of revelation is guided by the Holy Spirit (Jn 16:13; 1 Jn 2:20, 27). This sense of faith gives rise to and manifests itself in the *consensus fidelium* (Lat. "consensus of the faithful"), as a cause produces its corresponding effects. Those who have helped to develop this idea include John Henry Newman (1801–90), Matthias Joseph Scheeben (1835–88) and Johann Adam Möhler (1796–1838). See *Faith; Grace; Holy Spirit; Indefectibility.*

SENSUS PLENIOR (Lat. "fuller sense"). The way that the scriptures (e.g.,

OT texts) can have meanings which go beyond the literal sense (= the meaning explicitly intended by the original human author). Such meanings, intended by the principal author (God), have emerged in the light of later events in the divinely guided history of salvation. See *Senses of Scripture*.

SEPTUAGINT (Gr. "seventy"). The most important Greek version of the OT, known as "LXX" because of the legend that the translation was made by seventy (or seventy-two) scholars working independently. According to Jewish tradition, it was commissioned by Ptolemy Philadelphus (285–246 B.C.) for his famous library in Alexandria. While seeming to be a joint work of many translators, it was probably finished later—by about 132 B.C. In important respects it differs from the Hebrew Bible. Books which are simply not found in the Hebrew Bible (like Tobit, Judith, Wisdom, Sirach and Baruch) have been introduced, and some books (e.g., Esther) appear in a longer form. These traditional books and passages, called "Apocrypha" in the Protestant tradition, are considered "deuterocanonical" by Catholics and Orthodox. When citing the OT, NT authors often follow the LXX rather than the original Hebrew. Many early fathers of the church considered the LXX the standard version of the OT. See *Apocrypha; Bible; Canon of Scripture; Deuterocanonical Books; Old Testament; Vulgate.*

SEVEN ECUMENICAL COUNCILS, THE. Those general councils from Nicaea I (325) to Nicaea II (787) recognized as ecumenical by both Roman Catholics and the Greek Orthodox. They enjoy a unique importance in any dialogue between east and west. Although the Greek Orthodox later on held important councils like those of Constantinople in 1351 and Jerusalem in 1672, none of them were considered ecumenical. Roman Catholics have normally counted 21 ecumenical councils down to the Second Vatican Council. See *Chalcedon, Council of; Constantinople, First Council of; Constantinople, Second Council of; Constantinople, Third Council of; Council, Ecumenical; Ephesus, Council of; Nicaea, First Council of; Nicaea, Second Council of.*

SEVENTH-DAY ADVENTISTS. A group that broke away from mainline Adventists after William Miller (1742–1849) announced 1844 as the year for the end of the world and the second coming of Christ. Ellen G. White (1827–1915) was a prominent figure among the Seventh-Day Adventists. They observe the sabbath instead of Sunday, practice adult baptism by complete immersion, abstain from alcohol and tobacco, and live in expectation of the *parousia*, without, however, predicting a definite year for Christ's return. See *Advent; Parousia; Sabbath; Sunday.*

SHEKINAH (Heb. "abode, dwelling-place," formed from the verb "to pitch a tent"). God's glorious presence in our midst. Although it does not use the word, the OT refers to the Tent of Encounter in the desert where God's glory was manifested (see Exod 33:7–11; Num 11:16–25; 12:1–10). In the Talmud the term can be a reverent circumlocution for God. The fourth gospel uses the notion of the *shekinah* in speaking of the incarnation (Jn 1:14). See *Doxa; Glory; Talmud*.

SHEMA (Heb. "listen!"). The first word of a prayer which in its full form was composed from Deut 6:4–9; 11:13–21 and Num 15:37–41, but runs as follows in its shorter form: "Hear, o Israel, the Lord Our God is the Lord. You will love the Lord your God with your whole heart, with your whole soul and with your whole power" (Deut 6:4–5). Christ quoted the opening line of this prayer when answering a scribe's question about the greatest commandment (Mk 12:28–30). The *Shema* occupies in Jewish piety the central place that the "Our Father" does in Christian piety. See *Love; Prayer*.

SHEOL (etymology uncertain). The place in the underworld where all the dead lead the same shadowy existence (Gen 37:35; Num 16:31–34; Deut 32:22; Job 3:13–19; 26:5–6; Isa 14:9–11). Long life on earth is desirable, because the dead can no longer praise God (Ps 6:5–6; 88:3–6, 11–13; Isa 38:18). See *Eschatology; Heaven; Hell; Purgatory*.

SIMONY. Dealing with spiritual goods as if they were for sale. Selling or buying a church office or sacrament constitutes the sin of simony. The name comes from a magician Simon who wanted to buy from Peter and John the power to impart the Holy Spirit (Acts 8:9–25). At times simony has disfigured the life of the church, and has been repeatedly condemned (see DS 304, 473, 586, 691–94, 707, 751, 820; CIC 149, 188 and 1380). See *Office*.

SIMPLICITY. The characteristic of being indivisible and not made up of various parts. Being spiritual and entirely self-present, God is simple in this ontological sense (Jn 4:24; see DS 297, 800, 805, 1880 and 3001). In the moral sphere simplicity refers to the uncomplicated rightness of intention with which the truly religious person acts (see Matt 10:16). See *Immutability; Prudence; Suffering of God*.

SIMUL PECCATOR ET JUSTUS (Lat. "being sinful and righteous at the same time"). A phrase summarizing the Lutheran conviction that we always have to confess ourselves sinners, when we look at ourselves in the light of the accusing law and of our own natural possibilities. At the same time, we should admit that we are really justified when we believe

221

in God's promise of forgiveness and mercy. See *Depravity, Total; Imputation; Justification; Lutheranism; Protestant; Sin.*

SIN. Any thought, word or deed that deliberately disobeys God's will and in some way rejects the divine goodness and love. Starting from the sin of Adam and Eve (Gen 3:1–24), the OT tells a story of human sin and bondage to sin (see GS 37). Repeatedly denouncing idolatry and injustice, the prophets affirmed personal responsibility for sinful failures (Jer 31:29–30; Ezek 18:1–4). The OT calls sin *hatta* (Heb. "missing the mark"), *pesha* (Heb. "transgression of orders," "revolt against superiors") and *awon* (Heb. "guilt stemming from iniquity") (see Ps 51:3–5). Like the OT (Gen 6:5; 8:21; Jer 17:9) Jesus saw how sin comes from the heart (Mk 7:20–23). St. John's gospel understood sin as disbelief in Christ, a preference for darkness over the Light of the world (Jn 3:16–21; 9:1–41; 11:9–10). From the outset Christians acknowledged how Christ had died "for our sins" (1 Cor 15:3; see Rom 4:25; Heb 2:11–14). The Protestant tradition has been impressed by St. Paul's reflections on the power of sin to corrupt and enslave human beings (Rom 1:18–3:23; 5:12–21; 6:15–23). The Orthodox tradition sees how sin destroys *koinonia* (Gr. "communion") with God, with other human beings and with nature. The Catholic tradition, like western Christianity generally, has tended to think of the sins of individuals rather than of the community wounded by sin. But the 1987 encyclical of John Paul II, *Sollicitudo Rei Socialis* (see 36–37) witnesses to a renewed sense of the societal dimension of sin (see GS 25). See *Atonement; Expiation; Fall, The; Grace; Heart; Koinonia; Metanoia; Original Sin; Penance, Sacrament of; Reparation; Salvation.*

SIN, MORTAL AND VENIAL. A distinction between sins which "exclude from the kingdom of God" (1 Cor 6:9–10; Gal 5:19–21; Eph 5:5) and those which do not do so (Jas 3:2; 1 Jn 1:8; 5:16–17). A mortal (Lat. "deadly") sin means a deliberate and radical turning away from God which comes through clear knowledge and full consent in a truly serious matter (see DS 1537, 1544, 1680–82). It brings the loss of sanctifying grace and the risk of eternal damnation. Venial (Lat. "excusable") sins truly harm one's relationship with God and others, but do not entail a fundamental option against God. See *Fundamental Option; Grace, Habitual; Hell; Penance, Sacrament of.*

SIN, ORIGINAL. See *Original Sin.*

SINS, SEVEN DEADLY. The sins traditionally considered to be the root of all other sins. As developed by Evagrius Ponticus (346–399), St. Gregory the Great (ca. 540–604) and others, the list settled down as follows:

pride, covetousness, lust, envy, gluttony, anger and sloth. *"Sloth"* translates inadequately *acedia* (Gr. "indifference"), which means apathy, torpor or a distaste for spiritual matters.

SITZ IM LEBEN (German "place in life," "life-context"). Term popularized by Hermann Gunkel (1862–1932) and other pioneers of form criticism. It refers to the function a particular biblical unit (e.g., a hymn, saying or story) could have enjoyed in the life and worship of the community. In the case of the NT it refers especially to the way specific traditions about the earthly Jesus were shaped and handed on (orally or perhaps sometimes in writing) during the post-Pentecost period until Mark and the other evangelists wrote their gospels (A.D. 30–ca. 67). Sometimes scholars speak of the *"Sitz im Leben Jesu"*—that is to say, the historical circumstances in which Jesus told a parable, cured some sick person or pronounced on a given issue. See *Biblical Criticism*.

SOBORNOST (Russian "conciliarism"). Term which was used by Jurij Samarin (1819–76) in the Russian translation of the English and French works of Alexej Chomjakow (1804–60), Russian Orthodox layman and theologian, and which can be rendered by "conciliarity" or "collegiality" (from the Russian *sobor* meaning "gathering," "synod"). From the eleventh century the word *"soborny"* had been used in the Slavonic version of the creed to translate "Catholic" in "the Catholic Church." Chomjakow held *sobornost* to be the distinguishing characteristic of the Orthodox Church: the loving collaboration of the faithful and hierarchy in their life, belief and worship. He argued that Catholics have unity without freedom, Protestants freedom without unity, and the Orthodox freedom in the bond of love. *Sobornost* amounts to the collegiality of all church members. See *Catholicity; Collegiality; Eastern Churches; Orthodoxy; Synod*.

SOCIAL TEACHING. Church teaching concerning the rights and obligations of different members of society in their relationship to the common good, both national and international. Jesus' message of repentance called on the financially secure to care for the poor, the maimed, the lame and the blind (Lk 14:12–14). The future judgment should encourage us to attend now to the earthly needs of the hungry, strangers, the naked, the sick and prisoners (Matt 25:31–46). In general, the NT shows the same practical concern for needy people (Acts 4:32–5:11; Rom 12:8; 1 Cor 13:3; Heb 13:16; 1 Jn 3:17; Jas 1:27; 2:14–17). St. Ambrose (ca. 339–97), St. John Chrysostom (ca. 347–407) and other fathers preached the same message. For centuries church institutions stood almost alone in caring for the socially deprived like widows, orphans, the sick and prisoners, as well as in providing education through monastic orders like the Benedictines. St. Vincent de Paul (ca. 1580–1660), the Daughters of Charity, the Sisters of Mercy, Antoine Frédéric Ozanam (1813–53), Joseph de Veuster (1840–89), known as Father Damien, Adolf Kolping (1813–65) and many others spent their lives meeting the needs of the poor and suffering. The first great social encyclical was Leo XIII's 1891 *Rerum Novarum* (Lat. "Of New Topics") which addressed itself to such questions as just wages and private property. Forty years later in 1931, Pius XI took up these and related themes in his *Quadragesimo Anno* (Lat. "On the Fortieth Anniversary"). John XXIII's *Mater et Magistra* (Lat. "Mother and Teacher") updated the church's social teaching with an eye to state intervention in the case of the needy, whereas his 1963 *Pacem in Terris* ("Peace on Earth") advocated an international social order based on a thorough respect for human rights. The Second Vatican Council spoke out for religious freedom in its declaration *Dignitatis Humanae* (1965). The same council encouraged at every level a more specific and just social order (GS 9, 63–93), calling on church members to participate actively in social causes (AA 7, 8, 13). Although the mission Christ gave his church does not primarily concern the political, economic and social areas, religious faith heightens our obligations to neighbors in need (GS 42). In his 1967 *Populorum Progressio* (Lat. "Progress of the Peoples") Paul VI called an economic development that attended to the whole human person the new name for peace. Social justice, international solidarity and human rights have been constant themes of John Paul II's teaching, expressed, in particular, through his 1981 and 1987 encyclicals *Laborem Exercens* (Lat. "Through Work") and *Sollicitudo Rei Socialis* ("Social Concern"). See *Encyclical; Justice; Liberation Theology; Moral Theology; Option for the Poor; Rights, Human; Subsidiarity.*

SOCINIANISM. A religious system which denies the Trinity and the divinity of Christ and draws its name from the Italians Lelio Francesco Maria Sozini (1525–62) and his nephew Fausto Paolo Sozzini (1539–1604; his name was spelled differently from that of his uncle) (see DS 1880). Fausto Sozzini spent the last part of his life in Poland. Eventually many Socinians joined other forces to form the Unitarian Church. See *Trinity; Unitarianism.*

SOLA FIDES (Lat. "faith alone"). A basic axiom Martin Luther (1483–1546) gave to the Protestant reformation. Justification comes by faith in Jesus Christ (Rom 1:17) and not through the works of the law (Rom 3:28). See *Faith; Law and Gospel; Justification; Merit; Protestant.*

SOLA GRATIA (Lat. "grace alone"). A basic principle of the Protestant reformers expressing as a matter of fact the same conviction as "sola fides." We are justified only by God's mercy and Christ's merits, to which we cling by faith, and not by our own observance of the law and meritorious works. Catholic theology also teaches the absoluteness of God's grace, but stresses the importance of human "collaboration" with and within the all-embracing initiative of God's work. God and human beings are not in competition; every human success has God as its necessary inspirer and supporter. See *Faith and Works; Imputation; Justification; Pelagianism; Sanctification; Semi-Pelagianism; Synergism.*

SOLA SCRIPTURA (Lat. "Scripture alone"). Another reformation principle coming from Martin Luther (1483–1546) and recognizing the highest religious authority in the Word of God as witnessed to in scripture. In this sense, the principle can be aligned with the Second Vatican Council's statement that "the teaching office of the church is not above the Word of God but serves it" (DV 10). Luther's principle is unacceptable (and indeed unworkable) if it is taken to exclude the interpretative and actualizing role of tradition (DV 9, 21, 24). See *Bible; Magisterium; Revelation; Scripture and Tradition; Sufficiency of Scripture; Tradition.*

SOMA (Gr. "corpse," "body"). A living body (Mk 5:29) or a dead corpse (Mk 15:43). Over against Platonism and Neoplatonism, the biblical concept of "soma" shows no hostility toward matter, as if the soul were imprisoned in the body. In St. Paul's letters, unlike *sarx* (Gr. "flesh"), which may denote the whole human being as oriented toward sin, *soma* is more neutral. It can simply refer to the body as distinguished from "soul" or "spirit" (1 Thess 5:23). *Soma* is used of Christ's body in the eucharist (Mk 14:22; 1 Cor 11:24), of his church (Rom 12:4–5; 1 Cor 12:12–27) and of our earthly body that will be glorified and "spiritualized" through the resurrection (1 Cor 15:35–58; Phil 3:21). See *Body of Christ; Eucharist; Resurrection; Sarx.*

SOPHIA (Gr. "wisdom"). (a) A practical knowledge and discerning judgment, classically represented in the OT by Solomon (1 Kgs 3:1–28; 4:9–14). Revealed through creation and human history (Wis 10:1–19:22), *hokmah* (Heb. "wisdom") is personified as God's agent in creation and a prophetess (Prov 8:1–36) who invites to her feast those who are not yet wise (Prov 9:1–6). Wisdom is a sure and beneficial guide for life (Wis 6:1–9:18). The NT sees in wisdom a prefiguration of Christ (Matt 12:42; 1 Cor 1:24–30; Col 2:3), a wisdom, however, which expresses itself in the folly of the cross (1 Cor 1:17–25). (b) For the Valentinians and some other ancient Gnostics Sophia Prounicos and Sophia Achamoth had an important cosmological and ecclesial role. (c) The most famous church in eastern Christianity was *Hagia Sophia* or *Santa Sophia* (Gr. and Lat. for "Holy Wisdom"), dedicated to Christ as the personification of wisdom. Built in Constantinople and consecrated under the Emperor Justinian in

538, Santa Sophia became a model for many other Byzantine churches. After the fall of Constantinople in 1453 it became a mosque and later a museum. (d) A *sophiology* (Gr. "study of wisdom"), or theology in the key of wisdom, has been developed by Russian theologians like Vladimir Solovi'ev (1853–1900), Sergius Bulgakov (1870–1944) and Pavel Florenskij (1882–ca. 1943). See *Christology; Creation; Fools for Christ's Sake; Gifts of the Holy Spirit; Gnosticism; Valentinians; Wisdom Literature.*

SOTERIOLOGY (Gr. "doctrine of salvation"). The systematic interpretation of Christ's saving work for human beings and the world. Recognizing how Christ died and rose to save sinful humanity (Mk 14:24; Jn 11:49–52; Rom 4:25; 5:6–11; 1 Cor 15:3; 1 Pet 1:3), the NT holds together inseparably the saving function and personal identity of Christ as Son of God. Just as the NT applies various christological titles to Jesus, so it understands his saving work in a variety of ways—above all, as victorious liberation, expiation and transforming love (Jn 1:29; 13:1; 16:33). Through the influence of Philipp Melanchthon (1497–1560) and others, reflection on Christ's saving work was often partly separated from christology. Or else treatises on soteriology examined "objective" salvation apart from its "subjective" appropriation through grace. In general, recent western theology has tried to end the divorce between soteriology and christology. See *Atonement; Christology; Economy; Expiation; Grace; Love; Redemption; Salvation; Satisfaction.*

SOUL. The spiritual principle of human beings which survives their death. According to the OT the *nephesh* (Heb. "breath of life") comes from God (Gen 2:7) and disappears at death. "My *nephesh*" can mean "myself" or "my soul" (Ps 3:2–3; see Mk 8:34–36). Like the LXX the NT often uses *psyche* (Gr. "soul") as the principle of life (Rom 16:4; Phil 2:30). Toward the end of the OT Greek language and thought introduced a sense of the human soul as distinct from the body and endowed by God with immortality (Wis 3:1–9; 9:15; 16:13). Here and there the NT reflects a certain dualism between body and soul (Matt 10:28; Lk 16:22; 23:43; 2 Cor 5:6–10; Phil 1:23; 1 Pet 1:9), but primarily thinks of human beings as animated bodies destined for final resurrection. Under Stoic influence Tertullian (ca. 160–ca. 220) seems to have believed the soul to be material, whereas Origen (ca. 185–ca. 254), at the other end of the spectrum, held that our souls were not only spiritual but even preexistent. St. Thomas Aquinas (ca. 1225–1274) understood the soul to be the form of the body. This became official teaching at the Council of Vienne in 1312 (DS 902). Against the Neo-Aristotelianism of Pietro Pompanazzi (1464–1525) the Fifth Lateran Council taught in 1513 the individuality and immortality of human souls (DS 1440). See *Animism; Anthropology;*

226

Aristotelianism; Immortality; Matter and Form; Preexistence; Reincarnation; Resurrection; Stoicism; Vestigia Trinitatis; Vienne, Council of.

SPHRAGIS (Gr. "seal"). A word used in profane Greek for an official seal (e.g., that of the emperor) or a mark indicating the owner of something (see also Rev 5:1–9; 6:1–12). In the language of the Greek fathers of the church, the word refers to the cross made on catechumens during the rite of baptism to show that they belong to Christ. *Sphragis* also refers to what the Latins call the sacramental character. See *Baptism; Character.*

SPIRATION (Lat. "breathing"). A technical term based on John 3:8 and used in the doctrine of the Trinity for the way the Spirit proceeds from the Father and the Son. The NT calls the Holy Spirit the "Spirit of the Father" (Matt 10:20) and the "Spirit of the Son" (Gal 4:6). Latin theology adds that the Spirit is "breathed" from both (see DS 850; 1300), distinguishing between *active* and *passive* spiration. While common to the Father and the Son, active spiration does not make up a new person, whereas passive spiration is another name for the Holy Spirit, who is "breathed" but does not "breathe." In this way, the Latin church distinguished between the spiration by the Father, who is a principle without principle and an origin without origin, and the spiration by the Son, who is a principle originating from another principle, namely the Father. Most theologians of the Greek church, however, deny the Son's participation as origin in the procession of the Spirit, as this would impair the "monarchy" (Gr. "sole principle") or originless origin of the Father. Both the Second Council of Lyons (1274) and the Council of Florence (1439) specified that the Holy Spirit is breathed from the Father and the Son as through a single principle (DS 850; 1300). See *Filioque; Florence, Council of; Lyons, Second Council of; Processions.*

SPIRIT. See *Holy Spirit; Soul.*

SPIRITISM OR **SPIRITUALISM.** System of practices based on the belief that the souls of the dead can communicate with the living, especially through the help of a medium. While efforts to contact the dead were common enough in the past (e.g., 1 Sam 28:3–25), modern spiritualism goes back to 1848 and the abnormal experiences which Margaret and Kate Fox had in Hydesville, New York. Their influence spread séances with mediums across North America and the British Isles. Spiritualism has often been characterized by fraud and commercial exploitation. In 1882 Friedrich W.H. Meyers founded the Society for Psychical Research in London. The Society still operates and investigates parapsychological or abnormal phenomena. But the academic world at large is still reluctant to recognize parapsychology as a genuine science.

227

SPIRITUALITY. Systematic practice of and reflection on a prayerful, devout and disciplined Christian life. In its practice Christian spirituality has always called for an ascetical and prayerful life in which a spiritual guide and the light of the Holy Spirit help discern the direction in which individuals and communities are being led (1 Thess 5:19–22; 1 Jn 4:1). Schools or styles of spirituality have often followed the charisms of such orders as the Benedictines, Carmelites, Carthusians, Dominicans, Franciscans and Jesuits. As a field of study, spirituality involves theological (including liturgical), scriptural, historical, psychological and social elements. See *Asceticism; Contemplation; Devotion; Discernment of Spirits; Experience, Religious; Grace; Hesychasm; Holy Spirit; Imitation of Christ; Monasticism; Mysticism; Pneumatology; Prayer.*

SPONSOR. Another word for godfather or godmother: that is to say, the adult who supports a candidate for baptism or confirmation. Canon law lays down that at least one sponsor but possibly two, one of each sex, should be present for the ceremony or at least fulfill their task by proxy. The sponsors have to be appointed either by the candidate (if an adult), or by the candidate's parents or guardians, or by the parish priest. A sponsor must be a Catholic who has already received baptism, confirmation and the eucharist, should normally be at least sixteen years of age, and may not be a parent of the candidate. The names of the sponsors are entered in the baptismal register. Besides giving good example and encouragement in Christian living, the godparents take responsibility for the Christian education of those whom they have sponsored if the parents or guardians fail in their duty (see CIC 774, 851, 872–74). At confirmation it is desirable that the sponsor or sponsors be the same as at baptism, since the duties assumed resemble those assumed by the sponsors at baptism (CIC 892–93, 895). See *Baptism; Confirmation; Marriage Impediments.*

STARETZ (Russian "old man"). A monk leading a contemplative life to whom younger monks or other people go for spiritual guidance. This kind of direction has been important in Russian religious history, and also among the Greeks, who call the director *geron* (Gr. "old man"). See *Apophthegmata Patrum; Spirituality.*

STAUROLOGY (Gr. "study of the cross"). See *Theologia Crucis.*

STOICISM (Gr. "teaching of the porch"). A school of philosophy founded by Zeno of Citium (335–263 B.C.) and called after the *stoa* or porch in Athens where he taught. Stoicism proposed a harmony between the human being as a *microcosm* (Gr. "small world") and the *macrocosm* (Gr. "big world"). Logos (reason or a world-soul) governed the universe, and human beings needed only to control their passions so as to live in tune with nature and its laws. Primarily a moral philosophy, Stoicism held a pantheistic cosmology in which God and the divine energy pervaded everything. Dominant for centuries among intellectuals in the Graeco-Roman world, Stoicism numbered among its adherents Seneca (ca. 4 B.C.–65 A.D.) and the Emperor Marcus Aurelius (121–80). Its influence on Christian theology may be seen as early as St. Justin Martyr (ca. 100–165), who adopted the Stoic distinction between *Logos endiathetos* (Gr. "immanent word") and *Logos prophorikos* (Gr. "expressed word") to interpret God and the process of revelation by which the Father expresses the Word. Stoic ideas exercised some influence on the Cappadocian Fathers and in the Trinitarian and christological controversies. The Christian tradition of natural law owes much to Stoicism. See *Apologists; Cappadocian Fathers; Cosmology; Immanence; Logos; Natural Laws; Pantheism.*

STRUCTURALISM. A method developed by Ferdinand de Saussure (1857–1913) in the area of linguistics, used by Claude Lévi-Strauss (b. 1908) to analyze the myths of traditional societies and applied in such disciplines as psychology and sociology. In biblical exegesis structuralism is concerned neither with the genesis of a text and the meaning intended by the author (= historical exegesis), nor with readers and their search for self-understanding (= existential exegesis), but with the present meaning conveyed by the text itself. This method reflects on the deep structures of narrative and the symbolic function of language (e.g., in parables). See *Biblical Criticism; Exegesis; Existentialism; Hermeneutics; Senses of Scripture.*

SUBDEACON. A church minister who was/is on the way to becoming either a permanent deacon or a deacon and then a priest. Subdeacons existed as early as the third century. Considered a sacramental rather than a sacrament, the subdeaconate was abolished in the west after the Second Vatican Council. In the eastern Churches, it is considered to be a minor order, and the role of the subdeacon is mainly that of assisting the bishop during the liturgy. See *Clergy; Deacon; Sacramental.*

SUBORDINATIONISM. Assigning an inferior status to the Son with regard to the Father and to the Holy Spirit with regard to the Father and the Son. When the doctrine of the Trinity had not yet been worked out and theologians were trying to do justice to the Father's *monarchy* (Gr. "only principle"), the tendency to interpret the Son and Spirit as subordinate agents of an absolutely transcendent Father was shown by St. Justin Martyr (ca. 100–ca. 165), Tatian (d. ca. 160), St. Irenaeus of Lyons (ca. 130–ca. 200), St. Clement of Alexandria (ca. 150–ca. 215) and most of all

Origen (ca. 185–ca. 254). By denying that the Son was really and fully divine by nature, Arius (ca. 185–ca. 254) took subordinationism to an heretical extreme which was rejected in 325 by Nicaea I (see DS 125–26). When the *Pneumatomachians* (Gr. "denigrators of the Spirit") maintained a similar false subordinationism by declaring the Spirit to be created by the Son, Constantinople I (381) described the Spirit as being equal in dignity with, and worthy of the same worship as, the Father and the Son (see DS 150). See *Arianism; Constantinople, First Council of; Homoousios; Nicaea, First Council of; Macedonianism; Monarchianism; Pneumatomachians; Trinity, Theology of.*

SUBSIDIARITY (Lat. "assistance"). A principle consistently endorsed by the social teaching of the church according to which decisions and activities that naturally belong to a lower level should not be taken to a higher level. In social and civil life this means, for example, that the central organs of a state should not intervene unnecessarily at the local level. The Second Vatican Council appealed to the principle of subsidiarity in dealing with international cooperation in economic matters (GS 86), and in indicating the limits of the state's responsibility in education (GE 3, 6). Within the church subsidiarity has been an operative principle in many post-Vatican II reforms. See *Church and State; Education; Social Teaching.*

SUBSTANCE AND ACCIDENTS. A reality which remains the same under change, and the (often changing) characteristics which inhere in it. A *substance* (Lat. "underlying reality") can exist on its own, whereas *accidents* (Lat. "happenings") can exist only in a substance and not independently. See *Accident; Aristotelianism; Homoousios; Nature; Person; Transubstantiation.*

SUFFERING OF GOD. The question whether God can/does suffer, or remains "impassible," in the face of human misery. While God cannot change and suffer in the divine nature, by reason of his human nature the incarnate Son of God suffered and died on a cross. That appalling death expressed for all time God's loving concern for and real solidarity with human beings in their pain and suffering. See *Evil, Mystery of; Impassibility; Patripassianism; Process Theology; Theopaschite Controversy.*

SUFFICIENCY OF SCRIPTURE. The adequacy of scripture in communicating the foundational revelation that reached its absolute, unsurpassable completeness with Christ and the NT church. As long as Christians conceived of revelation as *primarily* a body of truths (plural) disclosed by God, the question of sufficiency became twofold. Do the scriptures "contain" all these revealed truths (= material sufficiency)? Are the scriptures "formally" sufficient, in the sense of being their own adequate interpreter? Recognizing the role of tradition (and the magisterium) in canonizing, interpreting, applying and actualizing the scriptures, even Catholics who accepted the material sufficiency of the scriptures rejected their formal sufficiency. When, however, the Second Vatican Council presented revelation as *primarily* being the personal self-manifestation to us of the triune God (DV 2–6), it no longer seemed appropriate to talk of this living reality as being "contained" in anything, even the scriptures. At the very least, appreciating revelation as an interpersonal event makes it difficult to inquire about the "material" sufficiency of the scriptures as either "containing" or "not containing" all revealed truths. See *Canon of Scriptures; Deposit of Faith; Magisterium; Revelation; Scripture and Tradition; Sola Scriptura; Tradition.*

SUMMA (Lat. "main part"). A systematic summary of what is known in one field like theology. In the middle ages a *summa* was distinguished both from *opuscula* (Lat. "small works") which debated particular issues, and from *Sentences* or collections of the views of church fathers on various topics. Those who produced a summa included St. Albert the Great (ca. 1200–80), Alexander of Hales (ca. 1170–1245) and St. Thomas Aquinas (ca. 1225–74). With his *Summa contra Gentiles* and the *Summa Theologiae.* Aquinas skillfully followed a dialectical method of first presenting two seemingly contradictory lines of evidence before developing his own response to the given question. See *Scholasticism.*

SUNDAY (Old English "day of the sun"). The "day of the Lord" (Rev 1:10) when Christians rest from work to remember joyfully Christ's resurrection (Mk 16:1–2), God's creation of the world and the coming of the Holy Spirit. Eastern Christians call Sunday "the eighth day," to recall how Christ's resurrection regenerated the universe. The NT indicates that Christians met for the eucharist on Sunday (Acts 20:7; see 1 Cor 16:2). In the early second century both St. Ignatius of Antioch and a Roman governor, Pliny the Younger, referred to Christians worshiping on that day. The Council of Elvira in Spain (ca. 306) legislated for Sunday observance, and in 321 Constantine the Great ordered abstinence from work on that day. Church law calls for attendance at mass on Sunday and a rest from work that allows for a proper religious and human enjoyment of that day (CIC 1246–47). See *Sabbath; Seventh-Day Adventists.*

SUPERNATURAL (Lat. "above nature"). A term coined by Dionysius the Pseudo-Areopagite (ca. 500) for God, who is *above* our categories, our experiences and our nature. From the middle ages the term refers to God's free and loving self-gift that already in the life of grace raises us above what is due to our human nature and that prepares us for the life of glory. See *Grace; Nature; Supernatural Existential*.

SUPERNATURAL EXISTENTIAL. The situation which was created for human freedom as a result of Christ's redemptive work. The term "existential" was coined by Martin Heidegger (1889–1976) to describe a situation which as a matter of fact pre-conditions the way human freedom is exercised. Karl Rahner (1904–84) adapted the term for theology. "Original sin" is an "existential," because it creates hindrances even before human beings can exercise their freedom. The supernatural existential is at the opposite end of the spectrum from original sin, because the supernatural existential means that, even before they accept grace, human beings are positively determined by it, and not merely confronted with an external offer of salvation. See *Grace; Original Sin; Redemption*.

SYMBOL (Gr. "something thrown together"). Something representing "naturally" (e.g., lion as symbolizing courage) or conventionally (e.g., flag as symbolizing a country) something else. By making other things present, symbols enter our imagination, affect our feelings and influence our behavior. Rational explanations will always fall short of the potential range of meanings expressed by given symbols. Particularly when we take up religious symbols which represent ultimate, transcendent realities, we can expect these symbols to prove inexhaustible in their significance. See *Creed; Cross; Sacrament*.

SYMBOL, THEOLOGY OF. View of the visible world as an image of the invisible. In his *Theaetetus* Plato (427–347), writing about the origin and constitution of the world, says: "Time is the moving image of eternity." His parables show how Jesus saw everyday things and events as windows on God and invitations to respond to the divine activity. Origen (ca. 185–ca. 254) developed a strongly symbolic theology. In his philosophical symbolism and biblical interpretation, St. Augustine of Hippo (354–430) gave a fresh impulse to the symbolic interpretation of reality. The Augustinian Hugh of St. Victor (ca. 1096–1141) interpreted everything in the universe as a sort of sacrament of divine realities. Hugo Rahner (1901–68) described the theology of his brother Karl Rahner (1904–84) as being a "theology of the symbol." A symbolic approach remains central in the eastern theology of the icon. See *Icon; Nicaea, Second Council of; Origenism; Sacrament*.

SYMBOLICS. The systematic study of the *symbols* (Gr. "creeds") and basic beliefs of different Christian confessions. Developed by Georg Callixtus (1586–1656), Johann Adam Möhler (1796–1838) and others, this branch of theology has been given fresh life through the ecumenical movement

232

—in particular through the bilateral dialogues (or dialogues between official representatives of two Christian churches) and the World Council of Churches' Faith and Order Commission (e.g., its 1982 report *Baptism, Eucharist and Ministry*). See *Augsburg Confession; Dialogue; Ecumenism; Faith and Order; Thirty-Nine Articles; World Council of Churches*.

SYMBOLUM APOSTOLICUM. See *Creed, Apostles'*.

SYMPHONY (Gr. "harmonious voices/sounds"). The theory in eastern theology that church and state should act in unison for the glory of God. See *Canon Law, Sources of Oriental; Church and State; Theocracy*.

SYNAGOGUE (Gr. "assembly of persons or things"). A Jewish school and place for worship. The corresponding Hebrew word was *knesset*, now used for Israel's parliament. Luke situates Jesus' first sermon in the synagogue at Nazareth (Lk 4:16–80), and we read of further visits to synagogues (Matt 9:35; 13:54; Mk 1:39; Lk 4:44; 13:10; Jn 6:59). St. Paul and other early Christians used synagogues for dialogue and debate with Jews (see Acts 13:14–43; 17:1–2, 10–12). First formed in the sixth century B.C., synagogues have remained the center for Jewish worship and instruction throughout the ages. Among modern Jews, the reformed speak of "temples," whereas the Orthodox refer to "schools." See *Israel; Judaism*.

SYNAXARION (Gr. "assembly book"). The brief account of the life of a saint or the meaning of a particular feast, read at the *orthros* or morning service in the liturgy of the hours of the Byzantine church. See *Liturgy of the Hours*.

SYNAXIS (Gr. "congregation"). An assembly for the liturgy of the word, the eucharist or some other religious function. Practically synonymous with "synagogue" (Gr. "assembly"), the word may have first been used by Christians to distinguish their worship from that of the Jews. See *Eucharist; Liturgy of the Word; Synagogue; Worship*.

SYNCRETISM (Gr. "combining of two Cretan cities against a third"). Any attempt to reconcile or even merge different or even incompatible principles and practices. Often superficial and transient, syncretism may occur between religions, philosophies and within Christianity itself. The first to attempt ecumenical syncretism on a large scale was Georg Callixtus (1586–1656), a Protestant theologian who aimed to reconcile Lutherans, Calvinists and Catholics on the basis of the Bible, the faith of the first five centuries, and the Apostles' Creed. See *Comparative Religion; Creed, Apostles'; Ecumenism; History-of-Religions School*.

SYNERGISM (Gr. "working together"). The teaching of the eastern church that God and human beings cooperate in grace and liberty. This doctrine has sometimes been rejected as "Semi-Pelagianism," because it is thought to detract from God's absolute sovereignty in the whole process of human salvation—from the first step toward conversion right through to final perseverance. However, this criticism wrongly presupposes that God and human beings are competitors, instead of recognizing how it is God's grace that enables human beings to repent and produce the fruits of conversion in liberty. A doctrine, similar to *synergism*, developed by the Lutheran Philipp Melanchthon (1497–1560), met with similar (unfounded) criticism. See *Semi-Pelagianism*.

SYNOD (Gr. "council"). An assembly of bishops and others meeting to determine matters of church doctrine and practice. The name is applied to any such official assembly, from a diocesan synod right through to an ecumenical council (CD 36–38). See *Council, Ecumenical; Collegiality*.

SYNOD, DIOCESAN. An official assembly of priests and laypersons convoked by the bishop of a particular diocese to help him in the government of that diocese (CIC 460–68). See *Bishop; Diocese; Ordinary*.

SYNOD OF BISHOPS. An assembly of bishops which represents all the episcopal conferences and usually meets every three years in Rome through the month of October. Its scope is to promote collegial union between the bishops and the pope by advising him in matters of faith, morals and church discipline (CD 5; CIC 342–48). The 1987 Synod discussed the role of the laity, the 1990 Synod the formation of priests. See *Episcopal Conference; Collegiality*.

SYNOPTIC GOSPELS (Gr. "overview"). The gospels of Matthew, Mark and Luke which very frequently parallel each other closely in content and phraseology. The term comes from the Protestant NT scholar Jakob Johann Griesbach (1745–1812), who printed the three gospels in parallel columns, so that one could see at a glance their major convergences and minor divergences. To account for the obvious literary relationship between these gospels, most contemporary scholars accept the Two-Source Theory, according to which Mark wrote first. Then Matthew and Luke drew on Mark and on a collection of Jesus' sayings (*Q* or *Quelle*), as well as having some other separate sources. See *Quelle*.

SYRIAN ORTHODOX CHURCH. Name for the church which Severus, (d. 538) Patriarch of Antioch and theologian, helped to organize in opposition to the Council of Chalcedon. Polemically labelled "monophysite" for its opposition to the council's formula regarding Christ's two natures (rather than to the two natures themselves), this church got its name "Jacobite" from Jacob Baradaeus (ca. 500–78). Ordained bishop of Edessa in 542 on the insistence of Empress Theodora, Jacob went around preaching and ordaining bishops. He wore rags to avoid capture; hence his nickname "Baradaeus" ("shabbily clad"). The designation "Jacobites" is first found at Nicaea II (787), but this church calls itself Syrian Orthodox. Its head bears the title of "Syrian Orthodox Patriarch of Antioch and all the East" and resides in Damascus, Syria. The liturgy of this Church, one of the seven major extant eastern rites, is known as "west Syrian" (or "Antiochene"). The west Syrian rite is extremely rich. It has at least seventy eucharistic anaphoras and many variant texts for other ceremonies. The main eucharistic liturgy is that of St. James, which may go back to apostolic times. In general, the liturgy is celebrated in the vernacular: Arabic is used in the Middle East, Malayalam in India and English in the United States. See *Anaphora; Church of the East; Edessa; Holy Week; Monophysitism.*

SYSTEMATIC THEOLOGY. The attempt to expound in a coherent and scholarly fashion the main Christian doctrines. While often coinciding in practice with dogmatic theology, systematic theology may differ by including a treatment of moral issues. It may also differ from dogmatic theology by paying even more attention to methodology, terminology, the use of philosophical principles, a strictly unified perspective, and issues concerned with the conditions and limits of theological knowledge. See *Dogmatic Theology; Epistemology; Fundamental Theology; Philosophy.*

T

TALMUD (Heb. "instruction"). The collection of Jewish traditions containing the Mishnah (oral teachings) and the Gemara (discussions about the Mishnah). There are two versions: the Palestinian Talmud and the longer Babylonian Talmud, both completed during the fifth century but including material that goes back much earlier. See *Mishnah; Haggadah; Halachah.*

TAOISM (Chinese "right way"). A system of religious and philosophical beliefs and practices which, along with Confucianism and Buddhism, has helped to shape Chinese history and culture. It was founded by Lao-Tse, an honorific title (= "the wise old man") for Li, a Chinese state archivist who lived around 600 B.C. or perhaps much earlier. He is credited with having written the *Lao Teh Ching* (Chinese "On the Primordial Principle of the World and Its Influence"), in which the Tao is seen as the way of ultimate reality—that is to say, as immanent in the way of the universe (the ordering principle behind all life) and the way human beings should order their lives in accordance with the Tao. Against the background of the social upheavals occurring while the Chou dynasty was in power (ca. 1127–ca. 256 B.C.), Taoism taught a harmony to be attained by bringing one's attitudes and conduct in line with the primordial principle. The system was further developed by Chuang Chou (ca. 369–286 B.C.). See *Buddhism; Confucianism.*

TELEOLOGICAL ARGUMENT (Gr. "study of ends and purposes"). The argument which moves from the orderly character of the world to claim the existence of God as the Designer and Final Cause of everything. In their different ways, Aristotle (384–322 B.C.), St. Thomas Aquinas (ca. 1225–74), and many others interpreted the universe as revealing intelligent purposes and pointing to God as the final end of all things. David Hume (1711–76) challenged trans-empirical causality in general, and Immanuel Kant (1724–1804) the viability of proofs for the existence of God in particular. The teleological argument had to face further objections when Charles Darwin (1809–82) explained biological design through the survival of the fittest. Mechanistic explanations of order in the world as simply resulting from the random operation of natural force had a long vogue. However, recent advances in astronomy, biology, physics and other sciences have shown just how massive and far-reaching is the order in a universe which has apparently existed for only a relatively brief time. The odds against such an astonishing order emerging by mere chance give a new plausibility to the argument for an intelligent Designer. See *Arguments for the Existence of God; Causality; Finality; Five Ways, The.*

TEMPERANCE (Lat. "moderation"). One of the four cardinal virtues, which enables us to moderate our appetites and control our passions. Expressed in Plato's (427–347 B.C.) image of a chariot drawn by three stallions whom the rider must keep under a tight rein if he is not to finish in a ditch, temperance was made a paramount virtue by Stoics. Later NT books encourage temperance (at times translated as "sobriety," "self-control" or "modesty") especially (but not exclusively) among church leaders and older people (1 Tim 3:2; Tit 1:8; 2:2,5; see also 1 Tim 2:9,15; Acts 26:25). Modern "temperance" societies, instead of educating people to be moderate, have required total abstinence from all alcoholic drinks. See *Abstinence; Chastity; Stoicism; Virtues, Cardinal.*

TEMPLE, THE. The central religious shrine of the Jews, built in Jerusalem, and the only place where sacrifice could be offered (see Deut 12:1–31).

First built during the reign of Solomon (ca. 970–ca. 930 B.C.), the temple was destroyed by the Babylonians in 586 B.C. The prophets Haggai and Zechariah encouraged the building of the second temple (520–515 B.C.; see Ezra 3:1–13; Hag 2:1–9, 15–19). After it was desecrated (Hag 2:15–19) by Antiochus Epiphanes in 167 B.C. (Dan 9:2–7; 11:31; 1 Macc 1:41–64; 2 Macc 6:1–6), Judas Maccabaeus purified and rededicated it (1 Mac 4:36–59). *Hannukah,* a yearly festival of lights, still commemorates this purification of the temple. Herod the Great, who ruled from 37 to 4 B.C., built the magnificent third temple, destroyed by the Romans in A.D. 70. On its ruins stands the Al-Aqsisa Mosque, the "Dome of the Rock" where tradition places Abraham's coming to sacrifice Isaac and Mohammed's ascent into heaven. For Muslims this is the second most sacred place in the world after El-Kaaba in Mecca. See *Islam; Jerusalem; Synagogue.*

TEMPTATION (Lat. "testing"). A valuable trial of one's worth (Jas 1:2–4,12) or else an inducement to commit sin (Jas 1:14–15). God is said to "tempt" Abraham (Gen 22:1–19; Heb 11:17–19) or allow Job to be "tempted" (Job 1:1–2:13). The weakness of the flesh (Mark 14:38) and difficult circumstances (Luke 8:13) can lead us to do wrong. As the great tempter, the devil tried to lead Christ into sin, especially during his period in the desert after baptism (Matt 4:1–11; Mk 1:13; Lk 4:1–13). Tempted as we are, Jesus, nevertheless, did not sin (Heb 4:15). Human beings can fail by "tempting" God, through demanding signs (Matt 12:39) and complaining about their situation (Exod 17:1–7; Deut 6:16; 9:22; 33:8; Ps 95:8; 106:32; Heb 3:8–10). Like Christ (Matt 6:13; Lk 11:4) church teaching recognizes our weakness when faced with temptation, and encourages prayer and asceticism as remedies (see DS 1533–35; 1574; 1576; 2192; 2217; 2224; 2237; 2241–53). See *Asceticism; Prayer; Sarx; Sin.*

TETRARCHY. See *Pentarchy.*

THEANDRIC (Gr. "divine-human"). Adjective coined by Dionysius the Pseudo-Areopagite (ca. 500) to describe the acts of the God-man Jesus Christ. Some used the term in a Monophysite and/or Monothelite sense, as if Christ had, respectively, only one (divine) nature and/or only one (divine) will. But St. Maximus the Confessor (ca. 580–662) and St. John of Damascus (ca. 675–ca. 749) used the term in a thoroughly orthodox sense. In and through his two natures, and two wills (which are neither confused nor separated) the one (divine) person of Christ performs divine-human acts. See *Chalcedon, Council of; Communicatio Idiomatum; Monophysitism; Monothelitism.*

THEISM (Gr. "God"). The belief in a transcendent, personal God who creates, conserves and intervenes (e.g., through miracles) in our world. Unlike pantheism, theism does not push the divine immanence to the point of identifying God with the world. Unlike deism, theism holds that God is not a mere remote creator but through providence, revelation and a variety of salvific acts is ceaselessly engaged on our behalf. A Cambridge Platonist Ralph Cudworth (1617–88) probably coined the term. Immanuel Kant (1724–1804) clearly distinguished between theism and deism. Despite their major differences, Christianity, Islam and Judaism may be bracketed together as theistic religions (NA 3–4). See *God.*

THEOCENTRICISM (Gr. "God-centered"). A way of thinking which systematically centers everything on God. It is often contrasted with "anthropocentricism" (Gr. "human-centered"), which takes human existence, experience and values as its center and guide. Exaggerated anthropocentricism ignores or even rules out God. At the same time, an exclusive theocentricism is unacceptable, since God made human beings in the divine image and likeness (Gen 1:26–27) and the Word has become flesh (John 1:14). In the area of Christianity and other religions, a theocentric approach (which sometimes overemphasizes pluralism and the value of any belief in God) is often contrasted with a Christocentric approach (which insists that, whether or not they acknowledge this truth, Christ is the revealer and savior for all human beings [Jn 1:9; 14:6; Acts 4:12; 2 Cor 5:18–19]). See *Anonymous Christians; Anthropocentricism; Christocentricism; Pluralism.*

THEOCRACY (Gr. "rule of God"). Government by God or by God's representatives. Many ancient nations believed their rulers to be invested with divine authority or even to be identified with divine beings. Flavius Josephus (ca. 37–ca. 100) created the term "theocracy" and applied it to a classic example, the Jewish people. The royal psalms, often composed for a coronation, celebrated God's dominion revealed and exercised through the king (e.g., Pss 2, 45, 110). Israel's laws (e.g., the ten commandments) not only expressed God's will but also carried civil sanctions, even the death penalty. After the time of Jesus theocracy showed up not only in new religious movements like Islam but also in Christianity itself. In the Byzantine Empire the ruler was seen as an image of Christ, the *Pantocrator* (Gr. "all-powerful"), and the state as an image of celestial order. Theocratic elements were to be found in the reforms of Pope St. Gregory VII (ca. 1021–85). Both Ulrich Zwingli (1484–1531) and John Calvin (1509–64) set out to establish a divine rule in Zürich and Geneva, respectively, examples followed by the Puritan Lord Protector Oliver Cromwell (1599–1658). See *Calvinism; Church and State; Decalogue; Islam; Pantocrator; Symphony; Zwinglianism.*

THEODICY (Gr. "justification of God"). Term introduced by the philosopher Gottfried Wilhelm Leibniz (1641–1716) in his response to Pierre Bayle (1647–1706), who had once again raised the question: If God is all good and all powerful, where does evil come from and what does it mean? The question is older than the book of Job and finds its most poignant restatement in Jesus' abandonment on the cross (Mk 15:34). How can believers account for the suffering of the innocent and the faithful? Auschwitz, Dresden, Hiroshima and further scenes of mysterious evil in modern times have more than kept the question alive. One can rightly point out that very often human beings, rather than God, should be put on trial for their murderous misuse of freedom. Nevertheless, a measure of mysterious, unmerited suffering remains. As we wait for the *parousia*, a provisional answer comes from the way Jesus himself suffered with us and for us. Nowadays, theodicy is often used in a broader sense, as a synonym for natural theology. See *Natural Theology; Evil, Mystery of; Parousia; Suffering of God.*

THEOLOGIA CRUCIS (Lat. "theology of the cross"). An expression coined by Martin Luther (1483–1546) to qualify the right way of doing theology. As saving and merciful, God is known only as hidden in Christ crucified and in all experiences of suffering and temptation that reveal the nothingness of human beings before God. God is revealed in a way that goes counter to our expectations—the powerful as powerless, the wise as fool (see 1 Cor 1:17–31). See *Lutheranism; Theologia Gloriae.*

THEOLOGIA GLORIAE (Lat. "theology of glory"). (a) Polemically contrasted by Martin Luther (1483–1546) with the "theology of the cross" and referring to scholastic and mystical theology. Luther sees in them ways of wanting to know God presumptuously by relying on our own possibilities and capacities, instead of humbly believing and trusting in God. "Theology of glory" means here a theology of human self-glorification. (b) In another context the term refers to eastern theology which highlights the glorification of Christ and our participating in his glory. This theology draws its inspiration from John's gospel: "The Word became flesh and dwelt among us, *and we have seen his glory*" (Jn 1:14). As understood by St. Paul, glory can be associated with Luther's favored theme of justification. "Those whom he [God] has called he has also justified, and those whom he has justified he has also glorified" (Rom 8:30). See *Doxa; Glory; Johannine Theology; Natural Theology; Scholasticism.*

THEOLOGOUMENON (Gr. "theological dimension/element"). A non-binding theological thesis which is neither found clearly in scripture nor in the definitive teaching of the *magisterium*. Theses of great theologians

239

can have the status of theologoumena and may later in some way enter the teaching of the church. The Orthodox sometimes use the word *theologoumenon* to distinguish the definitions of the first seven ecumenical councils from subsequent faith-pronouncements of the Roman Catholic Church. See *Councils, Ecumenical; Magisterium; Theology.*

THEOLOGY (Gr. "science of God"). The methodical effort to understand and interpret the truth of revelation. As *fides quaerens intellectum* (Lat. "faith seeking understanding"), theology uses the resources of reason, drawing in particular on the disciplines of history and philosophy. In the face of the divine mystery, theology is always "seeking" and never reaches final answers and definitive insights. It breaks up into a number of styles and sub-areas, some of which are indicated below. See *Apologetics; Apophatic Theology; Biblical Theology; Black Theology; Cataphatic Theology; Christology; Ecclesiology; Feminist Theology; Fundamental Theology; Hermeneutics; History; Mission, Theology of; Moral Theology; Mystagogy; Negative Theology; Pastoral Theology; Patristics; Philosophy; Political Theology; Positive Theology; Revelation; Spirituality; Systematic Theology.*

THEOLOGY, HISTORY OF. The orderly attempts to understand and interpret revelation which have continued from the NT to Vatican II and its aftermath. Even more than their OT predecessors, St. Paul, St. John, St. Luke and other NT authors have left us inspired theological insights and approaches but no treatises systematically structured through the use of philosophy. With the apologists and the struggle against Gnosticism, Greek culture began providing Christian theology with philosophical language and concepts. While remaining characteristically biblical, liturgical, doxological, catechetical and pastoral, the fathers of the church often developed their theology through great controversies, especially the Trinitarian and christological debates of the fourth and fifth centuries. By his powerful intellect and style, St. Augustine of Hippo (354–430) massively influenced subsequent teaching on such themes as sin, grace, sacraments and the Trinity. After St. Anselm of Canterbury (ca. 1033–1109) launched scholasticism, it was perfected by St. Thomas Aquinas (ca. 1225–74) and his synthesis of Aristotelian and Platonic philosophy with the data of revelation. Alongside the academic theology of the new universities, the monastic theology of St. Bernard of Clairvaux (1090–1153) and others continued the spiritual, liturgical tradition of the Fathers. Scholasticism declined into the nominalism of the late middle ages. The new humanism developed by scholars like Erasmus of Rotterdam (1469–1536) and the reformation itself revolutionized the study of the Bible and the fathers of the church. For Catholics the Council of Trent (1545–63) provided a clear basis for subsequent theology, which featured such outstanding figures as John of St. Thomas

(1589–1644), Denis Pétau (1583–1652), Francis de Suarez (1548–1617) and Gabriel Vázquez (1549–1604). First the Enlightenment philosophy and then nineteenth-century biblical and historical criticism, the theory of evolution, various forms of socialism, and the new disciplines of psychology and sociology brought massive challenges to Christian theologians. Not only great progress in philosophical and patristic studies but also the biblical, ecumenical and liturgical movements revitalized Catholic theology in the twentieth century, particularly in France, Germany and the Low Countries. Alongside the great Protestant teachers like Karl Barth (1886–1968), Rudolf Bultmann (1884–1976) and Paul Tillich (1886–1965) and the Orthodox theologians like Sergius Bulgakov (1871–1944) and Vladimir Lossky (1903–58), such Catholic theologians as Yves Congar (b. 1904) and Karl Rahner (1904–84) led the Catholic revival. Since Vatican II, both within the Catholic Church and beyond, theology has become more anthropological, dialogical and spiritual. Now less of a clerical and European monopoly, theology is being vigorously developed in the Americas, Asia and elsewhere. See *Alexandrian Theology; Antiochene Theology; Apologists; Aristotelianism; Augustinianism; Calvinism; Dialectical Theology; Doxa; Doctor of the Church; Enlightenment; Fathers of the Church; Gnosticism; Humanism; Jansenism; Kerygmatic Theology; Liberal Protestantism; Liberation Theology; Lutheranism; Modernism; Neo-Palamism; Neoplatonism; Neo-Scholasticism; Neo-Thomism; Nominalism; Origenism; Oxford Movement; Palamism; Platonism; Reformation; Scholasticism; Scotism; Stoicism; Thomism; Three Theologians, The; Trent, Council of; Tübingen and Its Schools; Vatican Council, First; Vatican Council, Second.*

THEOLOGY, METHODS IN. Coherent ways of doing theology which vary according to their characteristic questions, central aim, context, audience, use of sources and criteria. (a) North-Atlantic academics typically raise questions about meaning, look for the truth, prefer theology in a university setting, dialogue with professional colleagues, privilege written texts and use criteria suggested by reason. (b) Latin American theology of liberation represents another theological method which enquires about justice, does theology in a public context, privileges the voices of the poor and suffering, and respects the criteria of praxis. (c) A liturgical and monastic method of theologizing looks for the divine beauty, finds its home in the setting of prayer, aligns itself with fellow-worshipers, and takes its texts and criteria from the church. Each of these three methods can be broken down into sub-groups. Method (a), for instance, will be affected by the kind of philosophy it adopts (e.g., Neo-Thomism, various forms of existentialism, ordinary-language philosophy or process-thought). Method (b) will change if it is in contact with the Christian poor in Latin America or the Hindu poor of India. Method

(c) will vary according to whether it is practiced by Trappist contemplatives, Orthodox Christians in Russia or Buddhist monks in Japan. Ideally Christian theology can only be enriched by a proper pluralism in which the three major methods serve to complement each other. See *Beauty, Theology of; Doxa; Justice; Loci Theologici; Option for the Poor; Philosophy; Pluralism; Praxis; Schools of Theology; Truth.*

THEONOMY (Gr. "divine law"). An ethics, for which God's will mediated through our created intelligence and freedom, is the ultimate authority. See *Autonomy; Heteronomy.*

THEOPASCHITE CONTROVERSY (Gr. "suffering of God"). A controversy which continued from the fifth century until after Constantinople II (553), and which concerned statements about the Son of God suffering and dying for us. Granted that God as God cannot suffer, the union of the divine and human natures in the one person of Jesus Christ justified the confession of those Scythian monks who on a visit in Rome around 519, declared "One of the Trinity suffered for us." See *Communicatio Idiomatum; Constantinople, Second Council of; Suffering of God; Trisagion.*

THEOPHANY (Gr. "appearance of God"). A visible manifestation of God. While repeating that no one can see God and survive (Exod 19:21; 33:20; Judg 13:22), the OT refers to theophanies experienced by Moses and others (Exod 3:1–6; 33:17–23; 34:5–9; Isa 6:1–5). The gospels report quasi-theophanies at Christ's baptism and transfiguration (Mk 1:9–11; 9:2–8). In the early church the Epiphany or Christ's manifestation to the gentiles (Matt 2:1–12) was called a theophany—a usage that still continues in the east. See *Christophany; Doxa; Epiphany; Experience, Religious.*

THEOTOKOS (Gr. "God-bearer"). A title given to Our Lady and used at least as early as Origen (ca. 185–ca. 254) to express the fact that she gave birth to the Son of God. In Latin, although the exact equivalent is *Deipara*, the title often appears as *Deigenetrix* (Lat. "Mother of God"). When Nestorius of Constantinople called into question this popular title, the Council of Ephesus (431) condemned him and, in upholding the unity of Christ's person, proclaimed the legitimacy of the title *Theotokos* (DS 250–52). It was not just a man (or a humanity) that Mary begot but the Son of God himself. See *Ephesus, Council of; Mariology; Nestorianism.*

THIRTY-NINE ARTICLES. A set of doctrinal propositions adopted by the Church of England in 1571 which partly distinguish the Anglican position on controverted issues from those of Roman Catholicism, on the one hand, and continental Protestantism, on the other. These articles, which often allow for somewhat divergent interpretations, remain a

242

major witness to the faith of the Anglican Communion. See *Anglican Communion.*

THOMISM. The philosophical and theological teaching of St. Thomas Aquinas (ca. 1225–74). Enriched by the encyclopaedic knowledge of his teacher and fellow Dominican St. Albert the Great (ca. 1200–80), Thomas shaped a mass of insights that had been accumulating over the centuries, especially since St. Anselm of Canterbury (ca. 1033–1109). He created a remarkable synthesis between faith and reason. Although unfinished, his *Summa Theologiae* is the greatest achievement of medieval theology. Thomas is said to have baptized Aristotle (384–322 B.C.), drawing from the Greek philosopher such items as a theory of causality. At the same time, Thomas retained a number of Platonic traits, something connected with his extensive use of St. Augustine of Hippo (354–430) and Dionysius the Pseudo-Areopagite (ca. 500). From 1300 to 1500 interpreters of Thomas or "Thomists" were concerned with opposing Scotism, Nominalism and a revived Neoplatonism. With the sixteenth and seventeenth centuries came a golden age of Thomists who included Thomas Cardinal Cajetan (1469–1534), Sylvester of Ferrara (1474–1528), Francisco de Vitoria (ca. 1485–1546), John of St. Thomas (1589–1644), Melchior Cano (1509–60), Domingo Soto (1494–1560) and Domingo Bañez (1528–1604). Whereas the 1917 Code of Canon Law still considered Thomas to be *the* teacher for philosophy and theology in Catholic seminaries (see the old CIC 589, 1366), the 1983 code simply recommends him as particularly useful (see the new CIC 252; PO 16; GE 10). See *Aristotelianism; Augustinianism; Five Ways, The; Loci Theologici; Molinism; Neoplatonism; Neo-Thomism; Platonism; Scholasticism; Schools of Theology; Scotism; Summa; Transcendental; Trent, Council of.*

THREE CHAPTERS, THE. Three authors, accused of favoring Nestorianism, whom Justinian I had condemned posthumously ca. 534 as a goodwill gesture to the monophysite opposition to the Council of Chalcedon (451). The condemnation touched the works and person of Theodore of Mopsuestia (ca. 350–428), the writings which Theodoret, Bishop of Cyrrhus (ca. 393–ca. 466) directed against St. Cyril of Alexandria (d. 444) and the letter which Ibas of Edessa (bishop 435–49) sent in 433 to Maris, Bishop of Hardascir in Persian. Though summoned to Constantinople in 547, Pope Vigilius refused at first to subscribe to the condemnation. In his 548 *Iudicatum* he condemned propositions from Theodore, who had died in peace with the church, only insofar as they might lend themselves to a Nestorian interpretation against Chalcedon; and, most of all, Vigilius refused to acquiesce in a posthumous condemnation. When an ecumenical council was convoked, Constantinople II (553), the pope eventually signed the condemnation. The condemnation of the Three Chapters led to a serious schism in the west which was only healed around 689. However unfortunate the circumstances, this unusual censuring may be interpreted as a guarantee that there is nothing in church doctrine which would warrant the Nestorian error. See *Chalcedon, Council of; Constantinople, Second Council of; Monophysitism; Nestorianism.*

THREE THEOLOGIANS, THE. Those considered in the east to be the theologians *par excellence:* St. John the Evangelist, St. Gregory of Nazianzus (329–89) and St. Symeon the New Theologian (949–1022). (a) A prayerful contemplation of the glory of God revealed and experienced in Christ, the Son of God (Jn 20:31), John's gospel is the most profound of all the gospels. The author of the fourth gospel has been traditionally identified with John the son of Zebedee (see Jn 21:2) and the disciple "whom Jesus loved" (Jn 13:23; 19:26–27; 20:2–8; 21:7,20–24). (b) St. Gregory of Nazianzus attended the second ecumenical council, Constantinople I (381). He became Bishop of Constantinople during the council, but some time later resigned his see and retired to Nazianzus (in Cappadocia). His writings include "Five Theological Orations," in which he defended the divinity of the Holy Spirit, many poems and several letters against Apollinarianism. (c) St. Symeon the New Theologian (949–1022), after joining the Constantinopolitan monastery of Studios, left what he found to be a lax religious community, to become a monk and for about twenty-five years superior of the monastery of St. Mammas also in Constantinople. Considered the greatest mystical theologian of the Byzantine church, his original contribution consisted in the way in which he communicated his own experiences of God in hymns and poems centered on the theme of *deification.* See *Apollinarianism; Cappadocian Fathers; Constantinople, First Council of; Deification; Doctor of the Church; Johannine Theology; Philocalia.*

TIARA, PAPAL (Gr. "royal Persian turban"). A large beehive headdress with which popes were crowned and which they wore on solemn, extraliturgical functions. Pope Paul VI sold his tiara and gave the money to the poor. John Paul I refused to be crowned. His successor, John Paul II (b. 1920) declined to reintroduce the tiara and any solemn crowning at the beginning of his pontificate in 1978. See *Pope.*

TIME. Defined as "the moving image of eternity" by Plato (427–347 B.C.) and as the measure of movement by Aristotle (384–322 B.C.). Scholastics added that time was thus created by reason, because only reason can measure the before and after. The lived time when we wait, suffer, rejoice and rest is not properly measurable by a clock or even by the passage of day and night and the shift of the seasons. With their

244

memory of the exodus and messianic expectations, the Jews had a primarily linear concept of time and history. They remembered the past so as to hope for a fuller future. Wherever a sense of history's dénouement is lacking, the Greek cyclical image of history will prevail, which Friedrich Nietzsche (1844–1900) recaptured in "the myth of the eternal return." Christian eschatology highlighted the direction of time and history, which will culminate in Christ's *parousia* and God's final kingdom (1 Cor 15:20–28; Rev 21:1–22; 20). See *Advent; Apocalyptic; Eschatology; Eternity; Exodus; History; Kairos; Lent; Parousia; Sabbath; Salvation History.*

TITHES (Old English "tenth"). The tenth (or other) part of the produce of the land, contributed to maintain the clergy and support the church's mission through schools, hospitals, help to the needy and works of evangelization. Support for the maintenance of OT priests and places of worship (see Gen 14:16–20; Deut 12:6,11,17) was enjoined by law (see Num 18:25–32; Deut 14:22–29). The NT considers it only right that Christian communities should support those who proclaim the good news (see Matt 10:10; Lk 10:7; 1 Cor 9:7–14; 1 Tim 5:18). Eventually, after the conversion of Europe to Christianity, tithes became part of the taxes to be paid. Wherever states no longer recognize and support churches in that way, the mission has to be maintained by voluntary contributions. See *Church and State; Justice; Koinonia.*

TOLERANCE (Lat. "enduring"). Leaving in peace those whose beliefs and practices differ from our own. After suffering persecution from some Jewish authorities and then, for centuries, from Roman rulers, Christians gained religious freedom with the so-called "Edict of Milan" (312). Fairly soon and especially after Theodosius the Great (emperor from 379 to 395) made Christianity the state religion, Christians began showing intolerance toward others, including fellow-Christians (accused of being heretics or schismatics), Jews and later Moslems. With the reformation tolerance was proclaimed but was normally extended only to one's own party. John Calvin condemned Michael Servetus (1511–53) to death, and another Protestant theologian, Theodore Beza (1519–1605) upheld the decision. The Peace of Augsburg (1555), with its maxim *"cuius regio eius religio"* (Lat. "whoever runs the state determines its religion") tolerated in each country only one Christian confession, as practically was the case in England under the Elizabethan settlement. Some Baptists, Catholics, Puritans and Quakers fled from England in search of religious freedom in Europe and North America. The Enlightenment and the American War of Independence served to encourage, at least in the long run, a racial, religious and cultural toleration based on respect for natural human rights. Nowadays, at least in the area of religion, mere indifference to questions of truth and practice can masquerade as genuine tolerance. The Second Vatican Council encouraged all Catholics to live and proclaim the gospel, but always with loving respect for others (GS 28, 73, 75; AG 11; DG 1). See *Church and State; Crusades; Enlightenment; Freedom, Religious; Inquisition; Pluralism; Priscillianism; Rights, Human.*

TONGUES, SPEAKING IN. See *Glossolalia.*

TONSURE (Lat. "shearing") Having the hair of one's head cut to express separation from the world and complete dedication to God—a symbol found not only in Christianity but also in other religions such as Buddhism. When conferring minor orders (acolyte, exorcist, lector and porter), the bishop cuts some hair from the candidate's head—in recent times a mere tiny circle at the back of the crown. In the Latin rite tonsure was abolished along with the minor orders in 1972. However, in some religious orders, mainly contemplative ones, the ceremony of tonsure is still performed by the abbot. Immediately after baptism in the Byzantine rite, there is the ceremony of *trichokuria* (Gr. "haircut"), when hair is cut from four places on the head to show that the neophyte is completely dedicated to God. In the east clerics still receive the tonsure before receiving minor orders, as do monks before entering a monastery. See *Acolyte; Cleric; Exorcist; Holy Orders; Lector; Monasticism.*

TORAH (Heb. "instruction," "law"). The law God gave to Moses (Deut 1:5; 4:44) and the Pentateuch which contained it. "Torah" could also refer to parental teaching or authority (see Prov 1:8; 3:1; 4:2), instructions given in God's name by priests (Deut 17:11; 24:8; 33:10) and the law God writes in the human heart (Jer 31:33; Mal 2:7). The Samaritans retained as their Bible only the Pentateuch, an index of how the authority of the Torah was (and is) higher than that of the "Prophets" and the "Writings" (= the other parts of the Jewish Bible). See *Bible; Pentateuch; Old Testament; Sadducees.*

TRADITION (Lat. "transmission"). The process of handing on (tradition as act) or the living heritage which is handed on (tradition as content). Through the Holy Spirit (the invisible bearer of tradition) the whole people of God are empowered to pass on their memory, experience, expression and interpretation of the foundational self-revelation of God which was completed with Christ and the New Testament community. Thus tradition involves "the Church in her doctrine, life and worship" transmitting to the next generation "all that herself is, all that she believes" (DV 8). Identifying and unifying the Church, tradition secures continuity from its origins into the future. Within the whole people of

God, bishops and others have a special responsibility as the visible agents and interpreters of tradition. Particular traditions can fail to communicate the gospel and the need of reform (see Mk 7:1–23; 10:2–12). For the Orthodox tradition, expressed above all in worship, is indispensable for understanding any issue. Reception by the whole church indicates whether a new development is in line with its tradition. See *Sensus Fidelium; Deposit of Faith; Revelation; Scripture and Tradition; Sensus Fidelium; Sola Scriptura.*

TRADITIONALISM. A reaction against the rationalism and individualism encouraged by the Enlightenment. Traditionalism was classically expressed by Félicité de Lamennais (1782–1854) in his four-volume *Essai sur l'indifférence en matière de religion*. Others who held similar views included Louis de Bonald (1754–1840), Joseph de Maistre (1753–1821), Louis-Eugène-Marie Bautain (1796–1867), Gerhard Casimir Ubaghs (1800–75) and Augustin Bonnetty (1798–1879). The traditionalists maintained that a revelation was granted to humanity at its origins and then transmitted in an unbroken way through subsequent history. This revelation is the authoritative source of our philosophical, moral and religious truth. De Lamennais held that the common consent of humanity infallibly testifies to the original revelation. The First Vatican Council (1869–70) repudiated the traditionalists' claim that knowledge of God can only come through revelation and our faithful assent to it. By the natural light of reason human beings can also know God (see DS 3004–05, 3026). See *Enlightenment; Faith; Fideism; Natural Theology; Rationalism; Tradition.*

TRANSCENDENCE (Lat. "surpassing"). The otherness of God whose existence "goes beyond" the universe and is not to be identified with it. See *Apophatic Theology; Immanence; Incomprehensibility; Natural Theology; Pantheism.*

TRANSCENDENTAL PHILOSOPHY. A form of Thomism developed by the Belgian Jesuit Joseph Maréchal (1878–1944) in response to the critical philosophy of Immanuel Kant (1724–1804). After René Descartes (1596–1650) one could not ignore the question about the subject who asks and seeks to know, but is all too aware of the possibility of being deceived. Then David Hume (1711–76) rejected all knowledge which is neither analytical (tautological) nor experiential. Kant put metaphysics into question, in the sense that whoever makes claims concerning the existence of God, the immortality of the soul and its liberty must first inquire whether such an enterprise is at all possible. What we call "external" reality may be shown to be (at least in part) the product of our mind. In response to Kant, Maréchal defended the theistic realism of St. Thomas Aquinas (ca. 1225–74) by arguing that human beings and their (metaphysical) questions reveal a drive which leads them beyond the immediate data of sense perception toward an Absolute. Maréchal's transcendental method was followed by such thinkers as Bernard Lonergan (1904–84), Emerich Coreth (b. 1919) and Johann Baptist Lotz (b. 1903). See *Epistemology; Metaphysics; Philosophy.*

TRANSCENDENTALS (Lat. "things that surpass"). A word used by scholastics for those properties which belong to a being just because it is a being, and which thus "transcend" the categories for classifying things (e.g., essence, quality, time and space). Six transcendentals have eventually been listed: (a) reality; (b) being, (c) unity; (d) truth, (e) goodness, and (f) being something. A being is all this just because it exists. St. Thomas Aquinas (ca. 1225–74) names only three transcendentals: unity, truth and goodness. The scholastics often added a fourth (beauty), but were inclined to say that beauty is merely the harmonious functioning of unity, truth and goodness. However, Hans Urs von Balthasar (1905–1988) has argued for the priority of the *beautiful* as God's first way of attracting us in Jesus Christ. See *Doxa; Glory; Scholasticism; Transcendence.*

TRANSCENDENTAL THEOLOGY. A theological orientation similar to transcendental philosophy and associated especially with Karl Rahner (1904–84) and Bernard Lonergan (1904–84). It asks about the possible answers which open up when we consider the human subject. To use Rahner's own example, penance is not simply an objective duty to be carried out but a virtue impelling the subject to change. Every objective question has its subjective side, which, when explored, throws new light on the theological issues at stake. See *Method, Theological; Penance, Sacrament of; Theology, Methods in.*

TRANSFIGURATION. That episode in Christ's life when on a mountain (probably Mount Tabor near Nazareth) Peter, James and John saw him radiant with glory and in the company of Moses and Elijah (Matt 17:1–9; Mk 9:2–10; Lk 9:28–36; 2 Pet 1:16–19). Representing, respectively, the law and prophets, Moses and Elijah had both seen God's glory (see Exod 24:12–18; 33:7–23; 34:29–35; 1 Kings 19:1–18). In Oriental mysticism the "light of Tabor" became synonymous with the deepest experience of God which completely transforms our being after the arduous climb to the mountain (our asceticism). However, the predominant note is/was not the indispensable effort, but the ever-greater glory which is ours if we let God change our being (2 Cor 3:18). In this assimilation to God's own glory through purification (see 1 Jn 3:2), the Byzantine mystic St.

Gregory Palamas (1296–1359) saw God's energies at work. The feast of the Transfiguration highlights Christ himself, the Son of God by nature whose eternal glory revealed through suffering supports the Christian pilgrimage in time to God. At least as early as the fourth century, Greeks celebrated this feast, which became widely adopted in the east by the year 1000. Pope Callistus III made the Transfiguration a feast of the universal church to thank God for the victory over the Turks on August 6, 1456, at Belgrade. See *Doxa; Hesychasm; Mysticism; Palamism; Theology.*

TRANSFINALIZATION (Lat. "change in purpose"). A term used by some theologians in trying to illuminate what happens in the eucharist when bread and wine are changed into the body and blood of Christ. Instead of invoking the terminology of substance and accidents (which also applies to subrational beings), they look to the area of interpersonal relationships and note how our human experience changes when something assumes a radically new purpose. Some also speak of a eucharistic *transignification* (Lat. "change of meaning"), in that the bread and wine undergo a deep change in meaning, and express Christ's giving himself to us. In his 1965 encyclical *Mysterium Fidei* (Lat. "the Mystery of Faith") Paul VI warned that these theories can at best complement the traditional church teaching on transubstantiation and on some points seem at odds with it. Do "transfinalization" and "transignification" indicate a change in the bread and wine that allows us to confess the real presence of Christ? See *Transubstantiation.*

TRANSMIGRATION OF THE SOUL. See *Reincarnation.*

TRANSUBSTANTIATION (Lat. "change of substance"). The change (through the eucharistic words of consecration) of the substance of bread and wine into the body and blood of Christ, with the appearances of bread and wine remaining. Lateran IV (1215) used the word "transubstantiate" in the eucharistic section of its profession of faith (DS 802; see 782, 1642, 1652). At the reformation Ulrich Zwingli (1484–1531) took a purely symbolic view of the eucharist, and denied that any change took place, a view anticipated by Berengar of Tours (ca. 999–1088) who rejected transubstantiation and denied the real presence (DS 700). Martin Luther (1484–1531) held that, while the substances of bread and wine remain, the body and blood of Christ do become present for the believer. This view is called *consubstantiation* (Lat. "with the bread"). In its eucharistic teaching the Council of Trent restated the belief that by their consecration bread and wine are transubstantiated into the body and blood of Christ, and should be adored (DS 1651–54, 1356). The Greek Orthodox Church uses *metabole* (Gr. "change") or

249

metousiois (Gr. "change of essence"), instead of "transubstantiation," but the only real dispute with the Roman Catholic Church concerns the moment of consecration. See *Accident; Constance, Council of; Consecration; Epiclesis; Eucharist; Lateran Council, Fourth; Real Presence; Zwinglianism.*

TRENT, COUNCIL OF (1545–63). Convoked by Paul III to meet the grave need for reform, held in the northern Italian city of Trent, and considered by Catholics the nineteenth ecumenical council. The great council of the counter-reformation, Trent clarified church doctrine and renewed discipline. It met over three periods. The first eight sessions (1545–47) treated such major themes raised by the reformers as the relationship between scripture and tradition, original sin, justification and sacraments (see DS 1500–1630). Tension between Emperor Charles V and Paul III led to a suspension of the council which resumed under Pope Julius III in a second period (1551–52). The achievements of sessions 9 to 14 included decrees on the eucharist, and on the sacraments of penance and extreme unction (now called the anointing of the sick) (see DS 1635–1719). After various princes revolted against Emperor Charles V, Trent once again adjourned, and finally met again in a third period (1562–63) under Pope Pius IV. Its sessions 15–25 defined doctrines about the eucharist, the sacraments of order and matrimony, and purgatory. Disciplinary measures covered such items as the "form" of marriage, indulgences, the need for an index of prohibited books, and a range of church reforms (see DS 1725–1861). The decrees of the Council of Trent, approved by Pius IV in 1564 (see DS 1862–70), laid a solid and clear basis for subsequent Catholic teaching, theology, institutional reform and spiritual renewal. See *Anabaptists; Anointing of the Sick; Baptism; Calvinism; Counter-Reformation; Eucharist; Grace; Justification; Lutheranism; Marriage Form; Penance, Sacrament of; Protestant; Reformation; Sacrament; Scripture and Tradition; Sola Fides; Sola Gratia; Sola Scriptura; Zwinglianism.*

TRINITY, THEOLOGY OF. An attempt to understand and interpret the central Christian mystery of one God in three distinct persons, Father, Son and Holy Spirit (Matt 28:19; 2 Cor 13:13). Drawing on the operations of our intellect and will for his "psychological" model of the Trinity, St. Augustine of Hippo (354–430) interpreted the generation of the Son (or Word) on the analogy of human self-knowledge, whereas true self-love illuminates the origin of the Holy Spirit, the "personified" mutual love of Father and Son. Over the centuries theologians have followed Augustine or else taken up such other analogies from experience and philosophy as the "I-Thou-We" of the personalist thought developed by Martin Buber (1878–1965). All such approaches to the tripersonal God can be helpful. Nevertheless, through being drawn from *created* human reality and common experience, they are not immediately rooted in the self-communication of God in salvation history that reached its climax with the paschal mystery. The famous trinitarian icon of A. Roublev (ca. 1360–1430), which is now kept in a Moscow gallery, represents the scene of Abraham's *philoxenia* (Gr. "hospitality") with three angels seated around a table (Gen 18:1–15), a scene which brings to mind for a Christian the ineffable trinitarian mystery. A chalice on the table links this mystery with the eucharist, hence with the saving story of Christ's passion, death and resurrection. That icon reminds us of a basic truth about trinitarian theology: it should move from the Economic Trinity (revealed in salvation history) to the Immanent Trinity (where analogies from created reality can help us) and not vice versa. In the theology of the Trinity, as elsewhere, the order of redemption takes precedence over the order of creation. See *Constantinople, First Council of; Economy; Filioque; Generation; Immanent Trinity; Modalism; Mystery; Nicaea, First Council of; Paschal Mystery; Person; Processions; Relations, Divine; Spiration; Tritheism; Unitarianism.*

TRIODION (Gr. "three-odes"). The book of seasonal propers in the Byzantine liturgy for the divine services from the fourth Sunday before Lent till Holy Saturday inclusive. During this period normally only three odes or canticles, instead of the usual nine, are sung at matins. See *Chant; Lent; Octoechos.*

TRISAGION (Gr. "thrice holy"). An ancient refrain ("Holy God! Holy! Mighty! Holy! Immortal! Have mercy upon us!") stressing Christ's holiness, power and immortality against those who ascribed suffering to him in his divine nature. Indeed, we come across the first (documentable) use of the Trisagion at the Council of Chalcedon (451), which carefully distinguished between the divine and human natures in Christ, but without separating them (DS 302). Then opponents of the council, apparently led by Peter the Fuller (d. 488), "Monophysite" Patriarch of Antioch, added to the hymn, after "Immortal," the words: "who was crucified for us." The supporters of Chalcedon reacted by addressing the prayer to the Trinity, rather than to Christ. With or without the addition, the prayer is found in all the ancient liturgies, normally in the opening rites. Until recently in the Latin rite, the *Trisagion* was sung in Latin and Greek during the adoration of the cross on Good Friday. See *Aphthartodocetism; Chalcedon, Council of; Monophysitism; Theopaschite Controversy.*

TRULLAN SYNOD. A synod convoked by Justinian II and held at Constantinople (692) in the *trullus* (Gr. "domed room") of the imperial palace. Its aim was to deal with some canonical matters, since the fifth ecumenical council, Constantinople II (553) and the sixth, Constantinople III (680–81), had not enacted any disciplinary measures. For this reason, the synod is often called the *Quinisext* (Lat. "fifth-sixth"). The legislation concerned marriage impediments, the age of ordination, clerical marriage and clerical dress. It also prohibited representing Jesus under the image of a lamb, considered to be a monophysite aberration. At the same time, it was a hint of coming iconoclasm. From the viewpoint of eastern canon law, the synod was one of the most important, even if it met resistance in the east itself and its legislation was never fully approved by Rome. Only Hadrian I (Pope, 772–795) gave its canons some approval, after they were mistakenly presented as the canons of Constantinople III. See *Constantinople, Second Council of; Constantinople, Third Council of; Canon Law, Sources of Oriental; Iconoclasm; Islam; Monophysitism.*

TRUTH. A characteristic of (a) knowledge, (b) being and (c) activity. (a) Knowledge is true when one's judgments are logically coherent and correspond to the way things are. (b) All reality is true, inasmuch as it is intrinsically knowable and known by God. (c) Our words and deeds are true when we faithfully witness to what we know, live according to our beliefs, and find our theories verified through their practical consequences. The Hebrew word for truth (*emet*) is cognate with *amen*, and indicates lived fidelity. God is called "rich in grace (*hesed*) and fidelity" (Exod 34:6; see Ps 117:2), an OT refrain echoed when John describes the Word made flesh as being "full of grace and truth" (Jn 1:14). As the perfect revelation of the Father, Christ is *the* truth (Jn 14:6). His Holy Spirit will lead us into all truth (Jn 16:13). Believers are set free to "do" the truth (Jn 3:21; 8:32). Where philosophy has interpreted "truth" as a property (of knowledge, reality and activity), the NT understands truth in a deeply personal way—in terms of Christ, the Holy Spirit and believers. See *Hesed; Holy Spirit; Revelation; Transcendentals.*

TÜBINGEN AND ITS SCHOOLS. Several quite different orientations in theology, which came to be identified with the University of Tübingen. When founding this university in 1477, Count Eberhard of Württemberg was helped by the scholastic, Gabriel Biel (ca. 1420–95), whose nominalism significantly influenced Martin Luther (1483–1546). In 1534–35 the faculty of theology became Protestant. Luther's second in command, Philipp Melanchthon (1429–1560), had studied in Tübingen. Other, later students included Georg Wilhelm Friedrich Hegel (1770–1831) and Friedrich Wilhelm Joseph von Schelling (1775–1854).

Between 1573 and 1581 three Lutheran theologians Jacob Andreae, Lukas Osiander and Jakob Heerbrand as well as the Greek scholar Martin Crusius, all from the University of Tübingen, carried on a correspondence with the Ecumenical Patriarch Jeremias II of Constantinople, to whom a Greek translation of the *Augsburg Confession* had been sent in 1573–74. In spite of the patriarch's friendly reaction no agreement was reached.

In the early nineteenth century Ferdinand Christian Baur (1792–1860) founded a renowned "Tübingen school," which included Adolf Hilgenfeld (1823–1907), Albert Schwegler (1819–57) and David Friedrich Strauss (1808–74). Applying to Christian history and theology the Hegelian dialectic of development (*thesis-antithesis-synthesis*), Baur argued that in early Christianity the dialectic of the Jewish party of Peter and the Gentile party of Paul was overcome by the emergence of Catholicism in the second century. The Baur school declined after the departure of Albrecht Ritschl (1822–89) and Adolf von Harnack (1851–1930). A Catholic "Tübingen school" emerged when a Catholic faculty of theology moved there from Erlangen in 1819. Important figures in the first period included Johann Sebastian Drey (1777–1853), Johann Baptist Hirscher (1788–1853), who moved to Freiburg in 1837, and Johann Adam Möhler (1796–1838). In the second period of the Catholic Tübingen School we come across Johann Evangelist Kuhn (1806–87), Franz Anton Staudemeier (1800–56), who later moved to Freiburg, and Karl Joseph Hefele (1809–93), the famous historian of the councils and Bishop of Rottenburg. A third period was distinguished by the teaching of Paul Schanz (1841–1905), Francis Xavier Funk (1840–1907), Karl Adam (1876–1966) and Josef Rupert Geiselmann (1890–1970). While the programs differed, common themes included the kingdom of God, dynamic tradition, the church as organism and the critical study of history. Through the influence of Johannes Michael Sailer (1751–1832), these Catholic theologians of Tübingen were enabled to overcome the Enlightenment by "baptizing" it. After the Second Vatican Council one can hardly speak of "schools" in Tübingen. But significant Catholic teachers there have included Joseph (later Cardinal) Ratzinger (b. 1927), Hans Küng (b. 1928) and Walter Kasper (b. 1933), later Bishop of Rottenburg. Among the important Protestant professors one should mention Gerhard Ebeling (b. 1912), Eberhard Jüngel (b. 1934), Ernst Käsemann (b. 1906) and Jürgen Moltmann (b. 1926). See *Augsburg Confession; Enlightenment; Schools of Theology.*

TWO-SOURCE THEORY. (a) The widely accepted hypothesis that the gospels of Matthew and Luke had two major sources: Mark's gospel and Q (a collection of Jesus' sayings). (b) A view commonly held from the sixteenth century down to the Second Vatican Council that there are two "materially" separate and equally valid "sources" of revelation, one being tradition and the other scripture. See *Quelle; Revelation; Scripture and Tradition; Synoptic Gospels.*

TYPOLOGY (Gr. "study of images, prototypes"). Way of interpreting events, persons and things as "types" foreshadowing the NT "antitypes" that fulfilled revelation and salvation. Thus Adam and Melchisedek are types of Christ (Rom 5:14; Heb 6:20–7:28). The story of God's people in the exodus from Egypt prefigures the challenges which Christians face and the sacraments they receive (1 Cor 10:1–11). The flood foreshadows baptism (1 Pet 3:20–21) and the manna in the desert anticipates "the bread of life" (Jn 6:48–51). St. Irenaeus (ca. 130–ca. 200) and then the school of Alexandria were attuned to this typical sense of scripture, which Origen (ca. 185–ca. 254) developed in an allegorical direction. In the west, typological interpretation was adopted by St. Ambrose (ca. 339–97) and then by St. Augustine of Hippo (354–430) from whom it passed down to the Latin middle ages. See *Alexandrian Theology; Allegory; Antiochene Theology; Origenism; Senses of Scripture.*

U

UBIQUITY OF GOD. See *Omnipresence.*

ULTRAMONTANISM (Lat. "beyond the mountains"). Contemptuous name used by Gallicans for those who maximalized papal authority and looked for all solutions "beyond the Alps" to Rome. The Ultramontanes reacted against such movements as Febronianism, Gallicanism and Jansenism, which in their different ways supported the jurisdiction of local churches over against the central authority of Rome. Representative ultramontanists included Joseph de Maistre (1753–1821), Félicité Robert de Lamennais (1782–1854) for part of his life, Louis Veuillot (1813–83), Cardinal Nicholas Wiseman (1802–65), Archbishop of Westminster, his successor Cardinal Henry Edward Manning (1808–92) and William George Ward (1812–82). The restoration of the Jesuits in 1814, the unsettling revolutions of 1830 and 1848, the long pontificate of Pius IX (1846–78) and other factors encouraged many to look for authority as the answer to almost every question. The ultramontane movement culminated in the definition of papal infallibility at Vatican I in 1870 (see DS 3065–75). The qualified terms of the definition, however, implicitly criticized the exaggerations of the movement. Through its teaching on the collegiality of all bishops with and under the pope, Vatican II (1962–65) produced a more balanced account of papal authority (LG 22–25). See *Church; Febronianism; Gallicanism; Jansenism; Traditionalism; Vatican Council, First; Vatican Council, Second.*

UNIATES. The name given to the Ruthenians who, at the synod of Brest-

Litovsk in 1596, accepted full communion with Rome. The term, often used in a pejorative sense, was then extended to other eastern Christians in union with Rome. The Orthodox often consider Catholics of the eastern rite a treacherous stumbling-block on the way toward the one church which Christ wants—examples of false *proselytism* rather than real ecumenism. However, in the official theological dialogue with the eastern Orthodox there is a sub-commission on the eastern Catholics of the Byzantine rite in union with Rome whose purpose is to study this question of proselytism and uniatism. Eastern Catholics are taking full part in this dialogue. See *Armenian Christianity; Eastern Churches; Maronites; Melchites; Proselytism; Ruthenian.*

UNITARIANISM. A view that rejects the divinity of the Son and the Holy Spirit and, in defense of a strict monotheism, accepts only one divine person. Although various doubts about the divinity of the Son and the Holy Spirit emerged repeatedly in the early history of Christianity, Unitarianism is really a modern heresy, developed by Martin Cellarius (1499–1564), Michael Servetus (1511–53) and Faustus Sozzini (= Socinus) (1539–1604). In the United States the intellectual prestige of Unitarianism came from such figures as William Ellery Channing (1780–1842), Ralph Waldo Emerson (1803–82) and the reformer of the Harvard Divinity School, Charles W. Eliot (1869–1909). Unitarians have no formal creed and have dwindled in numbers. Many have either become agnostics or else returned to mainline forms of Christianity. See *Adoptionism; Arianism; Monarchianism; Monotheism; Pneumatomachians; Socinianism; Subordinationism; Trinity, Theology of.*

UNIVERSALISM. A conviction emerging after the Babylonian exile that through Israel God's salvation was being offered to all the nations (Isa 42:6; 49:6; 52:10; see Jonah; Lk 2:30–32; Jn 8:12). "Universalism" also refers to the view that all human beings will eventually be saved. See *Apocatastasis; Hell; Israel; Salvation.*

UNIVERSALS. General concepts like rose, house, justice and creature. With a kind of exaggerated realism Plato (427–347 B.C.) argued that eternal, subsistent forms or ideas in a higher world serve as models for the universal terms we apply to individual things in our changing, visible world. The opposite view is the nominalism of William of Occam (ca. 1285–1347) and Gabriel Biel (ca. 1420–95). Only individual beings are real; universal terms are more or less an arbitrary convenience. The moderate realism of St. Thomas Aquinas (ca. 1225–74) argued that general concepts exist in our mind, but are based in the real nature of things. See *Nominalism; Philosophy; Platonism; Thomism.*

UNIVOCITY (Lat. "one voice"). Being predicated of different subjects, including God, in exactly the same way. As this procedure may imply no essential difference between God and creatures, the consequence could be monism in philosophy and pantheism in theology. See *Analogy; Equivocity; Monism; Pantheism.*

V

VALENTINIANS. Followers of Valentinus, who founded one of the most important Gnostic sects in the second century. He seems to have been born in Egypt and to have led the Gnostics in Alexandria before leaving for Rome around 135. He stayed there for about twenty years, and at one point apparently hoped to become the Bishop of Rome. He taught a complicated system of aeons, which originally formed the *pleroma*. Later, through *syzigies* (Syriac "coupling," "marrying") Sophia, a female goddess and one of the lowest aeons, gave birth to the Demiurge or creator of the universe, identified with the (evil) God of the OT. This system was vigorously challenged by St. Irenaeus of Lyons (ca. 130–ca. 200) (see also DS 1341). See *Demiurge; Dualism; Gnosticism; Marcionism; Platonism; Pleroma.*

VALIDITY (Lat. "strong," "efficacious"). A term which entered the standard vocabulary of the church with the Council of Trent (DS 1809) and Pope Benedict XIV (1675–1758) and which concerns the conditions that have to be observed for some act to be efficacious—also in canon law (see CIC 124). Sacraments, for example, besides being primarily signs of Christ's covenantal love, have their essential elements, and thus may be valid or invalid. A condition for validly receiving any of the other sacraments is the prior reception of baptism (CIC 842). Invalidity is synonymous with nullity; an invalid act may be described as null and void. The valid reception of a sacrament means that it counts; fruitful reception means that grace is imparted or augmented. A Christian who gets married according to the conditions required by the church but does so in the state of mortal sin is valdily married, but has not (yet) received the grace of the sacrament. See *Grace; Marriage Form; Marriage Impediments; Sacrament; Sin.*

VATICAN COUNCIL, FIRST (1869–70). Convoked by Pius IX (Pope 1846–78) and intended to treat many themes including the eastern churches. (The Orthodox patriarchs had been invited to attend the council, but they declined.) Proceedings were suspended when Italian troops occupied Rome in September 1870. By then the council had produced two constitutions: *Dei Filius* (Lat. "Son of God") on God the Creator, revelation, faith and the relationship between faith and reason (DS 3001–45); and *Pastor Aeternus* (Lat. "Eternal Shepherd") on papal primacy and infallibility (DS 3050–75). Against fideism and traditionalism *Dei Filius* taught that from the works of creation God can be known with certainty. In the OT and NT there has been a "supernatural" revelation of divine truths or mysteries (plural). The definition of papal infallibility prompted the schism of the "Old Catholics," and was misused by the "Iron Chancellor" of Germany, Otto von Bismarck (1815–98), in his *Kulturkampf* (German "cultural fight"), an attempt to subordinate the church to the civil government (see DS 3112–17). Vatican I strengthened Catholic faith and papal authority, but its teaching on revelation and infallibility was to be filled out by Vatican II's teaching, respectively, on faith's personal response to the divine self-communication and the collegiality of bishops. See *Fideism; Infallibility; Old Catholics; Primacy; Rationalism; Revelation; Supernatural; Traditionalism; Ultramontanism.*

VATICAN COUNCIL, SECOND (1962–65). Convoked by Pope John XXIII (1881–1963) and considered by Catholics the twenty-first ecumenical council. Meeting for one session under Pope John and three under Paul VI (1897–1978), the Council aimed at an *aggiornamento* (Italian "updating") of the church's life and doctrinal formulations. Instead of defining new dogmas, it wanted to teach pastorally and encourage the cause of Christian and human unity. The unprecedented number of non-European bishops present led Karl Rahner (1904–84) to divide Christian history into three periods: (a) the church at her origins in Jewish Christianity; (b) the church of a specific culture, Hellenistic or Latin (European), which lasted for centuries; and (c) the church of all nations, which started with Vatican II. The council was attended by over two thousand Catholic bishops and by non-Catholic observers from the main Christian denominations, enhancing its value as a platform for dialogue and a point of reference for all. On December 7, 1965, Paul VI and the Orthodox Patriarch of Constantinople issued a joint declaration, expressing their regret for nine centuries of division and hopes for future reconciliation. The first of the council's sixteen documents was *Sacrosanctum Concilium* (Lat. "The Sacred Council") (December 4, 1963), a constitution on the liturgy, which endorsed reform through (a) a return to earlier and simpler forms and (b) the use of the vernacular or language of the place. The decree *Inter Mirifica* (Lat. "Among the Remarkable Things") (December 4, 1963) drew attention to the importance of the communications media. The second session brought the dogmatic constitution on the church, *Lumen Gentium* (Lat. "Light of the Nations"), one of the council's major achievements. It was approved on the same day (November 21, 1964) as the decree on the Eastern Catholic Churches, *Orien-*

talium Ecclesiarum (Lat. "Of the eastern Churches") and the decree on ecumenism, *Unitatis Redintegratio* (Lat. "The Reestablishment of Unity"), declarations committing the church to ecumenical work which was to bear fruit in subsequent unofficial and official dialogues. At the fourth session the council issued a decree on the pastoral duty of bishops, *Christus Dominus* (Lat. "Christ the Lord"), a document which also aimed to renew synodical structures in the church. On the same day (October 28, 1965) the council promulgated two other decrees, *Optatam Totius* (Lat. "Desired [Renewal] of the whole [Church]") on the training of priests and *Perfectae Caritatis* (Lat. "Of Perfect Charity") on the renewal of religious life, and two declarations: *Gravissimum Educationis* (Lat. "The Extreme [Importance] of Education") on Christian education, and *Nostra Aetate* (Lat. "In our Age") on the positive relationship of the church to non-Christian religions. On November 18, 1965 Vatican II approved two further documents: *Dei Verbum* (Lat. "God's Word"), a major contribution on divine revelation which also dealt with faith, scripture, tradition, biblical truth, the interpretation of the gospels and the role of the scriptures in renewing the whole church; and a decree on the ministry of lay people, *Apostolicam Actuositatem* (Lat. "Apostolic Activity"). On December 7, 1965 the council issued its last four documents: a declaration on religious liberty, *Dignitatis Humanae* (Lat. "Of Human Dignity"), a decree on the church's missionary activity, *Ad Gentes* (Lat. "To the Nations"), a decree on the ministry and life of priests, *Presbyterorum Ordinis* (Lat. "Of the Order of Priests"), and the longest text of Vatican II, *Gaudium et Spes* (Lat. "Joy and Hope"), a pastoral constitution on the church in the modern world. On December 8, 1965, the council, the greatest event in the life of the Catholic Church of this century, ended with a solemn liturgy. See *Byzantine Christianity; Council, Ecumenical; Dogma; Synod; Synod of Bishops; Vernacular.*

VENERATION OF SAINTS. A devotion which is shown to dead persons of outstanding holiness, seeking to imitate their lives and obtain their intercession before God. Saints are venerated in a special way by the Catholic and Orthodox Churches (UR 15), and, to a lesser extent, by the Anglican communion, in particular since the Oxford Movement. The Jews drew inspiration from the great figures of their past history (Sir 44:1–50:21; see 2 Macc 15:12–16), a theme taken up by the letter to the Hebrews which lists many OT heroes and heroines of faith (Heb 11:1–12:1). The early Christians revered the Blessed Virgin and the martyrs; Origen (ca. 185–ca. 254) was the first to reflect seriously on devotion to the saints. The first nonmartyrs to be venerated were St. Antony the Abbot (ca. 251–356) and St. Martin of Tours (d. 397). Both at Nicaea II (787), against eastern iconoclasts, and at Trent (1545–63), against Protestant iconoclasm, the Catholic Church asserted the importance of venerating saints. Altars are consecrated only after relics of saints have been fixed in them. In the eastern church, the eucharistic liturgy is celebrated on the *antimension* or a piece of cloth containing relics which is placed on the altar and functions like the Latin *corporal* (= cloth on which the paten and chalice are placed). See *Beatification; Canonization; Communion of Saints; Hyperdoulia; Martyr; Miracle; Nicaea, Second Council of; Oxford Movement; Pilgrimage; Relics; Saint; Trent, Council of.*

VERNACULAR (Lat. "dialect, language of the people"). The language of the people used in the liturgy. Liturgies usually started with the local language, except when another language was introduced by missionaries or imposed by a conquering nation. But liturgical history constantly illustrates a deeper, religious phenomenon: the tension between the people's need to understand the texts and the desire to acknowledge God's mysterious otherness by using a classical, numinous language. In the west, Greek was used in the liturgy for the first few centuries until Latin gradually took over. Rome encouraged Sts. Cyril (ca. 826–68) and Methodius (ca. 815–85) to employ the vernacular among the Slavs in central Europe. The reformation leaders, while often continuing to use Latin in theology, introduced the vernacular for public worship. In 1963 the Second Vatican Council officially approved of the vernacular for Catholic liturgy (see SC 36, 54, 63, 101) in the Roman rite. In the east, the various national churches used the people's language: Arabic, Armenian, Coptic, Ge'ez, Greek, Syriac and so forth. But with the passage of centuries, the liturgical texts have become archaic and are no longer readily understood. Many eastern Christians in the USA, Canada and Australia, for example, have simply switched to English. The issue of using an archaic language or the vernacular in the liturgy will never be fully and finally resolved. See *Liturgy; Liturgy of the Hours; Evangelization; Reformation, The.*

VESPERS (Lat. "evening-star"). Evensong or evening prayer in the liturgy of the hours. In the 1970 reform of the Latin rite Vespers have the following structure: (a) an introductory verse; (b) a hymn corresponding to the day, the feast or the liturgical season; (c) three psalms, one of which is sometimes replaced by a biblical canticle; (d) a short reading from scripture; (e) a short responsorial hymn; (f) the Canticle of Our Lady or *Magnificat* (Lat. "Magnifies") (Lk 1:46–55); (g) the Intercessions, followed by the Lord's Prayer and the collect of the day; and (f) a final blessing. In the Byzantine rite, evening prayer is called *hesperinos* (Gr. "evening prayer"); during Lent, it introduces the Mass of the Presanctified. See *Lauds; Liturgy of the Hours; Mass of the Presanctified.*

VESTIGIA TRINITATIS (Lat. "footprints, traces of the Trinity"). Hints of the tripersonal being of God to be found in the created world and especially in human beings. St. Augustine of Hippo (354–430) saw the Trinity mirrored in human knowing and loving. Other such hints of the Trinity include the "I-Thou-We" of interpersonal relationships, the father-mother-child structure of a family, and the human search for the fullness of life, meaning and love. See *Analogy; Creation; Glory; Image of God; Natural Theology; Trinity, Theology of.*

VIA AFFIRMATIONIS, NEGATIONIS, EMINENTIAE (Lat. "way of affirmation, way of negation, exalted way"). Three rules for speaking analogously about God which were classically formulated by St. Thomas Aquinas (ca. 1225–74). Our experience of human goodness, for example, allows us to predicate goodness of God. At the same time, God is *not* good in the limited way that human beings may be said to be good. Finally, being Goodness itself, God is good in an excellent way that transcends our understanding and language. See *Analogy; Apophatic Theology; Cataphatic Theology; Five Ways, The; Negative Theology; Transcendence.*

VIATICUM (Lat. "food for the journey"). Holy communion given to those in danger of death to prepare them for the next life. Church law lifts every restriction when Christians are dying so that they may confess their sins and receive the eucharist (see CIC 566, 844, 865, 867, 883, 913, 921, 961). See *Eucharist.*

VIENNE, COUNCIL OF (1311–12). The council which was convoked by Pope Clement V (1264–1314) and met at Vienne in southern France. French by birth, the pope had transferred his residence to Avignon, southern France, in 1309; there the popes were to stay till 1377, in what is called the "Avignon Captivity." Wanting to seize the property of the Templars, an order of religious soldiers founded by Hugh des Payens in 1119, King Philip IV ("the Fair") forced the pope and council to condemn them on what seem to have been trumped-up charges of immorality and heresy. The council censured the Beguines, sisters who led a semi-religious common life, and their male counterparts, the Begards, for holding that one could see God through natural effort (see DS 891–99). The council ordered a levy for a crusade, but the money ended up in the pockets of Philip IV. Without naming Petrus Olivi (ca. 1248–98), the leader of the spiritual Franciscans, the council condemned a series of propositions attributed to him, and taught that Christ really suffered, because he had a complete human nature, that the soul is the form of the body, and that it is necessary for their salvation to baptize infants (DS 900–04). See *Beatific Vision; Council, Ecumenical; Crusades.*

VIRGINAL CONCEPTION OF JESUS. The act by which Mary conceived Jesus through the power of the Holy Spirit and without the intervention of a human father. On the basis of the gospels (Matt 1:18–25; Lk 1:26–38), the Christian tradition and ordinary church teaching have always held that Jesus was so conceived—a belief which is at least implicitly affirmed by the Apostles' Creed: "He was conceived by the power of the Holy Spirit and was born of the Virgin Mary." The fact that Jesus was born of a woman points to his humanity. The fact that he was conceived through a special intervention of the Holy Spirit points to his divinity; he is "Emmanuel, God with us" (Matt 1:23). See *Christology; Holy Spirit; Incarnation; Mariology.*

VIRGINITY. A state of abstention from marriage and sexual intercourse. From the time of the early church, communities of men and women have practiced a life of consecrated virginity, following Christ, living a program of constant prayer, serving the needy and acting as a sign of God's final kingdom (see LG 42; PC 1, 12; OT 10; CIC 604). See *Bogomils; Cathars; Celibacy; Chastity; Encratites; Monasticism; Religious Life.*

VIRTUE (Lat. "force"). A habit of good behavior which enables one to do what is right with ease, pleasure and consistency. The opposite is vice, or the habitual inclination to do evil. See *Chastity; Ethics; Fundamental Option; Habit; Moral Theology; Personalism.*

VIRTUES, CARDINAL (Lat. "hinge"). Prudence, temperance, fortitude and justice, which together support the whole structure of the moral life. See *Justice; Moral Theology; Prudence; Temperance.*

VIRTUES, THEOLOGICAL. The faith, hope and love which are directed immediately toward God as being infinitely trustworthy and lovable, the One to whom we should commit our whole life and future (1 Cor 13:13; Gal 5:5–6; Col 1:4–5; 1 Thess 1:3; 5:8; DS 1530–31; DV 5). See *Agape; Faith; Hope; Love.*

VISIONS. Unusual experiences in which other-worldly beings are manifested and which may be merely subjective hallucinations or else genuine communications from God (Isa 6:1–5; Lk 24:23; Acts 7:31; 10:17,19; 11:5; 12:9; 16:9–10; 2 Cor 12:1–4). The official church has pronounced worthy of credence only a few visions of the Virgin Mary like those to Blessed Juan Diego, an Aztec peasant, at Guadalupe, Mexico (1531), to St. Catherine Labouré, Paris (1830) at La Salette, France (1846); to St. Bernadette Soubirous at Lourdes, France (1858) and to Lucia, Francesco and Giacinta at Fatima, Portugal (1917). Visions are corporeal when something is seen, imaginative when the inner imagination is affected (but not the outer senses), and intellectual, when the visionary receives a sudden and unmediated grasp of divine truths. Authentic visions never add new "content" to the deposit of faith. Instead, they remind Christians of what has already been revealed in Christ, and/or give practical encouragement toward moral and spiritual reform. Alleged visions which, at least in the long run, do not produce "the fruit of the Spirit" (Gal 5:22–23; see Matt 7:15–20), are for that very reason suspect. See *Appearances of the Risen Lord; Deposit of Faith; Mysticism; Revelation.*

VOLUNTARISM (Lat. "will"). Any doctrine which stresses the will at the expense of the intellect. The serious discussion of voluntarism was launched in Plato's (427–347 B.C.) dialogue *Euthyphro*, when Socrates raised the question: "Do the gods love the law because it is holy, or is it holy because the gods love it?" Affirming the second alternative would be voluntarism. For voluntaristic systems God's will or the moral agent's preferences have tended to be decisive in establishing moral values. Voluntarism has also played a role in metaphysics: for example, in Scotism and Nominalism. See *Ethics; Metaphysics; Moral Theology; Nominalism; Scotism.*

VOW. A promise freely made by an adult to do something good which is not already required by God's commandments, church law or other obligations. To fulfill one's vows comes under the virtue of religion (see CIC 1191–98). In the OT vows were practiced (Lev 27:1–33; Deut 23:22–24; 1 Sam 1:11), sometimes with tragic consequences (Judg 11:30–40). The possibility of taking vows continued in the NT (Acts 21:23–26). Vows may be private or public. Vows are public if pronounced in the presence of witnesses, as is the case with the first, simple (= nonsolemn) vows which members of religious institutes take immediately after the novitiate. If these public vows bind for life, they are called perpetual vows. If they no longer bind after a certain period of time, unless renewed, they are called temporary vows. Perpetual vows which are solemn make more severe demands on the one who pronounces them, are recognized as such by competent church authority and may be dispensed from only by papal authority. See *Chastity; Novice; Obedience; Poverty; Religious Life.*

VULGATE. A name deriving from *vulgata editio* (Lat. "popular edition") and referring to the most widely used Latin translation of the Bible. When the need for a common translation was felt in Rome, St. Jerome (ca. 340–420) undertook to revise some of the already existing Latin translations of the NT. Forced to leave Rome, Jerome learned Hebrew and began translating the OT as well. By 404 he completed translating (or revising existing translations of) the whole Bible. In 1546 the Council of Trent declared the Vulgate to be the "authentic" Latin translation of the Bible (see DS 1506). A revised edition of the text was published under Sixtus V (1590), and another revision under Clement VIII (1592). In 1908 work was began on a new edition of the whole Vulgate, but will now end with a revised edition of the OT only. See *Bible*.

W

WALDENSIANS. Members of a renewal movement which started in the twelfth century, and eventually emerged as a church with a Calvinist creed. In 1174 a rich merchant of Lyons, [Peter] Valdes (d. before 1219), after hearing Christ's invitation to the rich young man (Matt 19:21), distributed his wealth among the poor and began preaching the gospel in the south of France. By their frequent attacks on the worldliness of the church, he and his followers provoked constant friction. After the Third Lateran Council (1179) failed to win them back, they were excommunicated at the Council of Verona (1184). Their rejection of any use of violence, refusal to take oaths (DS 913), and preaching without official church approval (see DS 809) made the rift too wide to heal. In 1207 Innocent III launched a crusade against the Albigensians that also affected the Waldensian bases in southern France. Many Waldensians migrated to Spain, Germany, Bohemia, Poland, Savoy and Piedmont. The Waldensians who returned to the Catholic Church in 1207 were required to make a profession of faith touching the disputed issues (see DS 790–97). Italian Waldensians looked for contact with the Protestant reformation at the Synod of Chanforans (1532), and they adopted the Calvinist confession of faith. After the 1655 massacre of Waldensians, mourned by John Milton in his sonnet, "On the Late Massacre in Piedmont," a few mountain communes received permission to practice their religion freely. After 1848 they enjoyed real political and religious freedom. In 1922 the Waldensians moved their school of theology to Rome, just a few blocks from the Vatican. They are a church of about 30,000, the strongest Protestant group in Italy. See *Calvinism; Hussites; Protestant; Reformation*.

WEST SYRIAN CHURCH. That church often called (polemically) Monophysite or (on account of its origin) Jacobite, but which prefers to call itself the West Syrian Orthodox Church. It represents one of the four main streams of the Syrian tradition, all of which have a strong monastic tradition: (a) the West Syrian Church, based in Antioch; (b) the East Syrian Church, based in Edessa; (c) the Melkite Church, which is united with Rome and uses Greek in the liturgy; and (d) the Maronite Church, united with Rome and based in Lebanon. Liturgically the West Syrian Church is extremely rich, having at least seventy eucharistic anaphoras and many variant texts for other ceremonies. The main eucharistic liturgy is that of St. James, which may go back to apostolic times. Its special features are an incense ceremony after the Liturgy of the Word and a farewell prayer to the alter at the very end. This liturgy is usually celebrated in the vernacular; Arabic is used in the Middle East, Malayalam in India and English in the United States. See *Anaphora; Church of the East; Holy Week; Maronites; Melkites; Monophysitism.*

WILL OF GOD. The supreme principle by which all human beings should let their lives be guided (Matt 6:10; see 6:33). Based on God's infinite wisdom and goodness, the divine will is a personal project of love for all men and women which aims to bring them to their full and final happiness. Not always easy to discern in practice, the will of God can at times call for painful sacrifice (Mk 14:35–36). See *Conscience; Decalogue; Discernment of Spirits; Holiness; Moral Theology; Perfection; Providence.*

WISDOM LITERATURE. A genre of literature which was developed in the ancient Middle East (and elsewhere) and to which belong five books of the OT: Job, Proverbs, Qoheleth (or Ecclesiastes), Sirach (or Ecclesiasticus) and Wisdom. (Sometimes the Song of Songs and the Psalms are added to the list). The Hebrew word for wisdom is *hokmah,* and can refer to the skill of a craftsman (Exod 31:6), administrative ability (Gen 41:39) and political leadership (Deut 34:9). While not avoiding ethical and religious questions, ancient wisdom often highlighted useful maxims for advancing one's career. Israel's wisdom went deeper and even wrestled with such mysteries as the unexplained suffering of those who, like Job, are blameless before God. King Solomon (d. ca. 931) was considered the wise man *par excellence* (see his famous judgment in 1 Kgs 3:16–28). True wisdom comes from God and helps human beings discern between good and evil (1 Kgs 3:5–9). It is one of the spiritual endowments of the messiah (Isa 11:2). Like the word of God, wisdom tended to be personified in the OT, foreshadowing the NT revelation of the eternally preexistent Son of God (Prov 8:22–31; Wis 7:22–8:1; Sir 24:1–22). Christ's parables reflect OT wisdom; for instance, the parable of the unjust steward (Lk 16:1–8) and that of the wise and foolish virgins (Matt 25:1–12). Yet God's wisdom is folly to the wise (Matt 11:25; 1 Cor 1:18–2:5). See *Fools for Christ's Sake; Sophia.*

WORD AND SACRAMENT. God's word and its correlative sign, symbol and/or event. In John's gospel the words (3:34; 5:24; 8:31; 15:3) and signs (Jn 2:11, 18, 23; 3:2; 4:54) of Christ harmonize to communicate "truth" (revelation) and "life" (salvation). Origen (ca. 185–ca. 254) associated word and symbol in his theology of the preexistent and incarnate Word who manifests the Father to us. As regards word and symbol in Christian life, St. Augustine of Hippo (354–430) spoke of a sacrament as visible word. The reformation, especially in the Calvinist tradition, brought a one-sided stress on word at the expense of sign and sacrament. The Second Vatican Council understood God's self-communication as coming, neither by word alone nor by significant event alone, but through the interplay of words and events (see DV 2, 4, 14, 17). See *Revelation; Sacrament; Symbol.*

WORD OF GOD. God's self-revelation in history (DV 1–5, 26), as (a) uttered, (b) written and (c) incarnated. (a) God's word is creative (Gen 1:1–2:4) and effective (Isa 55:10–11). God spoke through the OT prophets (Heb 1:1; 2 Pet 1:21). Jesus proclaimed the word of God (Lk 5:1), as did his apostles (Acts 13:5; 17:13; 1 Thess 2:13) and those who follow them in truly preaching "the gospel of God" (1 Thess 2:9), a reality that is simultaneously revealing and saving (Rom 1:15–17; 1 Cor 1:18; 2 Cor 2:14–16). (b) Written under the special inspiration of the Holy Spirit (Rom 15:4; 2 Tim 3:16; 2 Pet 1:20–21; see DV 11), the scriptures are the word of God which enlightens and nourishes the church's liturgy, teaching and life. (c) The preexistent Son of God is the Word who "became flesh" (Jn 1:14), the personal self-communication of God. See *Inspiration; Logos; Pre-existence; Prophet; Revelation; Word and Sacrament.*

WORLD. The universe created by God (Matt 25:34; Jn 17:5,24). "World" can also mean the field where the gospel is to be proclaimed (Mk 16:15), and even those who do not acknowledge Christ (Jn 1:9–11) and are hostile to him and his followers (Jn 8:23; 15:18–20; 17:14). Satan is the prince of this world (Jn 12:31; 14:30; 16:11), but out of love God sent the Son into the world (= humankind) to save it (Jn 3:16–17). The longest text from the Second Vatican Council was *Gaudium et Spes*, the Pastoral Constitution on the Church in the Modern World. In line with the consistent Christian opposition to Gnostic forms of dualism, this document affirmed the essential goodness of the created world. Far from being a screen between God and human beings, the world should be a point of mediation, as the use of matter in the sacraments illustrates (see DS 800; 3025). See *Cosmos; Dualism; Gnosticism; Liberation Theology; Manichaeism; Oikumene; Political Theology; Sacrament.*

WORLD COUNCIL OF CHURCHES. A fellowship of churches that was formed by the merger of the Faith and Order Movement and Life and Work at the first assembly of the WCC in 1948 (Amsterdam). The main purpose of the WCC is to call churches to the goal of visible unity in one faith and in one eucharistic fellowship. At the same time, the WCC

265

considers itself a provisional expression of that unity, and as such it is a forum for encounter and collaboration between Christian churches. General assemblies were held in Amsterdam (1948), Evanston USA (1954), New Delhi (1961), Uppsala (1968), Nairobi (1975), Vancouver (1983) and Canberra (1991). The Geneva-based WCC has 314 member churches of various Christian traditions: Anglican, Orthodox and Protestant. Since 1965, the Roman Catholic Church, though not a member, has enjoyed regular contacts with the WCC through the Joint Working Group. See *Dialogue; Ecumenism; Faith and Order.*

WORLD RELIGIONS. Those religions which command world attention because of their age, many adherents and sophisticated teaching. Any complete list could be debated, but at least Christianity, Judaism, Islam, Buddhism, Hinduism and Taoism belong among such religions. See *Anonymous Christians; Buddhism; Christianity; Dialogue; Hinduism; Islam; Judaism; Taoism.*

WORSHIP. Adoration of God which expresses itself in praise, thanksgiving, self-offering, penitence and petition. Personal worship of God can take place anywhere and at any time (Jn 4:21–24). Public Christian worship is the liturgy which is centered on Christ, who as great high priest has offered on our behalf the sacrifice of the new covenant (Heb 4:14– 10:25). Our worship means sharing in Christ's priestly act on our behalf (SC 7), which calls for the living sacrifice of our daily existence (Rom 12:1). See *Adoration; Covenant; Hyperdoulia; Impetratory Prayer; Liturgy; Liturgy of the Hours; Penance, Virtue of; Priest; Sacrifice.*

Y

YAHWEH (origin uncertain). The proper name for the God of the Jews, also frequently called *Elohim* (= the common Semitic name for God). The name "Yahweh" turns up in the creation and patriarchal narratives (see Gen 2:4; 4:26; 12:8; 26:25). But this may be an anachronism, a name for God antedated when the original traditions and texts were later edited by a redactor called the Yahwist. According to another redactor (called the Elohist because he had hitherto used "Elohim" for God), Yahweh as God's name was first revealed to Moses and "explained" as "I am who I am," or "I will be what I will be" (Exod 3:13–15). However, instead of receiving the name "Yahweh" through a special revelation, the Israelites may have taken it over from others. If understood causatively, as "he who causes to be," the name points to God as creator and Lord of history. Toward the end of the Babylonian Exile (587–538 B.C.), the Jews stopped pronouncing the name, which was written as the tetragrammaton YHWH (Gr. "word of four letters"). In its place they said "Adonai" (Heb. "Lord") when the tetragrammaton appeared. A similar reverence for God's name is shown by English versions which translate "Yahweh" as "the Lord." See *Israel; Jehovah; Pentateuch.*

YOM KIPPUR (Heb. "day of atonement"). The only obligatory Jewish fast-day, celebrated in September/October (Lev 16:1–34; Num 29:7–11). To expiate Israel's sins, an elaborate rite was performed in the temple. The observances of the day are now regulated by the Mishnah. The letter to the Hebrews uses the imagery of Yom Kippur to express the meaning of the redemption and especially the fact that Christ, having once and for all died for our sins, expiated them and so made the whole ceremony of Yom Kippur superfluous (Heb 9:6–10:18). See *Atonement; Expiation; Mishnah; Temple.*

Z

ZEALOTS. Jewish freedom fighters who fought the Romans at the beginning of the first century A.D. and then during the war that led to the destruction of Jerusalem in A.D. 70. There is no reliable evidence that the Zealots were active at the time of Jesus. The nickname "Zealot" applied to Simon, one of the twelve (Lk 6:15), probably referred only to his religious zeal (see Jn 2:17; Gal 1:14). See *Pharisees; Sadducees; Scribes.*

ZEN (Sanskrit "meditation"). A form of meditation which has flourished in the context of Buddhism. Apparently started by Bodhidharma, an Indian monk resident in China, Zen is now mainly associated with Japan. It involves such practices as the tea-drinking ceremony and the art of archery, ways of attaining peace of soul by being "lost" in things. Many Christians like the Jesuits William Johnston (b. 1925) and Makibi Enomiya (Hugo Lassalle, 1898–1990) have tried to show how Zen as a method (without the Buddhist credo) is compatible with Christianity. A 1989 letter from the Congregation for the Doctrine of Faith, while recognizing how Zen could help Christian meditation, warned against dangers and abuses. See *Buddhism; Contemplation; Meditation; Prayer.*

ZWINGLIANISM. A movement within the Protestant reformation, initiated by Ulrich (or Huldreich) Zwingli (1484–1531) with his reformation of the city of Zurich. Rejecting the authority of the pope, the mass as sacrifice, the invocation of the saints and the celibacy of the clergy, he tried to establish a theocracy at Zurich. His interpretation of the eucharist as entailing a purely symbolic presence led to a fruitless dispute with Martin Luther (1483–1546) at Marburg in 1529. Zwingli recalled to Christian attention that the eucharist is also a community meal (see DS 1635–61). He died carrying the banner in Zurich's war against the Catholic cantons. See *Calvinism; Lutheranism; Protestant; Real Presence; Reformation, The; Theocracy; Transubstantiation.*